AMY
JOHNSON

AMY
JOHNSON

CONSTANCE BABINGTON SMITH

SUTTON PUBLISHING

This book was first published in 1967 by Collins

This new edition first published in 2004 by
Sutton Publishing Limited · Phoenix Mill
Stroud · Gloucestershire · GL5 2BU

British Library Cataloguing in Publication Data
A catalogue record for this book is available from the
British Library

ISBN 0 7509 3703 3

Typeset in 10/12pt Bookman.
Typesetting and origination by
Sutton Publishing Limited
Printed and bound in Great Britain by
J.H. Haynes & Co. Ltd, Sparkford.

CONTENTS

AMY JOHNSON

PART THREE: THE VICTIM

PREFACE

Thanks to the cooperation of Amy Johnson's family and friends this account of her life is based to a very large extent on original material, notably her letters, as well as on the memories of some of those who knew her best. It was on the initiative of the elder of her two surviving sisters, Mrs Trevor Jones, that I was invited to write the biography. Amy's father, Mr J.W. Johnson, was still alive at the time, and I want to record my appreciation of the interest and goodwill he showed during the early stages of planning. Mrs Jones and her younger sister, Mrs Ronald Falconar-Stewart, together inherited the responsibility for the many letters, papers, photographs etc. relating to Amy's life which were in the possession of the family. I am most grateful to them both for agreeing to make this material available to me. Other relatives of Amy's to whom I am indebted are Mr Wilfred Hodge, the late Mrs Annie Campey, Mr and Mrs Humphrey Douglas, and the late Mr Eric Johnson.

Among Amy's friends who have helped me I must first mention the man – a Swiss – whom she long hoped to marry. He allowed me to borrow her letters to him, and agreed to my quoting from them provided his identity was not disclosed. For this reason I have substituted a fictitious name, 'Franz', for his own name throughout the book. I would like to express my warm gratitude to 'Franz' (and also to thank his wife and sisters for their many kindnesses to me). Other close friends of Amy's whose assistance has been invaluable and who have given generously of their time are Mr Jack Humphreys, Miss Winifred Irving, Sir James Martin and Mr Peter Reiss. I am also most grateful to the following, who were all of them friends or acquaintances of Amy's: Air Marshal Sir

Richard Atcherley, Captain Hubert Broad, Mr Sidney Cotton, Sir William Crocker, Mrs Arthur Dawson, Major Hereward de Havilland, Lady du Cros, Mr and Mrs Eric Exley, Mr Duncan Gillies, Mr Ian Grabowsky, Mrs George Heycock, Dr W. Alexander Hislop, Mrs Jennings, Mrs Ledaine, the late Mr John Moore, Mrs Harold Robins, Mrs Audrey Ronald, Mr A. Norman Schofield, Miss Mary Sheppard, Mr L. Stonehouse and Mrs Harry Venton.

As regards research and other aspects of my work on the book I am especially indebted to Miss Mary de Bunsen and Mr Michael Daunt; also thanks to Mr R.F. Drewery (Chief Librarian of the Hull Public Libraries) and his staff, and to Mr S.T. Thompson (Bridlington Borough Librarian and Curator). Others I would like to thank include Mr J.M. Brue, Dr A.W. Chapman, Mrs Denman, Miss Vera Douie, Mr L.A. Jackets, Mr Thurstan James, Mr W.D.M. MacAdam, Miss Gillian Mackay, Miss M.F. MacKnight, Mr Peter Masefield, Mrs Powls, Mr and Mrs James Priestman, Mr Jeffrey Quill, Miss Winifred Roberts, Mr Laurence Sultan, Mr O.J. Tapper, Mr A. Webster and Miss Rose Winslade.

Approval of the quotations I have made from letters belonging to them was kindly given by Dame Rebecca West, the executors of Mrs Charles Bullmore, Mrs William Courtenay and Mr John Brancker; I also acknowledge permission from Messrs. Faber and Faber to quote from *The Cocktail Party* by T.S. Eliot, from the Lawrence Wright Music Co. to reproduce the lyric of 'Amy', from Temple Press Ltd, to include an extract from *The Aeroplane*, and from Associated Newspapers Ltd, to quote a passage by Wilhelmina Stitch from the *Daily Sketch*.

Amy's original letters contain a few mis-spellings and slips of grammar and puntuation; these I have corrected, and in most cases I have expanded habitual contractions. In cables I have inserted appropriate punctuation.

Constance Babington Smith
Cambridge August 1967

Part One
Prelude

1

A CHILD OF HULL

1903–1914

Amy Johnson was born on 1 July 1903 at number 154 St George's Road, Hull. With its red brick and blue slate muted by soot, and a touch of privet by the front door, it was one of a long row of two-storied bay-windowed terrace houses stretching northward from Hessle Road with its shops and pubs, and the clattering fish dock beyond, towards Anlaby Road, Hull's main east-west artery, then set with the late-Georgian residences of the well-to-do, and enlivened by the tram-cars rattling along to the Paragon railway station. St George's Road, lined with young lime trees, was one of the better streets which had been run up in the 1880s, when the Newington district of Hull sprang into existence, a repercussion of the great boom in the fishery business that followed the advent of the railways: for the first time fresh fish could be marketed on a large scale at inland centres.

Amy's father, John William Johnson, had been fortunate to get the house when he married Amy Hodge (invariably known by her childhood nickname of Ciss) in September 1902. One of the Johnson's next-door neighbours was a minister, the other a marine engineer, and all along St George's Road lived the families of men connected with the sea and ships: master mariners, a skipper, a shipping clerk, a Humber pilot, a fish merchant. Will Johnson himself[1] – then a young man of twenty-six – also worked in the fish business, as market salesman in the thriving family company Andrew Johnson, Knudtzon & Co., which his father had founded in 1881.

It was in the days of sail, in the 1860s, that Amy's grandfather – Anders Jorgensen as he then was – had come to England from Denmark. The home he left behind was a humble one; his father, a well-digger, lived in the village of Saltofte near Assens, on the flat western coast of Funen. Anders went off to sea in his early teens; in those days the crews of the fishing vessels that sailed the North Sea always included one or two boys, whose life was sometimes as harsh as Billy Budd's. Before long he arrived in Hull, then in a turmoil of activity. The 'colonisation' by the Brixham fishing fleet was in full swing, and the owners of the famous red-sailed trawlers from Devonshire were bringing their families north and settling in the Humber port, within reach of the newly discovered riches of the 'Silver Pit', a stretch of the North Sea near the Dogger Bank where sole and turbot along with coarser breeds of fish had previously multiplied undisturbed (before the trawlers came Hull's fishing boats had busied themselves with off-shore drifting for herring).

Jorgensen served his apprenticeship to a Hull smack-owner, and by 1878, when he was twenty-six, he had settled in Hull, having taken British nationality and changed his name to Andrew Johnson. By this time he had worked his way up to become the skipper of a fishing smack, then owner of a smack which was called *The Flowers of the Valley* (later he acquired a second, *The Flowers of the Field*). And he had married a lovely girl from Devonshire, Mary Ann Holmes, or Polly as she was always called, the step-daughter of one of the Brixham skippers, Andrew Mudge (Polly's mother had married Mudge after the tragic death of her first

---

[1] In the family he was always known as 'Will', though he was 'Bill' to most of his business friends.

husband Thomas Holmes, a naval stoker who was murdered by Indians near Vancouver).

Amy's grandfather had a shrewd sense of business, and strong-minded little Polly had no illusions about the great grey widow-maker: in a terrible storm not long after their marriage thirty-six smacks and two hundred and fifteen lives were lost. Thus in due course Andrew Johnson decided to exchange the seagoing life for a venture in two specialised departments of the booming fish trade, the import of fresh herrings and salmon from Scandinavia and the export of salted cod and haddock. In partnership with a Norwegian named Knudtzon (who died a few years later) he launched the company which was soon renowned in the fish trade as 'A.J.K.', one of the most successful firms in its field. Thenceforth his business life was based upon his main office on the quay of St Andrew's Dock – the Hull fishmarket – but he could still satisfy his urge to travel, for he had to make frequent trips abroad to develop foreign contacts.

The time when Amy was a child, just before the first world war, was the heyday of the herring trade with Scandinavia. It was a seasonal trade; from December till May many thousands of tons of herrings packed in ice were unshipped in Hull and sent on immediately to inland markets or to the local smokehouses for curing. The other department of 'A.J.K.', the saltfish export trade, was also exceedingly flourishing;[1] to cater for it Amy's grandfather had set up a large fish-drying farm on the outskirts of Hull. Those who lived near it to leeward cannot have been in any doubt as to the magnitude of the enterprise; acre after acre was massed with long racks a few feet off the ground, on which were laid out myriads of salted haddock and cod before being packed into barrels.

For more than thirty years Andrew Johnson presided over the business and eventually retired (in 1914), a

---

[1] There was a constant demand for this saltfish in Spain and other Catholic countries, for *bacalao* was, and still is, one of the cheapest of Friday diets.

bearded patriarchal figure, the father of a family of ten. All six of his sons went either into the fishery business or to sea. His eldest son, Amy's father, who succeeded him as head of the firm, was temperamentally very much like his father – though considerably shorter in stature. He had the same forceful, stubborn personality, the same head for business, the same urge for travel – for adventure too. He had first started in the family business at the age of fifteen, earning five shillings a week, but when he was twenty-one, in 1898, he had felt impelled to seek his fortune on the other side of the world. With three friends, Chris Olsen, Albert Bell and 'Jack' Brown, he had set off from Hull amid cheering crowds to join in the Klondyke gold rush. He did not however succeed in making a fortune and after two years he came home again and settled down to marriage and to the humdrum routine of his regular job. But he loved to reminisce about the gold rush days, and cherished yellowing photographs of mountain tracks deep in snow and rivers foaming through pine forests, as well as a grubby working map of the Atlin Gold Fields (it was a blue-printed sketch map showing the route from Skaguay over the White Pass trail, with here and there log cabins and many 'high unexplored mountains'). He had kept, too, his free-miner's certificate issued in Victoria BC on 18 February 1898. But all the treasure he brought home with him amounted to four gold nuggets which he later had made into a brooch for his wife and a tie-pin for himself.

Will Johnson was a staunch Wesleyan and for many years held the position of Sunday School Superintendent at the St George's Road Chapel. Hull had long been a stronghold of Methodism, and before the first war the chapels were still the firmest bond that held the city's middle classes together. But chapel-going was not merely a token of respectability; the lives of the congregations were permeated by Methodism's puritanical code. In the sphere of politics, too, its principles of fellowship engendered a tendency towards Liberalism. Amy's father, though not politically minded, always supported the

Liberal Party.

Yet progressive ideas have usually taken hold in Hull rather later than elsewhere. Kingston upon Hull, as it was named by King Edward I when he granted the town a charter of incorporation, has always clung to an unspoken tradition of minding its own business, of being on its own, the centre of its own world,[1] despite the fact that as a major seaport (not merely a fishery centre) it is a gateway to Scandinavia, to Europe, and to the rest of the world. Securely established for centuries in its own little corner of England it is unique among the industrial towns of the north. Before 1914, from Manchester and Birmingham and other provincial cities, the livelier spirits were already gravitating towards London; in Hull this came only later. Before 1914 the life of most of the citizens of Hull was entirely confined to Yorkshire. Leeds was the great metropolis, London a place one read about in the newspapers – few of the Hull populace had ever seen it for themselves.

It is true that certain men from Hull have gone out into the world and become famous; Andrew Marvell and Wilberforce both came from Hull, and so did Joseph Rank. But most of the city's great men have been great within their own orbit: mayors, philanthropists, leading men of business. Hull was, and is, above all a trading city. You do not live there – for that matter you are unlikely to go there at all – except for reasons of business. This does not mean that the seaport of the Humber is devoid of charm (the older parts of the town near the ancient quays and docks, though dingy and down-at-heel, still possess a sturdy dignity and an atmosphere of leisureliness that is rare at the present day). Romantic lovers of the past have even gone so far as to call it 'the Venice of the North'.

[1] At the present time Hull is the only city in Britain to possess its own telephone system, independent of the GPO.

II

Amy's maternal great-grandfather, William Hodge, attained to Hull's highest dignities (he was Sheriff in 1859 and became Mayor in 1860) and in Victorian times the Hodges, for a short while, enjoyed notable success as small industrialists. But William Hodge's career began in a rural setting not unlike that from which Amy's Danish grandfather set out to seek his fortune: his father owned a small farm near Kilnsea, the southernmost village on the Spurn peninsula. At twenty he went to work in a linseed-crushing mill in Hull;[1] by the 1840s he was a mill-owner and had made a fortune. W. Hodge, Esq. and his family moved into a handsome 'villa', Newington Hall, set in its own grounds just outside the city limits on the road to Anlaby,[2] and there they lived in some style, with table silver bearing a newly acquired family crest, a wheatsheaf encircled by an adder.

Hodge was a moody, unaccountable man, oscillating between open-handed jollity and an equally open-handed Nonconformism. He gave so lavishly to chapel-building and to the poor that before his death in 1867 the family moved from their villa to a smaller house nearer to the centre of Hull, a terrace house in Coltman Street off the Anlaby Road. Nevertheless he left a considerable fortune to his six children, and his eldest son, Amy's grandfather, who was also named William,

1 The seed-crushing industry had long shared with the whale-blubber trade in providing oil for lamps, candles and paint manufacture. As the whaling trade dwindled the seed-crushing business expanded, and Hull, hitherto a major port for whaling-ships, was well placed to become a nucleus for the trade in vegetable oils.
2 According to Sheahan's history of Hull, published in 1866, Newington Hall, though 'remarkable' was not classed as a 'seat'. There was, at the time, only one 'seat' in the immediate vicinity of Hull, namely Holderness House, the home of the Jalland family.

inherited the main business interests. A gay irresponsible charmer, with the musical talent that ran in the family, the younger William Hodge was not interested in business except as a source of cash. One after another the mills were sold, and after each sale he disappeared abroad with most of the proceeds, leaving his wife (the former Edith Ada Hague) to look after his family which eventually totalled eight. Probably at the insistence of his more provident brothers he invested some of the money in the timber business (one of Hull's most thriving industries) but he was a natural playboy and spendthrift, unable to shoulder responsibility.

Amy's mother, who was born in 1881, had childhood memories of plenty, and as a little girl she was taught by a governess instead of going to school. She, and also two of her brothers, Alfred and William, early showed a strong taste for music, and were given every chance to develop it. But by the time she was twelve or so her father's prodigality brought about a drastic lowering in the Hodge's standard of living. This decline in family fortunes and the descent from a sheltered childhood to the struggle of making do seem to have left a deep mark on her character. Some of those who knew her well believe it contributed to the recurrent 'nerves' from which she suffered throughout her life. Gentle, petite and dainty, with refined tastes as well as great charm, she apparently lived under some sort of hidden strain which not even her natural gaiety or her courage and her tenacity could always vanquish. Perhaps one of the roots of the trouble was a conflict of loyalties: when at twenty-one she married Will Johnson she identified herself with a family which, in the eyes of the Hull of those days, was considerably less distinguished than her own.

Ciss Johnson clung proudly to the heirlooms which bore witness to her better days; one was an exquisite little oval sewing case made of ivory, opening like an oyster shell to show delicate embroidery scissors and a silver thimble. She was also fanatically houseproud, and spring cleaning each year, even with the help of the 'little maids' who were then two a penny, was a ritual that brought her almost to the verge of breakdown. For a long time no pets were allowed in the household because, she insisted, they would shed hairs all over the place. But depsite her fussiness her husband and little girls adored her (Irene, a second daughter, was born a year and a half after Amy). In later life Amy cherished a childhood memory of her at a big wash-tub, the sleeves of her red and white blouse rolled up to the elbow. She sang gaily as she worked, not the popular songs of the day, but snatches of her favourite hymns, or fragments of the *Messiah*. Music was her solace and delight; whenever a chance came she would slip into the front room to her piano and to Beethoven. As an organist she was so renowned that she was often invited to play at chapels other than the one the family attended in St George's Road (there she was the official organist). The whole atmosphere of the Johnson home derived from her cherishing, melodious, lively presence. Almost always she seemed to be busy with her washing and ironing and mending, or else preparing a meal amidst the aroma of newly-baked bread. The Johnson's bread and cakes were always made at home; in the view of Amy's mother it was a disgrace to be seen shopping at a baker's.

III

A lot of work and a little play all through the week; chapel and sunday school and family visits and hymn-singing on Sundays; occasionally an outing to a concert or social, a few seaside weeks in the summer in rooms at Bridlington ('Brid' had not yet become a teeming holiday resort; it was still an over-grown fishing village): so the years went by for the Johnsons during the first decade of Amy's life. The main landmarks were when they moved house, first in 1909, for a short time to the Boulevard – a street of somewhat similar type to St George's Road; then again in 1910, when she was seven, to Alliance Avenue, which was farther north. It was here, in 1912, that the Johnsons' third daughter Molly was born, and the new house (which was their home throughout the first world war) though of the same variety as their first, was a better, larger, and more modern one.

This last move must have seemed almost into the country, for Alliance Avenue was then at the edge of the flat open fields of the East Riding. It was also socially an upward step, for northwards meant farther away from the smelly fish dock and nearer to Pearson Park with its polo ground and the exclusive 'Avenues'. The Johnsons' housemoving probably served as a spur to Amy's adventurousness, and may well have been behind some of the running-away-from-home legends which were given prominence, after Amy became famous, in popular accounts of her life. According to one of these Amy (at an unspecified age) went off on her own intending to journey 'to the north'. Having spent money-box savings on provisions such as toffee she boarded a bus which would take her as far northward as possible, then continued on foot. Eventually she tired of walking and hailed a car for a lift. Poor Amy! The driver proved to be a friend of her father's who took her straight home.

There is also a legend that Amy several times took her sister Irene along with her 'to find a new home'; once they strayed so far among unknown streets that they lost their way and had to be rescued by a policeman. As a child, so it seems, Amy enjoyed being an elder sister, and pretty little 'Reeny' responded trustingly to her initiative (Amy herself was a sweet-looking child, with big blue eyes, a candid gaze, and curly brown hair in ringlets, but she was never as ravishing as Irene). Their father was sometimes stern with the younger child, telling her not to be silly and timid – he had always longed for sons – but her sister understood her better and tried to comfort her. We have Amy's own word for the affection between herself and her sister; she wrote of it in an essay that she contributed long afterwards to a

1 This book, edited by the Countess of Oxford and Asquith, was published in 1938.

collection entitled *Myself When Young*.[1] 'It seemed my job to protect her,' she wrote. 'For hours I would sit at night in the dark, with the firelight leaping and making terrifying faces on the wall, too frightened to move, but holding on to my sister's hand protesting with shaking voice that there was nothing at all to be frightened of.'

The two were constant companions, so she recalled, and even after she went to school her sister was her only close playmate. They both delighted in games of their own invention, unconventional and often boisterous games such as trying to make a circuit of the front room without touching the floor, climbing or leaping from table to chair to piano, and once, disastrously, attempting to swing from the ceiling gas fitting. They also loved dressing up as fairy-tale characters; Amy as a child was especially addicted to fairy stories. But playing at shops was the childhood game that she liked most of all – so she declared in a letter written years later.

The precise date when she started school is uncertain, but it seems that before she was twelve she had attended several of the small private schools which then abounded in West Hull. Every street had one or two of these little schools, where a handful of children from nearby families (girls of all ages and a few little boys) met for classes held by maiden ladies of the governess type. It was the half-way house between the education of the well-to-do who still employed resident governesses, and the board schools where children of the working class were sent from the age of five.

Only one of Amy's private-school reports has survived. It is for the summer term of 1914, when she was almost eleven and was attending the Eversleigh House School in Anlaby Road, an establishment with a reputation for 'exclusiveness' rather than for high academic standards. It shows that she excelled in Literature and History and that her Arithmetic was also 'very good indeed'; the report bristles with high marks and 'Excellents'. But since at this time the school in question, like most of the Hull private schools, was having a continual struggle to keep its numbers up, this glowing assessment must not be taken too liteally. It does nevertheless indicate that Amy was a bright child, and that her standard was well above the average. The concluding 'General Report', signed by the Principal, Miss Ada Knowles, reads as follows: 'Excellent progress continues to be made. Interest shown in all work'.

2

TO SCHOOL AND TO THE PICTURES
1914–1922

The first world war made little direct impact on Amy's life, and the usual round at Alliance Avenue continued much as before: the fact that her father's work was concerned with food supplies meant that he was not called up. But the Zeppelin raids, when the buzzer warning sent everyone into cellars or under the stairs or out into open country (which many thought safer) brought home that civilians were now 'in the front line'. There was plenty of time to take shelter because the 'Zepp' was usually picked up by the Flamborough Head searchlights, and after that nearly half an hour elapsed before it reached the Humber. The Hull docks and factories were important targets, and during the early part of the war, when the German naval airships were over Britain quite often, they were bombed again and again. The casualties and damage, though slight compared to those Hull suffered from the Luftwaffe, seemed very shocking at the time; in the worst raid twenty-five people were killed and a hundred injured.

For Amy the night raids meant the thrill of sitting up long after bedtime and drinking cocoa when all was quiet again. One of the occasions that stood out in her memory (according to *Myself When Young*) was the time when she was chased indoors by her father after slipping out into the street to catch a glimpse of the Zepp. As she stumbled down the steps of the cellar where the family was sheltering, with her father after her, it was a hysterical moment, and Irene added a final touch by collapsing into a coal bucket.

The Johnson children knew that something terrible was happening, far away in France, because their favourite aunt (Mrs Hamlyn Petrie, their father's sister Evelyn) was so white and silent – their Uncle Hamlyn was missing – but the horror was at many removes. To Amy and her sisters the most strange and terrifying event of the war was nothing to do with hostilities. Molly's memory of it is still vivid: in the spring of 1918 their father (then forty-two) went down with a severe skin disease, erysipelas, and the attack proved to be unusually acute: the war years had been a time of great strain for him; since 1914 he had been at the helm of the family business, in place of his ageing father. To the children it was not only alarming that a strange nurse should be living in the house to look after him, but almost blasphemous that the omnipotent Daddy should be lying prostrate and delirious in bed, his head and face obliterated by bandages except for the narrow slits for his eyes.

II

Most of the happenings of Amy's life during the war years were the normal events of early adolescence, set against the regular pattern of her life at home and the rough and tumble of a co-educational day school; when she was twelve her parents decided to send her to 'The Boulevard', the largest municipal secondary school in the district, with more than two hundred pupils. In those days the Boulevard was not quite up to grammar-school standard; only a few of the staff had graduated from universities. Most of the teachers (the children too) lived in terror of the Principal, Mr Frederick De Velling, a tall, ramrod-straight, frock-coated martinet. According to his lights he acted always in the best interests of the school, to which he was devoted, but his methods could hardly create a happy atmosphere. The fact that he believed himself a supreme exampe of the school's motto *Non Sibi, Cunctis* ('Not for oneself alone, but for all') was a matter of bitter amusement to the staff. His second-in-command, Miss Edith Clews, the headmistress, was an elderly spinster. Small and plump, she lacked any academic distinctions but was, nevertheless, obviously conscious of her own importance.

It was in the autumn of 1915 that Amy started at the Boulevard and she soon took to her new school. During her first term, when by chance she was put with younger girls, she jumped to the top of the class and there – so she claims – she threw her weight about and led 'rebellions' with gusto, like the heroines of the currently popular schoolgirl dramas of Angela Brazil. In the Boulevard's lower forms the boys and girls were kept strictly apart, but in spite of this (according to Duncan Gillies, a schoolboy friend of Amy's) and in spite of the bars that divided the asphalt playgrounds, there were frequent meetings in and out of school; often, for instance, at Mrs Goodyear's sweetshop where the children queued for their wartime rations of sticky toffee. Amy (so she says) was soon priding herself on her popularity with the boys and trying to compete with them. She preferred cricket and hockey to tennis because they were boys' games, and enjoyed being the only girl in the school to bowl overarm, while in the gymnasium she revelled in the most arduous athletics such as trapeze work and high springboard jumping.

III

The doings of Amy's second and third years at the Boulevard, 1917 and 1918, are spotlighted in minute detail by a diary her father kept at the time, and from it we know that when she was not quite fourteen she was given a bicycle. This brought a sudden opening up of horizons. At weekends during the summer she often went for rides with her father, and sometimes the whole family rode together to visit his sister Mrs Campey – 'Aunt Annie' – at Cottingham, then a country village. Another pleasant ride, to the west of Hull, began past the turning to the fish dock. Soon the Hessle Road led out on to the flats alongside the Humber, which on bright days shimmers silver and sandy gold like shot silk, with the distant line of Lincolnshire emerging clearly beyond. Then the cyclists took a turning to the right leading past stretches of barley and oats, between hedgerows bright with willowherb, and found themselves in the winding lanes that pass through the first villages of the Wold country: North Ferriby, West Ella, Kirk Ella and Willerby. Here and there they came to a dip in the road; a glorious swoop downhill, then a hard climb up the other side. And sometimes they came back through Swanland and Anlaby, past the gates of Tranby Croft with its fine tall trees.

There was also one very long ride on the opposite side of Hull, fifteen miles each way, to stay with 'Auntie Maud' (one of the Hodge aunts) at Withernsea. Amy and her father would start off through the city with its tram-cars and horse-drawn carts, past the statue of Queen Victoria and the glimpses of the docks, and out on to the Hedon road, the main highway into the countryside of Holderness. It was an easy ride, almost flat all the way, the road winding between hedges full of dogroses, with every now and then a distant view of a majestic steeple; first Hedon's massive tower, then the pinnacle of Patrington.

But Amy's bicycle was not only a means for family expeditions and for dashing quickly to school. It enabled her to share, on the sly, in a delightfully dangerous sport which, so Duncan Gillies says, was a favourite of the most daring boys at school. It consisted in riding full tilt towards a brick wall and at the last moment skidding violently sideways, as a speedway rider skids round a cinder track. The tomboy stage of Amy's schooldays is also indicated by an entry which her father made in his diary in January 1918: 'Amy hit over the eye with some ice thrown by boys at school.' That was not the only time she had suffered a horrid accident when a cricket ball caught her full in the face and smashed her front teeth, which had to be replaced by false ones.[1] According to *Myself When Young* these new teeth were a disfigurement that caused Amy agonies of self-consciousness. 'Dentistry in those days not being what it is now,' she wrote, 'there was no doubt that my looks were seriously impaired . . . The boys made fun of me . . . I became introspective and withdrew farther and farther into a protective shell of my own making.' Whether or not this accident was the sole cause, the fact that Amy was painfully shy at this time is confirmed by some of her fellow pupils and also by two of the teachers who were then on the Boulevard staff, Miss Sheppard, who taught Amy French, and Miss Hanby, who taught Latin. It does seem certain that for a time, or at least for recurrent periods during her later teens, Amy became miserably shy and awkward. In certain photographs taken at this time (she hated being photographed) her candid look has changed into a glum stare.

Meanwhile, as though to exacerbate her misery, her younger sister Irene was blossoming into a most attractive young girl, gay and sparkling, with laughing hazel eyes and graceful ways. She had followed Amy to the Boulevard, and there she gained a reputation for being well-behaved and also 'brilliant in patches' – this refers especially to the little plays she produced. We know from subsequent letters that at home Irene's brilliance was openly acknowledged; her mother worshipped her and it is hardly surprising that she became adept at wheedling her parents. Not in the least shy, and with a lovely voice, she seized any chance to sing before an audience, and was encouraged to assume that the centre of the stage and delighted applause were her natural right. Each New Year's Eve, so Molly remembers, it was a family tradition to act charades, which culminated with a representation of the old year's exit and the advent of the new. Everyone took it for

---

1 The date of the accident is uncertain, but in the autumn of 1917 Will Johnson noted in his diary 'Amy got her new teeth'.

granted that while Amy acted the old year – draped in long dark robes, with a bit of white rabbit fur as a beard, and hobbling to imitate an old man – the scintillating Irene, fairy-like all in white, should take the part of the new year full of hope and joy.

Christmas and New Year were always a time of parties and entertainments for the Johnson family, when all the children were taken to the pantomime and to the circus (often by their mother's kind old uncle Alfred Hodge). But already during Amy's early teens the steady diet of her imaginative mind was 'the pictures' – the cinema of the silent films. In *Myself When Young* she goes so far as to say that the cinema was 'the big influence' in her life at this time. Will Johnson's diary too confirms that she was a constant cinema-goer (at fourteen she saw mostly adventure films, and then as she grew older spectacular historical romances).

IV

At the end of the war Amy's family moved into the Pearson Park district – the most select in North-West Hull – to 85 Park Avenue, an imposing semi-detached residence in the late Victorian style, with two upper stories and behind it a small garden. Socially it was a leap upwards. Such a sudden ascent was made possible chiefly by the fact that Norway had remained neutral during the war, and in consequence the herring trade of 'A.J.K.' had prospered exceedingly. To Will Johnson's friends his new address – with solicitors, well-to-do merchants, and the American Consul as near neighbours – proclaimed his success in the business world, and he was soon elected a member of the city's Rotary Club. In keeping with his new status, his motor-cycle was replaced by a car, and before long the Johnsons ran two cars, a Standard saloon and a two-seater Morris Oxford. But in many ways affluence did not change him: during the football season he still liked to spend his Saturday afternoons in the jostle of Hull City supporters, while at home in the evenings his favourite hobby was, as always, his stamp collecting.

AMY JOHNSON

To Amy's mother the move to Park Avenue was a delight; a return at the age of thirty-eight to the standards she had known as a child. At last she had a home where the silver sugar bowl with the Hodge crest looked in place;[1] at last a drawing-room instead of a front room – a fit setting for the grand piano she soon acquired. Such was the home where, in May 1919, she gave birth to her fourth child Betty (thus there was a gap of about sixteen years between Amy and her youngest sister).

In the autumn of 1919 Amy moved into the Fifth Form at the Boulevard to prepare for School Certificate, and a year later, when she was seventeen, she succeeded in passing the Cambridge Senior Local Examination with second class honours in History and French. A letter which she wrote to her father just before she sat for it provides a glimpse of what she herself thought of her own abilities. 'I don't want you to expect too much from me,' she wrote, 'because I know you'll only be disappointed. I'm not at all exceptionally clever, but just of ordinary average intelligence, and it isn't as if I'd only my own class to compete against. There are centres for this exam all over the world.' One of her school reports at about this time shows that her estimate was probably not far out, although on the diffident side. Mr J.W. Waddy, her form master at the end of her year in the Fifth Form wrote of her general conduct: 'Keen, conscientious-all-round worker. Position well earned. Above average ability. Keen in school and on the playing field.' 'Keen on the playing field' relates mainly to hockey but also to cricket, and it is of interest that Amy distinguished herself at team games as well as in the individualistic achievements of the gym, though she probably gave a good deal more to

[1] Ciss Johnson's pride in this sugar bowl was a source of much amusement to Amy, who used to tease her mother by pretending that she thought the Hodge wheatsheaf (because of its similarity to the trademark of the Co-operative Society) signified that the sugar bowl had been bought at 'the Co-op'.

the latter. Throughout her schooldays, in addition to her regular practice in the school gym she often went with Irene to practise in the gymnasium at the Young People's Institute, and the two of them sometimes took part in the displays that were given there.

In the Boulevard's Upper School the boys and girls, all cramming for the same examinations, were no longer segragated. But as in the Lower School rigid rules were enforced as to when and where converse between the sexes might take place (no private rendezvous of any kind was permitted). This rule was of course often evaded though usually discreetly enough to avoid observation. Amy and Duncan Gillies, however, once made the mistake of walking together in Pearson Park, both of them in school uniform, and they were spotted by a form mistress and reported.

The strictness of the school regulations and also the negative attitude of the Principal exasperated Amy. A sport that she loved was swimming, and she initiated an attempt to start a girls' swiming club at the Boulevard. But the idea was crushed by De Velling who maintained that swimming was an unladylike sport. This incited Amy to take matters into her own hands. There was a bath in the Beverley Road where she and Irene often practised, and she persuaded her father to hire it so that she could stage a girls' swimming contest. She then invited Miss Sheppard to present the prizes, which put the teacher in an awkward position. After considerable heart-searchings she agreed to officiate, on Amy's assurance that no hint of the affair should appear in the local press. Amy kept her word. The contest went off without a hitch and also without publicity, and De Velling never mentioned it so presumably knew nothing of it.

The influence of Mary Sheppard may well have been the most beneficent in Amy's school life: the fact that French became one of her best subjects speaks for itself. Miss Sheppard describes Amy as an unusual girl, clearly with potentialities but always a 'lone wolf'. She made no intimate friends at school, belonged to no clique. In class she was not an easy pupil; it often seemed impossible to kindle a spark in her, to raise a laugh or even a smile. Possibly, so Miss Sheppard believes, she might have blossomed in the less restricted schools of a generation later; at the Boulevard as it was in her day she alternately withdrew into her shell and sallied out to embark on some original escapade.

The swimming contest is not the best known exampel of Amy's defiance of school authority. In the so-called Revolt of the Straw Hat Brigade[1] she tried to lead a rebellion against the hated straw hats, known as 'bangers', which all the Boulevard pupils had to wear. We do not know the exact date of this incident, but it was probably some time in 1920, when Amy was seventeen. For it was then that Irene was moved from the Boulevard to the more select Hull High School where the pupils wore soft panama hats. Amy made up her mind that the Boulevard girls should wear them too. Her resolve was not an unreasonable one: the teaching staff, who had to wear 'bangers' like the pupils, disliked them – so Miss Sheppard confirms – just as much as the children, for they were uncomfortable, impractical and ugly. 'Somehow or other,' Amy wrote in *Myself When Young*, 'I persuaded my mother to buy me a Panama hat, and to put around it my Boulevard ribbon and badge, and one fine morning I turned up wearing this hat, expecting to be supported by the whole class who had promised faithfully to do the same. I was the only one to turn up in a Panama!' Her excruciating punishment was to have to wait, seemingly for hours, wearing the offending hat, outside Miss Clews' door – the laughing-stock of the whole school. Perhaps Amy's ordeal taught her something of human nature but it did not damp her reforming spirit. Some years later she wrote to her sister Molly, then thirteen: 'Try a few Angela Brazil

[1] In the film of Amy's life *They Flew Alone* it is represented as typifying her childhood.

stunts. Get your form to refuse to work unless they'll give you at least two hours' games per week. It would be great fun, but you'd never get them to do it. When I tried to institute the wearing of Panama hats at the Boulevard no one would follow my example. The majority of schoolgirls have no gumption at all.'

V

Amy's parents decided that she should not leave school when she was eighteen, in the summer of 1921. Instead she stayed on for a second year in the Sixth Form and when she eventually left she was almost nineteen. Although at home with her sisters (so we know from letters she wrote to her parents when they were away) she was, at this time, happy and full of fun, her final year at school was intensely irksome to her as far as work was concerned. Having passed School Certificate she found no incentive in working for another examination of about the same level, the Oxford Senior Local (though when she took it, in March 1922, she passed with first class honours). According to *Myself When Young* she continually played truant or arrived late in the morning, and since any girl who came late had to offer an explanation to Miss Clews she became adept at inventing excuses. Pupils who stayed on for a second year in the Sixth Form normally became prefects as a matter of course, but since Amy was so often unpunctual she forfeited this privilege. Gwyneth Roulston, a girl from Hessle just younger than her, who first became acquainted with her while she was in the Sixth Form, and later became a close friend, remembers her as aloof and bored and solitary. At this stage Amy's shyness seems to have isolated her almost entirely, in spite of opportunities which came her way for making friends not only at school.

At about this time she became a teacher in the primary department of the Sunday School belonging to the Prince's Avenue Wesleyan Chapel, the Johnson family's chapel since they moved to Park Avenue (though not, so it seems, because of any special religious zeal on her part). Amy and seven other young Methodists, three girls and four boys of about the same age, formed a teachers' group which was also an informal club. Together they often went 'rambling' into the countryside and the eight also joined forces regularly for theatres and cinemas. Two marriages and several lasting friendships arose from these outings, but Amy always remained aloof. She was never an enthusiastic chapel-goer, so her sister Molly remembers, but it is of interest to find, in an essay by her which was published in *The Boulevardian* in April 1921, a chance reference which shows that she was nevertheless imbued with Methodist morals. The subject of her composition was 'New Year's Day in China', and the essay ends with the following observation about the holiday habits of the Chinese: 'A large portion of the people gamble, drink or smoke, and so frequently quarrel, thus marring what would otherwise be a period of rest and enjoyment.'

As the months of 1922 slipped by the problem of Amy's future became an urgent one, and within the Johnson family there was some diversity of views. But the Boulevard's Principal had no doubts. De Velling's daughter Elizabeth was reading Modern Languages at Sheffield University, as a step towards a teaching career, and to him it was obvious that no Boulevard girl who was eligible for a university could do better than follow her examle. Besides, the Board of Education offered a grant covering all university fees to students who undertook to go on into teaching. Amy herself (so her letters indicate) was pleased to fall in with this plan, and found the prospect of 'college' very exciting. No matter if she were nominally committed to teaching; she could evade that later on. Eagerly, in the summer of 1922, she prepared to set off from home for the first time.

3

'ROMANCE'

1922

Before Amy left for her first term at Sheffield in the autumn of 1922, when she was sixteen, she had fallen in love for the first time. The young man was not one of her Hull neighbours, but a newcomer from abroad, and his foreign accent and sophisticated ways gave him, in Amy's eyes, the glamour of a Rudolph Valentino. Franz was a Swiss, eight years her senior and accustomed to success with the ladies. Sturdily built and not very tall he had a squarish face and clear-cut features; his fine grey-blue eyes could be steely but they flashed with charm when he smiled. His smile also gave charm to his full lips though his face in repose could look sullen. There was a gay side to him, yet his frowning brow and dryly mocking manner betrayed that he was by temperament a worrier.

Franz had come to England early in 1921 to work in the Hull branch of a Swiss organization, and throughout the summer he commuted from Bridlington; it was there, at a tennis club, that he met Amy's Aunt Evelyn, and Amy was introduced to him at a party of her aunt's during the following winter. He did not at first pay much attention to Mrs Petrie's young niece, but for Amy it was worship at first sight, and she immediately took the initiative in trying to see more of him (partly through her aunt, partly by attending the meetings of Hull clubs such as the French Circle where she knew she might run into him).

Already by March 1922 – while she was still in the sixth form at the Boulevard – they were on a Christian-name footing, and Amy was writing to him to his office impulsively apologising for being 'horrid and bad-tempered' the day before. 'I daresay you've forgotten all about it, but I've not . . . Foreigners always seem to have such perfect manners, and I'm afraid you'll think I haven't any.' And then, in a PS, 'Please don't think I'm silly for writing, will you? It relieves my mind a bit.' Before the end of the summer, which for Amy was the interim between school and university, a flirtation was in full swing; Amy, coy but tenacious, leading the way, and Franz responding with reserve but at the same time a certain amount of amused interest. Although his life had been full of variety (he had served as an officer in the Swiss frontier force during the recent war) he was not accustomed to the genteel advances of an English girl such as Amy – a girl who was at the same time entirely inexperienced, determined to appear sophisticated, and steeped in the romantic lore of the cinema.

During the summer of 1922 Franz took Amy out fairly often, sometimes dancing or to the pictures, sometimes for an expedition when she rode pillion behind him on his motor-cycle. To her delight he taught her how to manage a cigarette, that daring symbol of feminine emancipation. She also enjoyed helping him with his English which incited him to tease her about her future as a school-teacher. To this she retorted (for she always liked to have the last word) that since he himself was planning to make a little extra by giving French coaching, he would soon be a school-teacher too. Tennis, a game she had formerly despised, became her favourite because Franz liked it, and she eagerly encouraged him to introduce her to his friends and acquaintances.

Although at first Franz evaded Amy's pursuit by gently making fun of her, soon after her arrival at Sheffield he sent her a snapshot of himself, and a regular correspondence began. Franz was fairly communicative about his doings but did not disguise the fact that his main object in writing to her was to improve his English, for she relished commenting on it in scrupulous detail. She also seized any chance that offered to throw in an arch remark such as 'If you're tired of boarding-houses, you know the remedy, don't you?' and 'I hope you've enlightened Mrs B—— [his landlady] as to "our engagement". The only engagement we've got is to write to each other, isn't it, *cher frère*?' One of her girl-friends had been telling her, so she reported coquettishly, that she ought to get engaged to keep her steady: 'She says I need tying down . . . She yearns for men's society (*même que moi*).' But Amy's letters, though primarily outpouring 'to relieve her mind', are also full of spontaneous and vivid accounts of the new life she was entering as a university student.

II

Her first impressions of Sheffield were as rose-coloured as the Virginia creeper that adorned 'the College' on Western Bank. As a new student devoid of any standards of comparison she did not realise that the university was then at a difficult transitional stage. It was no longer a raw amalgamation of technical schools, but, in a Sheffield severely hit by the post-war depression, it had not yet had the chance to become the flourishing provincial university it is today. The main problem was that the total number of students (by 1922 some eight hundred) had more than doubled since before the war, and many now came from outside the city area. There were more young women than ever before (nearly a quarter of the total) and the halls of residence provided nothing like enough accommodation for the girls whose homes were out of reach. The remainder had to live in 'approved lodgings'. This meant that about fifty girls, including Amy and two of her Hull friends, Gwyneth Roulston and Miriam Benham, who like herself had been bundled off from the Boulevard on teachers' grants, had to live a floating existence full of petty irritations.

But on the day after Amy arrived in Sheffield she

wrote to Franz in a glow of excitement from her lodgings in Grange Crescent Road, a drably respectable street off Sharrow Lane: 'Thank goodness I'm here and settled . . . I have decided irrevocably (will you have to look that word up?) to take French, English, Latin and modern European history . . . It is very pretty round here, and very healthy and bracing. The hills are lovely and there's a very pretty cemetery to walk through each day. The rooms are very comfortable and Mrs Skinner (the landlady) is nice and fat and kind. Wish I'd somebody here to take me out! When are you coming over? . . . The University is quite decent – lovely large rooms, long corridors, little towers etc. Quite romantic in parts. There's a sweet little fountain stuck in the middle of the quadrangle . . . The Dean of the Faculty of Arts [Professor Douglas Knoop] is charming. He wears a cap and gown and I took his photograph. He seemed quite astonished but I said "thank you" politely and retreated . . . If you come here Mrs Skinner will show you all her glass and china and antiquities. She collects ancient things. She had a lovely model of a Swiss chalet, and has been in Switzerland for some time herself . . . Please don't take my letters as models of English. They are *not*, quite emphatically. *Repondez en francais, s'il vous plaît.*'

Once or twice Amy tried writing to Franz in French, but after he had marked in red ink no less than fifty-nine errors of grammar, spelling and idiom in one of her letters she gave it up, though she still liked to throw in an occasional French phrase. She persevered for some time in advising him on English, and one interesting example of her tuition has survived. 'What are "co-spectators"?' she asked. 'We just say "the rest of the audience" . . . We don't say "Banal truth". It's purely a dictionary word and very rarely used. Do you mean "commonplace, everyday truths"? . . . What do you mean by "I have brought Arnold Bennett quite in fashion in my surroundings?" (By the way, I'm quite determined to read some of his books. I'm going to join a library here).'

But Amy had no time for novels in the whirl of her first term, when she was soon caught up in the current fashion for dancing and jazz – foxtrots were still the latest craze from NewYork.[1] 'We've got the gramophone on tonight and all I want at present is someone to dance with. I'm simply aching for a dance,' she told Franz during her second week. She also related that at her first formal dance she had cut a considerable dash. 'Being a fresher I was told I needn't expect to get any dances as the senior men didn't bother themselves with newcomers. But to my own astonishment (and incidentally to the other freshers' surprise and envy – now don't laugh) I got my program[2] full at the very beginning. One of the dear people on the committee (don't forget the *two* m's, will you) evidently took a fancy to me (again, don't raise your eyebrows and look sarcastic) and kindly introduced me right round . . . Really it was quite a triumph for a fresher . . . I had my yellow dress on! (perhaps that did it!).'

Among other new experiences that Amy enjoyed were the debates at the Students' Union. The first she attended, with Miriam Benham, was on the motion 'That Prohibition would be beneficial to the nation'. The two girls joined the opposition (which won) but Amy was not yet prepared to speak in public, though she was eager to argue about drink and Prohibition with Franz. 'You know very well that I don't believe in people drinking,' she told him. 'People can be strict teetotallers and yet not agree with Prohibition. I'm surprised at you

[1] According to the official history of Sheffield University 'a prolonged epidemic of dancing' was one of the most notable features of student life during the post-war years, and in addition to the many formal affairs with bands and programmes, 'unofficial dances were held, indeed broke out at odd times and places, especially in the lunch hour'. At one time the Firth Hall, the University's largest assembly hall, had to be kept locked against invasion. Just before Amy came up the mid-day dances had been banned, because of their alleged effects on examination results, but most of the students were still dancing-mad.
[2] American spellings frequently appear in Amy's letters of this period; presumably she picked up the habit from the silent films of which she saw so many.

drinking whiskey and am very glad you felt queer after it. Your phrase that "it didn't seem to agree with you in such quantities" gives me a vision of you rolling home at midnight.'

And then there was hockey – the glorious but anguishing excitement of playing in the University's first eleven, and the thrill of visiting other northern cities for away matches. Liverpool especially moved her. 'It was simply spiffing . . . the University there is heaps bigger than Sheffield and they have over a thousand students.' After the match and a memorable tea 'we went to the pierhead and watched the ferries going across. I enjoyed that the most of anything. It was a beautiful night with a half moon and it was fascinating watching the huge, long ferries gliding across the black water. All you could see of them were the lights and each one had a different coloured light. Crimson, blue, green, yellow and white. All we could see of the opposite bank of the river were rows and rows of twinkling lights. It was beautiful and fresh walking up and down and I didn't want to go away. If I lived in Liverpool I should go there every moonlight night.'

III

The crescendo of Amy's first term, with the lectures, the essays, the chapel-going she had promised her mother ('and it's half an hour's walk, and collection out of my allowance'), the hockey, the letter-writing, the irresistible lure of ragtime and of the pictures, reached a climax in early November when the Varsity Rag took place. Amy, Gwyneth, and Miriam disguised themselves as Red Indians. 'We did look fierce,' she wrote to Franz a few days later, 'but got quite a lot of money [for local hospitals] . . . In the evening we raided a theatre and went mad in general. I don't think I've quite recovered yet.' At this point her 'nice, fat, kind' landlady became less benevolent and lectured her about burning the candle at both ends: 'Mrs Skinner says I'm on the downward path in every particular'. To this she retorted that she had now reached the age of incorrigibility and avoided further argument by slipping out to the pictures. Franz as well as Amy had landlady problems, and when she learnt that he had moved to new lodgings she inquired whether his new 'all-round sporting landlady', as he had described her, was still living up to his expectations, 'or has she turned out to be as loquacious and tactless as the rest?'

After the Varsity Rag and the subsequent Varsity Ball it suddenly came to light that Amy had to take an important end-of-term examination. 'We're having exams . . . on which our future fate depends. If we don't do well enough, we're turned out of the Honors School, and if I can't take Honors I don't want to take anything.' She did not do well in this examination. The results came through when she was back in Sheffield after Christmas, and in deeply chastened mood she wrote to break the news to Franz. 'I've failed in French. I've never failed before, and it's a horrid feeling. Miriam has as well, but Gwyneth hasn't. She's awfully clever. We're trying to get the Faculty to let us take English Honors instead, and then you don't say you've failed, but simply that you've been transferred. That doesn't sound half so bad.' She was not permitted to take English Honours, but Professor Knoop, the stolid Manchester economist whom she had photographed on her arrival, was able to suggest an alternative that she was glad to accept. She could read for an Ordinary Degree if she took French, Latin and either Economics or Logic as her primary subjects. Amy, subdued and humble, chose Economics rather than Logic – in *Myself When Young* she claimed that she made this choice because Economics seemed 'much less learned and academic'.

On the day after she broke the news of her failure to Franz an unexpected package arrived from Hull; a box of chocolates from him, in gratitude for her help in improving his English. Amy doted on chocolates and as she savoured them – they were of a kind she had never tasted before – she may well have reflected that academic successes are not the only thing in life.

4

RED-BRICK

1923-1925

When the name Amy Johnson filled the headlines one of the Sheffield lecturers asked Professor Knoop whether he realised that the heroine of the day was a former student of his. 'Amy Johnson!' he exclaimed, 'Was she ever here? What was she like?' She was Winifred Irving's shadow,' replied the lecturer, and his answer neatly sums up not only the impression Amy left on the Sheffield staff but also the character of the friendship which proved the most enduring of her university years.

Her first term had been so full of excitement that she had not felt the lack of an intimate friend in Sheffield, but early in 1923, after the shock of having to give up hope of the Honours School, she was attacked by loneliness and confided her misery to Franz. It was a misery which, to her surprise, she had just discovered was shared by her father, then away on one of his trips abroad – 'the feeling of being alone in a crowd'. Soon after this Winifred Irving's name began to appear in her letters home and to Franz. 'I've made friends at Varsity with ever such a nice girl called Winnie Irving,' she wrote to her mother. 'She lives in Sheffield and it's her first year as well. She's taking Economics Honors and is a very interesting talker. She often speaks at debates.' To Franz she described her looks, or rather her sparkle: 'You'd like Winnie awfully – piles of character and personality, though not specially beautiful.'

RED-BRICK

Winifred herself can well remember the occasion when she first set eyes on Amy; they did not actually become friends until some months later. It had been at the freshers' dance during the autumn term. Winifred was with some of her Sheffield friends, and one of them drew her attention, with a disparaging comment, to a girl on the other side of the hall. Amy was at that moment laughing in a most amused way at a little entertainment that was being given, and Winifred was immediately attracted by the way she laughed.

The chance to become acquainted arose during their second term, when the two girls found themselves walking home after lectures by the same route. The Irving family lived in Nether Edge (a suburb almost two miles from Western Bank and then close to open country) while Amy's Sharrow lodgings were in the same direction though not nearly so far out. Winifred, who was three months younger than Amy, was already emerging from among the mass of students as one of the new leaders, and in the friendship between the two there was, on Amy's side, a strong element of hero-worship. Meanwhile Winifred was attracted by Amy's warm sweetness, a quality which hardly anyone outside her family was allowed to discover, for few were gifted with the knack of putting her entirely at ease. At twenty Amy possessed little charm; her shyness often made her seem either aloof or aggressive, and she suffered from occasional 'black moods' when she gave vent to pessimism and impatience.

Winifred was, like Amy, one of four sisters, but she was the youngest of her family not the eldest, and her home background was rather different. The Irvings were Plymouth Brethren, and Winifred's father, a Scottish engineer who had been trained on Clydeside and had taken a job connected with the Sheffield steelworks, seemed to his gay young daughter a dour spoil-sport, always against parties and amusements. Winifred kept quiet in his presence but once out of sight went her own way, dancing and smoking and flirting, like Amy and all the others. Among her own friends she made up for her silence at home, and as an idealist with an ardent belief in internationalism she radiated crusading zeal. Soon in the Students' Union she was on the Committee for European Student Relief and also secretary of the Debates Committee. Furthermore she took on the job of treasurer to the University Dramatic Society, a thankless task because the society was well on the way to decease. Besides all this she played hockey steadily in the university's first eleven, and later for Yorkshire. Everyone at Western Bank knew Winifred Irving, and if in 1930 someone had told Professor Knoop that *she* had sprung to fame as a woman pilot he would not have been in the least surprised.

In *Floreamus*, then the university magazine, her name recurred continually during the years she was up. During the same period there was only one mention of Amy, when she acted in *Lady Windermere's Fan* in the Lent term of 1923 (it was almost the last production of the Dramatic Society). 'The part of Lady Agatha Carlisle was played in a finished manner by Miss Amy Johnson, who also filled the less important role of Rosalie': this was the reviewer's comment, and several of Amy's Sheffield friends remember that she looked charming in costume. 'We have got into the habit of calling each other by the names in the play,' she wrote to Franz, 'and now I am greeted on all sides with "Agatha darling" to which I am expected to reply "Yes, Mama", as that was my special phrase in the play.'

II

At Sheffield in the 1920s women students who had been living in lodgings for their first year were usually given a chance to move into a hall of residence for their second. Gwyneth Roulston moved into Endcliffe Hall after a year in rooms, and so far as she can remember Amy could also have done so if she wished. But by this time the freedom of living out had become a habit and she preferred to be on her own. Early in 1924 she moved to lodgings in Thompson Road, a Sharrow

terrace overlooking the valley site of Wilson's snuff
factory. But she stayed there only a few weeks for she
found that the charges were beyond her – a guinea a
week for 'residence' plus another ten shillings for
board. 'The question of money worries me far more
than all my work put together,' she told her mother.

Was Amy an abnormally bad manager, or was her
allowance really inadequate? The official grant covered
her university fees, and she had a dress allowance of
something like a pound a week (which she often
overspent, though it should have been ample) but she
seems to have had to meet all other expenses, including
board and lodging, out of a living allowance from her
father (unfortunately no record of its amount has come to
light). By nature she was inconsistent about money. Most
of the time she was very careful – having been brought up
to be thrifty – but occasonally she indulged in a wild
shopping spree or bought some rashly generous present.
It is tempting to see here a manifestation of the Hodge
tendency to careless spending: in the family it
was affectiontately acknowledged that Ciss Johnson was
incapable of keeping accounts; Amy's musical Uncle
Willy was even more unrealistic as regards the cost of
living, and in the previous generation, too, Amy's Hodge
grandfather had shown himself unable to manage money.
But another point concerning the family's finances
may be relevant here. Will Johnson's business life,
depending as it did so largely upon the weather and
the catches, was essentially precarious. Several of Amy's
letters to her mother from Sheffield echo his anxieties.
'Hope Daddy's quite well and not too worried,' she
wrote in one. In another 'If he has as much worry with
his money proportionately as I have with mine, I'm
very sorry for him,' and in a third, 'Am sorry Daddy's not
very well. He does have such an awful lot of worry that
there's no wonder he gets depressed . . . I hope it will be a
big relief to him when I begin to earn for myself. It won't
be long now.'

She pined to escape from having to beg every extra.
Once a Bachelor of Arts (even with an Ordinary Degree)

– so she hopefully imagined – she would have no trouble in securing a well paid post. But she ignored the fact, or perhaps did not realise, that only a few professions were then open to women. She once surprised a fellow student who took the inevitablility of a teaching career for granted by announcing that she had no intention of teaching because she meant to see the world. So far she had seen very little indeed of the world. She had stayed several times in Leeds with her Uncle Willy, who was a music teacher there (his two step-daughters, Clarice and Olive Birkbeck, were very friendly to Amy), in the summer of 1923 she had holidayed with Irene in the Isle of Man, and there had been her visits to various northern universities. But her only glimpse of the south had been on a schoolgirl trip to London which left her with memories of the shops and the British Museum.

Of course the influence of Franz had sparked in her the ambition to travel abroad. But seeing the world was a tradition in the Johnson family, at least for the men,[1] and while she was at Sheffield there was a dramatic reminder of this. In January 1924 the Golden Wedding of her Johnson grandparents was celebrated with much pomp, and all ten of their children assembled for it with their families. Amy's five Johnson uncles had all seen distant parts of the world and several had settled abroad (her Uncle Tom had built up a successful salmon-canning business in British Colombia). With uncles to visit the idea of seeing the world could be regarded as an inviting possibility – not merely a tantalising daydream.

III

'When once you get soaked through, you really don't mind anything at all,' so Amy wrote to Franz during her second summer term at Sheffield. Her letter was

---

[1] Two of them had rounded the Cape under sail.

headed 'Fir-Tree Island, Fairy Glen, near Baslow',[1] and she hastened to tell him what she was up to. 'You'll probably think I'm quite crazy . . . but please allow me to explain that three of us are camping here. It's an absolutely heavenly spot – if only it were dry. I can imagine you sitting in a comfortable easy chair in your warm, dry, perfectly adorable flat,[2] smoking a Turkish cigarette, with a cup of hot real coffee on a table by your side. Now try to imagine me, perched on a straw pillow in a wee tent where you can't sit upright, smoking countless "Players" to keep the midges off, and attired in a grubby gym tunic . . . no shoes and stockings etc; they're all soaked. The sun's shining for the moment – Heaven be praised! But we can see the rain racing towards us . . . But really, in spite of the rain, dirty soaked ground, flies, beetles, spiders and other minor discomforts, it's really a most adorable place. If you've any soul left at all, you couldn't help but love it. We're surrounded by the stream – frightfully swollen – heaps of little waterfalls, trees, ferns, violets, bluebells, and the most glorious scenery all round . . . The people in Baslow – a dear little village – think we're quite mad. Suppose we are really, when you come to look at it sanely. Can mad people look at things sanely?'

Although Amy was by this time half-way through her three years at Sheffield she had only just discovered that the Peak District lay close at hand. 'I went the most heavenly walk I've ever been in my life,' she told Franz a few weeks earlier. 'Three friends and myself went a long tramp into the Derbyshire hills . . . I'd no idea there was such lovely country in England . . . You're a most unenterprising mortal. Coming from a glorious, heavenly place like Switzerland and being content to stagnate in a hole like Hull or Bridlington!! Really, you're an enigma. Of course, Hull's a topping

[1] A village in the Peak District.
[2] Franz, who by this time had decided to settle in Hull, had abandoned lodgings and moved to a flat close to his office.

place – it's the only place in England I'd live in besides, London, but there's no beauty there.'

It was entirely thanks to Winifred, whose idea it was to improvise a camp for the enjoyment of herself and her friends, that the chance to get to know the Derbyshire countryside had come her way. In the 1920s, when camping was still comparatively rare, and the Peak District unfrequented, the scheme was a bold and original one. The summer before, on one of the solitary bicycle rides which Winifred (like Amy) found consoling, she had discovered a 'camping site' – a glade with a stream, well shielded from the road by a thicket – in a valley full of boulders and sapling birches. Then, having made friends with the valley's self-appointed guardian, Miss Kate Beswick, an elderly spinster who had a cottage near by, she acquired a tiny tent, and in the spring of 1924 persuaded a former school-friend to join her in an alfresco reading party. This first experiment was a success, and now at the same spot, nicknamed Fir-Tree Island, Amy sat perched on a straw pillow to write to Franz.

After her initiation by drenching Amy was often at the camp at weekends, and there, with Winifred, Gwyneth Roulston and Constance Tupholme ('Tuppy'), a Sheffield friend of Winifred's she shared in the trial-and-error camping (none of them had been Girl Guides) and in acting hostess to their student friends at picnic parties. It was thus that she found herself becoming one of a close-knit foursome of intimates, and the companionship shared by these four throughout the remainder of their time together as undergraduates was one of the happiest features of Amy's life at Sheffield.

IV

The summer of Amy's first camping adventure was also the summer of her twenty-first birthday, and at this time, in almost every way, the example of Winifred dominated her outlook. Winifred, who had already been to France, travelled as far afield as Poland during the summer of 1924, to an international students' conference in Warsaw. Amy, with the urge to travel already in her blood, was more than ever set on 'seeing the world'. Winifred, reading for Economics Honours, was determined not to become a school-teacher: Amy, now adamant that she would not teach, had persuaded her father to refund the Board of Education's grant (totalling nearly a hundred pounds) and had decided, with wildly unrealistic optimism, to try for the Civil Service. Winifred was engaged to be married to a young Irishman. Amy, again with wildly unrealistic optimism, seems to have believed that she and Franz were on the way to an engagement and wedding bells.

Letters she wrote to him some time later indicate that at this stage, more than two years after their first meeting, Franz began at last to take the initiative. Around the time that Amy came of age her letters to him show a marked change of tone. No longer only coquettish she now became demanding and at the same time jealous and unsure of him, while emotionally ever more dependent. On better acquaintance she had discovered that behind his charm he was subject to unaccountable moods which she did not understand, and this depressed and worried her. Why was he so guarded? But some of her own letters were now guarded in the extreme; one or two are little more than cryptic notes, and she was still writing to him non-committally as 'Dear Franz' and signing herself 'Yours, Amy'. 'I quite agree with you now that it's best not to write letters,' she assured him in October 1924, 'as a thing written can't be unwritten . . . I won't write any more.' This resolve lasted for less than a week, but she was still careful to make only the most discreet references to the meetings between them that were now taking place not only openly as before, but also under the moon, and once, when they both had pretexts that coincided, in London.

The replies Franz wrote to 'Dear Amy' and signed 'Yours, Franz' were in turn so discreet as to appear brusque. Amy, re-reading some of them a couple of years later attributed their phrasing to his coldness and caution but perhaps that is not the whole picture. In 1924 Franz was still a newcomer to England and most of his letter-writing in English was business correspondence. Probably he lacked sufficient command of the language to express himself in other terms. But Amy, always hungry for affection and reassurance, did not consider this. 'I loved you then a lot more than you did me,' she reflected, pondering over one of the letters he wrote to her that autumn. 'It is such a curious letter – full of formal stilted phrases. And even then I was your mistress, and yet you didn't love me in your letters. I must have loved you very much.'

To her Sheffield friends Amy had previously boasted about 'my Swiss', but now, even to Winifred, she spoke of him with reserve. In the letters to her mother the occasional mentions of him were also made with caution but without any embarrassment. It is virtually certain that Ciss Johnson never realised – either now or later – that Amy and Franz were lovers. If she had, she would have been profoundly shocked and horrified. He was accepted in the Johnson family as Amy's 'young man' and her father was on friendly terms with him as one business man with another (after two years in Hull Franz had launched a small business of his own there, in partnership with a Swiss friend).

Amy's attachment to Franz made her somewhat aloof with other young men but she was much sought after, for her feminine attractiveness was exceptional (Winifred remembers a remark by a French woman who chanced to meet her at about this time: '*Elle a tout pour plaire aux hommes*') and by the time of her final year at Sheffield she had acquired a new self-confidence. In January 1925, under Winifred's tutelage, she was helping to entertain parties of visiting students. 'It's our Inter-Varsity debate and dance today,' she wrote to her mother. 'We've all been very busy seeing to the delegates . . . I looked after the Liverpool ones . . . There are thirty-five South Africans here this week from Cape Town University.' At this point Amy's other main news was that she was about to move from her current lodgings in Moncrieffe Road (which she found too far out) to Glossop Road, only two minutes' walk from Western Bank. She was to be the only lodger in the house of a lady masseuse and chiropodist, a widow called Mrs Fussell.

On arrival at her new lodgings Amy was greeted by a florist's messenger with a bunch of white flowers from Franz; this made quite an impression on her landlady, and Amy on her side was flattered by Mrs Fussell's attentiveness. Then later on, when Franz was planning his first, and only, visit to Sheffield for a students' dance (in February 1925) Mrs Fussell kindly invited him to stay. Amy and Winifred had been planning a party for the Shrove Tuesday Carnival Ball and Amy, not really expecting Franz would come, wrote begging him to join them. To her surprise he accepted and for the next fortnight she was in a flurry of nerves. 'Varsity dances are so rough and ready,' she warned him, 'not the kind you're used to.' Mrs Fussell was told that the friend who had sent the flowers was coming over, and she said he might use her visitors' room. After the visit Franz showed his heartfelt appreciation by sending Amy some exciting presents: first arrived some ripe pears which she described as 'deliciously surprising' and 'woefully extravagant'; then, better still, peaches, and with them a bunch of primroses. 'It was just simply delightful of you to want to send me the peaches when you saw how beautiful and fresh they were,' wrote Amy, enchanted. 'It is their *freshness* that you want me to realise, isn't it? They're too great luxuries, and almost too beautiful to eat. I quite see that the slightest rough touch would spoil a peach more than any other fruit.'

But Amy's doings in the early part of 1925 were not confined to Sheffield and Hull. During the Easter Vacation new vistas opened up for her, once more thanks to Winifred, when she accompanied eight other Sheffield students at Oxford, for a Congress organised by the National Union of Students. To her mother she wrote, 'We spent all Sunday seeing round Oxford. We went through lots of the Colleges, walked along Addison's Walk by the river and altogether spent a most interesting time. We've got to know some perfectly delightful people.' To Franz she was more explicit: 'Maybe I've fallen in love with an Irishman,' she wrote teasingly. Amy did not hesitate to boast to him of her flirtations though she was frankly not too pleased if he mentioned that he had been enjoying himself during her absence. By now she was much more tolerant regarding drink but she was worried quite a lot about rivals. 'You're not the ony one who gets jealous,' she told him. 'Whenever I hear of the dances you've been to, my imagination just won't stop working.'

V

The final term that Amy spent at 'beastly Sheffield' as she once called it – for she was prone to bouts of homesickness – was as hectic, in a different way, as her first. 'What if I fail my degree!' she exlaimed to Franz. 'I'd disappear, I'm sure.' Trying to study in earnest for her finals she became aware that her lodgings were noisy and sunless, and this distracted and depressed her. Then Winifred came to the rescue with an excellent suggestion. Why not move to some quiet place outside the city – Hathersage for example? The idea took Amy's fancy and without much trouble she found a 'dear person' in Hathersage who was ready to give her two rooms, a bedroom and a sitting-room. With only just over a fortnight until her examination she planned to do nothing but work, but even the tranquility of the countryside did not always help. 'It's so absolutely glorious where I am just now that I can't spoil everything by studying,' she wrote to Franz from a spot overlooking the Derwent. 'I'm sitting on a bank covered with daisies and bluebells and violets, and there's the river just below, the hills all round, and the sun shining most gloriously . . . Anyway, I'm almost perfectly happy – if I just had you, and was through my exam.'

Franz was abroad at the time, holidaying at home, and his thirtieth birthday was soon to take place. 'I hope you have an awfully nice birthday,' she wrote. 'But one doesn't bother with birthdays so much when one's getting so old, does one?' From what he had told her she could picture him with his four sisters and his only brother (like himself a bachelor home from abroad); the six of them gathered round their widowed mother, a beloved and respected matriarch. Amy must have realised that the approval of his mother meant much to Franz, for while he was at home she asked 'What will your mother think if I send too many letters; shall I not write so often?' Several of her letters dwelt upon a feature of her new lodgings that shocked and upset her. 'There's one blot on the landscape – beetles!!! And not decent respectable *black* ones either. They're horrible creepy, crawly wriggly ugly brown cockroaches!' She then went on to 'relieve her mind' on the subject, but at the end of the letter she hesitated. 'I'll keep this until tomorrow and write some more then. Three pages, all about beetles, are not worth sending all the way to Switzerland.'

While Franz was still abroad Amy's father, who was soon to get off on a three-months' business trip to America, stopped in Sheffield between trains to talk with his daughter about her future plans. A job was now the great question-mark in her life, for her ambition to enter the Civil Service had proved entirely unattainable and she had nothing else definite in view. A Swiss she had met through Franz had encouraged her to write to Brown Boveri, the engineering concern at Baden near Zurich, to ask whether they had any secretarial vacancies, and when they replied with an application form her hopes leapt ahead. But it had already occurred to her, for she was by nature a schemer, that her father might hear of good openings for her during his travels. 'Father's going to do his best for me in America,' she wrote to Franz, 'But he says if once I go out he's sure I'll never want to come back. I wonder. Do you think so? . . . Anyway, I'll go out of

England somewhere, sooner or later . . . I'm almost as fond of getting my own way as you are – and usually get it, though not ostentatiously.'

After this she had no more time for dreams or scruples: the exams were upon her. Both her mother and Franz did their best to help; Ciss Johnson advised a tonic, and Franz – on his return – kept her supplied with tablets from Switzerland, *Kola pastillen*, which she found, to her astonishment, freed her immediately from exhaustion and gave her an unfamiliar confidence. Twice at weekends he came over to Hathersage to cheer her, riding the seventy-odd miles each way on his motor-cycle. Between his visits she wrote to him almost every day, or rather every night. In the early hours, when she could no longer force herself to study, she wrote page after page to him, unburdening all her anxieties. But in a moment of candour she admitted that this was a mistake. 'I'm realising that it's very bad for me to rely so much on you, because I find I'm not so independent as I think I am. Whenever anything goes wrong I always want to dash to you at once or else tell you . . . I think I shall have a rough time of it if I go somewhere right away for a job, don't you? It takes me a long time to make friends.'

She could think of nothing but her own miseries and when Franz confided that he himself was not enjoying being back at work she was brusque and unsympathetic. 'Well anyway,' she admonished, 'be thankful you haven't to come into personal contact with beetles, and that you haven't to learn what Lucius Junius Moderatus Columella and Titus Calpurnius Siculus and a thousand others with equally terrible names, wrote. . . . This wretched Latin literature. I'll fail in that as sure as sure.' Economics was the subject with which Amy felt most at home but she never pretended that any of her studies were more than ephemeral; they were merely the means to a degree.

There were several nightmare moments during the examination: one when her head felt red-hot, and she realised she had taken a double quantity of *Kola* tablets; another when, aghast at the devilish demands of the Latin examiners, she found she had spilt ink over her hands, frock, handkerchief, and the paper itself. But a couple of weeks later when she was back in Hull a telegram came from one of her Sheffield friends – Norman Schofield, a law student – with the news that she had been awarded a Second Division Ordinary Degree in Economics, Latin and French. Delirious with joy and relief she dashed off a note to her mother, who was in Bridlington with her two youngest sisters. 'I'm through! Have just got a wire this very minute. My lawyer has wired straight away . . . Am just going out with Franz to celebrate.'

The finale of Amy's academic career was an embarrassing scramble. On the Saturday morning in July when the Degree Congregation took place she went over to Sheffield to receive her BA. 'It was awful when I got here this morning,' she wrote to her mother. 'I found I had to pay five pounds before I could get my degree and they wouldn't give it before I paid the money . . . I finally managed to borrow it . . . It was 11.29 and I had to find five pounds before 11.30 – it was awfully worrying.' Thus with less than five minutes to spare and on a borrowed five pounds, Amy became a Bachelor of Arts.

5

FALSE START

1925

'The typist who flew solo to Australia': this is what most people would say if asked to describe Amy Johnson in a word or two. But the label 'typist' is only partly accurate, for it ignores the variety of the posts she had before she took to flying. Nevertheless it is true that the first job of her career was as a shorthand-typist, and she rushed into it at once after Sheffield. She had made up her mind not to waste time with holidays. She meant to be in Hull, free to see more of Franz than usual while both her parents were away – her father in America, her mother at Bridlington. Besides, she was all agog to start earning, and while she waited for an opportunity abroad she intended to find work locally. Prostrate with exhaustion after her finals she was persuaded by her mother to come and rest at the seaside for a few days, but then at the end of June – just before her twenty-second birthday – she hurried back to join Irene in lodgings in Anlaby Road (the Park Avenue house was temporarily closed).

Amy was not the only one of the Johnson daughters who liked her own way and was already leading her own life. Irene, after leaving school, had for a time been a resident student at a teachers' training college in Hull, but she had to give this up, for the discipline did not suit her and she had a nervous breakdown. After she recovered her health she took a secretarial training, though she was meanwhile toying with the idea of a stage career which some of her admirers believed was her métier. By the time Amy left Sheffield she was not living at home, but had established herself in Hull lodgings. The circumstances of her departure from Park Avenue are uncertain but Amy, in one of her letters to Franz, mentioned her sister's delight in describing herself as 'the black sheep of the family turned out because of her wild ways.' It seems that Irene's new independence was financed mainly by her father; as Amy once said to her mother, 'Irene's a marvellous power of getting what she wants. That's what Franz meant when he said Irene's a lot cleverer than I am. She is.' But she usually referred to her younger sister in a tone of affectionate tolerance: she had earlier told Franz that she was looking forward to sharing lodgings with her because then they could have some fun. 'She's not going on the stage after all for some reason or other,' she added. 'I wonder what she'll do now. She says a Frenchman in her digs has fallen in love with her, and they're going to Paris together soon by aeroplane, and she's going to stay there and live a "wild Bohemian life". She'll wake up soon.'

II

As a first step towards a secretarial job Amy attended classes at Wood's Shorthand and Commercial College. But she must already have been fairly competent at shorthand as well as typing, for a year earlier she had reported some of the meetings at the NUS Congress at Oxford, and it seems likely that she attended secretarial classes during some of her vacations from Sheffield. When she joined Irene in Hull there was less than a month before Wood's College closed for the summer, but it seems that this was long enough for her to leave a lasting impression upon one of the staff. Mr L. Bourne remembers her as a good pupil, and also recalls the remarkable fact that a passage he happened to choose for her, in order to improve her Gregg

Shorthand speed, was an account of the Atlantic flight of Alcock and Brown.

After this brief refresher course Amy began answering advertisements for secretarial help, and to her surprise found there was little interest in her Sheffield degree. As usual however discouragement made her all the more determined, and at last (probably early in August, by which time her parents were back and she was living at home again) she was taken on as a shorthand-typist by a corporate accountant named Frank Hall. The figure of her salary is not certain but she probably started at a pound a week. The accountant's office was in Bowlalley Lane, a byway of Hull's business quarter, and this meant that she was now working every day only a few minutes' walk from Franz's flat in Wellington Chambers (where he was looked after by an elderly manservant) and his nearby office in Humber Place. Both flat and office were in a part of the old dock area which Amy, with reason, called 'a rotten neighbourhood', for it abounded in the warehouses and offices of wholesale greengrocers, jumbled together in shabby little streets and alleys – the business that Franz and his partner had started was a trading company dealing in vegetable oils and fruit. Franz was already finding the risks of his new venture a heavy burden, but he enjoyed the freedom and also the business trips. Often he had to spend a day or two in Liverpool (before long his firm opened a branch there) and during the summer of 1925 he and Amy met in Liverpool for a rendezvous which she remembered as a particularly happy one.

As summer merged into autumn, and Amy went week after week to work in Bowlalley Lane, she was able to meet her lover very often and during this time her letter-writing appears to have ceased. This absence of letters means a lack of contemporary evidence as to how she felt about her first experience of wage-earning, but in *Myself When Young* she described it in no uncertain terms. 'I hated the job,' she wrote. 'I was terribly unhappy. My shorthand was not up to standard and I did not dare to own up to this. I would sit in my chair dreading the bell. With trembling hand I took down straggly shorthand at a speed far in excess of anything I had done at college, with the result that I was unable to read it back and had to go to the dreaded Presence and ask for words to fill in the numerous blank spaces . . . The rest of my time was spent typing financial statements. I was not allowed to make a mistake as nothing must be altered or even erased. No matter how skilful I tried to be with my typewriter rubber, I was always found out. The result was a passion for accuracy and care . . . I was unpopular with the other girls in the office, probably both they and I instinctively feeling that I was different from them. For one thing I was older . . . For another my university degree stood between us. In those days it seemed so terribly important. After about three months of this life I had a nervous breakdown, and no wonder.'[1]

III

Amy's mother was convinced that she had been starving herself for the sake of her figure and that plenty of food and rest would put everything right. There was talk of a month's holiday, perhaps at Bournemouth, and Amy, tearful and ill but always hoping for the best, pictured herself luxuriating in some splendid hotel. For this she would need smart new clothes, so she opened an account at a Hull store, and also bought two frocks on credit from a little dress shop. But in the first week of October when she was packed off to Bournemouth she was not bound for a 'hydro' where she could preen herself. Her parents had arranged for her to stay with some cousins of her father's, the Eddisons, who lived in a comfortable house about a mile from the centre of the town.

[1] From subsequent letters it seems that the crisis came at the end of September 1925, when Amy fainted at the office and had to be taken home. She worked for Hall for about two months (not three).

The household consisted of Mr and Mrs Eddison ('perfectly kind and placid and old,' so Amy told Franz) and their youngest child Bunty, a little girl of five (almost the same age as her own sister Betty). 'The child . . . I don't think I can stand it for long,' she complained. 'Immediately I got in she chattered and chattered . . . helped me to unpack . . . every single thing had to be explained, my chocolates eaten, drawers opened and ransacked, scent sprayed all over her.' Franz, however, when he heard about Bunty, predicted that Amy would soon become attached to her, and he was right. 'She follows me everywhere and still insists on adoring me and calling me "Aunty Emly",' she told him before long with pleased amusement.

The Eddisons were househunting with a zest she found exasperating, and they insisted she should accompany them. But despite her impatience the sight of so many houses, 'beautiful styles, lovely gardens, and the prices £3,000 to £20,000,' prompted her to exclaim to Franz: 'Darling, don't you ever have the slightest ambition to live in a beautiful house – not big, but beautiful – surrounded by beautiful things, with lovely scenery and music, and a beautiful wife to look after you and make everything happy and gay.' Then she added a realistic remark which illuminates her whole attitude towards herself: 'I'm not beautiful enough, but perhaps I'd do if I'd very pretty frocks.' It was true that Amy was not beautiful but her looks were girlish and sweet and not at all unattractive – as Franz was reminded by a portrait photograph of herself which she gave to him at about this time. It shows a reflective Amy, the long oval of her face softened by bobbed hair draped sideways across the brow. As in most of her posed photographs of this period the lips are firmly closed; a smile would have revealed the front teeth that she regarded as a disfigurement (though as far as can be ascertained none of her friends – not even Franz – noticed anything wrong with them). In a sleeveless dance frock, bead-embroidered and straight, and wearing no jewellery, she looks an ingenuous, provincial version of the flapper of the 1920s. Her eyebrows are perhaps a trifle narrowed but not obviously plucked, there is only a touch of lipstick on her pretty mouth, and her figure is less boyish than that of a Michael Arlen heroine. She was a slender girl, but her shapely bust looked as if it might one day become a motherly bosom like those of her Johnson aunts.

Much to Amy's disappointment her dream of an ideal home failed to excite Franz. 'What do you mean in your letter by "everything worth having or living for is so far away", and "pleasure never seems to be at home",' she asked him. 'By the way, the homes I picture are never in Hull – they're always in Switzerland.' By this time she had extracted a promise that he would take her with him next time he went home for a holiday, and in letter after letter she reminded him of it. 'Now that I know I'm going – we are, aren't we, darling? I want to know everything you can tell me about it. But you mustn't run down England, because you haven't seen the best parts yet . . . it's not all like Hull.'

IV

Daydreaming of Switzerland she could forget the business worries that nagged at her conscientious mind, but afterwards they pursued her again. There were two main problems: must she return to her job, and how was she to pay those dress bills? After ten days at Bournemouth she wrote to consult her father about her job; it was the letter of a dutiful daughter, matter-of-fact, dispassionate, and in striking contrast to the rambling effusions to her mother and to Franz. Will Johnson advised her to leave the accountant's office and with rising spirits she wrote to give notice. She was surprised and touched when in reply she received a nice note from Frank Hall, and another from one of the girls in the office, who said that Mr Hall was quite concerned about her and not at all angry.

But there were still her secret debts. Obviously she must start earning again as soon as possible and she clung to the notion that she could do so by giving coaching in French grammar. In the meantime she decided to make up her accounts. The result shocked her so much that she wrote in great haste, at 1.30 am: 'Darling, I can't get to sleep. I don't know what on earth induced me to balance my money up before I came to bed . . . Do you mind if I tell you . . . I must confide in someone.' She then listed her debts which totalled £33 2s, a figure that flabbergasted her. 'The £33 might as well be £3,333, so far as it is within my means to find it . . . Can you suggest anything I can possibly do? . . . I'd no idea I was so extravagant on stockings till I added the various 10/11s up . . . Father says if I take pupils I can't keep the money. I must hand it over to pay for my board at home . . . These things do worry me dreadfully. It means I'm just driven to getting money by some means Father won't know of, to pay my debts . . . I'm an awful coward and hate to face things out. If only I can get this paid off I'm determined to pay cash down for everything else I get.'

By return of post Franz reassured her; he would gladly come to the rescue. 'It is just like you to offer to help me pay my bills,' replied Amy, overjoyed. 'You are the dearest darling there ever was.' She then made a remark which shows that although in debt she was not without private reseources; also that Franz, though increasingly fond of her, had not allowed himself to forget that a good Swiss never makes a loan without security. 'I'll hand you over some War Savings Certificates, but don't change them till 1928, because they're worth lots more then. And if I earn some money I can retrieve them before that date.'[1]

Her resolution to pay for everything on the nail had, however, caused Franz to raise an eyebrow. 'I

[1] These War Savings Certificates (probably to the value of about £40), which had been given to Amy by her parents when she came of age, were the aggragate of their savings on her behalf since the time of her birth (each of the Johnson daughters was saved for in the same way).

'absolutely mean that I shall always pay cash down for what I get in future,' she protested – but then she wavered. 'I'm glad you don't want a promise to that effect, because one never knows what eventualities may turn up. But I'll promise that I won't run up debts so thoughtlessly.'

V

At twenty-two Amy considered herself unlucky, buying books gave her even more pleasure than shopping for clothes, and she had come round to the idea that a married couple should have separate beds (rather than separate rooms). These sidelights, as well as many others which indicate her views, tastes, interests and feelings, were contained in the spate of letters which flowed back to Hull while she was convalescing at Bournemouth. She wrote more than usual to her mother but most of her letters were to Franz, who by this time had become demanding. 'You're quite spoilt in the matter of letters,' she chided. 'You're very greedy indeed wanting one every day. Nothing would induce me to give way to you, except that I want one myself every day from you . . . Mrs Eddison says I'm worrying myself far too much over letters, and wasting a big part of my holiday.'

Life with the Eddisons had at first seemed frustrating but Amy was thankful for the leisure: breakfast in bed every day, and no need to come down until lunchtime. Ciss Johnson had written to Mrs Eddison begging her to feed Amy up; this annoyed Amy until she discovered that her hostess was a very good cook. On her arrival she had confided to Franz, 'Wish I had that bottle of cocktail to give me an appetite' (an interesting remark in view of her former disapproval of drink). For a while her nervous exhaustion persisted and her black moods were worse than ever; Franz was told in relentless detail about her 'evil forebodings' and 'deadly fits of lassitude'. He replied advising Magnesia as a laxative (instead of Kruschen Salts which he had recommended when she was at Sheffield). But as the weeks went on she began to revive, and in more cheerful moments chattered away on any topic that came into her head. 'I really believe in an interpretation of dreams, do you?' she observed, after failing to recall one that had intrigued her. 'Much more than in fortune-telling, because I think there must be something ruling them. The only thing I can remember about this one was that I had that horrible feeling of trying to run and being held back – haven't dreamt that for ages. And I know you were in it. It's so very seldom that I dream . . . Do you remember the one I told you about our not being able to be married because I couldn't find the white gloves? I still think it has its significance. Do you?'

Amy, and Franz too, liked reading and discussing novels. At the cinema she revelled in conventional romances but her taste in books seems to have inclined towards the light and witty. She had mentioned earlier that she liked Jerome K. Jerome: 'There's a sort of playfully mocking cynicism in his writings which makes his somewhat ˋshallow ideas rather more attractive.' And now she had discovered a writer whose wit enchanted her – Rose Macaulay. While at Bournemouth she wrote: 'If you get a chance do read *Told by an Idiot* . . . It's splendid, though she's apt to repeat herself too often. You mightn't like it, but it's clever none the less. Will post it to you if you like.' A few days later however she revoked this offer. 'On second thoughts I'm not sending you *Told by an Idiot* to read. It has a nasty character in it with my name. Have you ever noticed that "Amy" is often used to portray this nasty type of person? That's one reason why I dislike it so much.' At about this time she found a way to avoid writing the name she found so irksome; she took to signing her letters to Franz "*Ta Chérie*".

When the two were in Hull they often went to the theatre and also enjoyed reading plays aloud together. Shaw was one of their favourites, and while Amy was away she conceived a passion for Ibsen. In an enterprising mood she went off alone to hear a lecture on him and a few days later wrote eagerly to Franz: 'I must tell you that I've got one of Ibsen's plays, darling. I so very much wanted to read one, because I felt somehow after the lecture that he would appeal to me very strongly . . . I passed a shop where they have lots of new and second-hand books so enquired if they had anything of Ibsen's. The boy searched and rummaged and at last brought quite a nice second-hand edition of *Brand* for 3s. After due consideration I bought it and brought it home to read instead of going to the pictures as I had thought of doing and which would have cost me nearly 3s. Do you ever have a most glorious feeling of possession when you've bought a new book? I always have that feeling much more with books than with anything else, even clothes. I was quite happy all the way home carrying my new possession. I've read the first two acts last night – stayed up till nearly twelve – and it's absolutely entrancing. But I'd rather read it on a mountain-side than in front of the fire. We'll read it again together, shall we, darling, and the others as well. I want to read them all. He's wonderful.'

During the lecture she had made notes and she proceeded to write them up, ostensibly to please Franz. What she really wanted was reassurance and praise, but this he was slow to give. A casual 'Hope they'll interest you,' was soon followed by 'I think perhaps, by degrees, you'll get a slightly higher opinion of my cababilities. You did like my Ibsen notes, at least, didn't you?', and then finally 'You won't destroy those notes on Ibsen, will you?'

It seems that Amy's leisure interests did not include following the news of the day. The Eddisons had a wireless with a loudspeaker instead of earphones, which pleased her so much that she wrote home urging her parents to buy a similar set. But her taste in programmes appears to have been confined to symphony concerts and dance music. And although we know she often glanced at newspapers and magazines she made no mention whatever of the hero of the moment, the Prince of Wales, who was receiving a rapturous welcome after his latest overseas tour. Nor is there any word of the flying accident which dominated the front pages one Saturday in October 1925, the disaster when Britain's racing sea-plane, the Supermarine S-4 crashed and sank during a practice flight before the Schneider Trophy contest at Baltimore. No: Amy was much more interested in the advertisements than in the news, and in *Myself When Young* she made special mention of her habit of browsing through them. It was a habit that before long was to have imporant repercussions.

VI

When the Eddisons were not viewing houses or shopping they went for expeditions in their car, a four-seater with a hood and open sides that let in the rain. They took Amy with them to Christchurch Priory, Wimborne Minster, the New Forest, and to the Bournemouth Races ('I said I'd never seen a steeple-chase race – fancy being twenty-two and never seen a horse jump a fence!') On one trip to Swanage they stopped for some sight-seeing. 'Bunty and I went a walk to see a ruined castle – Corfe Castle,' she told Franz afterwards. 'Awfully romantic, but utterly spoiled by palings round, guides, and entrance fees. Isn't it a shame! It's the district where Thomas Hardy wrote *Tess of the D'Urbervilles*. I'd love to explore by myself, when there are no other people there at all, and pretend I lived in the times when the castle was flourishing. You'd be my knight, of course, and kill nasty dragons (dentists etc.) and then we'd be married and live happily ever after.'

She also found plenty of enjoyment in Bournemouth itself. 'Darling it's simply beautiful here,' she wrote one sunny day from a deck chair on the sea-front. 'There's a long promenade lined with cars, bungalows galore, high red cliffs, bright yellow sands . . . It's a wee bit lonely (but I'd rather be by myself than display my legs like a girl near me is doing and try and "pick up" someone. My shoes and stockings look awfully nice, but they're only for you) . . . Never mind, we'll have a perfect time in Switzerland, won't we? If anything prevented our going I'd be bitterly disappointed. You said once I'd never had a real disappointment. You're not planning to test me, are you?'

Towards the end of six weeks Amy was well again, and was now writing to Franz, 'I feel marvellously energetic and fit. Went out this morning by myself – it was glorious on the cliffs. I ran down the zig-zag path again to the sea, startling the people on seats at the corners . . . I'm tired of leading an aimless existence like this and I want to be doing something.' But she was not looking forward to being home again, since her immediate plans for work were unsettled. Her mother had frowned on the idea that she should coach pupils privately and had also declined an offer of help in the house. Amy took this much to heart. 'When Mrs Eddison says she'll miss me very much, and my own Mother tells me . . . that she doesn't want me interfering with her home arrangements, and that I'd better get a post as it will be so long before I go to America, you've no idea how it hurts.'

'Before I go to America . . .' The possibility that Amy might cross the Atlantic had suddenly become more real, for a Boston friend of her father's, a fellow Rotarian, had written inviting her to come and stay while he helped her to find a job. Reading between the lines of Amy's letters, however, it seems doubtful whether she was genuinely in earnest about the plan. 'I have only to wait till I get a permit,' she told Franz. 'Do you mind awfully about my going? You see, I must go, because I've such a longing to see more of the world, and I couldn't settle down with that longing unsatisfied. But I'll go for a little while and then come back to you, shall I, darling?' Although she may possibly have been ingenuous enough to believe that Franz would wait for her while she took her fill of adventure, it appears more likely that by threatening to go out of reach she hoped to force him to prove his love by insisting that she should remain with him. A letter she wrote to her mother after he came to stay at the

Eddisons' for a weekend supports this likelihood. 'Mr and Mrs Eddison have taken a great fancy to Franz,' she announced. 'They say he's a very sensible man, with practical views and plenty of commonsense. Mrs Eddison advises me to take him whilst I've the chance and not go to America, but I don't at all agree.' To Franz himself she wrote: 'Mr Eddison says I'm very silly to go to America and risk losing you . . . He bet me £1,000 you wouldn't still be a bachelor in another twelve months. But you will, won't you, darling?' Then came an afterthought: 'When you go to Liverpool look out for a top-hole job for me . . . and then I'd probably not go to America. We'd have some fun together, wouldn't we darling?' In another letter she put it more tersely: 'I don't want to go home. I wish we two could run away and live all by ourselves. Why can't we?'

6

NEW DIRECTIONS

1925–1926

Amy returned to Hull in November 1925 just in time
for a dance that Irene had persuaded her parents to
give for her coming of age. It was a mortifying time for
Amy; when she herself was twenty-one there had been no
party. Furthermore when she was asked to list any
friends of hers who might be invited to Irene's dance she
was forced to realise, with some misgivings, that because
of Franz she had been missing the chance to acquire a
normal circle of friends. 'I know very few people in Hull,'
she admitted to her mother, 'and even those I do have
nearly all been introduced to me by Franz.'

The letters Amy wrote to her mother just before her
return show that relations between the two fluctuated
considerably at this time. Ciss Johnson, now in her mid-
forties, was sometimes quick to take offence. In
connection with the arrangements for the dance Amy
wrote bitterly to Franz, 'Mother never has and never will
understand.' An underlying reason for these tensions was,
of course, her very natural envy of Irene; to Franz she
confessed that although she was 'awfully fond of her' she
was yet 'hatefully jealous'. 'She's always breaking Mother's
and Father's hearts and bringing grey hairs to their heads,
and she's only to exert herself to be charming and they fall
over each other to please her. Irene has been for ages the
sole subject of conversation at home . . . Everyone,
including you, stands enslaved and enraptured by her
vivacity and charm . . . she always outshines me.'

At the time of the dance these feelings of inferiority were intensified by the fact that Irene was on the point of becoming engaged. The young man was a Hull friend, Edward Pocock, and the match was approved by the Johnsons. Teddy's winning manners and his talents as an amateur entertainer at the piano were so irresistible that even the paucity of the income he earned as an employer of Shell-Mex Ltd seemed unimportant to his prospective in-laws. The couple appeared to be deeply in love and when Franz, in a thoughtless moment, implied to Amy that her own love did not measure up to Irene's there was a torrent of resentment and sarcasm. 'Oh, but I'd forgotten – I have only to love you as much as Irene does Teddy. It's rather difficult, but I'll try . . . I'm glad Irene loves Teddy, it's made a marvellous difference in her – for the better . . . Goodbye, darling – Just as much love as Irene gives Teddy. *Ta Chérie.*'

But in spite of all this the two sisters remained the best of friends, and on Irene's birthday Amy gave her a lavish present, a black velvet evening cloak made by herself (she was evidently confident of her skill as a dressmaker, for she told Franz that her sister would never guess it was home-made).

II

It must have been soon after the dance that the idea of Amy's going to America petered out; from subsequent correspondence and the memories of friends we know that by the beginning of 1926 she had started on a new job – with a Hull advertising agency called Morison's. She clearly found the work there congenial for later on, when she had been with the firm for some time (she worked there for just over a year), and was encountering quite a few discouragements, she nevertheless wrote to Franz, 'I want to stick to advertising because I think it fits my temperament more than any other kind of business would.'

Why was Amy first drawn towards this kind of work?

From *Myself When Young* it appears that her habit of browsing through advertisements led her on to try her hand at improving their layout and wording, and soon she felt certain she would shine as a copywriter. She knew she would have to begin as a shorthand-typist but was confident that when her gifts were discovered she would be promoted. There seems little doubt that it was thanks to her own initiative, and her ability to make a good first impression, that she was taken on by Morison's at a time when jobs were exceedingly hard to come by, especially jobs in advertising. Agencies organised on American lines first began to flourish in Britain in the mid-20s but their status was still precarious; many firms regarded their help as an extravagance – something to be dispensed with when trade was bad. Hull however had several of them, and Morison's Advertising Agency was the largest, with a staff of about twenty and offices occupying the whole of one of Albion Street's tall Georgian houses.

Amy was engaged as secretary to the Manager of the Press Department, Mr Rowbottom, but the terms of her employment were unusual. According to her own memory she arranged to barter her secretarial services for the chance to learn the art of writing copy and planning advertising campaigns, and aside from this to receive a 'nominal salary' of thirty shillings a week. But one of her friends at Morison's believes that another factor entered the picture. Rowbottom wished to expand the scope of the agency to the Continent and Amy no doubt flaunted her Sheffield degree. Translations were expensive, and Morison's may have been glad to engage a shorthand-typist who might develop into a copy-writer but in the meantime could be useful as a French interpreter.

When Amy started work at Albion Street she found herself with three other girls in the typists' room. One of them (Nancie Readhead) well remembers liking her, but the other two, so it seems, were jealous of her 'imagined privileges' and tried to humiliate her by petty tricks such as making sure that she had the worst typewriter. They may well have resented the obvious affluence of her home background and perhaps also envied her eye-catching clothes. Most of the staff at Morison's were men and several of them have memories of Amy. Denis Carlill (then a junior in the Art Department) liked her, thought her 'quite attractive and unassuming', and can recall various details of her appearance: at one time she favoured a 'quaint' hair style with coils over the ears, and she used a rather heavy perfume so that one knew when she had been in the room. But although she often dressed for effect she impressed her male colleagues as quiet and shy and standoffish. Some of them imagined she was still heart-free, but the more perceptive noticed that a young man with a motor-cycle was often waiting to meet her after work. In any case she did not encourage advances in the office; once when a political argument was raging one of the men put his hand on her shoulder to emphasise a point and she made it clear that this familiarity was unwelcome.

As far as the work at Morison's was concerned, the indefinite scope of her job had advantages and also snags. On the one hand, in spite of the stigma of starting as a shorthand-typist she did after a time attain to writing copy, and Leonard Stonehouse (then a junior in Morison's Copy Department, now himself head of a Hull agency) says that she had quite an aptitude for the work, though she never really settled to it. Unfortunately no examples of her copy have been identified, but Stonehouse remembers that when she became famous a firm of Leeds grocers resurrected one of her efforts and diplayed it with the caption 'This advertisement was written for us by Amy Johnson.'

The chief drawback of Amy's uncertain status was that nobody hesitated to inflict extra chores on her, and even after she had been with the firm for almost a year (in November 1926) she complained to Franz: 'I have again become an addressing machine at the office . . . In two days I have done nothing but address a thousand envelopes and a hundred post-cards.'

Increasingly restive she asked for a rise, but after a long delay was told that although by rights her salary should be increased, business was so bad that nothing could be done for the time being. Her father advised her to stay on for the sake of experience but to Franz she confided: 'They're a queer lot at Morison's. I've given up trying to understand their methods. I'm going to write to some London agencies . . . and then to a few large shops and firms with advertising departments of their own . . . I want to induce them to give me an interview, so I shall say I shall be in town on such and such a date.'

III

Amy, at twenty-three, had visited London only once or twice but it was already 'town' to her. This despite the fact that Hull was still the centre of her world because Franz was there – sometimes. Business was now frequently taking him abroad, and her letters followed him to Germany, Italy, Czechoslovakia, Switzerland. In return she expected him to write constantly and her appetite for endearments was avid. 'I do like you to say you wish I was with you. I'm hoping you will write from somewhere to say "I'm not coming back to Hull any more. Catch the first steamer and come and live here with me happily ever after" – as in all fairy stories!' In one of her letters at this time (written while Franz was snatching a holiday with his family) she told him that an unusually exciting party was in the offing. For the first time the Advertising Club of Hull was to stage a Gala Dinner and Dance. Her parents were taking a party but she was hoping Franz would be back in time to escort her. He replied that although this would be impossible he was disturbed to think of her going without him. 'You are a dear funny boy,' she teased. 'You are away all this long time travelling in foreign countries . . . and then you hate to think of me at the Gala Night. But I love you much more for hating it . . . You needn't worry about my having anything to drink, because there won't be anything – at any rate not for me. But I should have been good anyhow, you believe that, don't you darling? . . . I love you far too much to bother about other people. I haven't found anyone yet so nice as you, and no one could be so good, even if they were handsomer and wore smarter hats.'[1]

She went on to describe the fancy dress she was making for herself; her taste for fussy detail had run riot. 'I am going as Vanity. The skirt has Molly's ballet skirt for a foundation with white muslin over it. All round are strips of black velvet . . . with lots of little round mirrors pasted on . . . There is a little hat with violets at the back . . . The bodice is tight and of black velvet with a bunch of violets pinned on with my diamond lace pin. Then I shall have two strings of pearls round my neck, and lots of bracelets and rings and powder puffs, etc . . . Can you imagine what it will look like, and do you approve or not?' She already knew the answer. 'I think you would admit it is a good idea, but I think you'd sooner see it on someone else.'

The morning after the party she wrote to say that it had been 'about the best "do" Hull has ever had.' 'I didn't win a prize but I was *specially* mentioned in the papers,'[2] she went on, 'but I didn't really enjoy it very much. Everybody had their own partners and looked so happy with them, and although I danced every dance it wasn't the same as if I'd had you to look after me. I was wanting you awfully the whole time and thinking I'd rather have you cross – as you usually are at dances – than not at all.' Then she gave him the latest news of her job, which was not good. 'Things are slack just now at the office. My copywriting has become a mere farce. I began with about eight small accounts and have only two left now – each having one advert per week.'

It speaks strongly for her penchant for advertising

[1] The 'continental' hats which Franz usually wore seemed oddly conspicuous to Amy.
[2] 'Miss A. Johnson was very dainty as Vanity.'

that she still wanted to stick to the work. Her hopes rose when she came on an article in a Sunday paper by that authority on advertising Sir Charles Higham; he spoke of the profession as a career for girls, and portrayed it as very lucrative. 'So I wrote to him,' Amy told her father, 'and he says if I am in town he would like to see me.' This first feeler towards a London job came to nothing. A few weeks later, after Sir Charles had returned her portfolio of copy and layouts, she wrote in crestfallen mood to Franz, 'He has no vacancy and doesn't consider I know enough yet for him to make one for me, but advises me to keep on "pegging away". That's all the advice he gives.'

The frustrations at Morison's were helping to spur her towards London. But the decisive impetus which took her there was to come from another direction – from a crisis in her mother's attitude towards Franz. During most of Amy's time in the Hull agency her attachment was still taken for granted at home, although Molly remembers that when Franz visited Park Avenue he seemed serious and unsmiling, and she says that the atmosphere often seemed charged with some vague tension she did not understand. Molly herself was in awe of Franz and sometimes critical of him, but they were on friendly terms, and she and Betty made so bold as to give him the nickname 'Pansy'. Though still a schoolgirl plump young Molly, with her dark curls and beautiful brown eyes, may have sensed her sister's predicament more accurately than she herself knew. 'The other day,' Amy related to Franz, 'I told Molly I might be going to London, and of course she doesn't want me to go. She is quite attached to me for some reason. Then she said suddenly that if I went I should have to be good. I said "Why?" and she replied "Because Pansy will be sure to come over often and give you a little surprise!" So you see, even if I do I shall have to be very good.'

Amy and Molly, in spite of the nine years between them, often went out together (especially of course when Franz was away). Irene's engagement had also brought them closer. Together they frequently went to plays, cinemas and lectures, and also to outdoor events such as the Hull Fair. And it was in company with Molly, in the autumn of 1926, that Amy – for the first time in her life – experienced the sensation of flight: the two sisters were taken up together in a 'pleasure aeroplane' from a field outside Hull.

Since the war ended the joy-riding business had been thriving in Britain; ex-service pilots had been touring the country with their aircraft, and wherever they went they proclaimed the news that 'going up' could be both enjoyable and safe. Thus it was that 'The World's Premier Joyriders', as the Surrey Flying Services called themselves, arrived with three 'pleasure aeroplanes' at the Endike Lane 'flying ground' off the Bevereley Road, and invited the citizens of Hull to 'fly with us in safety and enjoy the Wonders of an Air Tonic.'

Amy's chief hope when she set off for Endike Lane with Molly was to savour a new kind of thrill, for she relished physical excitement; of all the side-shows at the Hull Fair the giant swing-boats were her favourite. Molly, on the other hand, found them scaring. Surrey Flying Services charged five shillings a head for ordinary circuits and an additional five shillings each for looping the loop. The sisters produced ten shillings between them and were taken up together for an ordinary circuit.[1] Molly can

[1] The aircraft in which Amy first flew was almost certainly an Avro 536, a modified version of the Avro 504K intended specially for joy-riding, with a fuselage widened to take as many as four passengers in the rear cockpit (sitting side by side in pairs). Surrey Flying Services made four of this type, and a photograph of one of the 'pleasure aeroplanes' in the Hull papers at the time shows an Avro 536 with the registration letters G-EBOY.

remember glancing sideways and noticing that her sister looked serious and intent. In the open cockpit they could not talk while they were up, but back on the ground Amy was scornful. 'It was all over so quickly, nothing happened.' She would have liked to go up again to discover whether looping the loop was more fun but they had no money left, and the impression that remained with the sisters was that flying was a washout.

There have been various accounts of Amy's first flight, some of them far from accurate. Even her own rendering, in *Myself When Young*, is misleading for it implies she went up in summer and while still in her teens at school. Fortunately for the historical record Franz was away from Hull when the flight took place and Amy mentioned it in one of her letters (written on Tuesday, 9 November 1926). The allusion itself is brief: 'Sunday morning it was gloriously fine . . . In the afternoon Molly and I went up in the aeroplane. We both enjoyed it but I would have liked to have done some stunts.' The main importance of this fleeting reference is that it establishes the date of the flight as 1926 (when Amy was twenty-three), thereby disproving the legend that she first went up when a school-girl.

Mention must however be made of another episode relating to aeroplanes which Amy later said occurred during her schooldays. In *Myself When Young* she wrote (in the context of her addiction to the cinema) 'Once an aeroplane appeared on the screen in a news item, and, wildly excited, I sat through the whole programme twice just to see it again. For some strange reason that aeroplane appealed to me enormously. It seemed to offer the chance of escape for which I was always looking. I found that there was an aeroplane factory quite near to Hull,[1] and, time and time again, I cycled out to keep watch and try to see something of a plane. But I never had any luck. I never saw one close to the ground for I had neither the experience nor the courage

[1] The works at Brough belonging to Blackburn Aircraft Ltd.

to gate-crash.' When Amy wrote this she was doubtless describing genuine memories, but at the same time she must certainly have been tempted to make the most of her earliest links with flying, however tenuous they may in fact have been.

7

BRIDE-TO-BE?

1926-1927

Amy and Franz had already been lovers for two years when they first shared a holiday away together; they slipped away to Scotland for a weekend at Easter 1926. For Amy it was a blissful 'honeymoon'. She also viewed it as a step towards marriage, the aim in life that had now become an obsession. For ever since Irene's engagement to Teddy had become imminent 'people' – this probably means her mother and Irene – had been remarking on the length of her 'engagement', and her dreams of marrying Franz some day had given place to a compulsive urge to be married to him as soon as possible.

After Scotland she began preparing for another much more ambitious trip; she had at last coaxed Franz into agreeing to a definite plan for taking her to Switzerland (in June). But *was* the plan definite? Until almost the last minute she could not make out whether he was in earnest or not (this was partly because he spent some time trying, without success, to persuade Amy's father to finance her journey. Partly too perhaps because of the dislocation caused by the General Strike in May). Amy was maddened by the uncertainty, not only about the trip but also about their whole relationship. Whenever she tried to lead Franz into a serious discussion of the future he told her they must wait and see. Finally she could bear it no longer.

'Please excuse my speaking plainly, but I must,' she

wrote. 'The peculiar state of your nerves has been worrying me for some time now . . . I think the whole thing turns on the question of marriage, *our* marriage. It seems to me that you want to have me, and yet you don't want to marry me . . . You say I'm spoilt, but it's you who are – you know you have me anyhow. I do not like to say this, but whilst you're "waiting to see", as you are doing, you are utterly cutting out my opportunities and chances in any other directions . . . You have no wish to assume any proprietary right over me, although you are quick to be angry if I assume there isn't any and – have tea with my dentist, for example . . . For two whole years we have been almost constantly together, and yet you have never once of your own will mentioned the subject of marriage to me. I knew I loved you, and I couldn't help but hear people's talk, and it got on my nerves to such an extent that I opened the subject . . . It has always been a deep hurt to my pride that you have never asked me, although I suppose it was my own fault for not "waiting to see" long enough. I have tried again and again to get to know your views, but you can be as close as an oyster when you choose – which is almost always . . . Although you are taking me to Switzerland . . . you have never even mentioned me to your Mother . . . presumably, I should imagine, because you are not yet sure whether I really shall go, and you do not want to appear foolish before your people . . . Do you think it would do you any good if we each went our own ways for a time. You take out anyone you fancy and I'll do as I like.'

By means of this sort of bludgeoning she secured a promise that on her next birthday the future would be seriously discussed. In the meantime, on 20 June 1926, in company with Franz, she crossed the Channel for the first time. Next day, when she first set eyes on the Swiss mountains, and on the picturesque vistas of Franz's home town she felt – so she afterwards reflected – that she was entering a paradise which made the rest of her life seem like a bad dream.

Franz's family lived in a comfortable apartment up the hill at the edge of town; from its geranium-decked balcony there was a magnificent view over the many-dormered roofs towards the surrounding peaks. There Amy met Franz's mother, a tall *hausfrau* wearing the long dark clothes of widowhood; her strong, serene, almost beautiful face framed by masses of wavy grey hair. She possessed great dignity and calm and her manner was commanding, almost stern; since her husband's death eleven years earlier she had taken entire charge of family affairs. She assumed that Franz had brought Amy home because he was hoping to marry her, and she welcomed the English girl with gentle courtesy though at first with some reserve. Amy on her side was much attracted and impressed.

Three of Franz's sisters were at home, one of them on holiday from her job as a governess in Paris, and they too accepted Amy without question as their brother's future bride. With unaffected frankness they showed their liking for her, and Amy – her shyness forgotten – responded with happy warmth. She seemed completely at ease, but hardly mentioned her own home or relatives. Conversation was not too difficult for although Amy knew no German all the family spoke English. They also spoke fluent French, but 'Mademoiselle Johnson', or 'Mademoiselle Amy', as Franz's mother took to calling her before long, could not converse easily in French (her academic studies were no help here). During her stay of just under two weeks Amy was often out with Franz, but from time to time he had to keep various appointments, and then she shared the companionship of his sisters. In the evenings, after a simple meal, they all gathered round to chat and do their needlework; Amy set herself to make dainty household odds and ends, as befitted an expectant bride. Sometimes one of the sisters played the piano, while Franz sat at ease smoking cigarettes in a long holder, and his mother – always dominating the scene – busied herself with one of her hobbies. She collected stamps and also excelled at embroidery and other traditional Swiss skills; when Franz gave her a spinning-wheel she even learnt to spin. His attitude towards her, affectionate and respectful, was echoed by Amy herself. 'I love her and admire her,' she later declared, 'and I should like to be like her when I get old.'

Franz's mother and sisters were pious Catholics (their Canton was one of the main centres of Swiss Catholicism) and when Franz was at home he attended Mass to please his mother. On Sunday morning Amy too accompanied the family to church. This was probably the first time she had ever encountered incense and the images of saints; certainly she had never before attended a Mass celebrated before a baroque high altar of gilded black marble. With her Methodist upbringing, only a smattering of Latin, and no German at all, she cannot have followed either the ritual or the sermon. But she must have found the atmosphere congenial or she would hardly have returned here to pray a few days later, as we know she did.

III

Franz introduced Amy to several of his closest friends. One of them, Hermann, a handsome, sturdy Swiss of almost the same age as himself was a lawyer and already married. The two men had been friends since childhood, and in their early twenties they had been officers together in the Swiss frontier force. Franz looked back to that time as the happiest of his life – a time full of adventurous activity before he settled down to the grind of earning a living. He had a hoard of Army snapshots and had given one or two to Amy who in turn treasured them, for they showed a boyish Franz glowing with health and gaiety; sunburnt, laughing, merry-making, flirting, riding, setting off on motor-cycle patrols, scaling crags roped to four or five equally lusty young men. Something of the same happy boyishness seemed to reappear in him when he was at home with his mother and sisters, so Amy noticed.

She was intent on doing some 'mountaineering' while she was in Switzerland, and Franz and Hermann agreed to take her with them on the seven-hour climb up the highest of the local mountains. She had not envisaged the need for strong shoes or boots, and proposed to make the climb in high-heeled sandals. One of Franz's sisters thereupon came to the rescue, and in a snapshot of Amy taken near the summit - knapsack on back and stick in hand, posed as though battling her way through a snowfield – she is wearing suitably sturdy footwear. 'Here I am floating on a mountain top on a sea of mist,' she scribbled on a postcard to her mother. 'I've been climbing from 4 a.m. till 11, and difficult as well. Franz says I do all right which is good.' She had succeeded in reaching the mountaintop, but there had been a critical moment on one of the upper paths, a zig-zag scratch on almost vertical rock, which both Franz and Hermann well remember. Amy became paralysed with fright and could not move, either forwards or back. Experienced mountaineers know that if a beginner loses his nerve like this, shock treatment is sometimes the best sort of remedy, either by means of a very sharp smack or a yell; in Amy's case Franz had to scream at her more than once before she was able to continue. However she seems to have made a good recovery, and in the snapshot looks cheerful, indeed triumphant.

A couple of days later, just before the end of her stay, there was to be a party to celebrate her twenty-third birthday. She was looking forward to the day but also dreading it for she had a premonition that Franz would ignore his promise to discuss their future. The morning slipped by with no chance of a tête-à-tête. At midday she and Franz and a few of his friends assembled for the birthday lunch at one of the town's most ancient and famous inns, and at the party there were exciting presents for her: Hermann and his wife brought a blue vase, and another of Franz's Army friends two pictures of local scenery. Overcome by so much kindness Amy burst into tears. Hermann's wife, a vivacious brunette, told her she was the dearest girl she knew and invited her to stay with them if she came out again the following year. It seemed to Amy there could now be no doubt that Franz's friends regarded her as his bride-to-be; the birthday gifts were so obviously meant for their future home. Little did she know what had passed between Franz and Hermann beforehand when in lighthearted vein they had been planning the seating for the lunch table. Franz wanted to enjoy the company of his friend's lively wife and Hermann had consented to sit next to Amy and flirt with her. Franz also remembered, so Hermann says, that he had no intention of marrying Amy, although she unfortunately seemed to have set her heart on it.

When the party was over and the guests had dispersed Franz too slipped away on some pretext. Alone and once more tormented by fears, Amy made her way through the town to the church where she had attended Mass with the family. And there, as she herself later put it, she 'prayed to God that he would make Franz remember.' Towards evening they chanced to be alone together on the stairs outside the apartment; still he said nothing. Then her patience gave way and she reminded him of his promise. 'Even right up to the moment on the stairs when I asked you about it, I made myself believe that you had merely forgotten,' she wrote to him later, after they were back in Hull. 'But at that moment I knew you had forgotten on purpose . . . Perhaps you thought I wanted and expected we should get engaged, but I had no such thought: I know perfectly well you are afraid to commit yourself to such an extent. But I did think and expect (with justification, I believe) that you would at least talk things over with me. Tell me plainly whether you did really want to marry me ultimately and ask me if I was prepared to wait for you for some years and help you till we could afford it, or whether you had changed your mind and didn't care to take on such responsibilities and ask me if I would still be your friend. But no . . .'

BRIDE-TO-BE?
IV

A month had passed since their return from Switzerland when Amy wrote this. The euphoria of 'abroad' had long vanished and by now her impatience was once more at boiling point. Homecoming had been a sad anti-climax. They had travelled back via Paris, pausing long enough to attend the races at Longchamp, but after that they came straight back to Hull. At once Amy felt wounded by the way some of Franz's English friends cold-shouldered her, and work at Morison's seemed more frustrating than ever. She also became convinced that Franz was deliberately trying to mock her. Miserable beyond endurance she turned once again to the idea of escaping to America. As before, her underlying motive was to force Franz to insist that she should stay with him. He believes she had ideas of joining one of her uncles in Florida, but at the last minute the Swiss Consul in Hull, whose opinion she much respected, advised her emphatically against going.

She did not leave for America in August 1926, but she got as far as writing a dramatic farewell letter to Franz. 'I can't let you go out of my life for always without saying a few things to relieve my mind a bit,' she wrote. 'You think it's a huge joke that I go to America. I've never seen you look so relieved. You've been waiting for me to take the decisive step, so that it will be I who have gone away and left you and not you who have thrown me over . . . It solves your difficulties beautifully doesn't it, and without any hurt to your pride – i.e. in the eyes of your friends. Now you will nod your head wisely and say "How sensible of me to wait and see" and you will pat yourself on the back, and think how clever you are . . . Even now, although I feel so hurt and bitter, I simply can't believe that I have been mistaken in putting all my faith and trust in you . . . Why did you think I wanted to smash the vase *your* friends gave to *both of us*. I love it and I hate it. It was given with the idea that when we were married it would look nice in our home. How can I love it when it reminds me that even *your* friends don't yet know you as you really are . . . I know you will find this letter just as funny as you find the rest of my most intimate feelings. When I tell you you've hurt me, you laugh. But I think some day you will have something to answer for. You say you love me, but what is your love worth when you let me go away for always without an effort to stop me. I still love you and I can't believe that all I have written is true. If only you could tell me it isn't.'

V

After the emotional storms that followed the Swiss trip had spent themselves Amy became temporarily more settled, and a much more balanced attitude sometimes showed itself in her letters. This may partly have resulted from the fact that towards the end of the 1926, at the times when Franz was in Hull, she was prevented from seeing him as often as usual because the manservant at his flat had become 'disapproving'. But her newly calm frame of mind (when she was not in a black mood) may well reflect the serene influence of Franz's mother, with whom she was now keeping in touch by letter. 'Yes,' she wrote to Franz at this time, 'your love seems to have settled down now into the "quiet, steady flame of affection"; perhaps I am the same, I don't know.' She had just been re-reading some of his earlier letters, and was moved to comment: 'How quickly your moods change – we are so much alike in that. One day we both can write all sorts of delightful things to each other, whilst at other times we find it almost impossible to say nice things. Being so much alike on that point, I think we ought to make an effort to understand each other better, don't you?' One can hardly imagine her writing thus a year earlier, before she had met Franz's mother.

The solacing friendship of his family naturally encouraged her hopes of marriage. But Franz's mother, in writing to her, had come straight to the point as regards her Protestantism; if she were going to marry

Franz she would have to become a Catholic. 'Two people can't be really happy together unless they are of the same faith,' she explained. Amy hastened to reassure her. 'I wrote to your Mother and told her I entirely agreed with what she said on the subject of my faith,' she later admitted to Franz, 'and that she had not to worry because I would promise her not to "set a bad example" in her family . . . I knew what a big thing it was in her eyes, and I didn't want her to be unhappy thinking about it.'

At Christmas Franz went home and Amy wrote to him wistfully: 'I hope you will have ever such a good time . . . and go to church with your Mother. I do wish I could be with you . . . I can imagine your Mother and your sisters all loving you and caring for you . . . Please give them all my love . . . and especially to your Mother . . . Last night I dreamt that she had taught me to look after you properly – I think I must have been living at her house, because you suddenly came and gave us a surprise, and I was so happy that I knew how to care for you, and you were glad as well, but the dream was spoilt because you forgot to kiss me.'

She clutched at every token of the family's affection, such as the dainty embroidered trifles that Franz's sisters sent her for Christmas, and the lines inscribed in German from his mother (she could almost understand them for she was now studying the language at evening classes). On Christmas morning she slipped out early to Mass, and wrote afterwards to Franz that she felt much closer to him if she prayed in a Catholic church. Then she added: 'But it is difficult to get away from home – they don't understand.' This last remark was indeed an understatement. To 'them' – to Amy's parents, and especially to her mother – Roman Catholicism was anathema. Ciss Johnson would have been scandalised, outraged, if she had known that one day when she was absent from Hull two Roman priests called on Amy at Park Avenue (Molly, then fifteen, recalls that one of them helped her with her homework).

In Switzerland that Christmas, or soon afterwards,

Franz's mother evidently talked with him about Amy's faith, and asked him to discuss it with her himself. He was a dutiful son, and despite the awkwardness of the situation (Amy had by now abandoned hope of thrashing out plans for the future with him, and marriage was a 'forbidden subject') he did raise the matter not long after his return. Confronted by this unexpected opening she 'let the opportunity slip.' For with a jolt she realised that she did not fully understand what conversion would involve, and she was unwilling to commit herself while her ideas were 'utterly unformed'. 'Moreover,' she rationalised afterwards, 'I was entirely in sympathy with your wish to bring up any children of yours in the Catholic religion, so that there really wasn't much for me to say then.' After this she started to think the matter over more seriously and to investigate Catholic doctrines. Whereupon she discovered certain things (we do not know which) that she could not bring herself to accept.

A little later in London, almost certainly at the suggestion of Franz's mother, she and Franz attended High Mass together (at Westminster Cathedral) and afterwards discussed the sermon. This experiment was a failure, and to Amy, eager for reassurance from Franz – who she had imagined was at heart as ardent a Catholic as his mother – it brought painful disillusionment. Looking back on the occasion she wrote: 'I was awfully keen to go to a Catholic Church with you and it was rather unfortunate that the sermon just emphasised those very points which I had found so very difficult to face in that religion. When we came out I very badly wanted to think things over and adjust my ideas a bit and then somehow your, as it seemed to me, superficial remark on the excellent quality of the sermon jarred on me awfully. Instead of finding in you someone to whom I could confide my difficulties and get help I suddenly discovered that our minds were absolutely antagonistic and out of harmony and sympathy with each other. Instead of sensing my difficulties and tactfully helping me you were as nasty to me as you could be.'

Nevertheless she still clung to the hope that he might be able to guide her. 'Don't you feel strong enough in your religion, darling, to help me solve my doubts and difficulties?' she pleaded. 'I have been extremely sceptical lately and there are so many things I've decided I don't believe . . . It's difficult for me to discover anything I do sincerely believe in. I know that I can't stay at this stage believing in nothing, and I know that I must go on pursuing these thoughts until I have thought out my own creed. I can't just say I'm of a certain faith and I believe so and so without ever having thought about it. You can help me a lot if you only will, darling. Otherwise I must go on fighting it out myself.'

Now it was Franz's turn to let an opportunity slip, and Amy had no choice but to fight it out for herself. Her battlings overflowed into her letters, and there we can see her oscillating between her usual introspection and a naive attempt to formulate her ideas. 'It is universally recognised,' she wrote, 'that man must worship something . . . In its journey the mind, or soul, is fed on faith, and if this faith fails then I believe that particular religion loses its place as an ideal and becomes merely a disillusion. If the mind, or soul, is a vigorous one, I believe it will go on searching till it finds another ideal, more infallible than the last, where the faith will not be so likely to fail.' Then she made a defiant thrust at Franz. 'I believe that I have been making you my religion – I have been worshipping you, giving you the whole of my thoughts, acting on your code of right and wrong, confessing to you my sins. In my prayers you always have first place, and I am sure now that I've been doing wrong.'

'You will think all this nonsense,' she admitted, 'and I can hardly blame you if you don't understand what I scarcely understand myself. I only know that I love you differently from merely physically, and that often you disappoint my trust and faith in you . . . I still believe that you are always right, but I'm always a bit afraid that I may some time be forced to make the discovery that you're not . . . I am beginning to realise now why it is that man must worship a divine Being or an idol of stone or the sun – anything which is not another human . . . And that is why I am feeling I must have a stronger faith which won't let me down, and this I am trying to find, but it is difficult . . . and I have become so critical that I find flaws in everything, and it is no use expecting faith to make strong a religion which my reason prevents me from accepting . . . An infallible "something" must be found before the mind, or soul, can be satisfied once more.'

Poor Amy! Her 'mind or soul' remained dissatisfied. The drive towards finding the stronger faith she yearned for dwindled away, and the above letter, written some months after she finally left home, marks the end – so far as we know – of these spiritual gropings.

VI

But before following the course of Amy's career after she left Hull we must return to her parents' disapproval of Romanism. For at the beginning of 1927 it was this that precipitated a resounding family row, and speeded her departure from home. If Ciss Johnson had been gifted with more patience, and a subtler understanding of Amy's temperament, she might have anticipated that her daughter would in due course decide for herself that she could not face submission to Rome. But to the loyal Methodist mother it could hardly fail to be obvious that drastic steps had to be taken to save her child from an infatuation for a foreigner that was luring her not only to spiritual perdition but to social suicide. And if she would not voluntarily give up seeing Franz she must be forced to do so by some kind of banishment.

It must have been towards the end of February that the tempest broke, with lightning-flashes of temper and nerves from Amy's mother, and repercussions of wrath from her father. There is no doubt as to the virulence of the hatred towards Franz, the Papist villain, that had developed in little Ciss Johnson. 'I've realised lately it was Mother who caused all the trouble,' Amy confided to Franz after she had left home. 'I don't think Father would ever have acted as he did if it hadn't been for Mother . . . I really and honestly believe that given the opportunity and an excuse Mother could kill you. She's one of that sort.'

How *did* Amy's father act? It seems he delivered an ultimatum that she must either stop seeing Franz altogether or else leave Hull. But Will Johnson did his best to make things easier for his daughter; before the crucial talk he had enlisted the support of his brother Tom in Canada, and he pressed Amy to go out there to make a fresh start. But she had other ideas. For months already she had been trying for an advertising job in London; 'town' was where she wanted to be in any case. The family row merely accelerated her departure from Hull, but to an uncomfortable extent; when she gave up her post at Morison's and went south, in the first week of March 1927, she had as yet no definite London job in view. One of her letters indicates that she gratefully accepted some money from her father to tide her over until she was earning.

When she set off from Hull Franz was abroad; he was in Hamburg on business. Though his feelings about the crisis in Amy's life were doubtless mixed, it is possible that her decision to leave home was a relief to him, for he may well have foreseen that her presence in Hull was soon likely to be an embarrassment. He had quite recently decided to give up his flat, and had found lodgings where he was to start living after his return. While he was away Amy, determined to forestall any 'disapproval' on the part of his new landlady, had called and introduced herself as Franz's sister, explaining that she was living in lodgings elsewhere in Hull and was looking forward to evenings with her brother. The landlady was friendly but afterwards Amy felt scared at what she had done, and was tortured by worry until a letter came from Franz making light of it. Still, however, she was remorseful: 'I only make muddles of things . . . I think I must be a little mad sometimes, or perhaps as you say "I think too much".'

Just before she departed from Park Avenue she dashed off a note to Franz with her London address; she would be starting in a YWCA hostel. 'If I do not hear from you to the contrary,' she added, 'I will keep to the arrangements we made. Am looking forward ever so much to seeing you there.' The arrangement in question was that they would have a night together in London when Franz was returning to Hull from Germany, and 'there' was a West-End hotel.

8

LONDON

1927

Every evening by the glimmer of a nightlight Amy wrote page after page to Franz from her drab little room in the Bloomsbury hostel (the lights were turned off at 10.30 p.m.). She was surrounded by souvenirs of him: on the dressing table was his photograph and a motto 'Don't Forget' as well as scent and a new manicure set he had given her; on the mantlepiece over the gas-fire was a black cat for luck which was a present from him – 'I had to bring that if I wanted to get a job!' A job was of course her paramount need. During her first few days in London she approached various advertising agencies and put her name down with a Swiss employment house. She also wrote to John Lewis's store in Oxford Street emphasising her Sheffield degree, for she understood that they had launched a training scheme to attract graduates to retail selling. Almost at once she was given an interview, and then told that subject to satisfactory references she would be taken on at three pounds a week. Delighted at the chance of earning immediately, she accepted the engagement without bothering to study the conditions it entailed, as set out in a prospectus headed 'Learnerships at Peter Jones'.[1]

[1] These Learnerships were not, as Amy imagined, a scheme to prepare graduates for managerial posts, but a means of recruiting young women as salesgirls, aimed at replacing the traditional system of apprenticeship. The value of the Learner's

Just after she had taken this plunge her Aunt Evelyn came to London for a couple of nights, and she was reassuring about the Learnership. Amy, never having seen Peter Jones, imagined that the store must resemble the 1927 John Lewis's, which she described as 'an ugly, desolate place.' But her aunt told her that Peter Jones was 'a beautiful shop and very, very exclusive.' Matronly, warmhearted Evelyn Petrie was very fond of her niece, and probably came to London to make sure that she was not stranded. She took her to a matinée, helped her to find her way about, and gave her news from Hull, including the cheering information that both her Johnson grandparents disapproved of her father's dictatorial methods.

II

On the second Monday in March 1927 Amy reported to the Staff Manager at Peter Jones, along with half a dozen other Learners, and was put to work in the Silks Department, which she thought was 'next best to being in the Gowns . . . It is rather nice to be handling beautiful silks and satins.' That evening she wrote to Franz, 'I've had an awfully tiring day, not real hard work but a lot of running about . . . My brains will get slacker than ever, because there is no real brain-work involved. There are some intricacies in the process of selling, and quite a lot to learn, but it is simply a matter of getting accustomed to it.'

Franz replied reproaching her for impatience, and scolded her for wavering in her resolution to make good

---

services was assessed each week and charged against a 'remuneration account', from which a weekly advance of £3 was made. At first the weekly value of the Learner's services was far below the advance so inevitably a debt grew up, but in theory this would be worked off as the Learner's efficiency increased. In practice another source of income often helped to neutralise the debt; the scheme included a system of commission upon personal connection.

in London. This stung her to the quick. He was being entirely unfair to her, she felt, and she retorted in a long letter of self-justification. It is a fascinating record of her views on work in general and on her own capabilities, and it also shows the extent to which Franz dominated her outlook at this time. 'I do try to be patient,' she insisted, 'I know it takes a long time to achieve things that are really worth while . . . But I'm not the sort of person, dear, to achieve anything really great, as I hope of you. If you were not the ruling force in my life, then perhaps I might have the power to stick at a thing until I succeed. Because that's what I lack. I can't help living for the moment . . . If I were a man and knew that the business I took up had to prove my means of existence for my whole life, for myself and probably for a family, I should have the incentive to stick to it and make good, which I am sure I could do. But I'm afraid I haven't that incentive. You know that I've a horror of regarding my work as my "life's work". So long as I'm doing work which I feel is satisfying to my mind and my body . . . and which is bringing me sufficient remuneration to enable me to dress artistically, have decent digs, be able to attend classes (German and cookery in preference), have a very few amusements, and a little over for holidays, then I'm almost satisfied . . .

'Will you please tell me candidly if this is what you would rather have me say – "I intend to make my mark in the world and am going to do something worthwhile. I'll stick to my job in spite of whatever may turn up, and work and work until I have achieved a position I feel is worthy of my abilities, and a salary which will enable me to buy a car. Nothing shall stop me from achieving my ambitions, and I don't care if I devote my whole life to the task so long as I make good in the end." I couldn't say that, darling, and mean it, however much you wanted me to . . . Please don't be fed up. It's only because I have someone so worth while who fills my mind and my horizon.'

She made a point of telling Franz when others praised her. Soon after starting work at Peter Jones she wrote: 'They make me run all the errands . . . You've absolutely no idea how docile and obliging I can be . . . I couldn't be like this with you, I should have no pride left. I've none at Peter Jones – there's no chance to have any . . . Of course it is rather taken advantage of, but I had my reward today when I overheard the stock-keeper say, "Those other two are slow things – Miss Johnson is the only one who makes herself useful".' But she had to admit she enjoyed some aspects of the work. 'I can't help but regard this selling of silks as great fun,' she conceded. 'It reminds me so much of playing at Shop when I was little (my favourite game!). And I do so love arranging the silks and handling them. Already I have learnt a lot about them and can almost tell the exact price of a crepe-de-chine or georgette or chiffon just by the feel of it and the texture.'

Towards the end of the second week her zeal brought some exciting results. 'I've been extraordinarily honoured,' she told Franz. 'Next week I'll be stock-keeper and first sales of the Jap Silks and Shantungs. The girl in charge is having to move to Oxford Street, and they're giving me her place, as being very quick and promising – ahem!!! But really, darling, it's a great honour. I've been trying to find out what I shall be worth then, but haven't succeeded yet. Do you know what they valued my services at last week? Ten shillings!! So I already owe the firm £2 10s 0d'

By now she had studied the conditions of her Learnership and was gravely alarmed at the prospect of sinking ever more deeply into debt to her employers. A Learner was free to leave at the end of four weeks, but if she stayed on after that she was 'honour bound' to continue with the firm until her debt was paid off. She begged Franz for advice and also wrote to her father (the recent row had not estranged them) and was gratified when they both urged her to leave. 'But I think I'll stay the month,' she told Franz. 'In spite of being tired I've never felt miserable or unhappy . . . Everyone is so extraordinarily nice. I think shop-girls in a good class shop are amongst the nicest working girls there are. All I know in Peter Jones are nice – though of course not the kind one makes intimate friends of.'

Some of her experiences throw interesting light on the status of London shop-girls in the '20s. In particular there was an incident one Saturday afternoon when she was doing a round of hostel-hunting (she was stopping at the Bloomsbury hostel only until she could find something better). 'I've been to about six places this afternoon,' she related, 'all full up and only one would put my name down. One place I went to amused me awfully. She was a most talkative and inquisitive woman – wanted to know where I worked etc. I told her, because these places won't take you without knowing details, and then she said in a confidential whisper that she would give me a tip not to tell the other girls I worked in a shop, because they were rather snobbish and wouldn't have anything to do with shop-girls. I asked what sort of girls *they* were and she said most of them were teachers! When I got outside I laughed so much to myself that I'm sure some passers-by must have wondered what had happened to me! . . . What will all my dear relations and friends, Morison's etc., say when they know I serve in a shop? What a good thing I don't care!!'

III

Amy still believed that advertising was her vocation; in her heart she knew that the Peter Jones job was no more than a temporary expedient. Through a former colleague at Morison's she had an introduction to Harrod's advertising department, and her hopes rose to dizzy heights when she was asked to submit two specimen pieces of copy. When she wrote to Franz after composing them she evidently hoped they would win her a post.[1]

[1] One piece was on Spring Fashions and the other on Reproduction Antiques. The following is an excerpt from the latter. 'Walnut is the zenith of perfection in furniture. Our reproductions of rare and costly antiques nestle contentedly together in any room, and each piece finds itself in such delightful company that all whisper in unison their secrets of charm, elegance and good judgement . . .'

But after a fortnight Harrods returned them and told her they had no vacancy to offer. It was a crushing disappointment. The curtness with which she told Franz of her failure – 'Harrods don't want me, darling' – shows how much she took it to heart. After this she seems to have abandoned the idea of trying for any sort of advertising post.

In the meantime a different and quite unexpected possibility had arisen thanks to Olive Birkbeck, Amy's step-cousin from Leeds, who was already in London, working as an assistant in the stationery department of the Times Book Club in Wigmore Street (though she was leaving soon to be married). To Olive, who tended to exaggerate, Amy was something of a heroine – her clever cousin who had done brilliantly at the university – and she was keen to find her a better job. When Amy's mother came briefly to London Olive – short, dark and attactive – joined her and Amy for dinner at Gatti's Restaurant. ('I chose the wine,' Amy boasted to Franz, 'a half bottle of 1914 Bordeaux – I can't remember the name, but it was nice; not a bit sweet and heavy. I was so glad I knew a bit about it.') Olive was charming to Amy and encouraged her to try for a job in the Book Club library. Thereupon Amy, bold as ever, wrote to the manager and arranged an interview to discuss 'future possibilities'. She dashed to Wignore Street in her lunch hour but the expedition was a sad waste of time; the manager told her abruptly that he could do nothing for her. 'I saw Olive and she was amazed,' Amy told Franz. 'Of course I knew she was being far too optimistic . . . but I didn't think it would be so bad as that.'

This fiasco did not deter Olive and she proceeded to speak about Amy to a friend of her family's (who also knew Amy's father), Vernon Wood, a Manchester lawyer who was a senior partner in a firm of city solicitors, Messrs William Charles Crocker. They then dined with him at the Holborn Restaurant ('very nice but awfully expensive, Dinner 7s 6d'), and Amy showed him the Learnership prospectus and confided her anxieties to him. Next day he wrote to her giving his opinion of the Peter Jones system and it was not enthusiastic. As an alternative he offered her a post in his own office, starting on the typing staff at three pounds a week, and with the prospect of something better when she had acquired legal experience. A few days later she accepted this offer. It was a decisive turning point in her life. At Crocker's, where she started work on 11 April, she was soon to find herself in a job where she felt she was really valued, where she could at last settle down and give of her best.

IV

On the day when Lindbergh set off over the Atlantic, 20 May 1927, Amy was in high excitement. But writing to Franz she made no mention of the flight; she was far too much absorbed by a happy turn of events in her own life. 'I've got a ten-shilling raise today,' she announced, and added the thrilling news that she was to be promoted to the post of personal secretary to Vernon Wood when Miss Roberts, his present secretary, left to be married in the autumn. So far her work had consisted mainly of copy-typing, but she had sometimes been asked to do odd jobs for individual partners. She spent one busy day tracing stolen bonds in a criminal case. 'There were piles of papers to go through,' she told Franz, 'and it just suited me sorting everything out and getting all the facts clear. When I'd assembled all my evidence I made a beautiful schedule and it looked most professional. I find that the legal phraseology comes quite easily to me.' When Vernon Wood asked her what her off-duty interests were she told him she was fond of study, 'and I had a brainwave to ask him if there was anything I could study in the Solicitor's profession which could make me more useful to the firm.' He suggested Company Law (his own speciality) and she was overjoyed when he said she might borrow books from his bookcase. After this he asked her an occasional test question and her confidence grew as she found herself able to produce the right answer. Soon for the first time he told her to draft a letter to a client. Secretly alarmed she studied the relevant points of law and then did her best; to her amazement he did not touch the draft and she hoped for praise; but none was forthcoming. 'I suppose he's so used to writing letters, he doesn't think there's anything hard in it,' she groused to Franz, 'but there is for me. Never mind, I'm still pleased with my achievement.'

Such triumphs compensated for the grind, the frequent high pressure and the late hours. Furthermore her liking and respect for Vernon Wood were increasing; so much so that he now provided her with a standard of comparison for Franz. 'I like working for him and he isn't always fault-finding like you are,' she could now say. 'I wouldn't like to work for you.' When Franz disparaged her new-found dedication to work she replied with spirit. 'It's not nice of you to insinuate that I've put business first since going to Mr Wood's . . . You know perfectly well that you've always come first. But that isn't to say you always will . . . I'm going to put first whoever needs me most, and Messrs William Charles Crocker really do appreciate me and make the most of my abilities.'

She was not being unduly sure of her employers' confidence. Sir William Crocker[1] has confirmed that Vernon Wood (who died in 1957) had much faith in her potentialities. And when recently asked to give his recollections of Amy as an employee, his reply included the following interesting evaluation: 'Having a good brain and a marked power of concentration she proved competent but not sensationally so. My partner's idea was that if she should improve satisfactorily and show a sincere desire to be a Solicitor he would take her under Articles of Clerkship and enable her to qualify.'

Amy's work was not always in the five-storied office

[1] William Charles Crocker was knighted in 1955.

close to the Mansion House;[1] sometimes she had to attend the Law Courts or make trips to Somerset House. Nor was she always at the same desk, but her usual place of work was a small inside room with no windows, which seemed to her very claustrophobic and made her feel starved of fresh air. 'The girls there don't seem to mind,' she grumbled, 'they say it's warm in winter (which I call stuffy) and cool in summer . . . I must try not to let it get on my nerves.' With the summer ahead she pined to join a tennis club, but decided the expense was beyond her. Repeatedly she told Franz that she longed for air and exercise, and there was one day when she exploded, 'I just hate streets and houses and tubes and buses and people and stuffy rooms and typewriters. I wish I could climb up a mountain and be high above all these things . . . where there's light and air and sunshine.' But such outbursts were rare, for London was growing on her. 'I don't think I'd be happy in a quiet place, even though I grumble often at the noise and bustle,' she admitted. 'The intense "aliveness" gets hold of you somehow.'

On Saturday afternoons when the weather was fine she liked to take a book and a writing pad and go off alone to some park; 'I can think much better and more clearly in the open air and hot sunshine.' One spring Saturday she discovered Kew, another time she settled to her letter-writing near Rotten Row, alternately observing the riders and sharing her musings with Franz. 'It was lovely in Hyde Park,' she wrote. 'There were some ripping horses out, but not many good riders – though I know nothing about horsemanship. But surely it's not right either to flop like a jelly with legs going up and down and out like sawdust legs, or to sit perfectly rigid and bounce high in the air, with legs stuck like pokers through the stirrups? I liked to watch a few of them especially galloping.' Then she went on, 'I

---

[1] Number 21 Bucklersbury has been demolished since Amy's time and Bucklersbury House now stands over its site.

didn't exactly envy them, because perhaps they weren't perfectly happy with all their money, but it made me wonder if one has a chance in another life to do all the things one wants to do in this life and can't.'

Despite the wistfulness of this last remark, written during May 1927 (Amy's third month in London, when she was nearing her twenty-fourth birthday) she was in most ways enjoying her present life, and had already become far less restless. She had escaped from the austerities of the hostel after only three weeks, for Olive had done her another good turn by introducing her to friends in West Hampstead, a middle-aged couple from Yorkshire, who were on the lookout for a lodger. Amy was soon at home with them, and being treated as one of the family, while what impressed her most about them was their mutual affection. 'I don't think I've ever seen a couple so devoted to each other,' she wrote. 'It's most refreshing and I'm already losing a little of my cynicism towards marriage.' Her theories on the subject of marriage, based on those of Bernard Shaw, were quite distinct from her personal hopes.

V

At the time when Amy was at West Hampstead she had very few friends in London. Olive soon went home to be married (this was in some ways a relief, for she had taken to warning her against Franz 'for her good') and although Amy found the company at the office congenial, no special friendships had developed for her there. Of her Sheffield friends, Winifred and Gwyneth were working in the north and only 'Tuppy' was within reach (she had a teaching post at Leighton Buzzard, and Amy went several times to stay with her for weekends).

As far as men-friends were concerned, Franz insisted that she should have none but himself. This was flattering ('Whilst you want me I want nobody else,' she assured him) but she could not refrain from asking if he knew what 'dog in the manger' meant. Before long however a new possibility transformed the whole picture. Soon after Amy came to London Franz told her that he was planning to expand his business by embarking on a venture concerned with the import of potatoes; if it prospered he would have to come more and more often to London, in fact he might well decide to start living there himself in June. This prospect was, of course, intoxicating to Amy. At last, at last, so she immediately assumed, she and Franz would be able to live together, and the home they were going to share became the constant theme of her imaginings. She studied the advertisements in *The Sunday Times* and decided that when they pooled their resources (she intended to stay on at Crockers) they might be able to afford a small flat in the outer suburbs. But until he himself came and joined in the flat-hunt she could not convince herself that he was in earnest. 'When will you come and look for a flat?' she asked. 'I'm longing for that time. It doesn't seem a bit true, and often I think I'm just dreaming, as I have done ever since I knew you.' Then she consoled herself by remembering what had already been achieved. 'You don't think I've much will power – and yet I've made you love me, haven't I, because I've loved you so much. And when you come to London for good, I'm going to try to make you do something else – but I mustn't tell you what.'

Her anticipations were not all on the romantic level; finding herself suddenly keen to be a good cook she enrolled for a course of evening classes at the Regent Street Polytechnic. At home she had never been encouraged to help with the cooking; now it delighted her to be able to try her hand, and after every class Franz was told what dishes she had learnt. The technique of making an omelette fascinated her (she had never seen one made before) and after an evening devoted to fish she boasted 'I could even now teach Mother a lot.' She knew she could also teach her mother a lot about food values; at home her preferences for health-giving foods such as brown bread were called 'fads and fancies'. 'You've no idea how much I'm looking forward to doing my own cooking,' she wrote, 'and arranging the meals as I like them, and as you like them . . . *ça va sans dire.*' She shared with Franz many of the same tastes in food and drink, for he had long been educating her towards his own gourmet standards. But stubbornness was in her nature and even her daydreams were tinged with realism. 'We shan't of course quarrel at all,' she observed, 'but maybe we shan't quite agree on everything. Sometimes you'll win and have your way and sometimes I shall.' Doubtless living with a lover would be very different from her present independence. 'Whilst I'm on my own I go on a fairly calm way,' she reflected, 'but when you come I suppose I'll be again all ups and downs and violent happiness and violent depressions, but it's much more real life.'

During her first months in London she and Franz were able to meet every few weeks, for already he had to come south on business more than usual, and twice they had 'honeymoons' away together. At Easter it was Wales: Franz had suggested Stratford-upon-Avon but Amy was longing for mountains and could not resist an advertisement describing Dolgelly as 'The Switzerland of Wales.' To her family she said that she had been invited to spend the holiday at Southend by a girl she had made friends with at work. But to Franz she exclaimed: 'How I do loathe all this lying and deception. I used to think it fun, but now I'm afraid it irritates me. Shall I say the truth, darling? After all what does it matter to anyone but ourselves. And people may just as well get used to us now as in June. Don't you think so?' Franz did not agree. He advised discretion and Amy stuck to her white lie (she *had* been invited to Southend by an office friend but had declined). Yet she was still troubled. She could not bring herself to accept that lying was necessary, though in practice she found that the public opinion she thought she despised always had to be placated in the end, and at heart she was relieved to fall in with it. On occasions when she feared she might be pregnant she was of course especially tormented. 'When I'm with you I forget all about the consequences and just live for the minute,' she admitted, 'but I am quite certain we shall not be lucky always, and I can't help but think of the trouble and disgrace which would follow. I tell myself repeatedly I don't care what people think, but I know inside myself that I do care a lot . . . In spite of your teaching and my "advanced" reading I'm afraid I am all the same a bit priggish and old-fashioned.'

Before Whitsun there was quite a squabble. The weekend was to be at Hathersage but at the last minute Franz wavered; it was the sort of place where they might run into friends. 'I am disappointed but not surprised that you are making difficulties about our weekend in Hathersage which you yourself suggested,' Amy complained. 'I never could understand and still can't why you consider you have always done the right thing by me, and yet you're so afraid of anyone knowing how we stand towards each other.' She was certain, so she told him, that various people guessed at their relationship without knowing 'anything definite'. In this category she mentioned her Aunt Evelyn and her father but not – and this omission is significant – her mother. All the evidence of her letters indicates that Ciss Johnson never knew that Franz was her lover. As Amy herself remarked to him, 'Some people see us together a few times and conclude I belong to you, and others see us together for years and conclude nothing of the sort.'

Among Franz's friends there were some who tacitly accepted the relationship, who – as Amy euphemistically put it – accepted their 'refusal to bow down to English customs and be engaged.' There were others who ignored her and treated Franz as unattached, and this vexed her and wounded her. Any mention of these friends was apt to provoke a storm of irrational resentment: 'There is not one person . . . who has persuaded me to stick to you. Not a single one . . . They all say the same thing, "A charming boy, but not a marrying man." I don't care a damn whether you're a marrying man or not. Whatever difference does it make! . . . I'm so longing for you to come so that we can have our own little home and be ourselves absolutely, without any pretence or conventions or interference. You've no idea how much I want it.'

But Franz did not come to live in London in the summer of 1927. The potato trade proved to be much more precarious than anticipated, and as the weeks went on it became ever more obvious that he would not be moving south in the near future. 'I hate potatoes more than ever,' Amy exclaimed, 'they've been nothing but trouble to you since they entered the scene; they've made you severe losses, and they will insist on coming to Hull instead of London where they ought to come.' By midsummer her hopes of a London home with Franz had withered and died. But when she finally faced up to this disappointment she did so with philosophical calm. She could hardly have reacted in this unusual way had it not been for an unexpected and most fortunate coincidence of events which had been turning her thoughts in quite a new direction.

VI

Since leaving Sheffield she had almost lost touch with Winifred, for their paths had diverged completely. Winifred, whose engagement had been broken off, had been devoting herself to an arduous job which gave scope to her idealism and at the same time absorbed all her energies. Employed by the Women's Guild of Empire, a feminist organisation aimed at promoting public spirit among the women of Britain, especially working-class wives, she had been sent first to the East End of London, and was still there during the general strike, when the bitterness occasionally flared up into violence. Then she was moved to Kirkcaldy, and spent a sunless summer among the miners' wives. In the autumn she was transferred to Sheffield, her home town, and worked in the little towns and villages of the South Yorkshire coalfield. By the spring of 1927 she had decided to change to different work. Following the example of her eldest sister Isabel, who worked for the biscuit manufacturers McVitie and Price (and had by now become manageress of their Paris factory) she applied for a job with the same firm and was accepted; she was to be in the welfare department of their factory at Harlesden. At this point she wrote to Amy to tell her she would be coming to live in London. How would she like to join forces?

When Amy first heard the idea she did not consider it for she was then confident of setting up house with Franz, but when his coming was postponed indefinitely the thought of sharing with Winifred became extremely inviting. Winifred arrived in London early in July, and as she could not afford a flat she took a bed-sitting room in Marylebone Road; a small back room in a flat in Oxford and Cambridge Mansions belonging to a pleasant lady called Mrs Hodgkinson. Amy had by now become restive in her West Hampstead lodgings. Even before she had a definite alternative she had arranged to leave, and during the final days of July she joined Winifred in her tiny bed-sitter. It was much too small for two, but after a week or so of cramped improvision they were able to exchange it for a larger room in the same flat. Thus began a new stage of their friendship which was to prove exceptionally happy for them both.

By September 1927, when Amy had been in London for six months, her life was attaining some degree of stability. At work she received another increase in salary when she started as Vernon Wood's secretary; relations with her family were easier again,[1] and as regards her ménage with Winifred her letters to Franz show a state of mind that could almost be called contentment. 'Winnie and I are so happy and comfortable here,' she purred, 'and I think I'm awfully lucky to have such a cosy place I can really think of as home. I think we shall stick together, because I can't see anything that would separate us.' Nevertheless Amy

---

[1] She had not attended Irene's wedding in May, but she went home for the first time since her banishment for her parents' silver wedding celebrations on 11 September.

would not have been herself without some castles in the air. The only thing I would like better (much better) is a flat of my very own with all my own furniture and a small maid to do the work. If Winnie and I were each getting £5 (and we may soon . . .) and someone would kindly set us up with some furniture we could easily run a place of our own. That is what we are aiming for, though we probably shan't be able to do it for about three years . . . It is nice to have something in life to aim for.'

9

SHARING A ROOM

1927–1928

When Amy first came to London she bought writing paper by weight – it cost her fourpence-halfpenny a pound. Now the companionship of Winifred was little by little weaning her away from the need to 'relieve her mind' by writing unceasingly to Franz. 'It seems a long time since I wrote to you every day,' she now remarked to him casually. 'I've never found that absence makes the heart grow fonder.' She was still writing to him frequently but the tone of her letters was changing. Often now she was rudely critical, disparaging his personal tastes, and lecturing him on what she regarded as his extravagances (shampoos, hair restorers and shirts). She still asked for advice, but when he gave it she accused him of smugness and arrogance, and chafed at the 'master-and-pupil' relationship which she said she had outgrown. She complained loudly, too, because he seemed intent on keeping their discussions to a superficial level. 'I wish you would try to get below the surface sometimes. It would be worth it for you if you love me at all, and really do want me more than any other girl.' When she tried to initiate an exchange of views on 'really serious things' – religion, marriage, death – she failed to evoke much response. The subject of death came up after Franz had attended the funeral of a Hull friend and had made remarks that she dismissed as sentimental. She, it seems, preferred brutal realism. 'For myself . . .

I want to be cremated. I have no more fear of death than have you, but I don't like the thought of the worms.' As regards marriage, she insisted that she now had new ideas which he had not bothered to discover. 'When I first knew you I was a stupid ordinary girl who regarded every presentable man as a potential husband, and any one interested in her as a probable one. That's how I regarded you and you knew it . . . But the worst of it is, you still think that's my view . . . I would awfully like a home and I'd like some children to bring up and train and I think I'd be happier as a housewife than as a typist. But that's not my ambition and sole object in life.'

Some of the letters she wrote to Franz at this time contain fascinating insights into her thinking about herself. For example in one of them she expatiated upon her black moods – those fits of uncontrollable anger that afflicted her from time to time. In the days when she and Franz were often together she had blamed them on his influence, but after she settled in London she came to believe they stemmed from tendencies within herself. 'You are not altogether wrong or exactly right when you say that outbursts of temper seem essential to my happiness,' she explained. 'When I am quite happy I don't have outbursts of temper – it is when I am not happy, and little things accumulate to which sooner or later I have to give vent; and then when the storm's over I usually feel calmer and happier than for some time past . . . It's only once in a couple of months or more when I get these nasty moods.

'I do realise and have realised for some time that you're not . . . [their] immediate cause . . . These moods come from inside myself and have nothing to do with outside circumstances and influences, except so far as they are either aggravated or softened by the "petty worries" which you seem to think bring them on . . . The only real enemy I have to fight is in myself, and the only struggles I have are those with my own mind and ideas . . . I have noticed many times lately that I don't seem able to give expression to my feelings unless I am forced to by a bad mood or fit of temper or indignation . . . I only get the courage when in a bad mood . . . I'm not so level-headed and balanced as you are, and I sometimes find your calmness and balance and content awfully irritating, but in spite of my bad moods I don't think I'd like to change my mind for an equable, solid one of everlasting happiness and content – it would be far too boring . . . Do you really think I'm so unfit to face the "struggle of life"? You see life for me isn't a struggle – not so far. Sometimes it's highly interesting and worthwhile, and other times it's just "one damn thing after another".'

In a different letter, written just after one of her outbursts had failed to anger him, she protested that she didn't like him to swallow everything she said. 'It's somehow like hitting someone and they turn the other cheek in the proper Christian manner, and I can't help not liking that spirit . . . Have you ever felt in that detestable mood where you feel you must hurt someone you love awfully in order to make yourself feel better? I believe you have because sometimes you seem to want to make me unhappy just for the mere pleasure of it. Not lately, but many years ago! It isn't often I feel like that – hardly ever and I'm glad, because it's not the sort of feeling rational human beings ought to have, and I do feel sorry afterwards.'

She held the view that when her 'black' impulses came it was wiser to 'give vent' to them than to 'repress' them. But there was one exception to this, which in the context of her later life is an important one: she deliberately refused to let herself despair. 'I don't and won't give way to circumstances,' she once stated categorically to Franz, 'and if I don't like a thing I do my best to alter it instead of "grinning and bearing it" as I suppose you think I ought to. I've found I generally get my own way in the end if I'm sufficiently keen on getting it and I don't think there's anything that one can't change for the better if one wants to sufficiently.'

Apart from her direct references to her moods there is also, in one of her letters to Franz, an exposition of her theories on married life that is dominated by the idea of protecting each partner from the moodiness of the other. When she wrote it she had just been reading Shaw's *Getting Married*, and although she admitted she was influenced by his Preface, she stressed that this central idea was her own. 'Many years ago I more or less thoughtlessly declared that if ever I got married I should insist on separate rooms and weekend holidays from time to time,' she began. 'I have long since given up the former idea, but the germ contained in the latter seems to me sounder and sounder the more I think of it . . . The root of the idea is simply a refusal to be any man's permanent servant. It is unnatural to imagine that a marriage service is like a magic spell enabling two people to live peacefully together for the rest of their lives in complete love and accord. There are bound to be times when they quarrel, get on each others' nerves and even dislike each other, besides the times when one of other may be in a black mood and try to make himself or herself better by making the other one miserable. If both could be of angelic patience and forbearance they might be able to tide over these trying times . . . but these ideal people are rarely found . . . and so long as the marriage laws are so stupid as they are at present I think the only way to help these natural difficulties . . . is for a greater measure of freedom to be agreed on between the two than the words of the marriage service (hopelessly antiquated) confer . . .

'If a wife knew that she could trust her husband to be fair to her under all circumstances I don't see any objection to him keeping away from her if he feels a bad mood coming on . . . [in order to seek] other society which he feels will help him to combat this mood. Because after all, one undoubtedly does exercise more restraint on one's moods when amongst many people than in the privacy of one's home, and whilst some moods of depression seem to require loneliness, others are dispelled by the right society.' She ended this dissertation by remarking, 'I wish I could write a book bringing up problems of marriage and divorce. It's awfully interesting.'

Living with Winifred brought out Amy's home-making instincts. She bought cushions and made covers for them, and arrived back from a trip to Hull with her pictures of Swiss mountains and a couple of bright rugs she had borrowed from Franz. Although he had often impressed on her that she had no artistic sense she refused to tolerate drabness and was miserable if her belongings were out of order. Winifred, who had the talent for improvisation of a good camper, was more happy-go-lucky and lacked Amy's aversion to dust. But Amy, so it soon appeared, was almost as house-proud as her mother. At Mrs Hodgkingson's the cleaning was done by daily maids, whose standards were not up to Amy's. 'Only the surface is cleaned,' she grumbled, 'I do so loathe dirt, it depresses me.' She decided to tackle it herself. 'It's awfully satisfying somehow to have done some work and then look round and see how neat and tidy everything is and to feel that one has done that one's self,' she told Franz. 'I wasn't quite sure how far it was my real nature to be tidy, or how much of it was just because I knew I ought to be tidy and clean. But I know now that I couldn't do with things slipshod . . . The only thing is that when one does one's own cleaning the people who are supposed to do it marvel at the place being so clean and so do less than ever themselves.'

Amy and Winifred took the shopping in turns but the gas-ring cooking for their evening meal usually fell to Amy, since she was often back first. At weekends she was allowed to use Mrs Hodgkinson's stove and to her joy was able to bake a cake for Winifred's birthday. 'Most people seem to think they don't or shouldn't enjoy the things they make themselves,' she remarked, 'but I enjoy my cooking immensely, and I'm sure it's not so much that it's good as because I've done it myself.' Franz was not spared any details and was told, for instance, when she discovered that a chocolate blancmange was a good way of using up leftovers of milk. But he was well accustomed to minutiae; for years Amy had told him every time she washed her hair, laundered her clothes, or helped with 'washing up the pots.'

As the summer of 1927 turned to autumn she felt increasingly stale – despite the happiness of her new 'home' – for she had had no holiday and was missing Franz badly (he seldom came to London now). But she was still enjoying Crockers. After September, when she took over as secretary to Vernon Wood, she wrote to him, 'I've got much more status now at the office and am glad of it because I don't like to be just one of the crowd.' But the work was harder than ever. 'I'm there from nine till eight every day. But I love it . . . Mr Wood's frightfully particular. He won't have a single mistake or alteration in any letter and if a sentence doesn't sound just right he sends it out to be done again, however late it is.' At one point the pressure was such that she declared she would run away to Switzerland if it weren't for Mr Wood. 'I just work and work. I'm gradually getting very bitter and old-maidish and uninteresting . . . I'm always longing for someone near to love me and whom I can love . . . I'm not the "old maid" type and could never be content to lavish all my affection on cats and nieces (they seem to go together somehow) . . . If there were a God and he cared he wouldn't make it so impossible for you to be with me.'

By November she had slightly more leisure; she had been given an assistant and was usually able to escape from the office by six o'clock. So now once a week she and a girl from the office went swimming at the Marylebone Public Baths, but this indoor swimming was her only regular exercise at the time and she never seems to have considered taking up hockey again as Winifred did. She was trying to improve her diving and also learning the crawl, and was determined to persist until she excelled. 'I like to do a thing better than most people,' she told Franz, 'and not only as well.' She added that Miss Harms, the girl she went swimming with, was a good singer and was teaching her how to breathe properly; she was trying to get into training as she had dreams of a ski-ing holiday at Christmas. But she did not go to Switzerland that Christmas, and although Franz went abroad without her he did not go for winter sports: he was immersed in his business affairs which were now causing him considerable anxiety.

III

Amy's period of 'old-maidishness' came to an end before the year was out when a chance meeting in Mrs Hodgkinson's kitchen led on to an enjoyable flirtation. 'I found out a couple of days ago that I have a secret admirer in the flat,' she boasted to Franz. 'He's only seen me twice – once when I was cooking pork chops and onions in a white pinafore and again when I borrowed a lemon for Winifred who has a cold, so it can't be very serious as yet. He's only a boy, about six foot tall and nineteen years of age. Winifred and I agreed that for it to be really romantic I ought to be a rich widow. We have so little to amuse us, so you must excuse this childishness.' She then discovered that 'the boy' was a good driver – he took her out for several runs in a tiny Austin two-seater – and she admitted to Franz that she was lonely and 'badly wanting something to happen.' 'I still feel young enough to want some fun,' she declared (she was now twenty-four). 'Last night I suddenly felt very boisterous and wanted to romp and fight – the boy was in and we had a "rough house". In the end I fell on my little table and smashed it.' Perhaps the absence of embarrassment in her account of these pranks made it easier for Franz to break to her, shyly and gradually, some important news of his own. But the noncommittal manner in which he first told Amy that he had a new 'acquaintance' aroused her suspicions at once. 'I wonder why you do so enjoy teasing me,' she wrote, 'especially now when I don't get so insanely jealous . . . You forget I've changed and am much more sensible now.'

Such was Amy's state of mind when at the new year of 1928 a financial crisis arose for herself and Winifred

which threatened to bring their happy stay at Mrs
Hodgkinson's to an end. Winifred's share in the expenses
was proving more than she could manage. Amy had just
received another rise and was now earning £5 per week,
but Winifred's wage was still £4. One of the troubles was
that their hospitality had been running away with the
housekeeping money. For both of them it was a delight
to be able to entertain; neither had been able to do so
since the days of the Baslow camp. Amy's sister Molly
had stayed several nights with them, Gwyneth stopped
off on her way to a holiday abroad, they gave 'Tuppy' a
bed several times, and Winifred's sister Isabel stayed
once or twice when she was over from Paris. But the
expense which brought matters to a head was the
heating, for it was a cold winter. There were high French
windows on to the street which did not fit, and the gas
meter devoured the shillings.

Mrs Hodgkinson liked both the girls, especially Amy,
and did not want them to leave, nor did they want to go.
Winifred recalls that Amy went so far as to invite her to
live as her guest, but she felt she could not accept this.
There is no mention of the offer in Amy's letters to Franz,
but the following account probably refers to an ensuing
discussion. 'I had a talk with Winnie the other night, and
although I told her I wouldn't leave her and would come
wherever she went, she didn't seem very keen on the
idea. She said there was no point in my being a
"Christian Martyr" and I got the impression that she
wanted to be on her own so that she could save more
money . . . She says she's going to the cheapest place
she can find.' But after talking things over yet again they
agreed they could not bear to part. Amy's letters to Franz
made it clear that Winifred was at this time the only
person she knew, apart from himself, whom she found
'satisfying' – as distinct from 'congenial'. And on
Winifred's side there was an even deeper affection. Once,
since they had been living together, when Amy had been
laid up with a bad cold, Winifred had brought her a
bunch of grapes as well as some oranges and lemons
because, so Amy told Franz, 'she says she loves me and

is sorry I don't feel well. Winnie seems to love me a lot – although she's not at all demonstrative – and I really can't see how I attract her.'

'Goodbye to our little home,' she lamented, writing to Franz just before 18 January when she and Winifred moved to Ames House, a YWCA hostel near Oxford Circus. But she comforted herself with the thought of how much she would save, since the cubicles they had booked cost only nine shillings a week. Their plan did not, however, work. Ames House proved so unbearably bleak that the two friends went out as much as possible and of course spent much more than they had intended. 'It's the problem of evenings and week-ends that's the worst by far,' Amy explained, writing to Franz on a wet Sunday. 'It's too cold to sit up in one's cubicle for long and the drawing room is an awful place . . . Today I don't know what on earth to do. Here's one of the girls beginning to play hymns! The walls of the drawing room are covered with texts . . . I can see I'll be driven to Church on Sundays at this rate . . . This hymn-playing girl will send me crazy soon . . . oh dear and everyone's humming it!!'

One Friday Winifred returned to the hostel after work tired out and frozen and with only one objective – a hot bath. As usual she had been forestalled and there was no hot water left. She found she could scrape together the price of a return ticket to Paris and she told Amy she was going to spend the week end with Isabel. 'I'm coming too,' said Amy, and off they went. After this refreshing escapade they knew they could stand Ames House no longer, and an advertisement in *Daltons Weekly* led to their next step. A room in Maida Vale at thirty shillings a week sounded promising, and their first sight of it decided them. 'It's only a single room but very well furnished and comfy and overlooks gardens and a tennis court,' Franz was told. Just before the end of February 1928 the two turned their backs on the hostel and moved to number 24 Castellain Road. Once more they had a home of their own.

10

THE END OF THE AFFAIR

1928

It was in North Cornwall, in the cold brightness of early spring, that Amy first discovered she possessed an unusually good sense of direction; on long walks through the unfamiliar countryside and among the sand-dunes near Perranporth she came to realise with pride that she could find her way without any assistance whatever. This gave her special pleasure because in the past Franz had told her she was incompetent at this sort of thing. In March 1928 – a few months before her twenty-fifth birthday – Amy was holidaying alone for a week. She was badly in need of a break for she had not had a proper holiday since Switzerland (almost two years earlier), and as soon as she and Winifred had moved to Castellain Road she made her escape. Her choice of Cornwall was by chance – a boy who delivered eggs at Crockers' office happened to mention some cousins who ran a private hotel in Newquay – but it was a fortunate chance and the holiday was a happy and successful one although so brief. It was also an exceptional interlude for Amy, a departure from the habitual patter of her doings, which in the light of her letters to Franz may even be regarded as a seminal episode in the whole of her life.

Later on, one of the ever-recurring questions that she came to detest was 'Miss Johnson, *why* did you fly to Australia?', and she usually replied with a superficial answer that satisfied a superficial interest. In her own mind, it is evident, she came to recognise the motives that had carried her along when the urge to fly took hold of her. But so far as we know she never traced them back to their springs, or rather to that breathing-space on the Cornish coast, surrounded by fresh wild beauty – 'intense blue sky, green sea, white seagulls and brilliant sunshine' – when she had the opportunity to stand back from her life as she saw it and gather strength for new resolves.

She had never before spent a holiday alone. At first she suffered a twinge of loneliness and wished that Franz or Winifred were with her: they were 'the two people who usually help me to enjoy things more.' But almost at once she found herself relishing the solitude. On the evening of her first day she went for a walk by moonlight, venturing down the cliff steps to the beach, and groping her way into dark caves and over rocks. After this she started out each morning with a picnic lunch and spent the whole day in the fresh air.

'I've grown to love Cornwall so much,' she wrote to Franz towards the end of her stay. 'How I have enjoyed these whole-day tramps all by myself, hardly ever meeting a single person. In spite of your contempt for my "bump of direction" – or lack of one – I've gained a reputation in this hotel for my ability to find my way – which isn't easy in Cornwall. There are scarcely any sign-posts and the roads are hopeless . . . My walk yesterday was to Perranporth . . . after my lunch and a quiet read I decided to try and find St Piran's lost church in the sand dunes. I walked a long way along the sands – firm and hard and yellow and utterly deserted except for seagulls – miles of sand – until I came to the sand dunes and then I turned inland and found the church with very little difficulty . . . It is the oldest in the country with the four walls still standing. The remains are enclosed in an outer building and I could only peep through the door. The sand dunes were inhabited by hundreds of rabbits and it was almost possible to imagine oneself in the desert when down in the hollows of the dunes . . . It was bitterly cold although all the time I have been out walking without hat or coat – just carrying my mac in case of need. I crossed the dunes and with absolutely nothing to guide me found my way across marshes and through fields straight as a die for a wee village called St Cubert and thence to Crantock where I had been and knew my way . . . It was a glorious day.'

II

Two days later she was back at work, and there was a silence of almost a fortnight before her next letter to Franz. In the meantime she had heard from him, with the news that he was now taking his 'new friend' to theatres and dances. The letter Amy sent to Franz on 25 March 1928 was a serious and lengthy one, and it is by far the most striking of all those she wrote to him – which is saying a good deal.[1] She must have devoted hours to it, for she did not write important letters in haste. 'Sometimes I spend ten minutes or more thinking of the best way to put a sentence,' she had once explained. When she wanted to have something out, however, she preferred to do so by letter. 'I can't talk nearly as well as I can write,' she said. 'When I talk I speak before I've thought thoroughly. When I write I've had time to get my mind well in order first.' Certainly the tone of this crucial letter is deliberate, yet its vividness is nonetheless startling.

'I must try and explain as clearly as I can the lines on which I have been thinking for some time and the decision I have come to,' she began. 'I'll tell you first of all the decision . . . and then try to tell you why. My life up to now has occupied two volumes: (1) my childhood and schooldays, and (2) you. The first one finished when I went to Sheffield and it is now time to close the second one.

---

[1] Franz kept about three hundred of Amy's letters and they total over 200,000 words.

THE END OF THE AFFAIR

'From the age of eighteen until now, when I am nearly twenty-five (please correct me if I'm wrong) you've been the predominating factor in my life. I don't blame you for that – it was I who was the fool – and now that I'm so much older and more experienced I can look back on those years and see how utterly stupid I have been. I think I am now strong enough to cut it all out and that's what I intend to do. No more looking for letters that come less and less often; no more wondering when you'll come to London again to see me, or rather when you'll be coming on business; no more puzzling over the question of how much you really do care for me and what are the thoughts about me that must sometimes be going on in your mind . . . The decision I have come to is the result of a lot of hard thinking on my part . . .

'Let's go back to the beginning of all the trouble and look at things plainly. You made the first mistake by treating me in the way about which you once said "If a chap had treated one of my sisters like this I'd have killed him." Ironical, isn't it? I've had no brothers to help give me a saner, healthier idea of the relationship between the two sexes or to protect me in the good old-fashioned way. I wonder what made you say such words out loud – they've excused you for a lot in my eyes although you resolutely forgot them as soon as uttered.

'I made the next mistake in allowing you to treat me in such a way. But whereas you had no excuse at all for your actions, I consider I had a good deal. First, you were practically a god in my eyes, and anything that you did was right just because you did it. Secondly I knew practically nothing about men and the way they differed from women and I was ashamed of my ignorance and tried to cover it up by pretending to know everything. The few ideas I had were totally wrong and absurdly ridiculous. I can't help but smile now when I remember some of them. In a vague sort of way I felt that in yielding to you I was losing your respect for me, and yet my mind was full of unsolved problems and wonders and perplexities, and I awfully wanted to find out things and have actual experiences, and it being you who was there and ready and wanting to give me them just clinched the matter, and the more I got to know the more I wanted to know. See where I am now. The matter no longer interests me, I feel I know all there is to know. That's all men want with girls, you can see it all round you, in the painted faces of nearly all the girls you meet and in the staring, desiring eyes of the men who pass you in the street. How I loathe them all and how I despise myself for being just the same as they. But please don't mistake – I owe all my knowledge to you and I am grateful to you for your training and for the worldly knowledge you have given me. If I could, I wouldn't wish again to be the stupid little innocent I was when you first knew me – I used to think it was *hurting* you and I was so sorry for you and felt so tender towards you because I thought you were hurting yourself for the sake of giving me enjoyment. Oh, isn't it too funny.

'Ever and ever so many times I wanted to try and undo the harm but I wasn't strong enough and I used to think about it for hours and try to justify my conduct. First I tought just to love you so much was sufficient excuse, and then I thought out all the ethics of marriage and sided with the view that it was merely legal licentiousness and I formed my own little code of right and wrong: that, because we live in a wide and tolerant age, the mere form of marriage makes no difference to whether it is right or wrong to be a man's mistress. I decided that there was no wrong being done at all if the lover and his mistress really and truly cared for each other sufficiently to be satisfied with each other and never to go to anyone else for their pleasures – and that the form of marriage made no difference at all except to give legal recognition to the children if there were any.

'This, I remember, lasted me for a long time, and then I began to find holes in it. It was one day after you'd really said something fairly definite, for you; that you thought some day we might actually get married. I then dropped all my former line of reasoning, and merely based justification for my conduct on the ground that we should really be husband and wife some day and there was therefore no sense in waiting until that day, and we might as well carry on as we were doing.

'The last phase, and the one I hold at present, is that there is no justification at all, except that everyone is more or less weak and that the less weak should help the more weak. This is of course seldom carried out and everyone is despisedly weak when it really comes to those moments of physical feeling which, I suppose, the good benevolent Lord endowed us with for good ends. Pity he didn't see the bad ends as well before he pronounced his work good.

'You will perhaps be wondering what all this has to do with the present state of affairs and my new decision. Just this. All the time that you have known me you have found so many things to grumble at and find fault with – as I see it now, the only thing which has kept us together for so long has been your intense desire, and my reciprocating desire, for sexual intimacy (loathsome words). (Apart from this one thing, the whole of your instincts seem to be against a married life.) This has been all right for you so long as I was content to let things drift on and on as they were, and I've been for the greater part of seven years content to let them so drift because I thought there was something at the end of it. Always I've had before my eyes the picture of a home where there'd be no outside interference causing friction, and where I'd be surrounded by things which would all belong to us, for which we'd worked hard, and paid for and chosen, and where there'd be children of my very own whom I'd train up so carefully, remembering all the little things I've grumbled about and bemoaned in my own training, and trying to give them the advantage of my experiences. It's so silly, but this is what I've always wanted so much, and you being the only man in my life, was naturally the one to whom I should look to give me these things – apart altogether from the urgent desire I've always had for you yourself.

'Now, however, I can no longer persuade myself into

believing this is a possibility; it is too obvious that in every way you are getting to care less for me. Your letters come less and less often and get shorter and shorter and less and less affectionate. They are now merely scrappy news bulletins prefaced with "Darling" – the sugar coating the pill; and how empty and farcical it sounds now when you so obviously don't mean it. I have told myself once or twice it was most unlike you to write it if you didn't mean it, until I realized that you couldn't address me as anything else because to do so would be in some manner bringing you face to face with your change of feelings, and I've noticed several times your tendency to let things drift as long as possible sooner than stop and face them.

'It is always I who stops the drift and often I have done so foolishly. I can see it now. I wish to God I'd never mentioned the subject of marriage to you. I was a fool and have, I can see, defeated my own ends, but it seems that it was inevitable. I was impatient to know what was going to happen to my life and you irritated me so tremendously. You have often reminded me of the donkey I once took Betty for a ride on at Bridlington. It went so slowly and I was so eager to get back to my games etc., and then the more I urged and coaxed the slower it went until finally it stopped, planted its legs firmly on the ground and refused to budge. I pushed it and pulled it and almost got to kicking it I'm afraid, but no use. Finally I lifted Betty off and we turned round and walked back. The donkey followed a minute later.

'There is a difference however in this letter from the others [which] . . . I've written to you on what was to me the most important thing in my life. I'd better point it out in case you don't realise it for youself. Always before, I've made many and varied protestations of my deep love for you and told you frankly how much I wanted you (*not* sexually, as you probably thought) and how sure I was we could be happy together, and begging you to be quick to come to London etc. etc. Now I no longer love you, I no longer want you, sexually or any other way, I don't believe we could for a single moment be happy together, and if you came to live in London I should probably leave; not because I couldn't bear to be in the same city with you – I don't hate you, I'm just totally indifferent, as you've been so long – but because I'd be always afraid of meeting you and that would get on my nerves . . .

'I just want to say two more things. One, that I don't want this to affect my friendship with your people. I love them all very much and even though they probably only care for me for your sake, I still feel I want their friendship so much. I had some topping letters from them . . . the other day and they sent me some photographs . . . The second is that I still owe you £3 which I cannot send you at the moment, I'm afraid. I'll send it along as soon as I can . . . I am very grateful for the loan and for the way you've always helped me in money difficulties . . .

'As a last thing I want to tell you something which I can't put plainly (there'd be no need to tell you at all if you could "read between lines", but you're not good at that, as I've found before). I'll tell you in allegory.

'In a certain room of a certain house a beautiful fire had been kindled by a youth who lived there. It was his duty, and his pleasure, to keep it always burning brightly and this he loved to do. But gradually he got somewhat tired of always picking out the best pieces of coal and wood and he grew careless and threw on anything handy until by and by the fire grew duller and duller and got choked up by ashes. And there came a day when it was practically out and only then did the boy grow alarmed. As he was considering what to do a voice whispered "Just leave it, that's the easiest way. It will go out and if you want you can light another. But if you want this one to brighten up again you must do something at once and look after it continually. Another time it will go out more quickly."

'It is stupid I know to make up such a silly story. Oh well, once a fool always a fool I suppose . . . I wish you every success and lots of good luck.

Amy

'I have just read this letter through . . . Knowing pretty well your ways of reasoning it strikes me you'll at once jump to the conclusion that I've written like this because I've got another lover. But this is not so. I have no other men friends at all . . . I do not want men and have no intention now of ever getting married.'

It might seem there was nothing further for Amy to say. But in spite of all her clear thinking and her new resolve she could not refrain from leaving a loophole for Franz. At the foot of the letter she added a postscript: 'It isn't of course possible that I've totally misjudged you?'

III

Franz replied by protesting with some warmth that she had indeed misjudged him. If he had seemed neglectful lately it was only because he was distraught by business worries; he had already decided he must abandon his business, and was now searching for a new job, so far without any success. He had not disclosed to Amy the full extent of his troubles because he needed to discuss them with a confidante closer at hand; she was mean to grudge him the sympathy of his new friend. Amy, contrite, suggested that she should meet him for a talk when she came home for Easter. Nevertheless she was glad she had written that letter; in her own words 'now at last the barrier is down.'

At their Easter talk she and Franz came to a 'new understanding'; in future each was to feel free to embark on friendships elsewhere, but they would continue a running exchange of confidences by letter. This seemed to Amy a hopeful experiment, although after the bargain was made she found herself in some confusion of mind, particularly on the question of marriage. 'More than anything else, I know I want children,' she affirmed, 'but I also know that at present I definitely prefer life as I am and I don't want to get married.' Her next remarks show even more obviously how muddled her thinking had become, for she seems to have assumed that Franz's state of mind coincided with her own. 'I don't know how we'd like it,' she wrote, 'if either of us were to become engaged to marry someone else, and I don't think it would be right for each of us to remain single all our lives because we never dare test ourselves. Although that, I can see quite clearly, is what is likely to happen.' This wildly erroneous forecast was Amy's last word on the subject; thenceforth, in her letters to Franz, she abandoned all such ruminations and arguings.

IV

In Amy's social life she now dropped the last vestiges of her 'old-maidishness' of the year before. Cinema-going (of a new, more selective kind) once again became an addiction. In Soho she bought herself a new dance frock – 'a sweet little pale green one with high waist, tight bodice and full skirt,' and a present of money from her grandparents was spent on perfume. During the next three months she lived in a whirl of films, plays and dances, and she exclaimed to Franz 'I love the present style of dancing,' which meant the Charleston and Black Bottom. Her remark was something of a taunt, for Franz himself preferred the Viennese waltz.

She and Winifred decided to acquire a gramophone on the instalment system, and since she took to purchasing two new records each Friday they must soon have amassed quite a collection (the hits of the day included the melodies of *Show Boat* and songs such as 'A Room with a View', 'Sonny Boy', 'Chloe', and 'I can't give you Anything but Love, Baby.') Sometimes the two girls went together to dances and one of these was a Sheffield Old Students' Dance at the Astoria. Amy was impressed by the dance hall but not by the Old Students. 'They were awfully boring . . . they couldn't dance at all,' she told Franz. 'I can see now that you belong to their sphere – I'm much too frivolous for you. You'd be scandalised at half my doings – my private life doesn't bear investigation.'

She was making numerous conquests, so she bragged, and in various letters she detailed them: a new friend from the Board of Trade, a young German boy, a nineteen-year-old articled surveyor, 'the most interesting boy I think I've met yet . . . just back from Persia,' and 'a young gentleman just home from Africa,' who gave her a memorable evening out. 'It must have cost him an awful lot of money,' she observed. 'We had cocktails at the Criterion; then went to the Café Marguerite for dinner and then to Romano's for cabaret till 2 a.m. Finished up on whiskeys and sodas and pâté de foie gras – Winifred said it was enough to make her ill to think of it, but I felt perfectly all right. My friend admires me because he thinks I'm a "good girl" and seems greatly intrigued thereby – I think I've managed to keep up the impression . . . You must tell me off if you're not agreeing with my conduct etc., just like Winifred does. She leaves me alone more or less but her advice is often quite valuable . . . I usually take her opinions on things as she's wiser than I am . . . but I can do with yours as well, my dear friend.'

Amy's reporting of her gaieties was in accordance with the new agreement between herself and Franz, and he on his side wrote to tell her not only about his 'new friend' but also other young ladies. Soon his 'new friend' was being referred to as his 'new sweetheart' and Amy was commenting coolly: 'I am glad you have someone to interest you . . . Is she one of the "steady" friends you recommend to me? You see I've had one experience of a "steady friend" and I can't say I'm thrilled at burning myself twice. Anyway I've found a new friend who promises to be true and steady [the articled surveyor] . . . we have lunch together nearly every day . . . He loves to come down here – he thinks our life's like a picnic. Now we have the gramophone we can entertain better.'

When Amy's birthday – her twenty-fifth – arrived she decided on a sudden impulse to stage a party. 'I got on the telephone and invited about eight people down (all boys but two because I don't know any girls) and then I went out and bought lots of strawberries and cream and cakes and ice cream etc. We had a lovely tea and I think everyone enjoyed it. In between we had lots of splendid tennis [on the courts behind Castellain Road] and in the evening when tennis was finished they all came in again for dancing.' 'You would hardly know me now, I have changed such a lot,' she declared in another letter. 'I am enjoying life very well and on the whole getting a lot out of it. It is glorious to be alive when the sun is shining, but even when it's not I am still happy – in spite of very hard work and late hours recently at the office . . . London is a wonderful place to live in and I think it's only by living here that one can find out and appreciate the smallest part of its wonders. I know I often get fed up and long for peace and quiet, but peace and quiet are only attractive because of the comparison. I do not think I could now be happy anywhere else but London – not for long anyway.'

If one were to interpret the course of events solely from these letters, one might deduce that Amy's attachment to Franz dwindled through the late spring and early summer of 1928 until by about the end of July it came peacefully to a standstill leaving no trauma behind it. The last of all the letters she wrote to him is not a dramatic farewell; it is a short note enclosing the three pounds she still owed him, and asking that various belongings of hers should be returned to her home in Hull.

But Winifred has memories that reflect a deeper level of Amy's feelings than do these final letters. She remembers – she cannot forget – a summer evening in 1928 when Franz turned up at Castellain Road. He and Amy had not met for several months and they were now 'just friends'. They went out together for dinner while Winifred stayed at home. She was surprised when Amy returned alone as early as ten o'clock, with looks that showed she had suffered a very severe shock. Briefly she told the news: Franz had just been married to his new sweetheart. Then she threw herself on to her bed and sobbed as though the storm of tears would never end.

PART TWO

TRIUMPH

11

THE FLYING CRAZE
1928

I'm going to learn flying! I'm joining the London Aeroplane Club and then I can get tuition and always use their aeroplanes.' In much excitement Amy wrote this in the spring of 1928, just after she had made her way for the first time to the de Havilland aerodrome at Stag Lane near Edgware. She was writing to Franz, and it is very fortunate for us that her new craze for aviation found its earliest outlet while they were still corresponding. For the lively account of this first visit that she sent him not only establishes what happened, but also helps us to understand the motives that impelled her towards the step which was to be the most crucial of her life.

It was soon after her holiday in Cornwall that she first felt drawn towards flying. Winifred believes that she originally toyed with the idea merely because it was an outdoor sport which would involve joining a club; she had been looking for a tennis club but had not found one to her taste. The courts in the nearby gardens were hardly a step away, but this little club had no social amenities, and to Amy's mind a tennis club that did not run dances was a poor affair. At this point she thought of trying something different. Why not take up flying – if it were not too expensive?

In the later part of the 1920s flying as a sport was in the news, with its races and 'pageants' and aerobatic contests, while private flying (for those who could afford it) was a fashion that seemed to promise an exciting future – some said that the light aeroplane would soon come to supersede the car as a rapid means of getting about. Aviation offered other attractions too: for the more poetically minded it opened the way to a new kind of exaltation, to something of the sense of freedom associated with the flight of birds, as well as to the aesthetic joy of viewing crystalline cloudscapes. This was also a time when few doubted the beneficence of the aeroplane, for military aviation was in eclipse (except to those immediately concerned). The role of the pilot seemed essentially pacific, as well as heroic in the extreme. One after another the pioneers were risking their lives to span the continents and the oceans, and each successful flight was a triumph of endurance as well as a victory over the forces of nature. The dew was still on the whole idea of flight, and it was a time when anyone might find that he – or she – had caught 'sky fever'. At such a moment the 'aviation bug' was liable to attack men and women of the most diverse characters, from a poet like St Exupery to a comedian like Will Hay, from duchesses and the wives of millionaires to the daughter of a Hull fish merchant. And once the flying craze was in one's blood it usually became an obsession.

II

Amy's first move was to write to de Havillands at Stag Lane to ask for details of their training courses. The name and address may have caught her eye in some newspaper or magazine, for the Moth – 'the motor-car of the air' – that sturdy, practical light aeroplane which Geoffrey de Havilland had designed at exactly the right moment, was deservedly in the limelight. By 1928 Moths had been shown in several London stores, almost half of the sixty or so light aeroplanes that were privately owned in Britain were products of the factory at Stag Lane, and those enthusiasts who could not afford £600 or more for machines of their own usually flew in Moths belonging to the flying clubs.

THE FLYING CRAZE

It was probably soon after Easter that Amy wrote to Stag Lane, shortly after she and Franz had agreed to be 'just friends'. As we know she was then in a mood to show off, and the writing of this letter was a token of her new independence. For although flying was a fashionable sport it was still regarded as something very unusual, and a sign of bravado, for a woman to become a pilot. This first feeler towards learning to fly led to nothing, entirely for financial reasons. When Amy wrote she had not realised that at Stag Lane, in addition to the de Havilland factory itself, there were two quite separate organisations which provided tuition, the de Havilland School of Flying[1] and the London Aeroplane Club. A reply to her letter came from the former establishment, with the news that the cost of instruction was five pounds an hour. Amy's salary was five pounds a week (with no additional allowance from her family) so for the time being she accepted defeat. Only later did she discover that the London Aeroplane Club, one of the clubs that benefited from the Government's current scheme to promote airmindedness, gave flying instruction at a very much lower figure. At this stage she knew nothing of subsidised clubs, nor of the international air rivalries that had brought them into being, nor, probably, of Air Vice-Marshal Sir Sefton Brancker, the Air Ministry's dynamic Director of Civil Aviation, who was later to play an important part in her career. It had been largely as a result of Brancker's zeal that the scheme for making grants to light-aeroplane clubs for the purchase of aircraft, and for each pupil who qualified as a pilot, had been initiated three years earlier.

The next relevant event in Amy's life is mentioned in one of her final letters to Franz: during the last week of April she saw the film *Wings*, which was being hailed as Hollywood's most effective portrayal of the war in the air. She was deeply stirred by its aerial sequences. The

[1] One of the largest civilian flying schools in the country, catering mainly for RAF Reservists.

new realism of its air-to-air photography, and the brilliant flying of the ex-operational pilots who battled and crashed in the biplane 'crates' made it a classic of its genre (as did also the banal love story, a triangle with Clara Bow as heroine). There is no doubt that *Wings* revived the allure of flying for Amy, but as a thrilling spectacle rather than as a possible hobby for herself.

Two days later, on the afternoon of Saturday 28 April, she happened to be alone with nothing to do. Winifred was out playing hockey, and she was feeling lonely but abnormally full of energy. We may guess, too, that her mind was full of adventurous ideas, for she was reading, with much enjoyment, Robert Graves' *Lawrence and the Arabs* (Vernon Wood had lent her his copy). It was a lovely spring day and she set off on an open-top bus for Hendon, hoping to see some flying.

Her expedition did not finish at Hendon. She explored further and eventually found herself at the entrance to the de Havilland aerodrome. Next day she related the whole story to Franz. 'Yesterday it was a wonderful day,' she told him, 'and I was so lonely and miserable . . . Winifred and I have decided that utter boredom is responsible for more crimes than wickedness – however, as I knew of no crimes to commit, I finally decided to go for a ride on the top of a bus to Hendon to see if I could see some aeroplanes. I went a long way round, by Golders Green and Hendon, and thence to Stag Lane Aerodrome which I finally discovered is near Edgware. There were lots of aeros up and I was wishing so much I could afford to learn. There was no one to stop me going in, so I went through the gate, down the path, past the sheds where aeroplanes were in various stages of construction, and finally came to the open space where the machines were taking off – there were lots of sheds and a pavilion with deck-chairs in front.

'There were lots of people about but no one questioned my right to be there; finally I saw down and watched . . . [and] I plucked up courage to speak to one of the pilots – he of course took me for a member of the [London Aeroplane] Club because otherwise I'd no right to be there – but he was awfully nice and told me, to my intense surprise, that I could join the club at an entrance fee of £3 3s 0d [and a] Subscription of £3 3s 0d and then lean to fly at the rate of 30s per hour. After about seven or eight hours' tuition, one can enter for a pilot's certificate (having previously passed tests for nerves) and then one can always use the club's machines at the rate of £1 per hour and enter for races, competitions, displays, stunts, etc. It is too good to be true and I can hardly credit such good fortune. I'm going up one evening next week to sign the papers and I'll probably have my first lesson next weekend. I'll play tennis at these courts here now, because I'll have to be as careful as possible with money to save it for flying lessons.'

She obviously hoped that her daring project would shock Franz, for in her next letter she remarked with evident disappointment, 'I'm surprised you approve of my wanting to learn.' She had also informed her parents, but so far they had made no comment ('I shan't mention it again now they know'). But the lack of any stimulating opposition from Hull did not cause her to waver; on the following Saturday she went again to Stag Lane. There however her hopes of getting quickly into the air were dashed, for she learnt that the club had a long waiting list. With a handful of aeroplanes and only two instructors no attempt could be made to keep pace with the queue of applicants. 'There are no vacancies until June at earliest,' she lamented to Franz, 'so I've joined as an Associate Member and can go down to the grounds, etc. and must wait in patience.'

Her patience gave way often during the next few months. She wrote more than once to Lieutenant Commander Harold Perrin, the gruff, intimidating secretary of the club,[1] trying to persuade him to let her

---

[1] Perrin was also, and more importantly, Secretary of the Royal Aero Club (to which the Stag Lane club was affiliated), the chief authority in Britain as regards flying activities; from his office off Bond Street he held sway over the destinies of hundreds of pilots.

jump the queue. But all in vain. June came and there was still no vacancy: Amy's turn did not arrive until mid-September.

III

In the meantime her life was not uneventful. It was, of course, half-way through the summer of 1928 that she suffered the shock of hearing that Franz had married. But fortunately for her morale she still had the companionship of Winifred and there was also, just ahead, a holiday she had been looking forward to for months: she and Winifred and Gwyneth were going for a walking tour in the French Alps. Together they pored over maps and Amy equipped herself with breeches and boots. This was the first time she had prepared for an open-air trip abroad. After a fortnight in the mountains with her friends, and a few days with Franz's sisters (her affectionate relations with them had not been spoilt by his marriage) she returned to London glowing with sunshine and enjoyment. This was a few weeks before her first flying lesson.

But before following Amy into the air, we must look briefly back to the early part of the summer, for it was then, in advance of her plunge into the outdoor world of flying clubs, that she became acquainted with an indoor corner of the world of aviation and was first introduced to air politics. Not very much is known about this transitional stage of her flying enthusiasm, but its importance must not be overlooked: it brought her closely into touch for the first time with air propaganda both civil and military, and undoubtedly influenced her thinking.

During the summer of 1928 (before her birthday) she went seldom to Stag Lane, for it was tantalising to be at the aerodrome merely as an onlooker (she fell back on tennis for fresh air and exercise). Nevertheless it was almost certainly in the club room there that she chanced to pick up the May issue of a monthly called *Air*. From it she learnt of an unexpected way in which she could associate herself with aviation. The magazine was the official organ of the Air League of the British Empire, a body which set out to spread airmindedness in the context of Empire politics. The membership of this grandiosely named organisation included the titled, distinguished and rich, but its aim was to convert both high and low. The future of Britain – so the League reiterated – would depend on her total strength in the air, and this meant the strength of her airlines and flying clubs as well as her Air Force. In that May issue some sinister figures were given: Germany, although prevented by the Treaty of Versailles from overtly building up an Air Force had an Air League with a million members (compared to the British Empire's six thousand), while the mileage flown by British civil aircraft was only a twelfth of the German equivalent.

But a paragraph in *Air* which caught Amy's eye had more personal implications. 'DO YOU KNOW' – the question was asked in bold capitals – 'That the Secretariat of the Air League is finding it increasingly difficult to cope with the ever-growing volume of work and that funds are not available to engage additional staff . . . If you are willing to help please DO IT NOW.' Amy did it then. She wrote to the impecunious Air League and offered to donate her secretarial services in the evenings after her work at Crocker's.

IV

By means of this voluntary work for the Air League, Amy doubtless became familiar with the names and reputations of the outstanding pilots of the day. These included several remarkable women. There was nothing stereotyped about the leading women pilots of the '20s and their only common denominator was affluence – almost all of them possessed aeroplanes of their own. Foremost among them was Lady Bailey, daughter of an Irish peer and wife of Sir Abe Bailey, the South African industrialist, who showed that to be a good pilot a woman did not have to ape manishness; her efficiency was disguised by an endearingly offhand manner. Within a year of learning to fly she had taken part in several air races and shared in establishing a world's height record.[1] The elderly Duchess of Bedford added prestige to the ranks of women who flew, but she did not attempt to lead the way as a pioneer pilot (during the expeditions she made, most of the flying was done by pilots she employed such as C.D. Barnard). Winifred Spooner, on the other hand, good-looking, serious, and quietly reliable, earned respect not only for herself but for women flyers in general by her ability to handle an aeroplane, as also did the courageous Sicele O'Brien, who re-qualified as a pilot after losing a leg in a crash. Most idiosyncratic of them all was Lady Heath (the former Mrs Elliott-Lynn) an attractive Irishwoman already well known as an athlete and feminist, who thrust herself and her flying into the public eye in a way that sometimes excited ridicule. But she was certainly, in her time, the outstanding campaigner for the rights of women pilots.

Just before the end of May 1928 a luncheon was given in London in honour of Lady Heath, to celebrate a pioneer solo flight she had made from South Africa to England. In her speech she put forward the idea that scholarships to help women to learn to fly should be made available under the auspices of the Air League, and she announced that Sir Charles Wakefield, the oil magnate, had already agreed to give £300 towards the scheme.[2] The plan went ahead and scholarships were

[1] She had also been awarded the title of Lady Champion Aviator of the World by an American organisation, the International League of Aviators, a notable tribute in view of the large numbers of American women who had already taken to the air.

[2] As Governing Director of C.C. Wakefield & Co. he was well known for his benefactions to flying. He became Lord Wakefield of Hythe in January 1930.

allocated to five clubs, to be awarded to the candidates chosen by the clubs' committees as the most deserving. The London Aeroplane Club was one of the five, and to Amy this seemed a chance intended especially for herself; the ony drawback was that her application would have to be submitted to Perrin.

Knowing that he was impervious to her letters, she forced herself to call on him unannounced at his office – this in spite of the embarrassment we know she felt, now that she was in London, about her Yorkshire accent (she remarked earlier to Franz that another Hull girl who was finding her feet in London 'talks much more nicely than I do'),[1] Apparently she hoped to convince him that she was the most deserving of the scholarship applicants, but she did not succeed.

Only some months afterwards, when she had abandoned all hopes of being nominated and had started flying lessons at her own expense, did she learn the name of the woman to whom the scholarship had been awarded; Miss Audrey Kidston, daughter of Lady Windham and sister of the wealthy sportsman Glen Kidston (currently in the news for his purchase of a Fokker aircraft for a big-game hunting expedition). At the time, so it seems, Amy assumed that Miss Kidston must like herself have been burning with a frustrated longing to fly, and she accepted the apparent snobbishness of the allocation in a philosophical spirit – Amy's outlook was not tained by class bitterness.

[1] It is not true, however, that she had a broad Yorkshire accent. In the film *They Flew Alone* and also in various broadcasts her accent has been much exaggerated.

13

TAKING WING

1928–1929

Amy's first flying lesson, so eagerly awaited for so long, was not a success, and when it was over Captain Matthews, the junior flying instructor at the London Aeroplane Club and a young man noted for his brusqueness, did not hesitate to tell her that she was no good. Later on, when she was famous and he in turn was setting off to make a flight to Australia, some of the press stories gave him a truly ironic twist. If she had been any less stubborn in temperament, and if Matthews had been her only insturctor, the discouragement he gave her might well have extinguished her hopes of becoming a pilot. More than once, after a flight with him, she came back to Castallain Road almost in tears. But in fact no less than three instructors contributed to Amy's initiation. Unfortunately not one of them is now living, so they cannot be asked for their memories of her as a pupil, but her progress can be followed by means of other evidence, including of course the entries in her pilot's log book.

The date of that first half-hour with Matthews was 15 September 1928, and we can picture Amy sitting helmeted and goggled in the deep cockpit of the Cirrus II Moth. Since she was not tall[1] her forward view above the dashboard and windscreen must have been chiefly

---

[1] Her height was 5 ft. 4 ins.

the back of Matthews' leather-covered head. When they were up, through the movements of his rudder pedals (linked to those under her feet) she was meant to learn how to keep the aircraft flying straight; then, when she had grasped this, she was supposed to practise similar movements, thereby making the 'straights' that are the first entry in most pilots' log books. The procedure was very similar to the elementary stages of learning to drive on a dual-controlled car, verbal guidance was given by means of a speaking tube which connected with ear-pieces in the pupil's helmet.

Amy, like many another novice, had not realised the importance of a well-fitting helmet. She had got hold of one that was far too large for her, so the earphones were in the wrong place and Matthew's remarks incomprehensible. 'When I was up in the air I could only hear a confused sound in my neck instead of what should have been lucid instructions,' she later reminisced. 'For my next lesson, I took care to have my own helmet to fit properly, but I was scared stiff of my instructor who never seemed to lose his first idea that I was a born idiot.' If Matthews had been a more experienced instructor, or if his character had been more sympathetic, he might have made sure before take-off that his pupil's earphones were in position, but it seems that he cannot have done this.

Fortunately for Amy, the club's chief flying instructor at the time, who also took a share in her earliest tuition, was a man of gentler temperament, and furthermore an exceptionally gifted teacher who later became recognised as one of the great British flying instructors of his day. Captain Valentine Henry Baker, MC, AFC (who was killed test-flying in 1942) reached the peak of his fame at Heston in the 1930s, although at Stag Lane, where he worked for ten months from the summer of 1928, he was already establishing a reputation for his ability to teach the unteachable. Some of his methods were individualistic – in the air he often conveyed his meaning to a pupil by means of mimed hand signals – and he believed that one could learn to fly only by being allowed to take risks (within reason). He could be just as outspoken as Matthews, but knew how to reprove without giving offence and lavished praise when it was deserved. When he worked at Stag Lane he was just forty, but looked far younger. Few would have guessed that the dark, unassuming Welshman with a quiet voice, who had flown in the Royal Flying Corps and then for Vickers before he turned to instructing, was old enough to have been earning his living as a bank clerk before the first world war.

Of Amy's first ten lessons five were with Baker and five with Matthews. Each Saturday until the beginning of November, and sometimes again on the Sunday, she went up for twenty minutes or half an hour, learning and practising the control movements while the Moth meandered along at about seventy miles an hour over the suburbs of north-west London and the countryside of Hertfordshire. And it seems that she was somewhat slow to master the elements of the art which Lady Heath had proclaimed were ten times easier than riding a bicycle. Both of her first two lessons with Baker were concerned with 'straights', and this suggests that at first her touch on the controls was too heavy for their delicate response. Even the lightest pull on the control column of a Moth and she is climbing, a finger-push forward and she is diving, only a touch on stick and rudder and she is in a bank.

After her first six lessons, on 13 October, Amy wrote a letter to her father which as a record of her attitude towards flying at this stage is of unique interest. When he was in London on business they usually had an evening together,[1] and at their last meeting she had evidently been holding forth on the delights of aviation. 'I note your remarks re my flying,' she wrote. 'The first time I talked to you about my ideas when you were in London I thought you were really interested and quite

---

[1] He often combined a day or two in London with visits to his firm's Lowestoft branch (which he himself had built up since the early 1920s).

approved, or I should not have enthused so much this last time. It makes me happy to be taking these lessons and gives me an interest in an otherwise very monotonous life and gives me a chance to meet people. Except for the one hour per week I spend at Stag Lane, the whole of my life is devoted to the office, coming home merely to eat and rest – I am always far too tired to study . . . I do not know what are your ideas as to how I should live my life – I am very grateful to you for making it possible for me to take a University degree, and for helping me to come to London, and looking at the result from merely a money standpoint I don't think I've done so badly as I earn more than any of my friends who were at Sheffield at the same time as I was.[1] I think you will agree I shall be happiest living my life in my own way and learning through my own experiences, and so long as this doesn't entail my having to fall back on you financially, I shouldn't think you will object. You see, I have an immense belief in the future of flying.'

II

'Turns' are first mentioned in Amy's log after she had flown for three and a half hours, when she was up with Baker during the first weekend of November. Another of his pupils has described the occasion of one's first steep turns as 'a solemn moment, this moment when the machine ceases to function merely like a motor car or a boat but begins to behave like a bird.' As the pupil's left foot presses the rudder, and simultaneously the stick is moved over to the left 'one's sense of stability and equilibrium is assailed with a majestic but rather sickening swing.' The left wing sinks and the right wing rises in the sky and a voice comes over the earphones, 'Stick central . . . steady . . . Don't let her nose down', a comforting reminder that Baker is there

---

[1] She was now earning £5 per week plus bonuses.

and will save the situation if one has really boobed. But after those first turns there was a pause of two months in Amy's training. With Christmas ahead, shortage of cash may well have been one reason for this. She had already spent over £12 on her flying[1] – all out of her five-pound-a-week salary – but another reason was the onset of stormy weather. In November the aerodrome was often a morass and the gales were so violent that some of the sheds were almost blown away.

But whatever the weather Amy was still at Stag Lane at weekends, especially at midday on Sundays when 'the crowd' foregathered. At the turn of the year the London Aeroplane Club took over new quarters, with simple restaurant facilities instead of a kettle-on-a-gas-ring and cups of tea; there was also a more comfortable club room and a better bar. A thriving bar was, of course, one of the essentials of a successful flying club, whether subsidised or not. Even when the London Aeroplane Club earned the maximum Government grant of £2,000 per year, the bar profits were very necessary to its financial health. And in the late 1920s when the club's total membership was about five hundred, almost half of these were associate members – or 'social members' as those who were not pilots were usually called.

Amy had once been a mere 'social member' herself. Learning to fly gave her a new status in the club where (as she once put it) 'everyone knew everyone else and no introductions were given or needed.' Now, to her delight, she could lose herself in the easy, cosy atmosphere of flying lore and flying jargon and slang; her shyness vanished as she mixed with 'the crowd' while they swopped stories over their beers and pink gins in the cigarette haze. Amy herself did not smoke much, nor did she drink much at this time. Several of her friends, looking back to Stag Lane, remember that she seemed to prefer coffee to beer or spirits, though she genuinely enjoyed good wine, and intrigued her new acquaintances

[1] This included the cost of full membership of the club.

by showing that she knew something about vintages. The gaiety of 'the crowd' much attracted Amy. 'The people at the club are awfully jolly and I get on well with them and know lots,' she wrote to her mother early in 1929. 'Sir Sefton Brancker, Director of Civil Aviation, was down yesterday. It is great sport out there, and I should like to take you some time when you're in London as I'm quite sure you'd be interested if you could be on the spot.'

The above remarks show clearly, and perhaps surprisingly, that the attitude of Amy's mother towards her flying was not a disapproving one. Indeed the letters Amy wrote to her at this time abound in evidence of mutual trust and understanding. Relations between mother and daughter obviously became easier once Franz was married.

III

At Christmas Amy had gone home to Hull, but as soon as the London Aerodrome Club reported after the holiday she was back there, and in the second week of January 1929 she started flying lessons again, now always with Baker. During the first two months of the year however she was able to go up only five times, for again the weather was atrocious; in February the frost and snow were the worst for years. But before the cold spell, on 10 February, when Amy's total flying was up to six hours, Baker was starting her on landings.

It has been said that the whole art of flying is to come down to land again. Even the most optimistic instructor has to admit that landings are difficult, and every aspiring pilot has to practise them again and again. All the other basic techniques that the instructor demonstrates and the pupil copies – the take-off, the glide, the side-slip, taxying, even the recovery from a spin – all of these are child's play compared to the making of a three-point landing – in pilot's slang a 'daisy-bender'. The aim is to bring the machine stalled on to the ground with wheels and tail skid touching down simultaneously, and this involves both accurate judgment of speed, height, and distance, and the making of exactly the right movements at exactly the right time. In every case the circumstances are slightly different; this is why landing is not a drill that can be learnt by heart. It is always a challenge to the pilot, however practised he may be.

In March 1929, when the weather relented, Baker made Amy concentrate on landings in lesson after lesson. Round and round the aerodrome they went, coming down every few minutes. If she misjudged her approach and landing Baker opened up the throttle and they roared round the aerodeome for another try. One of Baker's Heston pupils, Filson Young, has described (in his book *Growing Wings*) his feelings at this same stage of 'circuits and bumps'. 'I could see what to do on landing but could not know how to find the "when" of it in relation to the "how". I must not look over the side or guess how near I was to the ground. I must keep her nose pointing to the far fence of the aerodrome and then, at some vital moment, most difficult to me to estimate . . . begin easing the stick back by tiny movements, with a pause between each, saying: 'I won't let her land – I won't let her land – I won't – I won't – I won't – I won't – I won't – I won't – ". Bump. We are there. But I must see that the nose doesn't get up again, for the disgrace of landing is bumping. The tail must touch the ground at the same time as the wheels. Oh, dear me, shall I ever be able to do it?'

Some pupils are scared at the prospect of going solo for the first time, and cling to the dual stage, but Amy was pining to reach her first solo, not only for the satisfaction of proving herself but because after it flying would cost her less. But when she seemed to be on the very brink weather again intervened. One Sunday in April Baker told her that she could go solo that day if she did two good landings with him. The landings satisfied him but in the meantime a fog developed and he told her she must wait. Amy's disappointment was especially bitter because Baker was just leaving for his new post at Heston, so at this crucial stage she found herself back with Matthews, and he decided she was not yet ready to fly alone. After four more periods of dual including one devoted to spins and stalls Matthews said she could go solo the next time she came to the aerodrome, but in the meantime he was taken ill and was away for several weeks.

Baker's successor as chief flying instructor had by this time arrived at Stag Lane. Major H.G. Travers, previously chief instructor at the Cinque Ports Flying Club at Lympne, was a cautious man – some called him 'a nice old boy', others 'an old woman' – who tried to protect his pupils from making mistakes or taking risks. 'I couldn't get used to his ways,' Amy later wrote. 'I seemed further than ever from going solo, and from seven hours when I had been ready . . . my dual time had crept up to thirteen.' When Matthews reappeared she was almost glad, and after two more periods with him he sent her off alone. She made her first solo flight of five minutes on 9 June 1929. That evening she wrote to her mother: 'I don't know whether you will be interested to know, but I am very excited tonight as I had just successfully accomplished a first solo at the Aerodrome. Now I should very quickly get through and obtain my "A" Licence[1] and then I am qualified to take you both for rides – if an aeroplane were available!'

Experts differ as to how many hours of dual should be necessary from first flying lesson to first solo. Some pupils have been known to go solo after three hours, others have been known to take thirty or even more. Cautious official estimates give ten to twelve hours as an average. Frank Swoffer, an experienced flying instructor, in his book *Learning to Fly*, published in 1929, said he had found that 'those pupils who are likely to become pilots go solo after about eight hours dual instruction . . . If a pupil is not solo after about

---

[1] The Private Pilot's Licence, as distinct from the 'B' necessary for professional flying.

sixteen hours dual, he had better give up trying, for he becomes very trying to his instructor.' Amy's log book shows that when she made her first solo she had spent fifteen hours and forty-five minutes in the air: eight hours with Baker, four and three-quarters with Matthews and three with Travers.

The delays in Amy's progress have sometimes been blamed upon her difficulty in finding money for the lessons. According to her own account, however, this problem only became acute in the spring of 1929, when with the better weather she wanted to fly more often. Looking back over the whole of her training, she wrote that she would never advise anyone to learn to fly in winter because delays between lessons tend to set one back. But in her own case she never regretted it because she thus acquired early experience of bad-weather flying conditions, Baker had pity on her disappointed eagerness, and took her up in misty rain, high wind, or cloud. 'What I ought to have done, no doubt,' she reflected, 'was to have saved up my money during the winter and learnt to fly in the spring, but my patience had been exhausted by my long wait through the previous summer, and so long as I was in the air I didn't care whether it was fine or not.' One may also add that if she had waited until the fine weather she would not have had the benefit of Baker's help with her landings.

For Amy landings were always difficult, not only when she was a pupil at Stag Lane. Fellow pilots who had occasion, later in her career, to watch her coming in have commented with a friendly laugh that Amy Johnson was an 'arriver' not a 'lander'. The truth is that she was not gifted with the natural coordination and sensitivity of touch that distinguished the born pilot – a pilot such as Baker, for example – whose flying is a harmony of movement. Her determination, her pride, her tenacity, her thoroughness were the qualities that led to her achievements, not any excellence of flying skill. It is all the more remarkable that she achieved what she did.

13

BEFRIENDED

March–September 1929

What keeps an aeroplane in the air? Why does the engine sometimes falter? How do the compass and instruments work? Such questions arise in the minds of most flying pupils, but not all follow them up with as much initiative and persistence as Amy did, when in the spring of 1929 the technical aspects of aviation first drew her interest. If she had been taking her training at the expensive de Havilland School of Flying she could easily have slaked her thirst for knowledge; there lectures on aerodynamics, mechanics and so on were thrown in free between flying lessons. The London Aeroplane Club could afford no such trimmings, and she had to fall back on her own resources.

When she tried putting 'sensible and intelligent questions' to the hard-pressed flying instructors they tended to fob her off. So she edged her way into the club hangar and seized any chance that offered to put her problems to one of the ground engineers, the licensed mechanics whose job it was to prepare the club aircraft for flight in accordance with the Air Ministry's safety regulations. It was not usual for a lady member to insinuate herself into the rough, cheerfully blasphemous world of 'the shops', and we can appreciate the flavour of the situation from the following account of a typical scene at the end of day's flying, written in retrospect by Amy herself. 'A plane had made a heavy landing and was brought round to the hangar for an inspection . . . I never dared walk up openly to the crowd of mechanics who for their part were sincerely hoping nothing would be found damaged, but wormed by way gradually into the group hoping I wouldn't be noticed. This particular time I remained there unmolested for several minutes whilst the engineers feverishly examined the machine, and the pilot impatiently waited for their inspection to be finished. I caught scraps of conversation – a glance at me, then "Dear, dear, this bolt is bent." Another glance at me, then "Oh bother, that means a hard day's work tomorrow." Another glance and one of the engineers whispered a word in the pilot's ear. The latter came over to me, touched my arm and said that supper was ready in the clubhouse, whither he proceeded firmly to escort me. This sort of thing often happened, and I used to wonder whether there was some part of the machine I shouldn't see. Of course, now I know that engineers don't like having to use strange words like "bother" and "dear, dear".'

Although at first Amy probably made herself something of a nuisance, her irrepressible enthusiasm and spirit won over the chief ground engineer, 'Jack' Humphreys, a good-natured and tolerant man, and he did not take steps to banish her. On the contrary he liked her for her cheek, and Amy and he soon became friends. Charles George Hubert Stuart Humphreys, to give him all his Christian names (which he never used) was only two years older than Amy, and at twenty-eight was quite young to be a chief 'GE'. A married man and a dedicated Freemason he had been in aircraft engineering for about eleven years when Amy met him.[1] He lived for

[1] As a boy of sixteen he had enlisted in the Royal Flying Corps as a fitter-mechanic, and in the summer of 1918 served on the Russian front with the RAF. In 1924 he joined the aircraft industry and worked first for Shorts at Rochester and then for de Havillands. His job with the London Aeroplane Club began in 1927.

his work and was usually to be found in the hangars in the shabbiest of oily overalls, doing routine maintenance on an aero-engine or signing one of the 'DIs' (Daily Inspection Certificates) without which no pilot might take off in a club machine. His tall brow – the most characteristic feature of his looks – was usually hidden by a flop of thick dark hair, or by a cloth cap crammed on top of it, so that one noticed first the grin and the military moustache and the friendly glance. His blue eyes were sometimes thoughtful, never cold or hard, though they more often had a cheery twinkle.

If Amy had ever had a brother he might have played the part in her life which Humphreys was soon to play. Indeed it may well have been her lack of any brother-and-sister relationship (not only the mistrust of admirers which accompanied her rebound from Franz) that drew her to find help and support in his camaraderie. After the years of rows and tiffs and misunderstandings with Franz, the company of Jack Humphreys, with his direct manner and docile unruffled temperament, his jolliness and good humour and warm heart, must have acted upon Amy like healing ointment.

Her acquaintance with Humphreys started up while she was still having flying instruction from Baker. The two men, as the club's chief flying instructor and chief engineer, were constantly in touch, and it was in the company of both of them (so Humphreys recalls) that the seed of an idea of flying to Australia was first sown in Amy's mind. This must have been even before she had made her first solo, since Baker left Stag Lane before it took place.

One day in the club hangar, when the trio were chatting and chaffing in their usual bantering manner, the talk turned towards the subject of women in aviation, and Amy lamented to Baker that anti-feminist prejudice seemed an almost insuperable obstacle for a woman who wanted to become a professional flyer. Baker said that to be accepted a woman would have to find a way of 'winning her spurs'. 'How?' asked Amy.

With a laugh Baker replied 'Oh, by flying to Australia for instance.' He could have made his point as well if he had said 'by flying round the world,' and there is little doubt that the remark was a casual one. But Amy, like all Baker's pupils, knew that his flippancies were often worth pondering. And certainly pioneer flights between England and Australia were in the news; Bert Hinkler's of the previous year was still being talked about. It had attracted special attention because he was the first pilot to accomplish the 11,000 mile flight alone in a light aeroplane. No woman had so far attempted such a feat.

II

At Eastertime 1929, just before Baker's departure for Heston, Amy decided that to save money for more flying lessons she must economise on her living expenses, and this led to the major decision that she must part company from Winifred and move to lodgings that were cheaper and nearer to the aerodrome. The friendship between the girls was still as close as ever; their confidences were so prolific that on evenings when they were both at home they had to resort to turning out the gas-fire to force themselves to bed. Furthermore their landlady Mrs Riddle was friendly and kind, and Amy enjoyed the tennis. So it was a wrench to leave, and the fact that Amy did so shows the extent to which her flying was already taking precedence over all else. But the break came about more easily because Winifred too, by this time, was tending in a new direction. She had just won a scholarship to train for a Social Science Certificate at the London School of Economics, and this would mean living at the Women's University Settlement in Southwark. So a parting was ahead in any case.

Amy searched for lodgings and found an opportunity that appealed to her: a young couple called Perceval, living between Golders Green and Hendon, offered free board and lodging to a young lady who would occasionally keep an eye on their two small children. At the end of March she left Castellain Road while Winifred, for the time being, stayed on. She liked her new home but out of her vast experience of lodgings she was mildly critical. 'My new digs are really funny,' she told her mother. 'They are only young people . . . and they have never had anyone staying there before and don't seem to realise their responsibilities at all; they're all going to Ireland next week for their holiday and have intimated to me that they want to close up the house . . . Winifred says I can easily go back there for a time, but it is inconvenient because my car is garaged at Golders Green.' It may seem startling that at a moment when Amy was cutting down expenses she should have become the owner of a car. But this was, by an irony of chance, a direct result fo her move to 'economical' lodgings.

The desire to possess a car had been growing since she joined the London Aeroplane Club, for most of the members drove to the aerodrome while Amy arrived on foot, after a bus-ride and a walk of nearly half a mile. Then one day in mid-April, when she had been with the Percevals only a few weeks, she learned that they had decided to get a larger car and wanted to sell their maroon two-seater, a 1926 Morris Oxford. She wrote straight off to her father asking for a loan, and after some hurried correspondence Will Johnson sent her a cheque for seventy pounds (to be repaid by Amy in small weekly instalments). About a fortnight later she wrote to him in high spirits: 'The car is running very well indeed . . . It uses rather a lot of petrol at present but I'm going to fit an air-trap[1] to make it more economical. I want to do this myself. I already understand quite a lot about the engine and can tune up a magneto and carburettor and clean jets and plugs, etc. Shall soon be an experienced mechanic!' These last remarks reflect the influence of Jack Humphreys for already he was imparting to her some of his professional knowledge. And it was after he taught her how to care for the engine of her Morris Oxford that she became fired the with ambition to learn

---

[1] Air filters were a novelty in the late 1920s.

more about aero-engines. Soon this was to lead her on to the idea of qualifying as an engineer as well as a pilot.

III

At what stage did Amy's parents become aware that their daughter's new hobby was liable to develop into something more serious for her? Probably in the early summer of 1929 – just before Amy's twenty-sixth birthday – when they returned from a tour of several Mediterranean countries (they began and ended their trip by air-liner between London and Paris). For it was then that Amy wrote to them, 'It is just possible I shall leave Crockers in the autumn.' This is the first hint in her letters that she had thoughts of making aviation a career. She also told them that she was shortly going to have a quiet summer holiday, but refrained from mentioning that it was to be spent at Stag Lane.

The idea had come to her that instead of going away she would fly as much as possible and between-whiles devote herself to an 'engineering course' – an unofficial apprenticeship in the club hangars. Major Travers, who by now had succeeded Baker, said he had no objection to the plan if she could 'get round' the chief engineer. As Amy and Humphreys were by now good friends this condition did not present any difficulty, although Humphreys' chief assistant, Eric Mitchell, at first jibbed at the prospect of a woman 'on the floor'.

When it came to the moment of her first plunge into the masculine world of the ground engineers, no longer as a lady member of the London Aeroplane Club but as one of themselves, she received treatment that might have frightened her off if she had been any less enamoured of aviation. The first hours of the day's work were the busiest for Humphreys and his team of three engineers and three apprentices, since at 10 o'clock the instructors arrived, and some of the aircraft had to be ready for them to test before any club flying could begin. When Amy turned up on her first Monday morning she was ignored. 'At last I asked outright for a job of work,' she later wrote. "You can sweep the hangar," I was laconically informed. "All right, where's the brush?" "Look for it." I started work full of vim and made such an upheaval of dust that everyone coughed and choked and had to clear out of the shed. "Hi chuck it, you —— fool. Jim, show this angel from heaven how to sweep the floor." I stood by and watched Jim fetch a bucket of water and spray the concrete floor before beginning to sweep.' Nevertheless by the end of her fortnight she had been accepted. She had survived the long hours of standing on concrete, the aches in her arms from scraping carbon off pistons and cylinders, the blisters and bruises and cuts, the humiliations and curses. And in spite of it all, so she wrote later, 'I had never been so happy in my life.'

The joy of her 'apprenticeship' was complemented by the encouraging progress of her flying; during her holiday she went up more and more often alone, and also took the tests for her 'A' Licence. Her total flying time was just over nineteen hours (only about three hours of this was since she first flew solo) when she took the Altitude Test and the 'Figure of Eights' Test. In the first she had to show that she knew how to lose height and make a good approach, and in the second that she could make steep turns with a fair degree of accuracy, but in both tests the landings were of crucial importance. Her performance must presumably have satisfied the Royal Aero Club's observer, and her oral replies to the questions (on the rules and regulations of the air) must have been 80% correct, for on 6 July an 'A' Licence (number 1979) was issued to her by the Air Ministry, and she was thereby authorised to pilot 'all types of flying machine.'

A week later came the exciting moment of her first cross-country solo, but it proved a nerve-racking occasion; she got lost and had to make a forced landing at Stony Stratford. After this her log book shows that she practised compass courses repeatedly, and Jack Humphreys is of opinion that the Stony Stratford incident was a very good thing, for it fightened her and made her take her navigation seriously.[1]

After her holiday, when Amy went back to work at Crockers she knew it would not be for long. Her mind was made up: a career in aviation was to be the aim of her life. In this decision a compelling factor was Jack Humphreys' faith in her; he had even gone so far as to offer – quite casually, as was his way – to give her all the help he could to qualify as a ground engineer, while she accumulated the hundred hours' flying she would need for her Pilot's 'B' Licence.[2] The programme that Humphreys envisaged would take all Amy's time and energy for months or even yers and would cost a lot of money. But 'Where there's a Will there's a Way': Amy, like her mother, often found consolation and support in threadbare proverbs. And it seems that she knew her mother was in sympathy with her unusual ambitions, for in mid-July she wrote to her, 'I had most of the day off as I could do no work [she had hurt her thumb] and went to the Aero Show at Olympia. It is awfully good. I was intensely interested. I am going again on Monday. I go with the Engineer from the Club who explains everything to me. Shall you be proud of me when I'm the second lady ground engineer in the world. Lady Heath is the first and only one at present![3] Oh for plenty of money and then I'd do wonders.'

[1] In Amy's time, however, the 'navigation' used by most pilots of light aeroplanes was of a very sketchy kind. When flying cross country one usually, in theory, followed a compass course, but in practice one relied mainly on landmarks (and as a last resort on the names of railway stations).
[2] Only during the previous three years had one or two British women obtained 'B' Licences, which permitted them to fly 'for hire or reward', subject to more frequent medical checks than male pilots. An aggressive campaign by Lady Heath had helped to bring about the rescinding of the post-war ban – an international and absolute ban – on women as professional pilots.
[3] She had obtained her licence in the United States.

London in July 1929 endured one of the heat waves for which it is never prepared: 'the city is a terrible place in heat like this,' Amy complained to her mother. But the ardour of her enthusiasm for flying did not wilt. As soon as she could escape from the stifling office she was off to Stag Lane, and before dusk, in the cool of the evening, was often up for a short solo. These mid-week flips were in addition to her weekend flying, an added expense but increasingly a delight. 'It was only after I had my "A" Licence and flew solo that I really grew to love flying for its own sake,' she later wrote.

Through those parching weeks it was not only after work and at weekends that Amy made her way to the aerodrome. She took to rising at about five o'clock so as to be able to spend an hour or two working in the hangar with the engineers before going on to Bucklersbury, where she was due at 9.30. Sometimes, unable to tear herself away promptly enough, she had to slink into the office after ten – once even as late as eleven. And there was no disguising the reason for these lapses. Each day, as she typed and took shorthand and brought papers to Vernon Wood, it was obvious that her beautifully shaped hands, formerly well manicured, were becoming more and more like a mechanic's. And after the occasion when she damaged her right thumb (so badly that she lost the nail) she could not work properly for several days.

Amy had now been at Crockers for a little more than two years. The pleasure she had once derived from the work had ebbed away and she was now frankly a clock-watcher, while her admiring deference for Wood had given way to intolerance. 'I am getting on somewhat better with Mr Wood these last few days – I have hardly seen anything of him!' she told her mother at about this time. 'I have heaps of work to do which he has left me fairly free to get on with. I wish it was always like this!' In another letter she observed that 'Mr Wood is really changing very much.' From Wood's point of view it was Amy who was changing very much; she was no longer the dedicated secretary he needed. Nevertheless an interest in the firm's activities and in the business world was by now an integral part of Amy's outlook, as shown by the following remarks in a letter to her father. 'We are very busy at the office over this new Company we are forming for "talkies". I think it will be quite a good thing and if I had any money to invest I should most certainly take some shares . . . When you see the Prospectus issued for First International Sound Pictures Ltd why not take a few shares for a spec?'

It was probably before the end of July that Wood had a candid talk with her on the subject of her divided interests. He put it to her that if she continued as at present she would do justice neither to her work nor to her hobby: she must choose between the two. The ultimatum led her to the brink she had long been viewing from afar. The only obstacle that now deterred her from leaving Crocker's was lack of funds to finance the training she would need to become a professional pilot. Clearly she must tackle her father and somehow win his support. She resolved to write to him presenting her case, and planned to follow up her letter with a weekend trip home for discussions.

V

In the meantime however, before the end of the month, and just after the heat-wave had broken in a thunderstorm of exceptional violence, she received news from Hull – bad news – that sent her rushing north in shocked distress. Her sister Irene had committed suicide. She had put her head in a gas oven while her husband Teddy Pocock was away for the day. It was an utterly unexpected bombshell. Amy had not seen very much of Irene since she herself left Hull, but her sister had quite often made jaunts to London, and had sometimes persuaded Amy to make up a party with her for an evening out. And to Amy, as to everyone, Irene's married life had seemed 'perfectly happy'.

Irene, and Teddy too, had liked to live in a whirl of activity – there had never been any question of her settling down to a quiet domestic round as wife and mother. Often in the evenings they had earned good fees with their cabaret turns together (Teddy at the piano, Irene playing the part of a soubrette with song and dance). Besides this she had worked in the daytime for the *Hull Evening News* as private secretary to the editor, Mark Goulden. Here too she had seemed both successful and happy; a journalistic atmosphere suited her and in the office she was admired as a 'glamour girl' and also valued as a keen worker.

At the inquest Will Johnson voiced the feelings shared by everyone: 'It has come as a thunderbolt. We felt that she was happy in every way.' It seemed that the only clue was the period of mental difficulties she suffered about five and a half years earlier, when she gave up training as a teacher; then she had talked of trying to drown herself. 'We were a little afraid on that occasion,' her father said. The Coroner's verdict was 'Suicide whilst of unsound mind.'

It appears that in a note which Irene left for her husband she asked that no mourning black should be worn for her. In their sorrow the Johnsons did not concur with this wish. 'In spite of what Irene said,' wrote Amy to her mother when she was back in London, 'one can't go about in coloured clothes so soon afterwards because people on the whole attach such great importance to customs of that kind, and besides I couldn't myself feel comfortable at the moment in anything bright, although I suppose I shall soon feel better about it.' Winifred remembers her looking drawn, almost shrunken, in the little black frock her mother had given her for the funeral.

Yet at first the grief and strain, far from prostrating Amy, brought out qualities in her that helped to steady the rest of the family; exhaustion and neuralgia-headaches did not afflict her until a few weeks later. In that same letter to her mother, written the day after her return from Hull, she said, 'At the moment I can't imagine ever feeling cheerful and jolly again, but I know I shall be, so am not worrying. It's just a matter of hanging on until things get brighter and I think one can always rely on that, don't you? . . . Please, Muth, rest as much as possible and don't do any more work than is necessary. I'm sure no one will mind living on bought bread for example, for a short time, to save you a little work . . . I wouldn't like any telegrams saying anyone has collapsed!! . . . I'll write you often.'

Later, on the eve of Irene's birthday, she returned to the subject of her sister's death in another letter of tender sympathy to her mother, which provides some interesting glimpses of her optimistic and 'commonsense' views. 'It is the folk left behind who have the hard part to bear, and you, of course, are bound to suffer more than any of us,' she wrote. 'I wish Daddy or I could be with you tomorrow . . . I try to think of Irene as simply living in some place rather a long way off but where she is happier than she ever was before . . . Please, Muth dear, try to think that although it doesn't seem so to us, yet probably everything has been for the best and that she may thus have been saved from many illnesses and troubles. Nobody seems to get through life without illness and troubles and Irene, at any rate, is now through with them all.

'Her birthday will, of course, mean more to you than to the rest of us, but please don't think too much about it because that won't help at all and will only make you miserable, and if you're miserable, what about poor Moll and Bee! You've still got three girls left and I think this trouble has bound us all still more closely together . . . The great tragedy about Irene is that, to us, it seemed so unnecessary – and yet to her it was evidently the only way out.'

VI

Amy's philosophising may well have helped, in some small measure, to console her mother. But it is hardly surprising that her father, stunned by the death of his second daughter, should have felt disinclined to encourage his eldest in her passion for such a dangerous pursuit as flying. No one could deny it was a risky business, even for the most experienced. Only a couple of days after the tragedy at Hull two aircraft from Stag Lane collided in mid-air near the aerodrome and three men were killed (one of them was Captain A.S. White, chief instructor at the de Havilland School of Flying).

The letter Amy wrote to her father, pleading for financial help so that she could leave Crockers at once, had probably been posted to him before the weekend of Irene's death. And it seems that before Amy came south again she must have discussed her situation with him to some extent, and without any success in winning his support. For when she returned to the office on the Wednesday after Bank Holiday she was miserably resigned to staying on there. That evening she wrote to her mother, 'I can't say I'm delighted to be back at the office . . . The whole of this year I'd been sort of expecting to leave this autumn, but as it is much the best thing to keep on I suppose I must make the best of it.'

Nevertheless only a month after Irene's suicide Will Johnson had reversed his decision, had given his approval to Amy's wish to become a professional pilot, and had made it possible for her to leave Crockers immediately by promising to give her a small weekly allowance for the next six months as well as a sum (probably £100) to cover the expenses of her aeronautical training. This change of heart must be attributed to the intervention of Jack Humphreys, who now met her father for the first time. Will Johnson was on a visit to London and Humphreys remembers that they had a long talk at Stag Lane and also lunched together to discuss Amy's future. Doubtless the fact that Will Johnson had just become a Freemason was a bond between the two men, and they were later to become close friends.

Humphreys had not heard from Amy herself about Vernon Wood's ultimatum, but her father talked openly of it; then he went on to confide his very natural anxieties lest Amy, who in some ways had similar tendencies to Irene (there were her occasional 'black moods' and there had been the nervous breakdown that ended her first job) should some time be tempted by the opportunities of flying to throw away her life.

But, as so often, the viewpoint of someone who is outside the family, yet at the same time sincerely interested, can put such anxieties into a new, less disturbing perspective. The confidence in Amy's prospects of a man who looked you as straight in the eye as Humphreys did, a man whose interest in Amy was respectful as well as admiring, did not fail to have its effect. Humphreys tried to convince Amy's father that she would not be happy – indeed that she would suffer from lasting frustration – if she were not helped to go ahead towards earning her living in the flying world. And by this time he had seen enough of her abilities to feel justified in ancitpating success for her. He says that when he took Will Johnson to King's Cross for his train, the older man thanked him warmly and assured him that he would give further serious thought to Amy's future; he now realised that flying was 'what she really wanted'.

On 2 September 1929 Amy wrote to her mother in jubilant mood, 'You'll have heard the great news already from Daddy!! I'm leaving the office on Friday. I can't say how glad I am. Everyone is most intrigued and they want me to come and see them often and report progress. Everyone seems to think I'm going to do wonderful things so I mustn't disappoint them. Also I mustn't let Daddy down because he's being most awfully good to me over this affair, and of course without his help I couldn't have done it. Really, though, Muth, I couldn't stick this much longer. It gets on my nerves too much. I should have left long before except that the salary was so good and helped me to achieve my ambitions in aeronautics. I couldn't have done the flying I've done if I hadn't had so good a salary. I must have spent about £80 or £100 already all of which I've earned myself. I want to economise as much as possible,' she went on, 'and I shall therefore keep the car at the aerodrome and use it for running about (a trip to Hull sometimes, perhaps!!) and shall get digs within walking distance of the aerodrome. That will be much more convenient and it is a nice district and I'd much rather be living there than nearer in town . . . I'm more relieved than I can say that I'm leaving the city for good and shall be living an open-air life on work that I love. I can never thank Daddy enough for making it possible . . . I shall be as happy as a lark once this week is over.'

14

WITH THE BOYS

September–December 1929

Hatless and without a coat – it was a warm September – Amy was one of a party of eight, six men and two girls, who watched the Schneider Trophy contest from an elegant speedboat belonging to some of her flying friends. 'It's goregous cutting through the water at such a speed,' she wrote home afterwards. 'The sunshine through the spray makes a perfect rainbow all the time. We had two big hampers packed by the Regent Palace for lunch and we had a splendid position in the Solent to see the race. It was most awfully exciting.' During the intervals between glimpses of the seaplane racers there was much clicking of cameras on board the speedboat, and fortunately quite a few of the snapshots have been preserved. So we can see how Amy looked at the time, in fact on the very day, when she left office work behind her and was at last able to look ahead to a future devoted entirely to aviation. Her health was currently in a bad state (throughout the summer she had been complaining to her mother of excessive fatigue and 'nerves') and doubtless Irene's death also contributed to her subdued demeanour, but in spite of all this her enjoyment of the occasion shows clearly in her smiles.

At this time Amy looked much more fair-haired than usual. She had been experimenting, so Winifred remembers, with a hair bleach which proved to be unexpectedly potent, and some of the Stag Lane members recall that the transformation gave rise to cracks about 'the Platinum Blonde'. It was an epithet that did not apply for long, since the colour of Amy's hair gradually evened out, but around this time more and more of her friends at the aerodrome were using another nickname which stuck to her for years; 'Johnnie' or sometimes merely 'John', was what Humphreys and his mates had taken to calling her when she was at work with them. It had been an obvious form of address for the anomalous female addition to their team, and Amy must have welcomed it as an escape from the girlish Christian name which she had once told Franz she loathed. As a member of the London Aeroplane Club – to the chief flying instructor Major Travers, for example – she was still Miss Johnson, but among the ground engineers and the apprentices she was now always 'Johnnie'. She was also 'Johnnie' at the lodgings she had found within walking distance of Stag Lane. There, in the evenings, she now intensified her 'swotting' for the engineering examination that was her immediate objective; if she could pass it she would acquire the first of the ground engineer's licences that Humphreys had advised her to try for (the 'C' Licence,which would qualify her to inspect aero-engines of a specified type before flight). In the context of her future the significance of her engineering can hardly be over-stressed. The technical knowledge and experience she acquired in 1929 probably contributed more to her later successes than did her ability as a pilot.

II

In September 1929 Amy was not yet thinking in terms of a long-distance flight: her aim was to become a professional pilot. And if she were going to earn her living by flying she would have to be an all-rounder; in aviation matters her bible at this time was a book entitled *The Complete Airman*. Its scope is shown by the following dictum, made by the author G.C. Bailey in his introduction: 'The ideal airman must necessarily be somewhat versatile. He must have in him something of the sailor, the engineer, and the scientist, added to which he must possess more than an average share of common sense.' Bailey might have added that he must also possess an encyclopedic variety of knowledge; thirty-one subjects are covered in his book, ranging from Aerial Manoeuvres and Aerodromes to Mechanics and the Theory of Flight, from Ignition Systems to the Physiological effects of Altitude.

Among the papers Amy kept from this period of her life there is a bunch of hand-written notes containing chunks of *The Complete Airman*, transcribed with her usual meticulousness and interspersed here and there with neat diagrams. These notes make it clear that she did not shy away from the mathematics that now confronted her – a remarkable fact because although she had once told Vernon Wood she liked figures, mathematics had not been one of her university subjects, nor even one of her 'distinction' subjects in School Certificate. Evidently her single-minded enthusiasm combined with Humphreys' help and encouragement carried her over this hurdle; he can remember that when he showed her how to use a slide-rule she acquired the knack with unusual facility, and from her quick grasp of the formulae of aerodynamics and kindred subjects he assumed that she must be well at home with equations. Later on, when she sprang to fame, he was quoted as saying: 'When that girl first came to Stag Lane I knew I had got a born engineer to deal with.' But Humphreys was not thinking primarily of Amy as a student when he said this; rather he had in mind her skill at the manual work of an engineer, the work that can often be cruel drudgery but which in time can become the art that has been called 'thinking with the hands.' 'She didn't know what it was to wear filthy overalls and get nails broken in an engine, but I taught her,' Humphreys told his interviewer. 'She never complained; she broke her nails with the rest of us . . . for months she did nothing but pull down engines, decarbonise, build them up

again, and take them out to test. Then she learnt the
carburettor, how to fit new jets, how to strip and
rebuild a magneto, and do all running repairs . . . she
learnt how to do everything for herself.'

For her forthcoming examination she had to
concentrate upon the Cirrus (Marks II and III), the
Hermes, and the de Havilland Gipsy. And the following
'Maintenance Schedule', which she apparently
transcribed from one of the relevant technical manuals
is given here to convey the kind of knowledge she had
to assimilate, and the kind of routine she had to carry
out again and again.

DAILY SCHEDULE

For aeroplanes flying five hours or more per day the
following Daily schedule should be carried out before
flight:

1. Wash engine down with paraffin (or petrol).
2. Check tapper clearance [she then noted the correct
   clearance for each type].
3. Charge rocker fulcrum pins with grease.
4. Grease valve stems and push rods with Graphite
   grease.
5. Test valve springs by hand for strength.
6. Turn engine by hand for compression.
7. Check contact breaker gaps – .012 in, and clean
   points with piece of emery cloth if dirty.
8. Clean distributor segments with cloth soaked in
   paraffin.
9. Check plug points – .015 in.
10. Clean petrol filter.
11. Test airscrew bolts for tightness on hub, and hub
    for tightness on shaft. (In hot weather propeller
    shrinks and bolts frequently need tighening).
12. Check all engine holding-down bolts for tightness
    and engine mounting screws.
13. Check all nuts, screws, pins, pipe joints and pipes
    for leaks.

14. Clean oil filter.
15. Check all wiring and switches.
16. Examine airscrew for truth, pitting at tips, torn fabric and cracks.

Such was the sort of work Amy meant when she wrote to her mother, during the first week of her full-time aeronautical career, 'Before the exam . . . I should put in as much practical work as possible,' and she went on to give details of her new working life. 'I must conform to all the rules of the staff and the discipline is fairly stiff. Hours are 8 a.m. to dusk including Saturdays and Sundays, with Monday holiday. I am starting on the proper routine tomorrow and have my own engine I am absolutely responsible for . . . I shall be awfully upset if I fail this exam, and all the engineers say I shall let them down if I fail it.' Then comes the following most interesting remark: 'Also I have just heard three other girls are taking it and I wanted to be the first woman ground engineer – have heard that Lady Heath has let her tickets lapse so isn't one now.' There is no further mention of the three other girls in Amy's letters, so one may guess that they did not prove serious rivals. Nor was Lady Heath any longer a potential one; only a couple of weeks before Amy wrote the above, the aircraft in which she was racing at Cleveland, Ohio had crashed and she had suffered injuries so severe that she was not expected to recover.[1]

But as far as Amy herself is concerned the chief interest of her remark 'I wanted to be the first woman ground engineer' is that it confirms the nature of her ambitions; all her efforts were set upon proving, to herself and to the world, that she could attain to unusual success in the unusual profession she had chosen. Years later, in various articles, she maintained that she had met violent anti-feminist prejudice, both

---

[1] She did survive for some years (she died in May 1939) but in a sadly incapacitated state.

at Stag Lane and in aviation in general, and had been fired to join the battle for equal rights. Although after she became a celebrity she was drawn into the thick of this battle there is no doubt that in 1929 her motives were personal ones. Nevertheless in another letter to her mother just a whiff of incipient feminism can be detected. In the context of her mother's keenness for playing the organ Amy wrote: 'I was interested in the Harvest Festival handbill and am proud to see your name as "Organist"! I like to do things out of the ordinary, don't you? And that is very much out of the ordinary for a woman.'

Amy's earlier training in the advertising business had no doubt impressed upon her the publicity value of the 'out of the ordinary', and Jack Humphreys shared her view that the more an aspiring 'lady engineer' could be 'advertised' the better it would help her career. Writing home again, in mid-September 1929, Amy reported: 'They [i.e. Jack Humphreys] seem very pleased with how I am getting on, and I appear to create quite a bit of sensation in my overalls and dirty face!! I have been told that four people today have asked who I am, one of whom was Major Beaumont, a director of Imperial Airways, and quite a "big" man! You wait a bit until I begin to get publicity.'

III

All Amy's letters home now glowed with optimism and exuberance, 'You mustn't worry now about my health,' she wrote, 'because hard work hurts no one, and I at last have the opportunity to get plenty of rest, good food and fresh air . . . I have just got home after a very hard day's work and although I am tired yet it's the healthy sort and not the depressed "headachy" kind I used to get.' Her new home in Roe Green, then an unspoilt village, for the moment seemed very delightful to her – as new lodgings often did for the first month or so. Not only was there a country walk to and from the aerodrome, but the room she had found was in a black and white timbered cottage with a thatched roof and pretty garden, and the landlady and her husband were congenial and kind. Mr Evans himself fixed up a fireplace in Amy's room so that she could make herself cosy in the evenings: 'I buy my own coal and have got 2 cwts to go on with at 2s 6d per cwt,' she told her mother. 'How does that go for price? . . . It will be heaps cheaper and nicer than gas or electricity.' Mr and Mrs Evans were also tactful: 'Johnnie' had explained to them that she had given up her well-paid job in a solicitor's office to become a professional pilot, and although Mr Evans later admitted that he and his wife had thought her 'a shade too ambitious' they did not at the time make any open criticisms.

There were others who regarded Amy's hopes, or rather the unorthodox behaviour arising from them, with much less tolerance. At the London Aeroplane Club she found herself for a while at loggerheads with the chief flying instructor, Major Travers. When an attempt was made, on the pretext that the club rules did not permit members to frequent the hangars, to put a stop to her engineering training, she attributed it to jealousy on Travers' part; according to one of her letters he himself would have liked to acquire a ground engineer's licence and Humphreys had declined to coach him. 'He's taken a dislike to me,' she complained, 'I detest the man and he is a rotten instructor. A row quickly blew up and early in October Humphreys and Mitchell (his number two, now an ally of Amy's) were summoned to the office of the Commander Perrin, Secretary of the Royal Aero Club. Humphreys recalls that they met Perrin's blustering reprimands with an ultimatum. If he did not like the way they were running the GE department at Stag Lane they would be glad to clear out. Humphreys went on to point out that Amy, who was so keen and so apt that she worked hard and well without any wages, was 'good labour on the cheap.'

After this her strange dual role of lady member and unofficial apprentice was accepted more or less

graciously by everyone at Stag Lane, and her aversion
to Travers subsided. Nevertheless she had learned a
useful lesson in flying-club politics. At the end of
October she wrote home, 'I am sitting in front of a huge
fire in the club house doing bits of studying and writing
letters and then doing some work in the hangars
(surreptitiously of course!!). Things are not too bad now
and the days slip by awfully quickly and happily.'

IV

There was still, however, the worry of her impending
examination: two months had now elapsed since she
applied to sit for it and she had received no word of its
date. 'The question of time is of first importance,' she
explained to her mother, 'both from the point of view of
finance and also because it's possible there may be a
splendid job for me about Christmas if I am through. It
is very much "in the air", but I want to push through
as quickly as possible to be ready in case of need. The
job would be that of demonstrator of an entirely new
machine which is being built now. All the people in the
concern are friends of mine and it will be ideal if it
comes off. However, one never knows with a new
machine. There is such keen competition to face from
the popular ones already on the market.'

This is Amy's first allusion to a project which was
destined to lead on directly to her Australia flight,
though her use of the word 'demonstrator' suggests
that at this stage she pictured herself as some sort of
test pilot. The 'entirely new machine' was the brain
child of a free-lance designer, a determined young
Irishman from County Down, whose supreme interest
in life was aeronautical design and invention. His
name, then, was Jimmy Martin; now he is Sir James
Martin, Managing Director and Chief Designer of the
Martin Baker Aircraft Company, world famous for the
ejection seats that have saved the lives of so many jet
pilots. In the summer of 1929, when he moved his
activities from a workshop in Acton to a war-time

hangar at Denham, and started a little business under the name of the Martin Aircraft Works, he had hardly any capital and only two employees, but inexhaustible reserves of faith in his own ideas and in his perfectionist standards of workmanship, as well as 'a passionate desire to make better aeroplanes than those existing.'

Jimmy Martin – a sturdy, bluff, thickset figure – was often about at Stag Lane (some months earlier he had been taught to fly by Baker) and he and Amy were already acquaintances before Humphreys produced his latest brainwave; if 'Johnnie' were given the chance to fly Martin's first prototype – it was to be a monoplane rival to the Moth, and it might be ready to fly in a few months – Martin would profit from the publicity attendant upon the doings of a 'lady pilot', and for 'Johnny' it would be a first job in aviation.

Once the scheme had been agreed upon Amy clung to it blindly. She had no experience of the vicissitudes that accompany the gradual advance of a prototype from drawing board to mock-up, from minor components to fuselage and tail unit and wings, from airframe to powered aeroplane. Always in the background of her thinking was the time limit of the 'subsidy' from her father, and through the winter months of 1929 many of her letters echo her sense of urgency. Time and again she turned up at the Martin Aircraft Works to see how Jimmy was progressing, usually having driven over from Stag Lane in Humphrey's Austin Seven. She had sold her own car, the Morris two-seater, at the end of the summer for £40, partly to raise additional funds for her flying (her father seems to have written off her debt for it) and partly because it so often broke down. The little Austin, so she said, 'is useful for running about once one gets used to the "unsafe" feeling. I like to have something solid under me.'

Amy's visits to the Denham workshop have remained lasting memories for Sir James Martin, and he also remembers a conversation he had with her on one occasion when he took her home to Roe Green. She asked him in for a few minutes and he noticed a picture of Swiss mountains in her room. When he remarked on it she told him about her disappointment in love, of the Swiss whom she had pined to marry. (He was not the first of her flying friends in whom she had thus confided; Jack Humphreys already knew that she was sorrowing for her Swiss, and he remembers noticing at about this time that despite her vivacity her face in repose wore a look of sadness.) Sir James recalls a vivid detail of Amy's story: she confessed to him that when the man she loved told her he had just been married to someone else – they were in the Strand when he broke the news – suicide was her immediate impulse, and she decided that the best way to accomplish it without upsetting her parents too much was to go ahead with learning to fly and then have a crash. But, so she assured Jimmy, she had come to like flying so much that the suicde idea had dropped away.

Early in November the word 'demonstrate', in connection with Martin's aeroplane, occurs for a second time in one of Amy's letters to her mother. 'Tomorrow I am going out to a place where a new type of aeroplane is being built!!' she wrote. 'It's all very secret but I am in the secret!! It's a machine I hope to demonstrate some day and if everything comes off as planned it's going to make my reputation!! And I'm going to make its!' Amy was learning something about the time it takes to build a prototype; the 'Christmas' of her previous letter had now become 'some day'.

Also early in November Amy learnt, only a few days beforehand, that the date of her engineering examination had been set. Much to her relief it was to be at Stag Lane not the Air Ministry. In 1929 the examinations for ground engineers' licences[1] were entirely viva voce; as Amy put it, 'there are five people on the board and they all fire "catchy" questions at

[1] Held by the AID (the Aeronautical Inspection Directorate of the Air Ministry).

you.' Yet after it she felt confident. 'It wasn't nearly so bad as I expected and they asked very easy questions – so "seemingly" easy in fact that I am wondering . . . if I have been caught over them.' But she had not been 'caught'; and a ground engineer's licence (no 1391) was issued to her on 10 December 1929.

Since then a legend has grown up to the effect that Amy was the world's first woman ground engineer.[1] It is true that she was the first woman to receive a GE licence from the Air Ministry, but Lady Heath had earlier trained as an 'air mechanic' in America, and had been licenced for this work by the US Department of Commerce. Nevertheless Amy did attain for a while to a unique status when she acquired her 'C'. Since Lady Heath had by then allowed her 'tickets' to lapse there was a period when Amy *was* the only woman in the world in possession of a Ground Engineer's Licence that was currently valid.

[1] Its origin can be traced to an oversimplification in a newspaper headline early in 1930.

15

THE AUSTRALIA IDEA

January–March 1930

'You who fly – Do you tell your friends of the joys you experience in the air, of the exhilaration of knowing yourself free and alone in the glorious freedom of the skies, of the wonders to be seen . . . Do you show them by your example as a fine, careful pilot, how safe it is to fly a machine so shining, clean and well-cared-for as your own? I hope you do – you will be helping to make Aviation History.' These words of Amy's, written so obviously from the heart, are from her first commissioned article, 'Joys of the Air for a Woman' (which appeared in the *Daily Chronicle* in January 1930). It shows not only her delight in flying for its own sake but also the intensity of her faith in her own will power. 'You who would like to fly, but – no money,' she went on. 'Flying is still pretty expensive because it is as yet a luxury for the minority instead of the pleasure of the majority. It is up to you to help bring flying within the means of all. Think Aviation, Talk Aviation, Read Aviation, and if you're only determined enough, your chance will come. I joined a Flying Club and had a half hour lesson per fortnight costing £1. I found I could save 10s per week out of my typist's salary . . . "The best things in life are free" – not always, unfortunately. But perseverance and enthusiasm are free, and will win for you all else you want.'

The invitation to write this article was one of the repercussions of a sudden whirlwind of publicity which burst upon her just after the New Year of 1930 – her first experience of being 'taken up' by the popular press. A reporter from the *Evening News* chanced to come to the London Aeroplane Club on 8 January to see an Indian pilot who was shortly to set off on a flight to his home country, and he happened to hear about the 'lady engineer' who was helping in the club hangar. On the spur of the moment he asked for an interview, and Amy hurried to consult Humphreys. 'I asked my "tutor" what I ought to tell him,' she wrote home afterwards, 'and he said "This is the chance of a lifetime to get some publicity which you can do with at the moment. Tell him what you've done *and* your plans." So off I went and the reporter asked me a few questions [such as] what I hoped to do with my certificate, to which I replied "Make a career in aviation"; if I wanted to do any "stunts", to which I said I hoped to make a long-distance flight. "In a Moth?" "No, in a new type of machine about which I cannot yet divulge particulars."'

No wonder the reporter made the most of his lucky find. Next day the *Evening News* gave a prominent place to his story under the following headlines:

GIRL TO FLY ALONE TO AUSTRALIA
THE FIRST WOMAN AIR ENGINEER AND HER PLANS
A SECRET PLANE

Amy was described as a 22-year-old blonde, the daughter of a wealthy Midlands family, 'a slim girl who despite her cumbersome clothing looked as if her place was in the ballet.' 'She has only a very small allowance,' her interviewer went on, 'but she makes a comfortable living by her skill with aircraft and engines.' Humphreys, when questioned about her, had spoken in superlatives of her skill as an engineer and pilot, and had given as his last word, 'If she says that she is going to break the record for flying to Australia, believe me she will do it.'

The date of this news story shows that Amy's plans to fly to Australia had come into being only very recently (during the weeks since she acquired her engineer's licence), for in November she had still been talking of 'demonstrating' the Martin prototype. Why did she decide, at the end of 1929, to stake her future upon a long-distance flight, with Australia as her objective? Sir James Martin has said that he can remember saying to her, 'Why don't you fly to Australia?' But in fact, once she had made up her mind to try to 'win her spurs' – as Baker had once put it – in other words to concentrate upon a newsworthy solo flight (it had to be newsworthy if she were to win the necessary backing) Australia became an obvious, an almost unavoidable choice. What alternatives were there? Africa? Women had already flown there solo. The Atlantic? Only a navigator of long experience could tackle it with any hope of success. In a sense Amy did not make any choice at all – there was virtually no other choice to make.

No one had yet improved upon Hinkler's record of 1928 though there had been several attempts to do so by men. No woman had even tried to rival it, but the time for such an attempt was ripe, indeed from the publicity viewpoint almost overripe. Flights between England and Australia were no longer regarded as pioneering. Even while Amy was being interviewed Francis Chichester, then an unknown young amateur who had just learnt to fly at Brooklands, was on his way to Australia in a Gipsy Moth, but his progress was attracting little attention.

Nevertheless the article in the *Evening News* sparked off a great flare of interest. 'Have you seen anything of the remarkable publicity I'm getting?' Amy asked her mother. 'I expect you have – it's all over London. There's my photo in every London paper today.' She was, so she said, furious with the reporter concerned. 'I asked him to use his discretion instead of which he's used his imagination much too freely. The whole article's absurd – I don't come from the Midlands. I'm not 22,[1] and I

[1] She was now 26½.

haven't made a penny out of aviation, never mind a "comfortable living".' But some of her complaints lacked conviction. 'Yesterday and today people have been ringing up the whole day long,' she boasted. 'I must have had fifty phone calls . . . This morning when I arrived [at Stag Lane] there were ten press photographers waiting for me – including the cinema news people . . . so look out for me on the films too!!! I'm trying to take advantage of this publicity to get some financial backing and on Monday shall visit some oil companies. This afternoon I went to see the Australian press, who wrote promising to help me as much as possible.' She had much to learn of the ways of the press and of potential backers; these were the first of many, many futile attempts to win support for her venture.

II

At this crucial stage of her career, Amy was seriously in need of a counsellor upon whom she could rely for advice on business matters. Jack Humphreys, though indispensable to her as 'tutor' and confidant, was not a business man. Thus Amy was fortunate in being able to turn to her father, and until she finally left for Australia in May she was in touch with him almost daily. Not since she first came to London, when she wrote every day to Franz, had her letter-writing been so intensive, and her father's replies, page after page of closely typed comment and admonition, outspoken but understanding, and packed with the shrewd commonsense that his critics have called money-madness, convey a happy impression of the newly intimate friendship that developed between father and daughter. One of Amy's more cynical friends has remarked that she had everything to gain at this point from keeping on good terms with her father, yet the candid and affectionate tone of the correspondence speaks for itself. Here is a passage from one of Will Johnson's letters, on the subject of his daughter's relations with the press. 'Really I think you have had a great stroke of luck,' he wrote. 'What has happened is this, Amy Johnson is now well known all over the country – true you haven't got anything out of it, but you are of public interest and up to the moment that is your ASSET. Now just a tip in regard to interviewing reporters; please remember they put anything in and don't care about the feelings of their informants; therefore you must only SAY anything which you are prepared to see in the paper; there isn't any such thing as a friendly talk with them – they report it all. If you have anything you don't want to be known then don't even whisper it to a reporter . . . Really you have caught the eye of the press and they seem very interested, therefore go in and make as much publicity as you can even if you don't get any money. Moreover owing to this publicity you will be able to make better contacts with oil people etc . . . therefore I don't advise you to be too awkward . . . [and] you needn't be too modest.'

This first surge of public interest subsided quickly, for which Amy declared herself 'devoutly thankful'. 'I don't want any more until I'm actually ready to go on my trip,' so she wrote to her mother. Through the ensuing weeks and months she drove herself cruelly hard, but she seemed able to draw upon phenomenal reserves of energy. Not only was she now enmeshed in a campaign to secure backing but she was cramming for her second engineering examination, attending a formidable course of lectures on navigation and kindred subjects, putting in as many flying hours as she could towards her Pilot's 'B' Licence, and continuing her unofficial work as one of Humphrey's 'boys' at Stag Lane, where she did not shirk the most arduous chores. One wintry day she wrote, 'The aerodrome is knee-deep in mud, and today it began to pour while the two boys were at lunch. So I helped . . . to bring in the six aeroplanes. They kept getting bogged in the mud. It was an awful job and I got rather wet.' Later she remarked, in a facetious article entitled 'A Day as a Ground Engineer', 'If I didn't do it all voluntarily and for nothing I should, of course, consider I was grossly over-worked, ill-treated, underfed and underpaid!'

In her room at Oldways, the thatched cottage at Roe Green, she plastered the wall behind her bed with maps and charts, and night after night she studied her text books and battered out letters on a typewriter which her father had lent to her. 'She always ran with her letters to the post – ran back, and was never slow in her movements,' her landlady's husband later recalled. 'We put it down to nerves . . . Curiously enough she was strangely reticent about talking of her great projected flight. On being questioned she said "I will do it; I mean to win through," and we knew she meant it. With that she would change to some other subject.'

Amy seldom now allowed herself to relax, and only on Monday, her weekly day off, did she sometimes abandon aviation to shop in Oxford Street or to meet one of her few non-flying friends such as Winifred. She hardly ever saw a film or a play although occasionally she indulged in an evening out with some of her flying-club friends, after which she would arrive late and sleepy-eyed next morning at Stag Lane, to the pretended disgust of 'the Boss' (Humphreys now admits that he secretly thought a few 'wild parties' were an excellent safety-valve for her). But it seems that her tastes in gaiety were changing; after the London Aeroplane Club's annual party, held that winter at the Park Lane Hotel, she told her mother that she had quite enjoyed it, 'but not so much as I used to enjoy dances in my youth!!' This remark must not however be taken to imply that Amy was no longer a centre of masculine attention. Her newly acquired outdoor-girl look of vigour and exuberance, combined with the potent feminine magnetism that had held Franz for so long, could hardly fail to win her a following, whether she was wearing a dance frock, or thick flying clothes, or her dirt-saturated working overalls.

Her admirers at the London Aeroplane Club included men of varied talents: the comedian Will Hay was one of them, another was the actor Norman Shelley, another was a professional juggler, Tom Elder Hearn, and she was also friends with Tim Rose Richards, the racing driver, who found her an appreciative companion when he displayed his expertise at the wheel. In carefree mood she wrote to her mother (then practising on the new family car, as was her sister Molly) 'Do you find the driving easy? I was telling Moll that she ought to know all the "finesse" of driving in order to keep the car in good order, because a bad driver can so quickly ruin an engine. I often drive in a car with a member of the club who is a Brooklands racing expert and he's a most wonderful driver. His gear changing is marvellous and he can deliberately make it skid anywhere he wants. He's saved himself from scores of accidents by deliberate skids . . . When I get out after a drive in his car I always say "Now I'm going back to flying – it's much safer" . . . But all the same there is a lot to know about driving that none of us understand . . . A really expert driver can change gears without declutching as he knows exactly the right acceleration required for the gear teeth to engage themselves.' Apparently Amy had been allowed to emulate this, but she added 'I wouldn't attempt it on my own.'

To Amy's father, the supercharged pace of his daughter's life was causing a certain amount of apprehension, but he knew her too well to try to force her to let up. 'I note you have your hands full with preparations for your exams and your other work at the same time,' he wrote coolly. 'I hope you are not taking on more than you can manage . . . It's all right as long as your health keeps good . . . a breakdown in health would annul nearly all you've done. Can't you steady up with your flying or the manual work until you've got through with your heavy studies? However you know best, I only throw these suggestions out for your consideration.'

The most immediate of the examinations ahead of her was for a Ground Engineer's 'A' Licence, which would qualify her to make pre-flight inspections of aeroplanes as distinct from their engines; it was thus complementary to the 'C' Licence she already had. As with her study of the Gipsy engine, the knowledge of the Moth that she now assimilated was to prove invaluable on her Australia flight. Yet by a twist of fate, at the very time when she was steeping herself in de Havilland handbooks she still expected that her long-distance flight would be made in 'the Martin'. The design of this new machine was so 'avant-garde' that many of the procedures she was learning would not have applied directly to it (at a time when all the world was flying biplanes Martin's aircraft was to be a low-wing monoplane; for its framework he was using steel tubing in preference to wood; and there was to be side-by-side seating, with the engine set behind the cockpit, instead of the usual tandem layout). Her second engineering examination worried her far less than her first. Much of the theory no doubt came easily to her since already she had seen so much of its practical applications – besides, she knew she could rely upon Humphreys to elucidate points that puzzled her: often in the margin of her notes is a pencilled scribble 'See Jack'. She was on such friendly terms with Humphreys and also with his wife that whenever she needed some coaching she merely dropped in at his home at Edgware (where in spare moments she amused herself by playing with his small son).[1]

Nevertheless there was a wide field of subjects to cover, and Amy had to be prepared for questions on such diverse matters as the correct tension of bracing wires, the number of ounces per square yard that each coating of dope applied to the linen wing surfaces of a Moth added to its weight, the functioning of the de Havilland differential aileron control, and the proper installation of an air-speed indicator. But we can assume that when the time came she again succeeded in satisfying the

[1] Humphreys was also coaching Captain R.S. Rattray, the anthropologist, who was planning to fly to the Gold Coast in a light aeroplane. Rattray was staying with Humphreys at his home at this time, and Amy became acquainted with him there.

examiners, for on 10 March 1930 an 'A' Licence (valid for Moth landplanes) was added to her ground engineer's certificate. The possession of both the 'A' and the 'C' Licences represented an important advance in her professional status, and qualified her to become an Associate Member of the Royal Aeronautical Society (she had already, in the autumn of 1929, joined the Society as a Companion, thanks to Humphreys' help).

III

Amy's chief worry during this winter as regards her studies was not her engineering, but the course of lectures which was to culminate in an examination for a 2nd Class Navigator's Licence in March. The need for this additional 'ticket' had been recently brought about by drastic changes in the regulations for professional pilots. Henceforward all holders of the pilot's 'B' Licence would have to satisfy new requirements as navigators.[1] Amy, boggling at the prospect, told her mother that the exam was a very difficult one: 'I need to know Morse, wireless, forecast the weather, steer by the sun, moon and stars and what not!!'

At Stag Lane the lectures took place at the de Havilland Technical School, and the class consisted mostly of men (to Amy's glee both of the club's flying instructors had to participate) but besides Amy there were also a few experienced women pilots, including Lady Bailey. It was thus that she and Amy became acquainted, and in March, a couple of weeks before the examination, she invited her to spend at evening at her house in Bryanston Square, so that they could practice Morse together. Amy relished this taste of a new social milieu. 'I enjoyed myself at Lady Bailey's last night,' she

---

[1] This meant mastering the following subjects: Form of the Earth, Maps and Charts, Meteorology, Dead Reckoning, Direction-finding. W/T Navigation, The Earth's Magnetism and Compasses, Visual Signalling, International Legislation.

told her mother. Was waited on by real liveried footmen! It was great fun. I made several mistakes at dinner, but Lady Bailey is awfully sweet and has the art of making one feel perfectly at ease. She's got a lovely house. I'm going again soon if it can be arranged. We're practising Morse for the exam which is only a fortnight off. Am very worried about it.'

Her anxiety was justified. Despite the thoroughness of her studying (as witnessed by the notebook in which she wrote up her lectures) she had, as her father had tried to warn her, undertaken far more than she could manage in the time. A few days before the examination she brought herself to admit this, and with the utmost relief decided not to sit for it. Her father made the consoling comment, 'It would have been foolish to take it knowing for sure you would fail,' and added that the requirements for the Pilot's 'B' Licence seemed very stiff.

IV

Amy's flying, during the last six months before her Australia flight, was oriented towards qualifying for her 'B'. Here too the revised regulations brought heavy demands. In 1928, at the time when she started learning to fly, the number of solo hours required was only thirty-five. One cross-country solo of 200 miles was stipulated, and one night flight, but the tests for flying skill were of the same elementary standard as for the 'A' Licence. If these rules had continued in force until the end of 1929 Amy might well have obtained a 'B' Licence that year, and this explains why she had hoped to fly Martin's aeroplane 'before Christmas' (her solo flying reached the 35-hour mark during the first week of November). But according to the new rulings the candidate for a 'B' Licence must have not less than a hundred solo hours to his, or her, credit. Evidently however there was an interim arrangement by which pilots were permitted to carry passengers after fifty hours, for when Amy was approaching that stage she mentioned, in writing home, that she had received a letter from the Royal Aero Club saying that her application to carry passengers would be considered at the next committee meeting. 'What a silly lot of red tape,' she added, 'when everyone knows it's Perrin and him only who has the say in all matters connected with the club.'

According to Amy's log book Jack Humphreys was her first passenger (on 13 December 1929), and then during the ensuing months she took her mother up, and also Winifred, and after giving a talk to the Aeroplane Club at Harrow School she offered a half-hour joyride as the prize for a club competition. All this was delightful and exciting to her, but even more so was the thrill, in mid-January, of earning as a professional ground engineer. 'It will be my first money earned in aviation,' she wrote with pride to her mother, and mentioned that to commemorate it she thought of buying a small memento such as a toastrack. Her client was a Stag Lane habitue,' Major Nathan, who had asked Humphreys if one of his men could do some work on a Moth which he was about to take to the West Indies. This was not an unusual request; although the engineers spent most of their time on the club's machines, when they were free they often undertook the servicing of privately-owned aircraft.

Nathan was at first taken aback by the suggestion that a young woman should work on his aeroplane, but he was won over by Humphreys' insistence that 'Johnnie's' work was as good as a man's. He soon discovered that this was true and also that Amy was a fanatically keen pilot; to her delight he allowed her to make several longish cross-country flights in his Moth, sometimes with himself as passenger. It was one of her solo flights in his aeroplane that inspired her article. 'The Joys of the Air for a Woman.' The prospect of her final flight in Nathan's aircraft before it was shipped from Southampton was not however such a joy because Nathan, not she herself, was to be pilot. Even though she knew he was 'very careful' she wrote beforehand to her mother, 'I hate flying with anyone else . . . I prefer to be dependent on myself and I know more or less how I should act in an emergency, whereas I don't know what presence of mind anyone else would show.'

During a recent visit to Hull she had promised her parents to adopt as her flying motto the slogan 'Be careful'. And the following remarks to her mother embody the essence of her aviator's philosophy at this time. 'I don't consider flying is dangerous if one takes reasonable care, and you may be sure I shall not take any unnecessary risks. So you won't worry, will you?'

16

THE MEANS TO THE END

February–April 1930

A thousand pounds! That was the minimum Amy reckoned it would cost to buy a light aeroplane and then fly it to Australia, so she told her father early in 1930. Their correspondence at this time is fascinating for the light it throws upon her feverish search for backing and also upon the character of the man who now found himself in the position of business adviser to his self-willed, flying-mad daughter. Will Johnson was now just fifty-four but looked older; he was tending to become portly and his hair had thinned almost to baldness. He smiled easily and with good humour, his regard was direct and masterful, and at times his fine brown eyes kindled with a glint of guile. Both at home and at work he was a benevolent tyrant. Combined with the acquisitiveness and the ability to bully that had brought him success in commerce was the generosity of one who believed that a cheque-book was the key to almost everything in life. In the course of nearly forty years in the family fish business, of which he had long been Managing Director, he had become a wily negotiator; in Hull he was recognised as a leader in his own specialised field, and he had been elected President of as many as three local fish-trade associations. It was therefore from a wealth of experience that Will Johnson was now able to offer to his daughter the shrewd advice she needed.

In February 1930 Amy's programme was as amorphous as it was optimistic. The recent publicity given to her 'plan' for flying to Australia had forced the idea out of the realm of day-dreams: she no longer vaguely hoped to attempt the flight some day, but took for granted that she would make it soon – as soon as Martin's aeroplane was ready and she could secure some backing. Meanwhile however she was painfully short of money for the day-to-day flying for her 'B' Licence, and she set about trying to devise some scheme whereby she would be able to earn immediate cash as a free-lance pilot, undeterred by the fact that this would depend on possessing an aeroplane of her own. At this point her father was cautious. 'You know I'm not a rich man and do really need a lot of money for my business,' he told her. 'Still I'm very, very interested in your future and am willing to do everything I possibly can to help you . . . I am quite aware you have now committed yourself to aviation, therefore you have to do something, and to do that you have to have some chances.'

Amy talked matters over with her former employer, Mr Crocker, and afterwards wrote to report his views to her father. As regards backing for the Australia flight, Crocker suggested that a lunch might be arranged with his friend Sir Basil Clarke who had influence with the *Daily Mail*. Will Johnson, when he heard this, made the prophetic comment 'If the *Daily Mail* takes you up you are made,' but he advised Amy to step warily in the event of meeting 'big men' such as Sir Basil. 'Don't tell them that Father can do this or that, you can even tell them that I can't afford it and it seems such a pity for one as clever as you to be wasted because you can't get the chance and so on. However, Amy, you have the right ideas so carry on and do your best and see how far you get . . . I do feel you have a very unusual personality and I think you should be able to get some influential people or a paper or something to back you.'

In this same letter he urged her to press for a formal agreement of some kind with 'the Martin Aircraft Company': 'I think you should begin to get down to brass tacks with them . . . You ought to know how you stand and even get it in writing as verbal doesn't carry far.' She lost no time in following this advice but a shock awaited her; Martin's company, so she learnt, was in the same unhappy situation as herself, 'a shuffle to get financial backing.' Jimmy's perfectionism as a designer was proving a costly virtue, and although he was still as keen as ever that she should fly his aeroplane there was no question of his 'giving' it to her for a long-distance flight.

'I must say I am rather surprised to learn that the New Company will not provide you with a plane,' her father commented. 'Really, Amy, it changes the whole complexion of your schemes; it simply means you have a desire to fly to Australia and want someone to finance it . . . Now Amy, my object isn't to discount your ideas or damp your enthusiasm but really you haven't done anything yet beyond getting your Engineer's Licence, therefore . . . you [cannot] expect anyone except a pure philanthropist to put the money down for such a venture . . . unless it was to advertise something or someone . . . Wakefield would be a likely man to advertise his oil but he seems to have had enough of this already . . . You must remember dear, that men, even very rich men, are not standing with their money ready to pay out to all and sundry.'

He then urged her to postpone her 'big trip' until the following year, on the grounds that she would then have time to recover from the stress of her examinations, to accumulate more experience of cross-country flying, and 'to find someone to do the finance which isn't arranged in one interview but must be worked up.' 'Your letter says everyone is so apathetic and so slow,' he went on 'while you are wearing your nerves down with worry and impatience. I quite understand it dear, but to speak plainly no one troubles themselves that you are impatient and wearing your nerves down, and further it's only a few who are REALLY keen in aviation matters. Take my advice and slow down a bit yourself . . . reconcile yourself to waiting till next year and go for some smaller fry, say try and find a plane to fly in the King's

Cup or other things . . . Look up to the top of the ladder by all means, but you can't jump up there all at one stroke, it has to come step by step . . . This sounds like one of Father's lectures but still you know there is a lot of truth in it.'

II

Amy was in no mood to slow down: pride was one of her most deeply-rooted characteristics. Ever since the *Evening News* had acclaimed her enterprise it had been clear that if she failed to bring off her Australia flight quite soon the public would forget her, and worse still, in flying circles she would be a laughing stock behind her back.

Her next move was to embark on an intensive campaign of personal appeals for help, in the form of letters to public figures and members of the peerage. 'I often post as many as twelve or fifteen letters at a time,' she told her mother. 'So far everyone has turned me down. I haven't many resources left – I'll write to Lord Nunburnholme when I can get hold of his address. There's no harm in trying, but so many people do not even answer my letters. I have given up hearing from Lady Houston.'

There was a flicker of response after she wrote simultaneously to Lord Rothermere, Lord Beaverbrook and Sir Thomas Polson, chief organiser of the new United Empire Party (a propagandist venture aimed at promoting Empire tariffs). She had offered to donate her services as a pilot to the Party with the object, so she said, of carrying messages of goodwill to the Dominions, and her stratagem won her a mention on the front page of the *Daily Mirror*. She hastened to follow this up by writing again to Sir Thomas, explaining how her personal aims as regards Australia would coincide with the interests of his movement. 'Lindbergh's Atlantic flight was financed by a house-to-house collection in his home town, St Louis,' she reminded him, 'and his plane therefore called the *Spirit of St Louis*. Do you not think a plane named *Spirit of England* flown through out Dominions would capture the hearts of the general public and "do its bit" towards Empire Unity . . . This appeal to the Empire Party is my last resort. If they turn me down – which would be through timidity and lack of enterprise, the very things they are denouncing, I expect I shall have to turn to some other country . . . America respects her women pilots and gives them splendid opportunities and positions.' But despite her eloquence she received no further encouragement from Sir Thomas, for in this same letter she informed him that she needed between £1,000 and £1,500 to finance her flight.

It is tempting to wonder why she does not seem to have thought – long before this – of turning for help (in the matter of introductions) to the man who was one of the most enthusiastic of all the leading figures in British flying at the time: the Director of Civil Aviation, Sefton Brancker. His reputation for initiative had been familiar to her ever since she worked at the Air League office; she must have kown him well by sight, for the dapper little man with a monocle, commanding in spite of his short stature, was often at Stag Lane where his sky blue and silver Moth was kept. But there is no evidence that thd idea ever entered her head before it was thrust upon her by a sudden opportunity which she herself had done nothing to plan.

On the evening of Monday 10 March Amy, as a member of the Royal Aeronautical Society, attended a lecture on Air Transport by a German expert, Major Martin Wronsky. After it the Soceity's President, the Master of Sempill, moved the vote of thanks, and the seconder was Brancker. In the course of his speech Sir Sefton said: 'It has been very interesting to see the amounts received from the various German states and even from the cities for the development of the air services. I wish England would wake up and try to do likewise . . .' The words 'I wish England would wake up' pierced Amy's consciousness like a sword. Their context was of no importance; all she cared about was that they epitomized so perfectly her own strivings and disappointments. Next day she wrote yet another letter pleading her case, and this time she knew she was writing to a fellow enthusiast.

'I heartily echoed your words,' she began. 'I have for months been fighting against the lack of enterprise and faith existing in Aviation circles. I have a great ambition to do something to help spread interest in Aviation in this country, but – I have no money and no influence . . .

'I want to fly to Australia, one reason being that I am certain a successful flight of this nature, by an English girl, solo and in a flight plane, would do much to engender confidence amongst the public in air travel . . . At last night's lecture you called attention to the leading article in *Flight*[1]. Did you by any chance look further through the book and see my appeal on page 284?[2]

'By my own efforts, and through many difficulties, I have trained myself for a career in Aviation, and I have its good most sincerely at heart . . . I can give dozens of names of people who, I am sure, will willingly vouch for my sincerity and capabilities; for example: Lady Bailey, Lieutenant Colonel Thwaites, Secretary of the Air League; Commander Kenworthy, MP for my home town, Hull; Miss Stella Wolfe Murray, author of *Woman and Flying*; Mr Spooner, Editor of *Flight*; Commander Perrin, Secretary of the Royal Aero Club . . .

'Everyone in Aviation circles speaks well of you and says how much you would do for Aviation if you only had a free hand. Can you not do anything to help me? I want between £1,000 and £1,500, every penny of which I will guarantee to repay on my return, if required. Do you not know anyone who could easily spare that sum? There must surely be hundreds of people in England who would miss it less than would I parting with 6*d*! I have written several people, but I either get no reply or merely good wishes . . . I am getting rather desperate about this matter of raising finance and I cannot do

[1] On the subject of the South American market for aircraft.
[2] This was an editorial paragraph headed 'The Right Enterprise', calling for help to enable Amy to acquire a British aircraft for her Australia flight.

anything worth while without it, I'm afraid. Also time is of great importance, because if I cannot set off before May, weather conditions will force me to postpone the trip until next winter, by which time it will have lost most of its publicity value, as I hope by then it will be a normal thing to fly to Australia.

'I shall be deeply grateful if you can do anything at all to help me. Just a reply to my letter would encourage me to further efforts.'

At the end of this appeal, by an unfortunate oversight, Amy failed to sign her name. How providential that she had mentioned her appeal in *Flight*! How fortunate, too, that Brancker was a man of such irrepressible energy and thoroughness, and also with such an interest in encouraging women pilots, that he took the trouble to follow up the clue she had unwittingly provided, and thus discovered that the writer's name was Miss Amy Johnson.

III

In the meantime, before she received his answer, another letter, written on the same day that Brancker spoke, brought her a heartening offer of help from her father. He and her mother, he said, had just been visiting her Johnson grandparents at Bridlington, and much sympathy had been expressed for Amy in her frustrating plight. Her grandfather, who although retired from business still dominated the family, is not mentioned by name in the letter, but between the lines one can read the influence of the old man who in his own youth had ventured abroad to make his fortune. 'Well now Amy,' her father announced, 'Mother and myself have decided that we will supply the aeroplane for you for this trip if you can't get it elsewhere (limit £800). Our idea is, if this week nothing definite develops in your plans with other people then you must begin negotiations to buy your own plane . . . I suggust you come through to Hull for next weekend so that we can go fully into all details.'

In response to this exciting offer Amy decided to fly solo to Hull and she booked one of the club's Moths. On the appointed day (19 March) the cautious Major Travers would not permit her to set off because, so he insisted, the clouds were too low. Amy was much disgusted but when she heard later that it had been snowing in Hull she admitted to her father 'It was just as well I didn't come, as there is nothing worse than a snowstorm. I'd sooner fly though anything than snow, and it really is quite dangerous.' Next day, in better weather, she was allowed to make the trip and her cross-country flight of 150 miles from Stag Lane to Hedon aerodrome outside Hull, which took two hours and ten minutes, was by far the longest of her flying career.[1]

The talks with her father consolidated her plans, but the Hull visit was disturbing in that Amy found her mother distressed and anxious on her behalf, fearing that her health would not stand the strain of a long-distance flight and that her skill and experience as a pilot were inadequate. Ciss Johnson was herself in very poor health at this time: she was now forty-nine and earlier in the winter had been prostrated by blood-pressure trouble, neuritis and headaches, and on doctor's orders had spent February very quietly at Bournemouth. Amy's father, however, was unperturbed. 'The fact is, Amy, Mother must worry about something or someone,' he wrote afterwards. 'At times it's me, at others it's you and so on, so don't take such matters too seriously . . . I know it is very silly of her and unfortunate that she feels that way but there it is . . . we are being very careful with her.'

Nevertheless Amy felt that something must be done by way of reassurance, and she accepted her mother's pressing offer of a 'cure' – a course of 'electric treatments'[2] at the hands of a Bournemouth nurse in whom her mother had great confidence; this in spite of

[1] She had by now flown 85 hours solo.
[2] Probably some sort of vibro-massage.

the inconvenience of the necessary trips. It was also largely to reassure Ciss Johnson that a few days after Amy's return from Hull Humphreys sent her father the following tribute to his daughter's capabilities: 'I have followed Miss Johnson's career in flying with the closest interest, and it was because I considered her capable of doing something really worth while that I encouraged her to aim for a somewhat ambitious project . . . I have flown as her passenger . . . with complete confidence . . . [and] of her engineering abilities I can really speak, for she has . . . mastered the whole situation of Aeronautics so well that I can be assured at all times that both engine and machine under her care is equal to my own maintenance and inspection . . . Miss Johnson is looked upon here as an Engineer as well as a pilot.'

'I must say,' Will Johnson replied gratefully, 'that whatever success she may achieve, a great amount of credit must be due to you for the great interest you have taken in teaching her so well. Your assistance has been more creditable by the fact that in these days so many men are ever ready to push the woman down rather than give her a lift up.' To Amy, at the same time, he wrote, 'Now don't get too excited, but simply carry on with your arrangements as though it was a trip to Hull; hold your own counsel and look well after your health.'

The arrangements which she found hardest to carry on with were those with the Martin Aircraft Works. At the end of March Humphreys estimated that the new aeroplane would be finished in six or seven weeks. Yet even if Martin's finances permitted this, and even if all went well with the first flight, there would still be essential test flights before the green, untried machine would be anything like ready for an expedition to the other side of the world. More and more it became obvious that if she stuck to 'the Martin' she would not be able to make her trip that year, for there was no question of starting on it once the season of the monsoons had set in. In her diary was pencilled a note against the date 5 May 1930. 'Best day to set off. Try for it.' But she clung to the idea of working with Martin partly because she believed it would ensure future employment for her in aviation, and she seems to have persuaded her father of the logic of this. Immediately after the family offer to buy an aircraft for her she looked into the possibility of ordering a new Moth from de Havilland, whereupon her father made the realistic comment, 'You cannot expect anything whatever in regard to the future from De H's.'

Amy snatched at any scrap of evidence that 'the Martin' was making progress, and in one letter to her father mentioned with some excitement that it was being equipped with 'a tank for 1,500 miles.' Will Johnson was not impressed and merely remarked 'I think I should let Mr Martin know the progress you are making re your trip in order to urge him on with the work.'

IV

Such was the state of Amy's plan when she was summoned to Gwydyr House, the offices of the Air Ministry in Whitehall, for an interview with the Director of Civil Aviation. Afterwards she wrote to her mother, 'Sir Sefton Brancker has been awfully kind . . . I called to see him and he said he would find out what my reputation was as a pilot, and if good he would write to Lord Wakefield . . . I said to Sir Sefton that if I really couldn't after all fly to Australia, I should either have to leave Aviation or change my name and start again, and he said, "Oh, don't change your name; it has made a profound impression on me" . . . Immediately I left him, he rang up the Club and Major Travers has evidently told him a good tale about me. It's an awfully nice letter, isn't it?' She enclosed a copy of the letter Brancker had written to Lord Wakefield: it was worded in cool, objective terms, calculated to hold the attention of the philanthropic oil magnate whose gift for sizing up personal abilities was known to govern his choices where benefactions to British flying were concerned.

'I write this as a letter of introduction, but not as an appeal for help,' Brancker began. 'You probably have heard of Miss Johnson, who has rather distinguished herself in the London Aeroplane Club both by the speed with which she has become a reliable pilot and by the keenness which she has shown in working hard on the ground and becoming a licensed ground engineer. She has done all this up to the present at the expense of her father, who is a business man in Hull. She is anxious now to win her spurs by taking on some considerable flight; her particular objective is Australia. Her instructors tell me that she is a very reliable, sound and sensible pilot with a really good knowledge of maintenance both of engine and aircraft. Her father has promised to finance any enterprise which she eventually decides on undertaking up to a point, but she still wants some assistance. I send her to you on the off-chance that you may find her proposals interesting. She is the type we want to help and support, and I think she is as reliable as most people who come forward with pioneering propositions. Anyway she has impressed me very favourably. Please forgive me if I have worried you unjustifiably and don't hesitate to turn her down if you don't like the idea of helping her.'

By this time Amy had learnt not to expect overmuch from celebrities. 'I refuse to give up my project even if Lord Wakefield won't help me,' she told her mother. 'Will you please tell Daddy I've written to two aeroplane companies in Germany just to see what they say – Junkers and Klemm.'

But Brancker's diplomacy bore its fruits. On 15 April, the Tuesday before Easter, Amy wrote again to her mother. 'This morning . . . I received a *wire* from Lord W asking me to meet him tomorrow at 11.15! . . . I daren't be too optimistic as I've had so many disappointments, but I shouldn't imagine he would bother to see me unless there was some hope.' Next day, after the interview, another note was dashed off. 'I was successful. Lord W will put up the rest of the money I need. I told him Daddy would give me £500 and he will give me the rest.' To Lord Wakefield she wrote with appropriate respect, but also in triumph. 'I cannot adequately express to you my thanks for your great kindness, but I will try to prove my deep gratitude by carrying out a safe flight and thus add some further slight prestige to the excellence of "Wakefield's Oil" – not that it needs it! I know you have the cause of Aviation much at heart, and if I can therefore do any small thing to help on that cause, I shall feel that it is also pleasing you. I'll do my utmost to prevent your ever regretting your help to me.'

This was followed by a letter from her father. 'Please allow me, as Father of Amy Johnson, to express my appreciation and thanks for your kindness and generosity . . . I must admit, at first, the approval of my wife and myself was given grudgingly to her flying activities, but after seeing her keen interest in aviation, and having heard such good reports of her abilities and caution, from sources which we consider quite reliable, I felt it right to give what encouragement I could to help her. I am therefore writing this letter to assure you she has the approval of my wife and myself for this venture . . . If I am allowed to express an opinion of my own daughter I would like to assure you [that] you are helping a straightforward, good and clever girl to obtain her ambition and at the same time forward aviation.'

17

THE START

April–May 1930

Oh yes, she will go far. And we know where she is going.
But what do we know of the terrors of the journey? . . .
She will be afraid of nothing; she will not even know
That there is anything to be afraid of.

These words[1] apply with strange aptness to Amy as she prepared to face the hazards of her flight to Australia. The journey was to hold plenty of terrors for her, but she was protected from any real apprehension of them by the facetious banter of her friends, the matter-of-factness of her father (with his advice to prepare for the trip as though it were a flight to Hull) and by her own ignorance and romanticism. She looked forward with relish to 'thrills and adventures' but her notions of them, so she later admitted, were those of a schoolgirl nurtured on film dramas such as *The Perils of Pauline*, in which the heroine always succeeds in escaping from the cannibals, sharks, 'torture-loving bandits' and 'wild beasts of desert and jungle'. Nevertheless in the rush of the last weeks before she left she had little time for day dreams.

The assurance of Lord Wakefield's support had suddenly quickened the tempo of her project up to, and past, its take-off speed – a blessed relief after the harsh joltings of the preceding weeks; and she was now thrust

[1] From T.S. Eliot's *The Cocktail Party*.

into a turmoil of preparations, foremost among them the purchase of a suitable aeroplane. There was less than three weeks before 5 May, when she hoped to set off, and she did not yet possess a machine. Obviously she could not wait any longer for Martin's aircraft (in fact owing to lack of funds he had to abandon work on it at about this time) but through her Stag Lane connections an excellent alternative presented itself. Captain W.L. Hope, a seasoned pilot who had twice won the King's Cup, and who was head of a firm called Air Taxis, was ready to part with one of his Moths (G-AAAH), and she jumped at the chance to buy it. At the Easter weekend a fortnight before her departure) she wrote to Mr Alonzo Limb, Manager of Wakefields' Motor and Aviation Departments: 'I have now made arrangements to purchase a machine for my flight, and have been fortunate enough to find just the right one I need. This is a plane belonging to Captain Hope which is already fitted up with special long-distance tanks and has made one journey into the Tropics and proved its suitability for long-distance flying. It is a Gipsy Moth machine, about two years old, and he is charging me £600 which I consider reasonable. I should therefore be much obliged if you would kindly let me have a cheque by return for £300 as promised . . . I shall ask my Father for the other £300.' What exquisite pleasure to be able to demand fat cheques by return of post! And during the next couple of weeks both Wakefields and Amy's father paid out very much more than this first six hundred pounds for her aeroplane.

The Gipsy Moth in question, like other Moths, was colloquially known at Stag Lane by its final registration letters, 'AH'. But Amy had already decided that her aeroplane, when she got it, was to have a new, much more personal name. Weeks earlier, immediately after her father had made his generous offer of financial help, she had suggested that her aircraft should be given the name of *Jason*, a contraction of 'Johnson' which was the registered trademark of the family fish business. Her father, much pleased by this gesture, assured her that the name *Jason* would bring her luck.

THE START

In the first thrill of ownership, however, she seldom referred to the Moth by name; it was simply 'my machine'. Two days after it became hers she wrote to her mother, 'I wish you could see my machine, but I will take some pictures of it, and . . . you will see it when I come home.' And then again, after the aircraft had been painted green (at the time of purchase it was dark red), and when Humphreys and his team were busy overhauling the engine, she wrote, 'My machine is progressing quite well, it looks awfully smart, bottle green about the shade of my suit, with silver lettering and "Jason" on each side of the nose. "Jason" isn't half getting talked of already, but I don't think anyone connects it with kippers!'

It seems a trifle amusing that Amy, at this particular stage of her career, should have identified herself with the colour green. Her taste in colours was changeable; some years earlier she had a mania for navy blue; later in her life there was a time when she wore nothing but black and white. But now everything had to be green. When the Ingersoll company, who were presenting her with an alarm clock for the trip, asked if she had any preference as to colour she replied, 'I should like green, please. My machine is green, as also everything else I could get to match, as green is my "lucky" colour.'

Certainly it was lucky for Amy, in her greenness, that the former owner of 'my machine' was a knowledgeable and travelled pilot as well as a kindly man, and she gladly accepted advice form the smiling, efficient 'Wally' Hope. He helped to prepare Amy for emergencies and tropical conditions by urging her to take a revolver, a mosquito net and sun-helmet, as well as a portable cooking stove, reserve provisions, medicines and a first-aid kit. But of course she could not add indiscriminately to the weight of her cargo, and priority had to be given to her collection of spares and tools. One of the spares was an extra propellor; this awkward item, which could not be. stowed inside the Moth and would have to be carried externally (lashed to the centre-section struts) had to be fetched from

Weybridge, and she relied thankfully upon Jimmy Martin to drive her there to collect it. Her decision not to wait any longer for his aircraft had not cooled their friendship and during this hectic time he often acted as chauffeur for her.

Captain Hope also advised her about flying maps: he himself favoured strip maps fixed on to rollers in a map-case, and she duly ordered a set for the whole of her journey, though the only maps available for some stretches of it were sadly inadequate. She had already some time earlier decided upon her route, after studying the flight made by Hinkler in 1928. The brilliant little Australian test pilot had established a record for his 11,000-mile trip by making it in fifteen and a half days. In 1930 this still held good and as Amy's father remarked to her in one of his letters, 'Every time Australia is mentioned then it is "Hinkler's time" that is referred to.'

II

In one aspect of her planning Amy believed she knew better than Hinkler. He and almost all the other pilots who had tackled the trip had set out over France and Italy and then crossed the Mediterranean, thereby avoiding the Balkan countries, where visiting pilots were apt to become entangled in red tape. She however, never having flown abroad before, decided to follow as straight a course as possible despite national boundaries, and she later wrote that she planned the first part of her trip by drawing a straight line on a map from London to Basra. She calculated that by means of this 'short cut' she would save nearly 700 miles, and would have a very good chance of improving on Hinkler's record.

For Wakefields she now had to compile a concise list of the aerodromes where she planned to refuel, or might need to, and she also sent her list of twenty-two aerodromes to the Shell-Mex company, who had agreed to lay on the needful petrol supplies (she had failed however to inveigle the company into providing them free; she, or rather Wakefields, had to pay in advance for the consignments). The twelve main stopping places she was aiming for were as follows: Vienna – Constantinople – Baghdad – Bandar Abbas – Karachi – Allahabad – Calcutta – Bangkok – Singapore – Sourabaya – Atamboea – Port Darwin. But the tidiness of this list, resembling as it does a present-day airline schedule, obscures the fact that in 1930 air travel was far from tidy; it also suggests, misleadingly, that the risks and dangers were the same throughout the trip. This was indeed not so. As far as India, in 1930, civil aviation was just beginning to establish itself, Imperial Airways were in course of initiating the 'Air Mail Route', and a solo pilot might feel optimistic about the chances of rescue in the event of a forced landing. But beyond India conditions were very different. Except for the Dutch air services in the East Indies there was virtually no civil aviation in South-East Asia, and – as Amy soon learnt when she made some hurried researches at the Air Ministry – she would be flying over vast stretches of alternating ocean and jungle which had barely been mapped, at a season when the monsoons might well be beginning, and where there was little or no hope of rescue if things went wrong. That experience-hardened pilot Sir Alan Cobham, when he made his pioneering flight from England to Australia in 1926, had chosen to fly in a seaplane rather than a landplane because, so he wrote afterwards, 'from Calcutta to Australia it is simply impossible to land anywhere but on a specially prepared aerodrome.' When Amy planned her flight this was still true, but ahead of her now, of course, was the heartening example of Hinkler, who had dared to attempt the journey solo in a landplane, pinning his confidence upon the reliability of aircraft and engine. Hinkler was a natural mechanic as well as a remarkable flyer, and his skill and thoroughness in maintaining his machine had been one of the main factors in his success. Amy, with her training as a ground engineer, intended to follow his example in caring meticulously for aeroplane and engine.

At the Air Ministry she gleaned what she could about her route, and also arranged that applications for flying permits should be sent to all the countries she planned to fly over. These formalities normally took about six weeks but under Brancker's auspices they were speeded. 'Turkey was being very slow as usual in granting a permit,' she told Mr Limb at Wakefields, 'but Sir Sefton Brancker has now himself got on the war-path so I am sure the way will be smoothed.' The letters she wrote during the final weeks before she left were full of confidence and zest, but those to her mother were also tactfully reassuring, for Ciss Johnson was still full of fears. And when Amy's parents suggested that she should take a parachute with her, she dutifully arranged to obtain one from the Irving Air Chute company, although in those days few except military pilots used these excellent life-savers and many flyers regarded a parachute as a badge of timidity. 'There is certainly no need to worry now at all,' Amy wrote to her mother, whose nerves had just been harrowed by the death of her mother-in-law and also of another relative. 'I have a parachute, and Pyyrene are lending me a fire extinguisher and the engineers are working extremely hard on my machine and engine, so you need have no fear. I'm taking every precaution, you may be sure.' 'The old Duchess did very well,' she went on, apropos the flight from Croydon to Cape Town that the Duchess of Bedford had just made in 10 days. 'Good thing our flights didn't clash. I bet she'll go to Australia next. It's certain to be her next move, but I shall get in first!'

To Mr Limb in the meantime Amy had written, 'It is nice of you to say you would like to be present when I leave England, but I am afraid that the time I have fixed for the start will prove very inconvenient – namely, from Croydon [where Customs could be cleared] Monday next, May 5th, at sunrise which is about 4.30 a.m.! I am trying to keep the date very quiet as I want to keep the press out of it until I have actually left, as I am sure a secret start is much better.'

For the weekend before Amy's departure her father came to London, and in a letter to her mother he described the doings of the Saturday afternoon: 'I arrived at Stag Lane about 2.30 p.m. Met Mr Humphreys, but Amy was in town in Mr Martin's car getting her maps etc., and she arrived at the Aerodrome about 3.15. My word it must have been a heavy time for Amy as there has been such a lot to arrange. However she has nearly completed it now. We stayed at Stag Lane till 5.0 p.m. where she was meeting several people. Then I went with her to her room and helped her to get cleared up there. I wrote eight letters for her etc., and then she felt as though she was getting through her rush. I left her at 7.0 p.m. as I wanted her to get some sleep.' On Sunday he continued: 'The arrangements are that Amy lays in this morning, gets finished up at her digs in the afternoon and goes to Stag Lane at 4.0 p.m. when Humphreys and Amy will take the plane round to Croydon and I shall meet them there at 5.0 p.m. We have booked two rooms at Croydon Hotel and the arrangements are that Amy leaves early Monday morning if the weather is right. Well darling, everyone feels sure Amy will be successful and she herself is feeling well and anticipating the trip . . . I will wire Monday morning.'

Ciss Johnson, in spite of her anxiety, had been trying to enter into the spirit of the occasion by showering Amy with gifts. Not only as usual with parcels full of her daughter's favourite chocolates and sweets and cakes, but in addition with a welter of good-luck tokens and charms. 'I seem to be surrounded by black cats,' Amy wrote to her on the Saturday evening. 'I'm very grateful . . . I'll take the elephant and lucky cat with me and am sure with all these tokens I can't help but have a lucky trip. Now, you mustn't worry at all . . . You'll have the news almost as quickly as anything is known of my arrivals and departures. It's been nice to have Daddy here and he's helped me a lot today . . . Very dearest love from Johnnie.' And then a jubilant PS: 'When you're reading this I expect to be half way to Vienna!'

It was a fine Sunday, and in the afternoon many of Amy's friends were at Stag Lane: the two instructors Travers and Matthews were there, also Gordon Store, a young de Havilland pilot who had helped Amy with her flying. And before she finally set off with Humphreys for Croydon – this was only the second time that she had piloted her new plane – someone suggested that her friends should give her an aerial send-off, and so they did, in an original and heartwarming manner. In five of the club Moths, all of them in formation, they escorted *Jason* on the half-hour flight across London. 'It was very thoughtful and sporty of you all,' Will Johnson wrote afterwards to Travers. The escorting Moths followed *Jason* down at Croydon and a snapshot of the party was taken before they flew back to Stag Lane. It shows Amy looking blithe and carefree among her well-wishers, her flying-jacket buttoned high under the chin, her short hair blowing in the wind.

Jimmy Martin came over to Croydon by car, and he and Humphreys were to stay overnight. They supervised the fuelling of Amy's aircraft (with its three tanks it had a petrol capacity of eighty gallons, more than four times that of a normal Moth and enough for about thirteen hours' flying), made sure that the machine was safely put away for the night in one of the Imperial Airways hangars, and then joined Amy and her father for an evening meal.

Afterwards, so Sir James Martin recalls, a bouquet of flowers arrived from Amy's mother; he also remembers that Amy entrusted to him the responsibility of trying to place the story of her flight with one of the London newspapers. She herself had earlier approached one or two, but despite the spasmodic press interest in her venture she had failed to convince anybody that her flight would be major news. Nevertheless it seems she was now so confident of breaking records that she was certain her story would soon command a good price. At this stage she was not only hoping to better Hinkler's time (by means of hops averaging about eight hundred miles she hoped to reach Australia in twelve days) but in her ignorance of the strains of long-distance flying she was also thinking seriously of flying straight home again after her arrival at Port Darwin, in order to establish an England–Australia–England record.

IV

When Will Johnson was called next morning, more than an hour before dawn, he slipped on his dressing gown and padded along to knock on Amy's door, reflecting meanwhile that he might be sending his daughter to her death. Amy, who had been kept awake by the Sunday-night traffic returning into London, was already getting up. At breakfast the weather report was discussed; there was fog over the Channel and this usually meant no flying. Amy made light of it. 'Fog doesn't worry me,' her father remembered her saying. 'I don't want to see the Channel anyway.' Winifred Irving, along with an obliging friend who had, like herself, risen in the early hours so as to drive over to Croydon, now came in and asked Amy how she felt. 'Lousy,' she replied, 'I couldn't sleep for the traffic.'

It was a very chilly May morning when *Jason* was wheeled out on to the deserted tarmac and run up. Among the men in heavy overcoats who clustered round the aircraft there were several new arrivals, incuding representatives from Wakefields and Shell-Max. Winifred was the only woman present apart from Amy herself. In spite of Amy's avowed hope of a secret start some pressmen had turned up, and also one photographer for whom she posed in her fur-collared Sidcot suit, her goggles at the ready over her flying helmet, a parachute strapped cumbrously below her seat, a happy grin on her face. One of his photographs shows Winifed close at hand smiling with excitement; in another Amy's father was reaching up to *Jason*'s cockpit to give his daughter a farewell kiss. But then: a hitch. When Amy settled into her seat she was alarmed to notice a smell of petrol that betrayed a leak somewhere; one of the petrol-pipe connections proved to be dripping. She switched off the engine and Humphreys and Martin hurried to investigate. To their relief they found that the connection could be made good without draining off the tanks, but even so the work would take several hours. Amy went back to her room to rest and it was not until about half past seven that she again settled into the cockpit.

She had never before taken off a heavily-loaded aircraft, but she had discussed the technique with various friends. So she must have known that the way to get such an aeroplane into position for becoming airborne was to put the stick right forward at the very start of the take-off run. She must also, presumably, have been warned that if the machine did not even then lift its excessive load, one must lose no time in throttling back, and holding it down, so as to slow up in time to avoid crashing into the far boundary. She taxied down wind across the grass as far as she could, then turned and began her run. As her speed increased Humphreys, cupping his hands, yelled towards her, 'Damn you Johnnie! Get your tail up!' But *Jason* was clearly not going to get off the ground in time. Amy somehow managed to avoid crashing into the far fence, but when she taxied baack Humphreys and Martin met her with anguished reproaches: she had kept her stick too far back; she had failed to go to the farthest extremity of the aerodrome before beginning her run. This really angered her. 'I'll take off *my* way!' she exploded, 'and get out of the way all of you!'

However nerve-racking for herself and the others, the unintentional trial run had probably been for the best, as she thereby got the feel of her ponderously loaded machine. When for the second time she taxied down wind, turned and then opened up the throttle, Winifred noticed that Humphreys was standing so tensely rigid, with his eyes fixed so intently upon *Jason*, that only the slowly gathering speed of the aircraft seemed to govern the slow turning of his head. This time *Jason*'s

DH 80A Puss Moth letters G-AAZV, named *Jason III*, in which Amy broke the record from the UK across Siberia to Tokyo, as well as the return flight, in July 1931. (Royal Air Force Museum AC77/36/7)

Amy in May 1930 on her arrival in Australia, after her solo flight from the UK in DH 80G Moth letters G-AAAH, named *Jason* (Royal Air Force Museum AC77/36/4)

Amy with her husband Jim Mollison and the aeroplane *Seafarer*. In June 1933 they attempted to fly non-stop from England to New York in this machine, but ran out of fuel and crash-landed sixty miles short of their objective. (*Aeroplane*)

Amy in her flying overalls before the unsuccessful attempt to fly non-stop from London to England. (*Aeroplane*)

A page from Amy's Pilot's Log Book held at the Royal Air Force Museum in Hendon. (Royal Airforce Museum)

Amy arriving at Brisbane aerodrome after her record-breaking flight from Croydon. (Science and Society Picture Library)

Amy photographed on 12 May 1930, during her historic flight from Croydon to Brisbane. (Science and Society Picture Library)

Amy with her husband Jim at Hatfield Aerodrome in Hertfordshire, after their ten hours test flight in the new *Seafarer*. Photograph by George Woodbine. (Science and Society Picture Library).

Amy and Jim crossing the Atlantic in July 1933. *Seafarer* is about to enter a patch of thick mist passing the Irish coast on route to America. (Science and Society Picture Library)

The Mollisons off to New York, 22 July 1933. Bathers wave good luck to Amy and Jim in *Seafarer* as they take off from Pendine Sands, Dyfed in Wales, at the start of their great double flight across the Atlantic.
(Science and Society Picture Library)

Photograph inscribed, 'Amy Johnson, the wonder airwoman.' (Science and Society Picture Library)

Amy in her flying suit, standing in front of her beloved *Jason*. (Science and Society Picture Library)

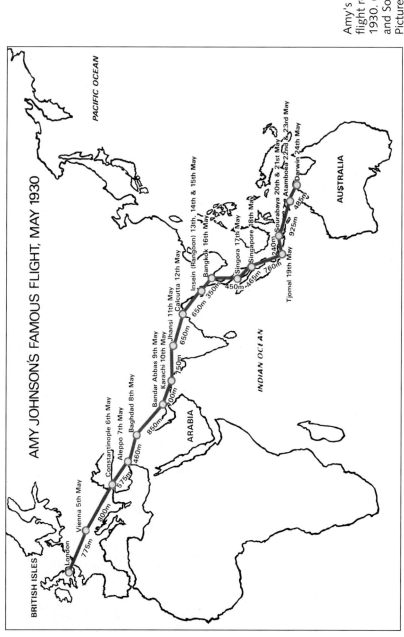

Amy's famous flight route, May 1930. (Science and Society Picture Library)

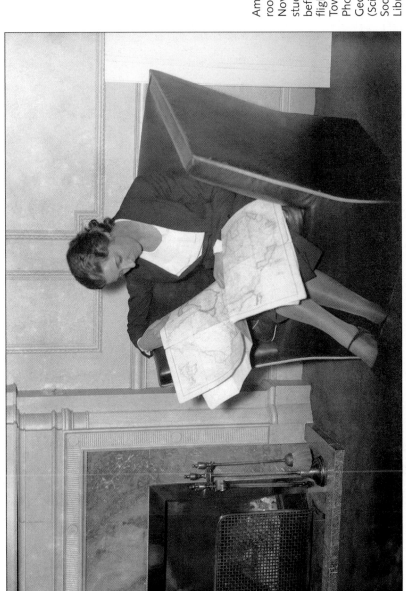

Amy in her hotel room on 17 November 1937, studying maps before her solo flight to Cape Town, South Africa. Photograph by George Woodbine. (Science and Society Picture Library)

Amy photographed with an aeroplane engine.
(Science and Society Picture Library)

New York City gave a tickertape welcome on Broadway to Amy and Jim after their transatlantic crossing in *Seafarer*. (Science and Society Picture Library)

Amy and Amelia Earhart. Amelia befriended Amy, and the two met often during the summer of 1933. (Wright State University Libraries)

Amy.

Miss **AMY JOHNSON'S LONE FLIGHT**

Left Croydon - - May 5th, 1930
Arrived Australia - May 24th, 1930

— -

85, Park Avenue,
Hull, *August*, 1930

Mr. and Mrs. J. W. Johnson and Family thank you and their many friends for congratulations upon Amy's successful flight from London to Australia. and appreciate very much all the kind wishes that have been expressed.

They felt the whole of the British people sympathised with them in the days of suspense and anxiety, and now are very happy to share with everyone the great joy they feel.

Thank you note from Amy's parents, to commemorate the support she received for her solo flight to Australia. (Wright State University Libraries)

Amy's pigskin flying bag, with the letters AJ inset in one side. It was one of the two pieces of luggage retrieved from the crash site in the Thames Estuary on 5th January 1941. (East Riding of Yorkshire Council)

Amy's CBE, which was awarded to her on June 3rd 1930, after her England–Australia solo flight. (East Riding of Yorkshire Council)

Photograph taken at Darwin, shortly after Amy landed on 24th May 1930. Amy is pictured in her famous Gipsy Moth *Jason*. (East Riding of Yorkshire Council)

Studio Portrait of Amy, a copy of which her father kept on his desk. After Amy's death her parents filled a room in their home at Beverley, Yorkshire, with souvenirs. In 1959 her trophies were given by her father to the Borough of Bridlington, and put on permanent exhibition at Sewerby Hall.
(Wright State University Libraries)

tail came gently up and the unwieldy Moth just staggered off the ground, cleared the aerodrome boundary and started climbing safely. 'Amy got away splendidly 7.45' was the cheery message Will Johnson telegraphed to his wife.

Back in Hull next day he wrote to Humphreys, whom he now for the first time addressed as Jack, 'I want to again thank you for all your kindness to Amy, which has extended over such a long period . . . Although she's my own daughter I must say she's a great girl, and I do hope every day will prove as successful as the first until we all meet again at Croydon to see the speck that we lost in the sky yesterday begin to appear again – what a day we'll all have.'

18

STRAIGHT TO INDIA

5–10 May 1930

If Amy's determination or her pride had wavered she might well have abandoned her flight soon after leaving Croydon. For the fumes which escaped into the cockpit whenever she pumped petrol into the gravity tank in the upper wing brought on such distressing attacks of nausea that she felt she could hardly carry on. 'The pump was a very old-fashioned one,' she later explained, 'the action being similar to pumping a bicycle tyre. I had to pump about fifty gallons of petrol every day . . . the only thing that kept me pumping was the ignominy of giving up the flight.'

These remarks are from a narrative lecture which Amy prepared soon after her return to England.[1] Along with another more technical one it provides a fairly reliable account of her trip; more reliable, at all events, than the many journalistic renderings that have since appeared. Some of the true facts about the flight will probably never be established. Her log book gives only the barest outline of her progress, and the log book of her aircraft was already missing when the machine was presented to the Science Museum. Even in her two

---

[1] She herself probably put the lecture together but much of it was indirectly the work of journalists. Some of its passages reproduce almost word for word passages in the 'exclusive story of her flight' which was written for her by newspaper representatives at her various stops.

lectures there are many discrepancies; she was habitually careless about figures, dates and details of fact. For example, as regards her first day's flying, in one of the lectures she states that she reached Vienna 'in good time with following winds,' in the other that she had slight head winds and only reached Vienna after ten hours flying; in her log book the flying time she first recorded was 8 hours 30 minutes but this was changed to 7 hours 30 minutes, while the London papers next day gave her time as 9½ hours.[1] Nevertheless with the help of surviving cables, letters, photographs and contemporary press reports, it is possible to follow the course of the flight more or less accurately, and Amy's lectures provide plenty of colour.

It was late afternoon when whe brought *Jason* down on to the grassy expanse of the aerodrome at Aspern, to the east of Vienna, and she made an excellent landing – an event so unusual that it remained vividly in her memory. 'I was still sufficiently a novice,' she later confessed, 'to regard a really good landing as a piece of luck rather than good management!' At the airport she found herself in an atmosphere of Austrian friendliness mixed with aggressive efficiency. 'The mechanics absolutely refused to let me do anything on my engine,' she related in her narrative lecture, 'and I danced hither and thither explaining what must be done . . . The mechanics meanwhile endeavoured to amuse me by a story of their last lady-pilot visitor who changed into overalls and mounted a ladder, insisting on looking over the engine herself. Now if there's one thing I cannot stand it's the idea of being laughed at behind my back so I left them to it, and went off to see about my passport.' She also had to see about overnight accommodation. There was no hotel anywhere near, and since 'Miss Amy Jason' (a Viennese

---

[1] The normal cruising speed of Amy's 100 h.p. Moth was 90 mph, but with the heavy airscrew she had fitted she flew at less than this.

rendering of her name) meant to start very early next morning she had to find some kind of improvised lodging. Here a kindly caretaker befriended her; he gave up his bed and looked after her 'in a most fatherly way.'

At four o'clock she was up again. 'I thought I was fortunate to find anyone up so early to open the hangar doors, but later never wondered at this because in other countries it seems the custom to start work early. We started up the engine but she didn't sound good, so out had to come my tools . . . and the plugs cleaned.' She was obviously much gratified at being able to find fault with the work of the bossy mechanics.

The second day of the trip took her from Vienna to Constantinople, and her chief memories of the eight-hundred mile flight were the stinging, soaking discomfort of the rainstorms she ran into, and yet more trouble with the petrol pump. A new leak had started and the pumping routine became even more of an ordeal because now at each stroke – and there were forty to every gallon – a jet of petrol spurted into the cockpit. 'I had to do all my pumping,' she admitted, 'with my face over the side of the ship.' (As the flght went on she became accustomed to the petrol fumes, but till the end she found the pumping a very irksome chore.)

She had planned her schedule so as to arrive at each of her main stops well before sunset, and she reached San Stefano, the aerodrome outside Constantinople, with an hour's daylight to spare. In 1930 aviation was still a novelty in Turkey, and the 'airport' did not deserve the name, yet Turkish officialdom was well in evidence and customs clearance took so long that by the time she was allowed to return to her machine darkness had fallen. 'A car was on the aerodrome, and I asked for its headlights to be lit and turned my way,' she related. 'By their light I cleaned and examined the engine and filled up with petrol and oil. The Turks helped me and after about three hours' hard work the machine was ready. No one spoke English, and I made signs to ask if it could be put in a hangar for the night. Before I could protest, several able-bodied Turks had lifted high *Jason*'s tail, and over he went on his nose, heavily weighted as he was in front with petrol and tools etc. Some intuition – or strict training – had caused me, two minutes before, to put the propellor horizontal, so no harm fortunately was done. Some ropes were fetched and *Jason*'s tail lassoed and brought gently to the ground.'

After seeing her aircraft installed in a hangar, Amy went off to the local hotel. 'I had to walk to the nearest village of San Stefano, carrying my luggage, and was directed to the only hotel – a brand new one – so new that they had scarcely any furniture in it, and in my bedroom there was a bed and nothing else. I felt very lonely here and missed my fatherly protector of the evening before.' There was another reason, too, for her forlorness that night. Awaiting her at the aerodrome she had found an unexpected cable from London; so far as we know this was the only one she received at Constantinople. It was a poignant echo from the past which read as follows: 'Best luck and wishes – Franz.'

Besides all this, nagging at her mind was the worry as to whether she would be allowed to continue her flight next day. She had no Turkish flying permit, for when she left England it had still not arrived. Brancker had, however, given her letters of introduction to two influential Turks, whose signatures would probably help her through. Soon after arriving she had persuaded the local Shell representative to take these letters into Constantinople along with her papers, and to try to secure the signatures of the gentlemen in question. He was to come to the hotel at 4 a.m. to return the documents. 'At 4 a.m., faithful to his promise, he arrived full of a long story of troubles and difficulties. One of the men to whom my letters were addressed was found to be in jail, the other one was in his bath and didn't wish to be disturbed. He had finally traced some personage of importance to a box at the theatre and in between the acts had managed to persuade him to sign his name on my papers.'

By 4.30 Amy was on the aerodrome, but to her disgust she was led into an office and told to wait.

'Having no alternative, I waited . . . in a frenzy of impatience, knowing that if I was delayed too long I could not make my scheduled hop for that day. I had intended to make Baghdad . . . I reflected bitterly on the unsportingness of people who could so carelessly spoil all my hard work . . . By 7 o'clock I was more or less resigned to having to make a shorter hop to Aleppo, which meant losing a whole day as there was not enough daylight in these lower latitudes to attempt to make up for lost time unless one flew by night, for which I was in no way equipped. At 7.30 . . . several Turks came noisily into the office and started the examination of my papers.' They obviously meant to be obstructive, and at first she did not hide her exasperation, but then, realising that she must humour them, she eventually won them over by presenting them with spare passport photographs of herself. 'By 8.30 my machine was out of the hangar and I was free to go, but first I had to see to the petrol leak. . . . I knew I couldn't make Baghdad anyhow so I went to rest while a French mechanic (conveniently working on a visiting French plane) mended the leak for me . . . It was 10 o'clock before I got away.'

From Constantinople she had sent a brief cable to her parents and also one to Jack Humphreys: 'All well. Engine fine.' But Humphreys was not relying only on messages from Amy herself for news of her. He had friends at most of the aerodromes on her route to India, and had arranged that they should send him progress reports. He had also undertaken to relay any information he received to Hull ('in case of bad news only phone the office,' Amy's father had warned him), and he was frequently in touch with both parents by telephone and also by letter. 'I understand that all the high Turkish officials saw her off from Constantinople,' he wrote to her mother. 'Martin and I are getting out our roses all ready and Johnnie is the talk of the aerodrome. Everyone is so very pleased about it here and I'm asked a thousand times a day for the latest news. Really it's a marvellous performance. I do hope she gets no reaction when it is accomplished, but in your care that will be OK, I know.' To Will Johnson he wrote 'Stag Lane is going mad with joy: really one hears everywhere "damn good effort" and it really is.'

II

The next stretch of Amy's journey, south-eastwards across Anatolia, was one that she was dreading for it meant crossing the Taurus Mountains. As she approached them she determined, with rash optimism, to try to climb above the cloud layer that hid the peaks. 'I climbed steadily to 8,000 feet, then 10,000 . . . and then more slowly to 11,000 . . . At this height my engine started an ominous coughing and spitting, and I realised that I couldn't go any higher. I descended to 10,000 feet and decided to try to follow the railway through its winding gorges . . . The cold was intense in my open cockpit, and I was glad of my thick Sidcot suit . . . The railway for the most part runs through tunnels and it is quite easy to lose it. In case of a forced landing one hasn't a chance. Even if one could get safely to earth . . . there would be wild bandits of the mountains to contend with . . . I had one very unpleasant moment when threading my way through an exceptionally narrow gorge with the mountains rising sheer on either side of me only a few feet from my wings and towering high above. Rounding a corner I ran straight into a bank of low clouds, and for an awful minute could see nothing at all. In desperation I pushed down the nose of the machine to try to dive below them, and in half a minute – which seemed to me an eternity – I emerged from the cloud at a speed of 120 with one wing down and aiming straight for a wall of rock. Once I could see where I was going it was easy to straighten the machine, but I was rather badly shaken, and not at all sorry to be through the range and out over a vast plain on the other side. I reached Aleppo without further incident.'

Aleppo was one of her happiest stops; everything went well there. At this time Syria was still under the

French mandate, and the Mouslimié aerodrome was a military outpost. Amy found the French Air Force 'most kindly and efficient'. Filling up was quickly carried out from pumps, which she was surprised to find in the desert, 'and as I'd landed fairly early I had plenty of daylight to finish the engine work by. With the aid of French mechanics I carried out an ordinary daily overhaul.' There was also time, just before sunset, for some photography. Amy, in the riding breeches, mannish shirt and pullover that she wore under her Sidcot suit, posed in front of *Jason* looking coy and happy.[1] At Aleppo she felt for the first time that she was 'on the road to adventure', because there she first set eyes on some 'real sheiks from the desert.' They were, she had to admit, 'so dirty and smelly that my dreams of romance were destroyed on the instant, but none the less worth staring at. The staring was quite mutual, but I gave up first as I suddenly remembered my manners. This was my first penetration into the East and I felt its glamour.' That evening one of the tiny cubicles in the officers' barracks was allotted to her, and she slept on the hardest bed she had ever known. 'I felt safe however,' she recalled, 'with bars to the windows and a sentry with loaded gun pacing up and down outside through the whole night.'

At dawn next morning, the fourth day of her flight, she left for Baghdad, nearly five hundred miles across the desert. She was wearing her Sidcot suit as usual, for she did not anticipate how unbearable the heat would be later in the day. And although she knew that such things as dust storms occurred in this part of the world, she was unprepared for the very frightning experience ahead of her. 'All went well until I was almost within sight of Baghdad. The heat was terrific and I was flying at 7,000 feet to avoid the worst of the

---

[1] This photograph was later sent on to her, with the admiring compliments of 'Le Chef de Bataillon Pitault et les Officiers de Mouslimié.'

heat and the bumps. The air was very hazy and visibility poor. Immediately ahead of me appeared a much thicker haze than any I had already encountered and I began to wonder whether it would be too thick for me to see through. Suddenly my machine gave a terrific lurch, the nose dipped, and *Jason* and I dropped a couple of thousand feet. The drop was so sudden and far that the propellor stopped for a few agonising moments, and I was terror-stricken at this unexpected happening . . . The machine dropped again with a sickening feeling as though I were in a lift with the machinery broken . . . again the engine choked and stopped and again picked up, only just in time for still a further dive downwards. In less time than it takes to tell I had dropped to within a few feet from the ground, and was helplessly being blown hither and thither at the mercy of some force I could not understand . . . Sand and dust covered my goggles, my eyes smarted, and I couldn't control the machine sufficiently to keep it straight. . . . I had never been so frightened in my life . . . All at once I felt my wheels touch ground although I could see nothing . . . I throttled down the engine and tried to steer into wind. The machine swayed and bumped and every second I expected to see it turn over or run into some obstacle. To my untold relief it finally came to rest and I switched off the engine and jumped out as quickly as I could, hindered as I was by my parachute . . . I pulled the machine round to face into the wind. The force of the wind started to push it backwards, and I hastily pulled out my luggage from the front cockpit to put behind the wheels. My next job was to try to cover up the engine to keep the dust and sand out of the carburettor, but . . . as fast as I tied down one side of my canvas cover and raced round . . . to tie down the other side, the first side would be torn from its fastenings. It must have been about half an hour before I had finally managed to get the cover fastened on. Then I climbed on the top of the engine and tied my handkerchief over the air-vent hole in the petrol tank . . . I couldn't see a yard in any direction and had no idea where I was or how far from civilisation. Turning my back to the wind, I sat down on *Jason*'s tail to try to keep it down, and settled myself to wait for some lull in the storm. Once I heard dogs barking and my terror broke out afresh as I had heard that these desert dogs wouldn't hesitate to attack and tear their victims in pieces. I therefore pulled out my small revolver and waited . . .

'After three hours the wind began to abate and soon I could see quite a distance ahead. In terror lest I should miss the opportunity, I raced round collecting my luggage and uncovering the engine, tools falling on the sand in my haste and getting covered up at once. . . . The engine started at the first swing of the propellor, and feeling devoutly thankful for this piece of good luck . . . I opened up and took off, going in the direction in which I thought Baghdad would be. If I had gone in the wrong direction I should have headed into hundreds of miles of desert . . .

'Within a short time I was in sight of Baghdad . . . I came in to land, but immediately *Jason* touched the ground he swung round and sank down on one wing. Jumping out to see the damage I found one of the undercarriage struts had sheared in two. I had probably strained it when landing in the desert at about 110 miles per hour . . . I set off to walk to the hangars I could see in the far distance. The heat was such as I had never before experienced, and I must have looked a pretty sight. . . . Before I had gone far a motor lorry came out to meet me and oh, the joy it was again to meet English people. This was the Imperial Airways aerodrome, and I was taken into a cool and comfortable lounge where I was stripped of my Sidcot suit and quickly given tea and cold drinks. The luxury of it! Suddenly I thought of poor *Jason* and his broken leg. But I was not allowed to worry. Efficient mechanics wheeled him into the hangar, and the damage was inspected. I was then informed of the sad news that the damage couldn't repaired, and that I couldn't get a new part in Baghdad. I must wait for a new part to be sent from Karachi, the nearest Moth depot. I was heartbroken. But the Manager of Imperial

Airways at Baghdad [Mr Phelps] was a most resourceful man, and he promised me to do what he could. He sent the broken strut over to the Air Force aerodrome at Hinaidi – quite near – and there about ten machines worked hard all night . . . to make me a new strut. When I came out to the aerodrome the following morning *Jason* was in excellent trim, with the engine overhauled and looking bright and tidy after a good wash. Without such sporting help as this I could never have accomplished my flight.'

It was at Baghdad that Amy first took to wearing shorts – a borrowed pair – as the most comfortable flying kit for hot countries. And for the first time since leaving England she was able to get away from the aerodrome and see something of the nearby city. 'At Baghdad I went for a drive and enjoyed a good dinner on the roof of the hotel overlooking the river,' she remembered. 'After this most refreshing change I felt much fitter for renewing my flight.'

III

As she flew on from Baghdad, following the Tigris towards the Persian Gulf, her father in Hull was writing to Jack Humphreys: 'Naturaly I do worry some, but will try and get your confidence and feel sure Amy will get there; really I do feel it, but of course there are some risks. Tonight's papers will be sensational as they have got some reports from the Press Association about her landing in the desert . . . Thanks for your phone messages; you have no idea how welcome your voice sounds.' In another letter, also to Humphreys, he wrote less anxiously: 'Glad to say we are managing to bear the suspense and excitement very well so far, but I can see it getting very keen before the end of next week. What a girl and what a trip; Hull is full of excitement over it, it is the main topic everywhere.'

This was now the fifth day of Amy's flight, and in Fleet Street the 'Lone Girl Flyer' was beginning to attract a certain amount of attention. And Jimmy

Martin – so a remark of Will Johnson's indicates – was already in touch with some of the London newspapers. 'Have had Mr Martin through in his car today and we enjoyed having a talk with him,' he mentioned to Humphreys. 'I told him if there was anything I could do in London re the *Mail* or anything else, I could come after next Thursday.'

Crossing with this letter was a scribbled note to Amy's father from Humphreys, which shows that at this stage her 'tutor' was being treated, by some of the press, as her spokesman-in-chief. In his excitement over Johnnie's adventure in the desert Humphreys was almost incoherent. 'This morning's news has surpassed me,' he wrote. 'I did not expect her to do so well she's great and I'm so very pleased that her efforts are so clever. And I think – as Martin – that her stories etc. are worth a good deal of cash to her, and since they would not help before they must pay afterwards. Pass on all cables and calls to your press and rub it in, making them realise all that this brave lass is doing. Do not sell anything for I've had some good offers so far but not good enough, and as the days go by the keenness will get greater for her story. Do you realise that she will break a record tomorrow if she arrives in India, the quickest time for a light aeroplane.'

IV

On 9 May, the day when Humphreys wrote, Amy's objective was Bandar Abbas, the fishing port at the eastern end of the Persian Gulf which she had chosen as a stopping place 'by the simple expedient of dividing the distance between Baghdad and Karachi in two.' 'The weather was excellent that day, and if it hadn't been for the engine spluttering all the way, I should quite have enjoyed my flight along the beautiful though dangerous shores of the Persian Gulf. The sea is a vivid blue, from which rise jagged mountains looking every bit like the teeth of a giant saw . . . There is, however, no single place where an aeroplane could safely land . . .

STRAIGHT TO INDIA

'I reached Bandar Abbas in good time. Circling round and round in the bumpy air I searched for an aerodrome. Finding none, I became anxious and looked out for a space large and flat enough to land. At last I found one – fairly large but not too level – near which was a large house . . . I landed fast, as usual, and rather heavily, also as usual . . . and to my horror the left wing drooped and trailed the ground. This time it was the bolt securing the top of the new strut which had sheared and I couldn't see any hope of help in such a God-forsaken place as Bandar Abbas . . . I landed with a very bad headache and I was tired and hot and dirty and worried about the engine. . . . Very slowly and wearily I started to walk towards the large house I had seen from the air. As I drew near, I saw a group of people coming out to meet me and I nearly cried with relief when I discerned a white man amongst them.'

The house was the British Consulate and the white man was the Consul, Mr G.A. Richardson, who explained that the aerodrome was no longer in regular use and that he had not been forewarned of Amy's coming. But he assured her that he had an excellent man called David who looked after his own car and who would do everything he could for her aircraft; he then led her into the Consulate and introduced her to his wife and daughter. 'My headache was so bad that they took me straight upstairs to a cool room where they made me lie down and massaged my head, and in a very short time I was fast asleep. I woke a couple of hours later much refreshed and with my headache quite gone, but to my consternation I found it was about dark, and I remembered poor *Jason*, abandoned in the middle of the aerodrome. Descending the stair I went outside, and to my immense astonishment saw *Jason* standing up straight on both legs. Running out to the machine, round which was a large crowd, I saw the Consul who introduced me to David. My first question was how had he repaired the broken bolt, and David told me in great pride and in broken English that many many years ago there used to be English RAF machines on this aerodrome. David, being very interested, had made it his business to hang round the aerodrome and learn as much as he could – incidentally he appears to have started a collection of spare parts, and from this hidden treasure trove he had produced the bolt for *Jason*. Too relieved to be critical, I laughed and thanked him.

'I was very anxious to start work on the engine, but the Consul insisted on my having dinner first, and he pointed out that later a full moon would rise which would be of great help. Returning to the house we were greeted by numerous white-coated Persian officials who had turned out in force to subject me to a rigorous customs examination. I had been warned that the Persians loved to exert their authority and think nothing of holding you up for really no reason at all. Sir Alan Cobham had been held up at this same place for two whole days for no reason he knew of. I was advised to be very polite and flatter them exceedingly, so I ran to fetch all my papers and smiled at them and generally tried to win them to my cause. After much talk amongst themselves they asked me where my health certificate was. I replied that I hadn't one and had never been asked for one before. They then informed me that I ought to be carrying all papers that a ship carries and that a health certificate was indispensable. I was then asked whether I had been vaccinated, and on hearing in the negative, I was told I should not be allowed to proceed until I had been both vaccinated and inoculated against smallpox, typhoid, etc., etc.. With the greatest difficulty I kept control of my temper, and endeavoured to explain that I should be hundreds of miles away from Persia the next day and that whatever diseases I might catch I should take out of Persia, and why should they go to such a lot of trouble and expense to protect another country, and so on. After nearly two hours' talking they suddenly capitulated and gave in on every point. Before I realised it, I was signing my own health certificate and the officials were bowing and bidding me good night. The

Consul said he had never known such leniency before and I was more than lucky.

'Next we went in to dinner which was a long meal because the electric lights went out in the middle – the man in charge of the power house had gone with the rest of the community to see my machine – and we had to finish by candle-light. It was 10.30 by the time we had finished dinner and I insisted on going straight out to work . . . The aerodrome was so bumpy that I was almost jolted out of the lorry which drove me across to my machine, and I no longer wondered that *Jason* had damaged himself landing on such sharp ridges . . . The moon had risen and shed sufficient light for me to see to work, helped by my electric torch for the "inside" jobs . . .

'David was waiting to help me, and balanced precariously on petrol tins we set about overhauling the engine. I soon found the cause of that day's rough running – the centre of one of the plugs had blown clean out. Work proceeded smoothly but rather slowly as we were hampered by the lack of light and the sand blowing over the tools, and the multitude of large and small insects creeping in and out amongst them attracted by the light of my torch . . . By 2.30 a.m. [this was the morning of 10 May] I had finished and went off to bed, not feeling in the least tired as the air was wonderfully cool and fresh . . . At 4.0 a.m. I was up again, eager to continue my flight as that day I expected to reach Karachi.'

Karachi was the first major point where Amy's time would be compared with Hinkler's, and it now seemed almost certain that she would break his England-India record. But she had an anxious day's flying, over the wild coastline of southern Persia, and then of Baluchistan, for during the seven-hundred-mile hop her engine again began spluttering and coughing. In spite of this she reached Karachi safely and landed in triumph; she had improved on Hinkler's record by a startling margin. He had got to India on the eighth day of his flight; she on her sixth. And this was not merely because of her 'short cut': Hinkler had averaged less than six hundred miles per day while she had averaged seven hundred. Soon the repercussions of her remarkable feat were to burst upon her, but just after she climbed out of the cockpit she was shaken by a reminder of the knife-edge between success and failure. She lifted the cowling of her aircraft to investigate the cause of the engine trouble. 'On the inside of the cowling,' she related, 'was a rainbow patch where one of the plugs had been shorting across. The most excellent David must have put two washers on one of the plugs instead of one, thus making it protrude beyond the others and almost touch the metal cowling . . . How lucky I had been again. Had the plug been one on the other side, there would have been grave risk of fire as the carburettor is on the other side of the engine. Even as it was, I had a very lucky escape, and all for so small a thing.'

19

THE WILL AND THE WAY

11–18 May 1930

THE BRITISH GIRL LINDBERGH . . . So the London headlines hailed Amy as soon as the news of her England to India record was out, and at once her name echoed around the world. Even during her overnight stop at Karachi she already found herself being treated as a celebrity. She was pressed to stay at Government House, and was able to do so on her own terms: 'Pleading fatigue and no clothes, I dined in my room and went to bed instead of attending the large dinner party to which I had been invited.' Meantime she had no worries concerning her aircraft for it was being serviced by experts at the Drigh Road aerodrome, and next morning she looked happy and refreshed when she was photographed clutching a bouquet presented to her by the Chief Officer of the Karachi Municipality.

It seems that only one small accident spoilt the enjoyment of her stay; she broke the chain of a swastika emblem, a good-luck token from her mother,[1] which she had been wearing round her neck since she left England. She could still wear it as a brooch but apparently believed that its efficiency was no longer so potent, for she later pointed out that 'by coincidence' it was only after this mishap that her 'real troubles' began.

[1] In 1930 the swastika was not yet identified with Naziism.

AMY JOHNSON

She was given a cheering send-off from Drigh Road; an aircraft of the RAF and also a Moth flown by the local de Havilland agent escorted her briefly eastwards. Then she was alone again, flying over barren, featureless stretches of desert towards Allahabad, nearly a thousand miles distant. Before long however she realised that she was not alone; huge birds were following her, flying at a great height and apparently keeping up with her easily. She noticed their bald heads and guessed they must be vultures. She hoped to recognise Allahabad from its position on the Ganges, and had been warned that the river would be much shrunken as it was the end of the dry season. 'Shortly before the time anticipated there lay ahead of me a sparkling river and a town. Gliding down I searched for the aerodrome, but couldn't find it. At last I decided to land in a large space, and no sooner had my wheels touched ground than an enormous horde of screaming natives rushed towards me . . . I sat tight and waited. Soon I saw an Englishman and I asked him where I was, Jhansi, he replied. How far was Allahabad? About two hundred miles. Thanking him I turned my machine round and took off rapidly before the crowd had time to spread over the open space. After an hour's flying, the petrol from my second reserve tank gave out, and I saw from the gauge in the remaining tank that I had only sufficient petrol for another hour's flying. Realising I must have had strong head winds I saw I could not possibly reach Allahabad in an hour, and I therefore very reluctantly had to decide to return to Jhansi. I didn't relish landing in the same place as before, and so looked about for a better spot. I chose the largest space I could find which was near houses and landed.'

The 'houses' were a military barracks, the 'space' was a parade ground, and as the time was late afternoon many officers and men were about. One of the officers soon afterwards gave the following lively account of her arrival. 'The plane was down. Down on the regimental parade ground, and charging at high speed towards the barracks. It twisted its way round trees, barely missed an iron telegraph post, scattered a group of men waiting to mount guard, smashed into the name board outside the regimental offices, and then came to rest wedged between two of the barrack buildings. There was a race to reach it. From the cockpit climed a figure – it was a girl – young, almost a child, fair, wearing only a shirt, an ill-fitting pair of khaki shorts, socks and shoes, and a flying helmet. The skin on her face, arms and legs was burnt and blistered by the sun, and tears were not far from her tired eyes . . . "I am two days ahead of Bert Hinkler's time so far," she said, "and now I'm afraid everything is ruined." Inspection of the plane, however, revealed that the damage was not irreparable, and a new light of battle appeared in her eyes. There was much to be done: the broken wing must be mended, the old oil replaced by new, petrol procured and poured into the almost empty tanks. Nuts and screws must be tightened and adjusted, and the sparking plugs changed . . . About 9.0 p.m. a halt was called. Miss Johnson was rushed in a car to a bungalow nearby, where a bath and a change of clothing awaited her. Then dinner . . . "I left London six days ago," she said, "and haven't once had more than three hours' sleep." And a little later, "This is my first meal today."[1] After dinner they returned to the aircraft and found it surrounded by a small crowd of Indian women, who begged that "Miss Sahib" would just touch them with her hand, a request which, tired as she was, Miss Johnson cheerfully acceded to.'

That night Amy slept little. 'Jhansi was hotter than I had ever imagined a place on earth could be. I found it impossible to sleep indoors, so dragged out my bed on to the lawn. I was overtired and I suppose it was being out in the open that kept giving me the illusion that I was flying and had fallen asleep . . . I kept sitting up frantically in bed thinking I was just about to crash.'

---

[1] While flying Amy kept herself going with sandwiches, fruit, tea from a Thermos, and occasional chocolate and glucose sweets.

But at dawn, as usual, she was up and off again. She landed at Allahabad to refuel, as she had not been able to take off from Jhansi with full load; then straight on to Calcutta. There, as at Karachi, the servicing of her aircraft was taken off her hands and next morning she again left early, despite local fog, hoping to reach Rangoon before evening, though she had been warned she would run into 'sticky weather' – in other words the first of the monsoon rains.

II

It was now that Amy's troubles started 'in earnest'. After crossing the marshes of the Ganges delta she flew southwards, following the jungle-smothered coastline towards Burma. At some point on the flight to Rangoon she had to cross the line of mountains just inland from the coast to reach the valley of the Irrawaddy, but she hoped to postpone this crossing until she reached the lower hills at the southerly end of the range.

'My plan however, was impossible as the weather ahead became so bad. Retracing my way, I then attempted to cross the mountains near Akyab . . . Climbing above one layer of clouds, I threaded my way amongst their enormous piled up masses, expecting every minute to run into a mountain I could not see. After half an hour I calculated I ought to be on the farther side, so began to come down through the clouds. It seemed almost a miracle that at this moment the clouds should part, and I saw far below the gleam of a large river. Circling round and round whilst gliding down, in order to keep this precious bit of river in sight, I was at last just over it and following its course southwards. I knew of course it must be the Irrawaddy and I was able to pick up my exact position on my map. After a time I had to leave the river, strike across country, and then pick up a railway. The rain was falling in torrents and I could barely see where I was going. When I reached the railway I flew almost touching the tops of the stations, scaring the people I could see waiting for trains, all with umbrellas up. At last I was nearing Rangoon . . .

'I had to land on the racecourse, and I had no idea of its position, except that according to my map it was near the railway and this side of the town. I flew on and on, right through the town and to the coastline beyond without seeing anything like a racecourse, except for one track which appeared much too small. In desperation I returned to this place and tried to land there as I couldn't find anywhere else and both daylight and my petrol were failing rapidly . . . Throttling down my engine, I glided in to land. Out of the corner of my eye I saw a large building with crowds of people on the balcony seemingly waving to me, and I was quite encouraged as I thought I had found the right place and was being welcomed. Too late, I realised that the space was much too small, and . . . at the last moment I saw goal-posts in the field and a ditch round the outside. The trees round were too high to allow me to open up my engine and take off again, I had no alternative but to land, *Jason* ran smoothly past the goal-posts head on for the ditch, into which he buried his head and came to a standstill with a loud noise and a great shudder. This was too much for me . . . I cried like a baby.'

She had come to earth on the playing-ground of the Government Technical Institute at Insein (five miles to the north of Rangoon); the oval she had mistaken for a racecourse was a running track and the large building was the Institute. The people who had waved were the teachers and pupils trying to point out the way to the racecourse itself. 'I was quite unable to cope with the situation that night, and begged to be allowed to go to bed at once. First of all, however, it was imperative to move *Jason* to a more sheltered place and this was a much harder job than it sounds. The damge proved to be a broken propeller, a ripped tyre, broken undercarriage strut and much damaged wing. We had to lift the machine out of the ditch, carry it across the compound, make a bridge over the ditch and carry it over into a grove of trees on the far side, where it was more or less sheltered. This done, I went to bed and refused to be disturbed even for dinner.

'Next morning I got up to think out what could be done. The Head of the Institute [Mr F. Shaw] was exceedingly kind and placed his own and his pupils' services at my disposal even though they were in the middle of exam time. None of them, however, knew the first thing about aeroplanes. With their help I took off the damaged wing and had it carried into the Insitute workroom. We stripped off the fabric, and found several of the ribs were completely shattered. The matter seemed hopeless. The rain was pouring in torrents, and we were all wet through, the thousands of insects were a torment and I saw my flight a hopeless failure . . .

'Then in walked an Englishman, and I was introduced to the Forestry Inspector. Picking up the bits of broken wood, he said "I'll see to this part if Mr Shaw . . . can see to the repairing of the metal parts." I hadn't much faith that they could do any good, but agreed to let them try. Picking up all the broken bits he took them away. Then we stripped the damaged metal parts and he set his pupils on to weld the broken metal, make new bolts and straighten out the bent fairing. In the meantime I set to work to put on my spare propellor and clean up the engine which was caked up with mud and dirt from the ditch . . .

'The following morning my Forestry friend returned bringing with him several new wooden ribs for the wing. He had glued together all the broken pieces, then chosen some wood as near like mine as possible and made new parts exactly to match. We at once set about fitting them in the wing and soon had the framework tacked and glued together. The next thing was to cover it with fabric.' But Amy's supply of linen for emergency repairs had been used up at Jhansi, and in any case a large piece was needed. Then someone remembered that the men's shirts in most common use at the time were made of war-surplus Aeroplane Fabric. 'With great glee about twenty of these shirts were produced which we tore into strips and joined together. We sent for several seamstresses from Rangoon who worked hard piecing them together and covering the wing. Even then out task was not finished. The linen cover had to be doped to stiffen and strengthen it, and I had no dope left, nor could we get any. We solved this difficulty by sending to the principal chemist in Rangoon a small tin . . . in which there was a very small portion of the dope left from the repairs at Jhansi. This chemist mixed up some stuff to match the smell, and although it was much too thin, yet two coats of it served our purpose.

'Now the repairs were complete, but as it was impossible to take off from the confined space of the playing field, the aircraft had to be transported to the racecourse some miles away. We borrowed the local fire-engine, carried the machine through the compound to the road, and there lifted his tail on to the back of the fire engine, fastening it as securely as we could and doing everything possible to lessen vibration as we were warned the roads were very bad . . . As many of us accompanied it as there was room for on the wagon, and the procession at last set out at a pace of five miles an hour, in torrents of rain, preceded by a native policeman on a bicycle who importantly cleared the road ahead of us of all traffic. We all had umbrellas up, even the policeman and every ten minutes the procession stopped whilst one of us got down to examine *Jason*'s tyre . . . The burst tyre had been vulcanised in Rangoon as we couldn't get a new outercover . . . Fortunately we were not too tired to see the funny side of it, and funny indeed we must have looked.

'Just as darkness fell we reached the racecourse so we tied *Jason* securely down and returned to get some sleep. At dawn we were all out at the racecourse again, and I prepared to take *Jason* up for test. I must admit I fastened my parachute on very carefully, as it wouldn't have been a bit surprising if the roughly repaired wing had collapsed when it encountered the strain of flying. I tested the machine thoroughly, and was quite satisfied although the new propeller was not quite so efficient as the other one which had been specially made for my flight. It was the greatest luck in the world that the machine flew "hands off" and didn't need any adjustment in the rigging, as we had no instruments to help us.'

III

Thus it was that on the morning of Friday 16 May, the twelfth day since Amy left Croydon, all was ready for her to continue her flight. The enforced stay at Insein had of course eliminated her two-day lead over Hinkler, who by his longer route had reached Rangoon eleven days after his start. But they were now neck and neck, and when she set out again, for Bangkok, there was still a hope – a very slender one – that she might be able to improve upon his record time of fifteen and a half days for the solo flight from England to Australia.

'From Rangoon to Bangkok I had to fly over similar country to that between Calcutta and Rangoon. I had to cross a mountain range, and again the weather was about as bad as it could be . . . I made for Moulmein, where I was told I should find a pass through the mountains. I couldn't even see Moulmein for the rain and clouds, never mind find a pass . . . If I was to get through at all there was nothing for it but to fly through the clouds. Climbing up to nine thousand feet I set off . . . expecting all the time to crash when I hit a mountainside . . . I was three hours flying through these mountains which, in fine weather, could be crossed in about half an hour. At last I emerged over the jungle-covered plains on the other side, only to discover that I was miles off my course, even off my strip map which only shows a small margin on either side of the proper course, with nothing but instinct to guide me. I knew that if I flew south I must reach the sea sooner or later. After flying for some time I saw ahead of me a network of canals which I could easily pick upon my map, and after that it was easy work to find Don Muang aerodrome at Bangkok.'

On arriving at Don Muang, according to news reports,

Amy seemed 'really dead beat'. Crowds of Siamese were waiting to welcome her and a special train was ready to take her into the capital where she had been invited to stay the night. But she declined all this and wisely remained at the aerodrome to supervise the servicing of her aircraft. After a meal and a short rest she found that the mechanics of the Siamese Air Force who had started the refuelling had done everything wrong, and there had to be much draining, filtering, and refilling. 'It was now quite dark and we had to work by the light of my small torch, which attracted enormous numbers of insects. It was dreadfully hot and everything was wet and miserable and I had the greatest difficulty in making myself understood. One man spoke English, and he had to translate what I said to a man who spoke French, who in turn translated it to the mechanics in Siamese.' Amy's helpers were cheerful and willing but most unreliable, as she discovered next morning when a few moments after take-off – again into stormy weather – her top cowling flew open. 'So down I had to come with full load, the first time I had had to do such a thing and I was a bit worried. I was devoutly thankful for the large aerodrome but the landing after all proved quite easy. The cowling was well and securely fastened and I took off once more.

'I had a long hop of nine hundred miles ahead of me to Singapore. I followed the coastline for hundreds of miles, flying so low that I was almost touching the waves, and keeping my eye glued to the narrow strip of sand . . . Once I looked at my compass and found it first pointing to North, then East, South, then West, and realised at last I was flying round and round a flooded field, having lost the coastline for one second. More by good luck than anything else I found it again and kept on . . . I couldn't wear my goggles as the rain made them impossible to see through, and my eyes were smarting terribly with the force of the rain. Suddenly I ran straight out of this terrible weather into a perfectly fine stretch, and below me I found Singora, where I decided to land, as it was getting late and Singapore was still 450 miles away.

'The sand on the aerodrome was so soft that *Jason* almost turned over on landing, and I couldn't taxi through it. For once I was able to carry out my overhaul in daylight but . . . I had to wait till the sun had gone down a bit, because there was no shade on the aerodrome and it was impossible to work in the mid-day heat. Fine sand was blowing all the time I was working and the Siamese brought picnic parties out and ice-cream stalls, squatting themselves round the roped-in ring made by the very efficient police. All these small people laughed at everything, and I even had to laugh myself at things which weren't really amusing . . . Fortunately there were petrol and oil supplies there which had been left over by some previous aviator, but there was no one at all capable of helping me fill up. This was the first time I had had nobody at all even to hand things up to me and unscrew nuts etc., and I found I hadn't the strength to undo many of the nuts and bolts which had to be unfastened. There was one Siamese who spoke English and who had been specially sent down by the Siamese Government to look after me. I asked him to find me a strong man and a Siamese was pushed out from among the crowd. So soon as he had undone one plug, or nut, or bolt, he ran away as though extremely shy, so that when I wanted something else undoing, I had to look round for him and ask for the strong man. This happened so often that the crowd round me learned these two words, and so soon as I looked round there was a general outcry for 'Strong man, Strong man", to everyone's intense amusement . . . Though I was hot and tired I found myself laughing with them.'

Amy had decided that since the surface of the aerodrome was so sandy she must use an adjoining bit of road for her take-off run next day and she enlisted the help of some of the onlookers in moving Jason into place at one end of it before the refuelling was done. 'I was on the aerodrome early the following morning, to be faced with a problem which awed me. Siamese in their hundreds, or thousands as it seemed to me, had flocked in . . . The narrow road was lined about eight deep with people in dazzling robes . . . on either side . . . Hundreds of children sat and laughed and played, behind them stood row upon row of saffron-clad priests, chattering women and curious men. Right in front were houses and a row of tall trees which had to be cleared before I was safe. Added to these difficulties was the fact that from the cockpit of a Moth aeroplane you cannot see straight ahead, but must look over one side . . . I shouted and waved, everybody argued and little by little the narrow lane was widened. But it was still most dangerously narrow, and not only was I risking my own life but the lives of perhaps hundreds of these ignorant and unsuspecting people. I started my engine and with my heart in my mouth I rushed between those human hedges. What a swerve meant I hardly dared to think. Worse was to come. There is a petrol vent pipe which leads outside my machine to the left, and because of which I had recently trained myself to look out to the right. But on this occasion, owing to the stress of the moment, I had returned to my long established habit of looking out to the left, and as I began to move I got a spray of petrol in my eyes which half blinded me. How I kept the machine straight and cleared those trees ahead of me I shall never know. My relief to be in the air was unspeakable. I turned and flew over the crowds below, waving to them and wondering if any had realised their danger.'

The flight from Singora to Singapore was uneventful. Amy's course should have taken her down the west coast of the Malay Peninsula, but she was told it had rained at Penang for a fortnight without stopping, so she chose instead to follow the east coast, where she found the weather 'not quite impossible'. As she neared Singapore she caught sight of several aircraft flying towards her, and was heartened to realise that they were Moth seaplanes which had come out to meet her.

Awaiting her arrival at the Seletar aerodrome, on the afternoon of Sunday 18 May, was a crowd of several hundred Europeans, the women dressed as though for a garden party; when she landed there was a waving of bright handkerchiefs and parasols while the men waved their topees. One of the reporters present was struck by the contrast between the appearance of Amy herself and that of the dressy ladies who had come to welcome her. 'Miss Johnson smiled through the oil on her face,' he wrote, 'looking more like an Indian than an Englishwoman. She was wearing a man's khaki shorts, mens' stockings, much oil-stained heavy brogue shoes, and a drill jacket, under which her long-sleeved purple blouse was pinned at her throat by her mother's swastika brooch. She had a pepper-and-salt topee, and her face and hands were burnt almost brick red . . . All started clapping their hands. It seemed as though Miss Johnson had just finished singing at a charity concert. It was a strangely quiet, dignified welcome. The now famous aviatrix waved a deprecatory hand, produced a large linen handkerchief from her pocket, and vigorously wiped the oil and perspiration from her face, turning to the women as if to say "Is it all off, dears?".' This vivid little sketch, revealing as a candid snapshot, shows that Amy, however exhausted she felt at the end of the fourteenth day of her flight, was enjoying the new experience of being a public figure.

20

'THE LONE GIRL FLYER'
18–24 May 1930

'Cannot break record, weather dreadful . . .'. So Amy cabled to her father from Singapore, on the fourteenth day of her flight, when she knew that she no longer had any hope of bettering Hinkler's Australia time. 'You are wonderful. Nobody worrying about record . . .' her parents cabled back, and their message echoed the crescendo of heroine-worship that was now surging across the front pages. Already for several days, all over the world, the press had been blazoning out news of the 'lone girl flyer' and already the spectacle of Amy's courage, as she battled her way across Asia, had seized hold of the public's imagination.

Just how and when did the press take possession of Amy? There are two main landmarks, the first during her enforced stop in Burma, when the *Daily Mail* bought the rights to the exclusive story of her flight, and the second after she reached Australia, when the same newspaper engaged her services for the period immediately after her return to England. The *Daily Mail* did not however bring off these coups unchallenged; in spite of a slow start the bidding had been quite lively. At first Jimmy Martin had hawked the rights to her story from office to office without success, but the interest that suddenly quickened when she reached Karachi caused a hurried sharpening of claws in Fleet Street, and by the day she crash-landed at Insein Martin had provisionally clinched a deal with the *News of the World*, subject of course to Amy's confirmation. On 13 May he cabled to her, 'Have disposed of world rights to your own complete story for splendid sum to *News of the the World* . . . please confirm my action by cable.'

She received this cable in the rain-sodden turmoil at Insein, while she and her helpers were feverishly patching up her damaged aircraft, and a hurried exchange of cables between herself and Martin took place. It was a complicated situation, for other newspapers, both British and Australian, were cabling their offers direct to her. Before she left Insein however the rights to her story had been sold for a much more splendid sum than the *News of the World* was prepared to give;[1] the *Daily Mail* had agreed to pay two thousand pounds for them.

In London Amy's father had joined Martin to handle the final negotiations with the *Mail* and on 15 May he wrote to Associated Newspapers: 'I hereby agree on behalf of my daughter, Miss Amy Johnson, for whom I have power to act, that in consideration of the payment of the sum of £2,000 to me on her behalf the Associated Newspapers shall have exclusively all rights in Miss Johnson's own story of her flight . . . I will attend at the *Daily Mail* offices tomorrow, when a formal agreement will be entered into.'

Next evening Amy's parents, and with them Jimmy Martin, celebrated at the Strand Palace Hotel, and they sent off a jubilant cable to Amy: 'Martin here. Story two thousand. Cheers! Never mind that ditch. Your luck is still in. Keep smiling.' But a second cable, sent off by Martin at about the same time had nothing to do with newspaper deals and was not jubilant. It brought Amy the distressing news that Jack Humphreys had had a

---

[1] Letters between Martin and the Sunday newspapers show that the splendid sum was five hundred pounds, with the prospect of another five hundred for the story of the return flight – if it took place.

most unfortunate accident and was in hospital: at Stag Lane an aircraft with its engine running had jumped the chocks when he happened to be near by, and his right arm (which he had raised to protect himself) had been struck by the propeller and badly broken.

These cables reached Amy at Singapore, along with a stream of congratulations. The trickle that started at Constantinople with good wishes from Franz had become a steadily increasing flow, which now included greetings from officials and celebrities; during her progress across India she received messages from Lord Thomson (the Secretary of State for Air), Field Marshal Sir William Birdwood (Commander-in-Chief in India), the Duchess of Bedford on behalf of the Air League, and a party of Women Labour MPs. At Singapore, too, yet more business propositions arrived, and Will Johnson cabled that the *Daily Express* was offering £500 plus expenses for ten aviation lectures. 'Leave all arrangements in England to you re lectures etcetera,' Amy cabled back. But it was far more difficult to deal with the Australian offers and invitations: she was being pressed to continue her flight to Sydney and had been offered as much as five thousand pounds for an Australian tour. By now she had finally abandoned the idea of trying to fly straight back to England from Darwin but she could not be sure whether by grasping at Australian opportunities, which on the face of it seemed very lucrative, she would be sacrificing prospects at home that would be even better if she returned promptly, while interest was still running high. She replied to Australia postponing her final decisions and at the same time cabled to seek advice from her father. Her urgent need for an adviser at closer range was fortunately met within the next few days when Wakefields offered to entrust the management of her affairs in Australia to Cyril Westcott, their General Manager in Australia and New Zealand.

AMY JOHNSON

II

At Singapore, where Amy stayed for the night of Sunday 18 May, she did not have the scramble of servicing her own aircraft, for she was able to entrust it to RAF experts. 'I told them about the wing damaged at Rangoon and asked them to examine it. It was fortunate I took this precaution as the rear spar was found to be cracked. Having a [Moth] wing to spare they kindly gave it to me, and I set off on my next day's flight with more confidence.

'I was so tired by this time, that my sole thought was to reach Australia so that I could sleep for as long as I wanted. My idea of bliss was to go to bed and have my sleep out, and I still had 2,400 miles to cover. This day when I left Singapore I had made up my mind to get to Sourabaya, a thousand miles away in the Dutch East Indies . . . But alas for my plans . . . I ran into such bad weather again that I wasted a lot of valuable time in following the coast instead of taking a direct course through the islands. At last I got to the tip of the Island of Banka, and decided that I would try to make up for lost time by a short cut across the Java Sea . . .

'The weather ahead seemed fairly clear and my engine was running well. After half an hour or so, when I was well out of sight of land, I ran into heavy clouds and rain and was forced lower and lower. The wind began to blow and the waves rose . . . the clouds got thicker and the rain fierce . . . It was equally black in every direction. I seemed hemmed in by blackness . . . Unable to go on, equally unable to turn back or to stand still, I circled round and round. I was more than terrified . . . I knew that thousands of hungry sharks were waiting . . . Then suddenly in one direction the sky cleared. The sun shone through and, outlined on the black cloud opposite, was a perfect rainbow. With thanks in my heart I darted for the clear patch . . .

'I had long given up my attempt to keep on a compass course across the sea, and merely tried to get to the coast as quickly as possible . . . Over the coast, the weather was better . . . My next problem however was where to land that night. I knew I couldn't reach Sourabaya . . . The country is a mass of rice-fields and sugar plantations and there isn't a hope of bringing off a successful forced landing. I was getting very anxious and thought of coming down on the beach when I saw what seemed like a large factory beside which was a fairly large and flat piece of ground.

'I came down and landed, and I had again a remarkable escape. Ahead of me I saw a wide ditch towards which I was racing at great speed. It seemed as though nothing could save a repetition of my misfortune at Insein, but to my surprise my speed was very quickly checked and in an incredibly short time *Jason* came to rest. Amazed but very glad I jumped out and saw that the ground was very heavy and sodden and I concluded that it must have been the state of the ground that had slowed me up . . . Only the next day quite by accident I discovered there were long rows of sharp bamboo stakes in the ground, which had struck in the lower wings as I raced over them, tearing the farbic and acting as a brake. I was not sorry, as the slits were easier to mend than would have been the damage had I fallen in the ditch again. I had to mend them with sticking plaster as I had no fabric left.'

She had landed on Java, about two hundred miles from Batavia and just alongside a sugar factory at Tjomal. The 'fairly large and flat piece of ground' was a plot which had been laid out for a new house for the factory's Dutch manager; the bamboo stakes marked the outline of the projected building. 'The Dutch were very kind to me and the following morning the Manager gallantly had all the stakes pulled up and the ditches filled in as I was worried about the take-off.' Amy's luggage was meanwhile taken by car to the nearest emergency landing ground and she flew there to pick it up, then flew on to the aerodrome at Semarang where she refuelled. Semarang was a stopping place for the three-engined Fokkers of the Dutch air mail service and one of them happened to be there; it was bound for

Sourabaya and the pilot offered to show Amy the way. She gladly agreed to follow him, but in her single-engined Moth she could hardly keep him in sight.

At mid-day on Tuesday 20 May, when she arrived at the Darmo aerodrome outside Sourabaya, she was given an uproarious welcome by the Dutch and English awaiting her. 'With one bound she was standing on the rain-soaked flying field,' wrote a local reporter. 'And then nothing else was seen but flowers, and laughing, enthusiastic faces, nothing else was heard but "cheers" and "compliments" and hearty good wishes.' The British girl, he added, looked 'very much tired out, but also very sporting.' After luncheon with the British Consul, 'Miss Amy' supervised the replacement of her reserve airscrew[1] – now much the worse for the monsoon rains – by one that a local Moth-owner had generously offered to her, and also the over-haul of her engine, which she told reporters was very tired like herself.

Next morning she hoped to leave early as usual, but when after starting up she tried each magneto in turn, she found that on one the engine stopped altogether. 'The coupling connecting the two magnetos had shrunk and was not doing its job. It was a long task to replace it, and I didn't have such a spare part with me.' So she had to abandon hope of pressing on that day, and she stayed at Sourabaya for a second night. The delay was fortunate in that she was able to get a little more rest. It was also fortunate for our understanding of Amy, because this unexpected pause gave her time to write to her parents, and the letter in question – probably the only one she wrote home during her flight – is of immense interest as a record of her personal feelings at the time. For although some of the remarks attributed to her by reporters ring true (such as her reply when reminded at Sourabaya that she looked tired: 'I shall go on to the bitter end. I'm tired, ever so tired, but I'm not

[1] The one which had been lashed to *Jason*'s fuselage when she started from Croydon, and which she had fitted as a replacement at Insein.

going to quit now.'), yet when she conversed with the press she was to some extent acting a part, whereas to her parents she was herself. And in the letter from Sourabaya she shows herself in a light which might have surprised those who read in the newspapers of her intrepid self-confidence. This letter makes it clear that the stresses of the flight brought out in her a child-like but strong trust in Providence. Although frankly denying that she was 'religious', she insisted that during the later stages of her flight she experienced a faith that sustained and consoled her.

'I hope that by the time you receive this letter I shall be safely in Sydney,' she wrote. 'I am getting very tired of my trip and a wee bit discouraged because everything seems to be going wrong. However, in many things I have been awfully lucky, and although I am not by any means religious, yet I am absolutely convinced that I have been watched over the whole way. It is comforting to feel this. I have had several narrow escapes and I am gratefully thankful for my safety even though my plans have all been spoilt.'

Later on, in Australia, she was quoted as having said that she was convinced she had been 'brought through' by Someone – a 'higher power' – who wanted her to reach Australia safely. She spoke, too, of her belief in the efficacy of her family's prayers, and said that on each morning of her trip she herself had prayed 'Please, dear God, see me safely through today.' And she also related that when, after she had made an agonized prayer for help at her worst moment of danger and fear (over the Java Sea) she was saved by the appearance of a sudden gap in the clouds, she was sure it was a 'happy manifestation'. Back in England she was less explicit on these matters, yet she mentioned several times in her narrative lecture that she was 'protected', and saved from disaster by her guardian angels. And although these later references were made rather flippantly, as if she were afraid of being thought superstitious, she had no need to include them unless she wished to.

'I am having trouble here with my engine,' the letter from Sourabaya continued, 'and do not yet know whether I can leave tomorrow. . . . Everyone is most awfully kind and has been all the way through. Here I am staying with a very wealthy lady who has the most beautiful house. She has lent me lovely clothes and at the moment I am surrounded by every luxury. I am having a good rest here today, but tonight am invited out to dinner to a Yorkshire man's house. Everyone makes a great fuss of me, and I don't quite know why because I have not yet accomplished anything and have no hopes of breaking the record. It is eighteen days already and I am beginning to despair of reaching Australia. Shall be so glad when the sea crossing is over which I dread. When one gets so tired I find one loses one's courage too. I am ashamed of myself and want so much to get safely to Sydney. Lord Wakefield has arranged an escort plane from Port Darwin through the bad country. It is topping of him and very thoughtful . . . I have heaps of invitations in Sydney and "Shell" are arranging all dinners, receptions etc., whilst Wakefields' representative will be my chief adviser. I could do with Daddy out here to advise me as I don't know at all the best thing to do. I have no idea what prospects there are in England and I have been offered a lot of money in Australia to make tours, public appearances etc. I should not like to hurry out of Australia and forgo such benefits to reach England and find no money there . . .

'At Sourabaya I had ever so many wonderful bouquets of flowers and hundreds of photographs taken etc. Everyone is so interested and I appear to disorganize the ordinary routine everywhere I go! . . . I wonder if interest has waned now in England as it is known I cannot break the record. I have had great difficulties. The monsoon broke earlier than anyone has ever known before and I struck the opening storms which are the worst.

'I do not think I can be in England before August – a month in Australia and five weeks on a steamer. God bless you all. Dearest love from Amy. Sourabaya is the "Paris of the East"! It is a big place and quite picturesque – complete with Talkies etc,!!!'.

III

Next day, Thursday 22 May, she was able to set off again, and she left Sourabaya intending to reach Atamboea on the Island of Timor before evening – a long day's flying of nearly a thousand miles, which would put her into position to make her final hop across the Timor Sea. She followed the islands of the archipelago eastwards, and during the morning flew past Bali. Then at noon she was sighted over Bima, on the Island of Sumbawa. 'I had been looking forward to this part of the trip, as this string of islands in the Dutch East Indies is noted for their beauty. The weather was improving and I almost enjoyed that day's flight until . . . darkness came on. There is quite a long sea crossing between the Island of Flores and Timor and it was rapidly getting dark whilst I was still over the water . . . Then the mountainous coast of Timor loomed up and I was lucky enough to pick up a tiny island which gave me my exact whereabouts. Turning inland I looked below me for the aerodrome . . . but I just couldn't see it . . . In despair I came lower and lower ready to put my wheels down anywhere as my petrol was practically finished. Seeing a bumpy stretch of grass I headed towards it, and once more had a miraculous escape. The field was a mass of ant-heaps about six feet high, but the machine ran safely in and out amongst them, coming to rest with one mound gently holding up the wing, but without breaking it.'

This time she had come down far from civilisation at Haliloeli, a native village near the boundary between Dutch and Portuguese Timor (the nearest white habitation was a Roman Catholic mission several miles distant). On landing she found herself outside 'a group of huts of mud and straw from which rushed a horde of yelling natives, with hair flying in the wind, and knives in their hands or between their red-stained teeth . . . In a minute I was surrounded and I pulled out my revolver, but I had no need at all to worry. With a deep salute, the leader came forward and gingerly touched first the machine, then me . . . Then he retired and everyone talked together in excited whispers . . . The leader then started to talk to me but I could make nothing of his language. Then I heard him say the word "Pastor" and I wondered whether this referred to a priest and if there was a mission anywhere near . . . As the darkness became more intense the leader took hold of my hand and with the utmost confidence I let them lead me to wherever they were going.

'At last we came to a large building made solidly of logs. Everything was in darkness . . . and in utter weariness I sank down on the steps and was soon fast asleep. I woke to find someone shaking me and looked up into the kind bearded face of the pastor. He spoke broken French and I had difficulty in explaining things to him. Inviting me inside, he quickly placed a frugal meal on the table, and I was very touched to see him open tins of cheese and bottles of wine . . . Whilst I was enjoying my meal, we heard the hoot of a motor horn, which sounded most incongrous in such a place. a moment later I was talking English to the Portuguese commandant of the aerodrome at Atamboea. It appeared that I had flown right over the aerodrome without seeing it – which didn't seem surprising when I saw it the next day in daylight. There had been a bushfire and the aerodrome was merely a blackened patch . . . They had watched where I had come down and followed me in their car. It was agreed they should take me back with them into Atamboea to get some sleep.'

IV

In the meantime, needless to say, the absence of news about Amy was causing much anxiety. Nothing had been seen or heard of her since she was sighted over Bima, half a day after leaving Sourabaya. That evening she was unable to report her whereabouts by telephone to the nearest British Consul, as she had done from Tjomal, for there were no such things as telephones within reach.

On the morning of the next day, Friday 23 May, the papers were full of it all. FLYING GIRL MISSING shouted the London placards, and Amy's family, as well as long-distance flyers who knew the area, were interviewed and re-interviewed for their reactions. Hinkler and Cobham agreed that one could reasonably be optimistic, since there were so many small islands on her route, and her father was emphatic that he had not given up hope. Yet for those close to Amy it was a time of real anguish and tension that was shared in a remarkable way by the general public. In Sourabaya meantime the Dutch East Indies authorities were also having a very worrying time, and a search expedition organised by the Naval Air Service was just about to leave when, on the Friday morning, news came through that Amy was safe.

By this time she herself, unaware of the extent of the concern for her, had been taken back to Haliloeli. 'I was delighted to see *Jason* again, surrounded as he was by a ring of grinning savages,' she later recalled. 'On this frail machine rested my one hope of getting away from this place, and it was *here* far more than when I reached Australia that I had the impulse to throw my arms around him as being the most faithful friend I had. The problems confronting me were, firstly, how to get petrol to my machine, and secondly, how to clear a long enough space to take off from. The second was easier to solve than the first, and we soon had bribed the whole village to set to work to rase the ant-heaps to the ground. Whilst they worked, we discussed petrol, and finally sent word to the village of Atamboea to bring out a couple of tins of motor spirit. It was mid-day before we saw emerging from the jungle a donkey with two tins of petrol tied on his back, but . . . it was so dirty and of such coarse grade that I was nearly two hours filtering two gallons, which was enough for ten minutes' flying.

'By this time a runway had been cleared which I paced and found to be barely long enough, but impenetrable jungle stopped any further extension. Pushing *Jason* back to the very edge of the cleared runway I started the engine. I daren't waste petrol running her up, and I wanted to take off with a flying start, which means that the wings are held back by two or three people whilst I open up the throttle, get the tail up, and then, at a given signal everyone leaves go and the machine rushes forward at flying speed and takes off in about half its accustomed space. But *could* I get these savage natives to understand what I wanted? . . . In desperation I had to risk an ordinary take-off, as I daren't waste any more petrol. As I opened up the throttle, the trees of the jungle rushed nearer . . . I am certain . . . that my wheels actually touched the tree-tops as I felt *Jason* give a lurch. For the twentieth time my guardian angels took me in their care, and in another second I was safely above the thick forest.'

V

At the so-called aerodrome at Atamboea ('it was very small, there were no hangars, and no markings') Amy set to work to overhaul her engine as thoroughly as she could in preparation for the sea crossing next day. 'The sun was intensely hot and there was no shade of any sort. Two or three Portuguese soldiers had come out to help me, but they were not much use. My petrol and oil supplies had not arrived. The only petrol was in huge casks, which had been lying on the field so long that they were covered with red rust. As we opened the casks and poured out the petrol it naturally collected all this rust, so I had to filter it out of the casks into smaller tins, and again filter it through two chamois leathers into my engine. I was very worried as to whether any particles of rust or water had gone through as the smallest fleck choking my jets – which are only pin-point holes – would have meant certain death on the following day's sea crossing. As for oil, by good fortune I had a spare gallon with me . . . It was long after dark before I had finished work.'

Next day, Saturday 24 May, the twentieth day of Amy's flight, as she prepared to start on her last lap, she received a heartening message from the Shell company: the oil-tanker *Phorus* had been instructed to stand by on her course, midway between Atamboea and Darwin. 'I taxied to the far side of the field go get the longest run. Turning round there was such a cloud of dust that I had to wait several minutes for it to clear. Then I saw how pitifully short the run was, and I had a full load of petrol on board. With a little prayer to my guardian angel I opened up and just managed to pull the machine off in time to clear the boundary trees. In about fifteen minutes I was over the coast and there before me stretched five hundred miles of shark-infested sea which I must cross to reach Australia . . . It was a quarter to eight by my watch, and I calculated it would take me seven hours to cross the water, making it a quarter to three when I should reach Darwin. I reckoned that after three hours I ought to sight the oil-tanker, if it was still there . . . At the same time I told myself firmly that I might get strong head winds . . .

The sea was calm and the sky a pale blue, with banks of cloud in the distance. Before long I had reached these clouds and, finding them very black and unpleasant, I made a detour round them. With my last experience over the Java Sea in my mind I was rather anxious, but on this occasion I was able to go round the storms. I got past three of them and then the weather improved. Relieved of the worry of bad weather, my mind turned to my engine. I fancied it was spluttering. It did really splutter; pulling back the throttle I opened up quickly to try to force out the foreign matter which I guessed was choking the carburettor. The manoeuvre was successful and black smoke poured out of the exhaust. This often happened . . .

'Resolutely not looking at my watch for what seemed like two hours, I found that ten minutes had passed. I counted as far as I could in French and then in

German. I receited all the nursery rhymes and poems I could remember . . . Three hours at last passed, and I strained my eyes to see a whisp of smoke . . . Right ahead of me was something . . . the oil tanker. Gliding to within a few feet of its deck I waved to the figures I could see hurrying about . . . I was wildly excited and forgot all danger.

'The smoke had given me the wind direction and I altered my course by a couple of degrees. Time again seemed to stand still, but I was comforted by the thought of the ship behind me and Australia ahead, and I seemed in some curious way to be protected. Another three hours passed and I began to climb so that I should see Australia quicker. Then I saw a dark cloud on the horizon . . . The cloud slowly assumed shape and after another half an hour's flying I made out an island, which I knew to be Melville Island and I was sure of my exact whereabouts. In another half an hour my wheels were touching Australian soil.'

21

AMY, WONDERFUL AMY

May 1930

'What a brave, wonderful daughter to be proud of. The perils she has gone through make one shudder' . . . 'The girl's glorious courage' . . . 'Her fame will live for ever' . . . 'When I read of her safe arrival I danced up and down the tram-car – the people thought I was crazy' . . . 'I want to be with her. I am prepared to give up everything, even my life if necessary, to fly with Amy' . . . 'Never!! has a single event so thrilled the whole world (and justly too).' Thus the tributes – there were sacks of them – that avalanched into Amy's home in Hull. 'Amy is a marvel' . . . 'I followed her each day from the moment she left Croydon, I knew she would do it. I prayed to our Holy Mother and to every Saint in Heaven to pray to God for her safe arrival' . . . 'I am an old Indian, belong to Medical profession. From the day your dear child started from here I am watching. God is great: am praying for her safety from bottom of my heart' . . . 'Following her progress from day to day makes me feel that I really know her. God bless her always' . . . 'I am very lonely but I prayed to God for her. Thank God she is safe. I went out for a paper before I had my breakfast. The first thing I saw on the placards was FLYING GIRL MISSING. I said to the paper man "Amy is quite safe but cannot give news of herself".' . . . 'Just can't help leaving off polishing floors to say how proud I am to belong to Yorkshire at this moment. I saw the news this morning that Amy

Johnson was reported missing, and later, on hearing "specials" out, ran to get one, and was quite overcome with emotion to see that your brave girl was safe. All the women down our terrace were out in no time, and just glorying in the good news' . . . 'This morning my husband came home to breakfast and said "Amy is missing", but I said "I had a funny experience during the night". In my sleep I saw your daughter coming down and I awoke. And it seemed so real as if she was with me, and she had bright lights all round her. So I said, "I'm sure she is quite safe" . . . my husband only laughed. I was more than overjoyed to hear she was quite safe on the wireless tonight' . . . 'My sister sent a wire saying Miss Johnson had arrived safe so that I would know before the news came on at 6.15 p.m. I felt like jumping out of bed!' . . . 'Your daughter's courage and endurance are simply wonderful. In these days when girls will not trouble to do things well it is splendid to feel your daughter has shown there *is* real grit still in our race' . . . 'I used to say to my husband every minute of the day "I wonder how Miss Amy Johnson is getting on". When I knew that Miss Johnson had arrived in Australia I cried with joy' . . . 'When the glorious news came through that she was *safe*, and how overjoyed you were, I am not ashamed to say I too cried with joy, hardened old Navy man that I am. I'm getting old now, but in all a long adventurous life, I've never heard of anything or seen anything to equal hers. I was down the Java Coast in 1898; you see I have been all that long journey myself and so have just a little idea of what it means. But then to do it alone, and in the air; it is more than wonderful, it is marvellous. God bless her, surely His angels have watched over her. An old sailor's best love to Amy when she comes home.'

Most of the letters to Amy's parents were, like these, from simple people who were profoundly moved by what she had done and what she stood for to them; in several she was compared to Joan of Arc. But not only the unsophisticated were moved. A great pianist, Harriet Cohen, sent this telegram to Hull addressed to

Amy: 'Heartiest congratulations. Being tied to piano all day must live adventures through wonderful beings like yourself.' And Stanley Baldwin telegraphed to Will Johnson: 'Please accept my warmest congratulations on your daughter's wonderful achievement which has stirred the imagination of all British people throughout the Empire. She has shown that the British spirit of adventure combined with initiative and courage still animates the youth of our country and you have every reason to be proud of her.'

For days the popular press brimmed with panegyrics, and in the *Daily Sketch* (which launched a Shilling Fund to buy Amy a new aeroplane) 'Wilhelmina Stitch' outdid herself in her column 'The Fragrant Minute':

'Oh! words, you are such wooden things when feelings are most deeply stirred! Now should you have bright golden wings; yea, every pulsing, thrilling word should rush to aid a rhymester's plight who longs to praise that epic flight.

'But one is silenced by your feat. All has been said by your lone trail, and we who live on Humdrum Street seek hard for fitting praise – but fail. We know we could not ever rise to match your noble enterprise.

'Endurance, courage and great skill – these words troop forth and tribute pay to your undaunted British will, and this the thought all share today, "You're Britain's pride. Brave girl, well done! The homage of the world you've won."

'Amy! For ever more your name will stand synonymous with pluck; and when we weary of life's game, or when we whine and blame "our luck", we'll think of your immortal 'plane and spread our wings and try again.'

The first outburst of hero-worship was followed by a spate of songs and verses. 'Queen of the Air' was the title of several of them, and others ranged in tone from the light-hearted foxtrot-song 'Aeroplane Girl' to the dramatic 'Johnnie, Heroine of the Air' in which she was compared to Grace Darling. Some radiated patriotic fervour, as for example a composition by William

Hodge, Amy's musician uncle in Leeds. It was entitled
'The Lone Dove' (Lindbergh had been nicknamed 'The
Lone Eagle') and its lyric ended with the words: 'Salute
the Queen of the Air, in the British Empire's Name.'
But the song that won far the most enduring popularity
was 'Amy', which became a hit in 1930, not only
because of its catchy tune by Horatio Nicholls, but
because the words (by Joe Gilbert) truly expressed the
sentiments of so many.

There's a little lady who has captured ev'ry heart,
Amy Johnson, it's you!
We have watch'd and waited since the day you made
    your start,
Amy Johnson, it's true!
Since the news that you are safe has come along,
Ev'ryone in Town is singing this love song:

Amy, wonderful Amy,
How can you blame me for loving you?
Since you've won the praise of ev'ry nation,
You have filled my heart with admiration,
Amy, wonderful Amy,
I'm proud of the way you flew,
Believe me, Amy, you cannot blame me, Amy,
For falling in love with you.

And then there was a second verse, which explained
with naive candour why Amy's sudden fame had
proved so popular:

You deserve a lot of credit for your daring deeds,
Amy Johnson, that's true!
You are just the kind of person that the country needs,
Amy Johnson, that's true!
Yesterday you were but a nonentity,
Now your name will go down to posterity.

Amy, wonderful Amy,
How can you blame me for loving you . . .

One of the most remarkable features of the explosion of rejoicing and adulation was its spontaneity. There had been no skilful build-up beforehand by public relations experts, as there had been for example in the case of Lindbergh. And although Amy would not of course have attracted the attention she did without the intense interest of the press towards the end of her trip, yet, in spite of the hyperbole of the journalists, she herself seemed an endearingly genuine figure, and her flight an impromptu adventure. This was very largely because she had not been boosted in advance. The subtle psychological barrier that separates the professionally publicised from the public was absent, and as a result she seemed to the man and woman in the street to be one of themselves – almost one of the family. Certainly she was much closer to them than the titled ladies who were usually in the news for their flying.

It was also this pseudo-intimate relationship between Amy and the public, along with the suddennesss of her ascent from obscurity to fame, which seemed to put flying all at once within everyone's reach – 'If a girl like Amy Johnson can do it, why can't I?' It also gave rise to the legend that Amy – a penniless nobody, a little typist – had stepped straight from a city office into an aeroplane and set off without any preparation at all to fly half across the world.

This was the legend which took root with the general public. But what of Amy's flight in the context of other pioneering flights? What is its place in aviation history? Merely as a flight from Britain to Australia – as a contribution towards the opening up of the future air route – it was not especially important, for it was only the ninth of its kind (the first was in 1919). Nor was it important as a demonstration that the trip could be made solo in a light aeroplane; Hinkler had already done that, and efforts to improve upon his time were a matter of sporting competition rather than pioneering. But as the first solo flight from Britain to Australia *by a woman* Amy's achievement was and is, of towering importance. It has given her a permanent place in air history as one of the first women in the world to become a pioneer pilot. This may seem a strange claim when she was the thirty-seventh woman to receive an aviator's certificate in Britain, nevertheless before she made her Australia flight there had been very few world-wide landmarks in the history of women's flying; in fact only four since the Wright brothers first flew. In 1909 the French Baroness de Laroche was the first woman to pilot an aeroplane; in 1912 an American, Harriet Quimby, was the first woman to fly the English Channel. After that there were no notable feminine 'firsts' until Lady Heath made the first flight by a woman from the Cape to England. This was soon followed by Lady Bailey's double flight from England to the Cape and back. Several other women had, it is true, made notable long-distance flights, but only as passengers. Mrs Keith Miller had flown from Britain to Australia before Amy but not as a pilot (and the expedition had taken five months). Amelia Earhart was passenger not pilot when she first flew the Atlantic in 1928 (she did not make the same flight alone until 1932). When Amy arrived in Australia one of the flying celebrities who was asked by the press to make comment was Lady Heath, then in New York and sufficiently recovered from her crash to be the President of the Women's International Aeronautical Association. Her comment was short and to the point: 'Miss Johnson's flight was easily the finest ever performed by a woman.'

At the time of the flight, however, as the letters and verses and songs that have been quoted show very clearly, Amy's success was predominantly a personal one, and this helps to account for the coolness, antipathy even, that was soon to arise towards her in some aviation circles. 'Amy, wonderful Amy' was adored by the public as 'a peach of a girl' who was also a brave flyer, not purely as a pilot. And it is perhaps hardly surprising that to some of those who took flying seriously this fact was not very palatable.

AMY, WONDERFUL AMY
III

In Australia Amy herself was at first amazed and thrilled but also bewildered by the acclaim. Not having seen newspapers recently, the mobbing and the cheering when she arrived at Port Darwin seemed quite inappropriate, for to her own mind her flight was a fiasco – she had failed to beat Hinkler's record. She later told her sister Molly that when, approaching the Fanny Bay aerodrome, she caught sight of the assembled crowds, and realised their vast size, she thought that her arrival must have coincided by chance with an Air Pageant.

But it was Australian habit to receive long-distance flyers with delirious enthusiasm. Ever since 1919, when for the first time an aeroplane had arrived from Britain, flown by Ross and Keith Smith, the Australians had welcomed each exhausted newcomer by air with exuberance almost amounting to frenzy. Even Alan Cobham had been overwhelmed when he arrived, the third England–Australia pilot, in 1926, and he now cabled to Amy: 'Give my love to Australia. They will give you greatest welcome in the world.' How right he was! All over Australia the praises of 'Johnnie' were being celebrated in verse and song.

'Johnnie!' There's a shouting goes up and down the land
'Johnnie's over Darwin!' And millions breathe anew
There's a plane high in the offing and a little waving hand
Johnnie's making Darwin! Johnnie from the blue!

The terrors of the Timor, the tropic seas are past
And a brave girl, a glad girl, is winging for the coast
A myriad hearts are easier, for Johnnie's here at last
To live in British history and be a British toast,
Where British men tell o'er again the deeds of derring-do,
    Here's a health to Johnnie! Johnnie from the Blue!

Amy delighted everyone on the evening of her arrival by insisting that she preferred to be called 'Johnnie' rather than 'Amy' and there were fresh outbursts of ecstatic doggerel:

AMY JOHNSON

You have opened up vistas of joy
  Yorkshire Johnnie!
For existence will always be bright
If a plane that is laden with some pretty maiden
From places like Hull, in its flight
  May alight
With an armful of laughing delight.

More than two hundred cables and telegrams had been waiting for her at Darwin (in anticipation of her safe arrival); by the time she left, after a day and a half, the local telegraph office had delivered six hundred more and had sent out 47,000 words of press reports. In the cables – from relatives, friends, strangers, royalties, politicians, celebrities, officials, businesses – the word that recurred most often was the same word 'WONDERFUL' that echoes through the telegrams to Hull. A message from King George V and Queen Mary ran: 'The Queen and I are thankful and delighted to hear of Miss Johnson's safe arrival in Australia. We heartily congratulate her upon her wonderful and courageous achievement.' Albert, King of the Belgians and his Queen, who prided themselves on being, with the Prince of Wales, the only royalties who 'frequently used airways', expressed their admiration for her 'wonderful skill and indomitable bravery and energy.' The British Prime Minister, Ramsay MacDonald, cabled: 'My heartiest congratulations on your wonderful achievement. We have followed your flight with the keenest interest and admiration. We are very proud of you.' Tributes also came from the Lindberghs, from Louis Blériot, the French aviator who first flew the English Channel in 1909 (his cable consisted of the one word '*Bravo!*'), and also from Francis Chichester, who cabled from New Zealand: 'Please accept heartiest congratulations on your great achievement of one of the finest flights in the history of aviation.'

Then ten days later there was a new wave of congratulations, for it was announced in the Birthday Honours on 3 June that Amy had been awarded the

CBE.[1] Lord Wakefield cabled 'Very sincere congratulations. His Majesty has interpreted the universal feeling throughout the Empire in honouring you.' It had in fact already been mooted in the press, both in Britain and Australia, whether a new honour might not be devised especially for acts of heroism by women; several men had been knighted for pioneer flights, but there was no feminine equivalent to knighthood. Why should it not be 'Lady Amy'? The Duchess of Bedford had been made a DBE for her services to flying; 'Dame', however, was considered too formidable a title for a girl in her twenties. In some quarters there was talk of an Air Force Cross, a decoration normally awarded only to Air Force personnel, for 'exceptional valour, courage or devotion to duty whilst flying, though not in active operations against the enemy.'

On rare occasions the honour had been conferred upon civilian pilots,[2] though never as yet on a woman.

It seemed however that 'Miss Amy Johnson, CBE' satisfied most people, though Lieutenant Commander Kenworthy, the Hull MP, proclaimed his disappointment and said he had been hoping for an Order of Merit. The Duke of Sutherland, President of the Air League, cabled to Australia with fitting pomp: 'Air League congratulates you on well-deserved honour and wishes you increased success in your endeavours to stimulate in the public a firm resolve for an Empire as glorious in the air as it has been on the sea.'

---

[1] Other more specialised honours were also conferred upon her at this time: she was elected an Honorary Member of the Guild of Air Pilots and Air Navigators of the British Empire, as well as an Honorary Fellow of the Society of Engineers.

[2] Hinkler had received it after his solo flight from Britain to Australia, and so had the great test pilot Harry Hawker after he 'returned from the dead' – he was missing for several days when attempting to fly the Atlantic in 1919.

Meanwhile in Lhasa, according to an apocryphal tale, an Englishman happened to mention what Amy had done, with admiration verging on awe, to the Dalai Lama. The priest-king considered the news gravely, then with a puzzled frown he asked, 'Why was the Honourable Lady in such a hurry?'

PART THREE

THE VICTIM

22

'AUSTRALIA'S SWEETHEART'
24 May – 7 July 1930

The six weeks that Amy spent in Australia were an exhilarating initiation into her new life as a public figure; at the same time they were an exceedingly gruelling ordeal. Darwin, Brisbane, Sydney, Melbourne, Adelaide, Perth. Receptions, luncheons, dinners; balls, galas, rallies; welcomes by Governors, by Lord Mayors, by women's clubs; by aero clubs, Rotary clubs, Freemasons; by feminists, Methodists, Yorkshiremen. And then there were the speeches, broadcasts, interviews, sittings, posings, signings; the gifts of fur coats, frocks and hats; of cash, jewellery and watches; of endless bric-a-brac; even of a baby kangaroo.

The Australians adored Amy for her girlish ways, her naturalness, and the affection for themselves and their country that she reiterated in every speech. 'Ambassadress of Empire' they called her, but she was also 'Australia's Sweetheart', and in the heroine-image that came into being there was not only the courage of the 'lone girl flyer' but the graciousness of a princess on tour, the sentimental appeal of a Mary Pickford, and the cosy informality of 'one of us'. 'The people love and admire her, as Amy, and as the girl who flew from England *just to see us*,' so wrote one of her Australian fans to her parents. 'Tell you what should happen. Let her marry one of the Princes and both come out here as Governor General and kind of "take charge of things".'

Amy on her side responded with genuine pleasure,

yet the strain of it all, on top of the strain of her flight, sometimes brought her to the point of collapse, and more than once after the crowds had rushed her she broke into hysterical sobs. Her bronzed skin, sunny smile,[1] and zestful handwaving gave an impression of health, but there were times when she had to be held upright as the open car that bore her crawled forward through the excited throngs. Reporters who met her wrote with sympathy of her eyes brimming with tears and her look of utter tiredness. It is astonishing that before she returned to England she did not suffer a complete nervous breakdown.

II

When she landed at Darwin (a few minutes before 4 o'clock on the afternoon of Saturday 24 May) she was – it need hardly be said – in desperate need of sleep and rest. During the weekend she did have one sleep of eleven hours, but on the Saturday evening, with hardly a pause after her arrival, she had to attend a civic reception and then a dance. It was at the reception in the Town Hall that she won hearts straightaway, after several speakers had referred to her as 'Miss Amy', by jumping up and interjecting 'Johnnie is my name in England. There they never call me Amy. So do please call me Johnnie.' Then came her own turn to speak. Only once before in her life had she spoken in public, when she had deputised for Lady Bailey at an Air League function in London. In the Darwin Town Hall, buoyed up by the enthusiasm of her welcomers, she replied with confidence ('She is a good speaker,' a local newspaper commented, 'and kept her audience's attention riveted.') Later she herself said that the warmth of her receptions in Australia made it easy for

---

[1] Many of the photographs of Amy in Australia show that at last she had forgotten to be embarrassed about her front teeth: her joyful grin was entirely without self-consciousness.

her to speak, but there is no doubt at all that she possessed a natural gift for making simple little speeches of the impromptu kind that were needed. 'I only wish to say a word of thanks to all for the absolutely marvellous welcome you have given me,' she declared at Darwin. 'It is well worth going through the difficulties I have had to face to get here. I was told I would have a marvellous reception in Australia, and that was why I was so anxious to get here. I was also told it was a wonderful country for flying, and as I am enthusiastic about aviation naturally I was keen to come out. I am certain that if you had aeroplanes coming through to Darwin regularly it would make a world of difference. It could be done easily if aviation were organized here. It is the best method of transport. You have such a marvellous country. The climate and everything else are just right, and I do hope aviation will be developed to the utmost.' As the reception was ending she again jumped to her feet. 'I say you people!' she exclaimed, 'I forgot to mention that I landed here on Empire Day. I am wondering if you will look on that as of very special significance. I think it is unique and so appropriate.'

At the dance that evening in the British Legion Hall most of her partners were of course Australians, but one of them was a tall, handsome young Englishman, well known for his talents as a flyer and also for his arrogance. C.W.A. Scott, formerly of the RAF, was the pilot of the plane that was to 'escort' Amy southwards (it had been chartered jointly by Wakefields and the *Sydney Sun*).[1] He had met her for the first time a few hours earlier on the aerodrome when, dishevelled and dirty from her flight, she asked him (so he wrote later in his autobiography) to 'look over' her engine. In the evening, wearing a summer frock, 'somehow or other she seemed to have changed . . . her hair was tidy and

[1] This aircraft was a DH 50J, the *Hippomenes*, a cabin biplane with a normal cruising speed of 110 mph.

her hands clean . . . there was a different atmosphere about her.' It would be interesting to know whether Scott spoke his mind to Amy at the dance about the state of the engine which she herself had serviced with such scrupulous care before the Timor crossing; if so it is hardly surprising there was a different atmosphere between them, for she was touchy about her skill as an engineer. 'Never have I seen an engine in such an appalling condition,' Scott wrote in his book. 'Compression was completely lacking in two of her four cylinders. The plugs, after the engine had cooled down, took two strong men and much perspiration to remove. The vent plug in the sump was only unscrewed by colossal strength and a huge spanner and tommy bar, and the propellor nuts were taken up anything from half to a complete turn . . . All that it needed however was adjustment and ordinary maintenance routine, and this I and another helper soon accomplished.' The other helper was Flying Officer Harold Owen, of the Royal Australian Air Force, an experienced mechanic who on the initiative of the Shell company (now vying with Wakefields in attentiveness to Amy) had flown to Darwin in the company's Gipsy Moth, especially to service the engine of *Jason's Quest*, as her aircraft was being called.

Charles Scott was well qualified to act as Amy's guide across the wilds of the Northern Territory, for as a pilot of Qantas Airways he had had to learn to find his way over the vast featureless outback where almost every aviator from Britain got lost – even such flyers as Ross and Keith Smith, Alan Cobham, Hinkler and Chichester.[1] But on the Monday morning, when

---

[1] Proper maps of this desert area did not then exist, and it must be remembered that in 1930 flying facilities throughout Australia were still primitive in the extreme. There were no ground-air communications of any kind, no control towers, no runways, no flare-paths for night landing, and the weather reports were (by present-day standards) hopelessly inadequate.

with Captain S.W. Bird of Wakefields and a reporter as passengers he set off ahead of Amy for Daly Waters and Alexandra Station, the first outposts where they were to stop, he did not prove a gentle 'escort', for he made no attempt to keep his cruising speed down to hers, and poor Amy had to chase after him at full throttle. Harold Owen, trying to act as a second escort, was also far outstripped. The reason later given for this lack of consideration was the necessity for pressing on so that the programme of welcomes which were being planned for Amy could be adhered to. But it seems probable that a contributing reason was commercial rivalry: it was obviously to the advantage of Wakefields' publicity that the Shell aircraft should be left far behind.

On Tuesday (27 May) Scott's plane, followed after an interval by Amy's, passed over the Queensland border, and not long afterwards they both came down to refuel at Cloncurry en route for Longreach, where Amy was to attend a function that evening. At this point, and for much of the rest of the time she was in Australia, interesting new light can be thrown on her experiences by the memories of a representative of de Havillands who now arrived on the scene. Ian Grabowsky, then Sales Manager and Pilot to the Australian branch of the company, had been sent from Melbourne by his Managing Director, Major Hereward de Havilland (brother of the late Sir Geoffrey), to meet Amy on behalf of his firm and to give her a warm message of welcome. Grabowsky was already at Cloncurry (having flown there in a racing Gipsy Moth, VH-UIQ, known as the *Black Hawk*) when Scott and Amy arrived there, and he happened to be in flight near the aerodrome when *Jason* came in to land. He noticed that Amy's propellor had stopped and proceeded to land alongside her; by this time she was out of her aircraft. Scott's DH50 was already being refuelled at the Qantas hangar some five hundred yards away and Grabowsky was rather surprised that no move had been made to come to her assistance. 'I walked up to her,' he remembers, 'introduced myself and gave her the message to which she said "Thank you. Thank you for some humanity." She looked so ill that I asked "How are you? Would you like a wash and a short rest?" Her reply was "I'd love a wash. I'm very tired. As luck would have it I'm experiencing the usual feminine problem. Those people have forced me to follow them with my throttle wide open." "Jump in," I said, "and I'll swing your prop." She smiled and climbed into the cockpit.' When the engine started she waited for him to get into his own plane and then both aircraft taxied to where the DH50 was standing.

'Knowing Scott and Bird I told them of the conversation,' Grabowsky continues, 'and suggested that as the only function that day was a welcome dinner at Longreach there would be ample time to drive Amy into Cloncurry and let her have a wash and a rest.' Bird's reaction to this was to the effect that 'she ought to be used to feminine problems by now – that's her business. Ours is to be on time at each appointment and we are leaving as soon as she's refuelled.' Grabowsky admits that this infuriated him, and he reminded the two men that while they had been sitting at Darwin Amy had been battling through the hardest part of her flight. He then asked Bird to wait until he himself had refuelled so that he could come along at the rear. But again the reaction was 'no waiting', and while the *Black Hawk* was being filled up Grabowsky watched the DH50 and *Jason* take off and set course for Longreach. His racing aircraft was much faster than the other two, and he set off intending to overtake them but engine trouble (a bent valve push rod) brought him down sixty miles from Cloncurry, and he did not see Amy again until several days later.

Meanwhile she followed Scott as best she could towards Longreach, the main township of the central Queensland sheep district and there a tumultuous welcome awaited her. For the first time she suffered the terrifying experience of being mobbed, and had to be carried to safety by four policemen. Afterwards she was feted at the official dinner, and was presented with a gift from local fans, a coat made of rabbit fur.[1]

On the third day of her trans-Australian trip with Scott (Wednesday 28 May) they were bound for Charleville – like Longreach a busy livestock centre – and were due to arrive in time for an official lunch. According to Scott's account *Jason*'s engine gave trouble and Amy was worried by the intense glare. 'On the way to Charleville we lost each other,' he related in his book. 'I saw her one minute, and the next minute, when I turned round to look for her . . . she had vanished . . . I flew round and round waiting for her to come up to me, I flew high and low . . . As there was no trace of her I continued my journey . . . I said to myself, "If this girl can navigate her way from England to Port Darwin, surely she will have no difficulty in finding her way".' When he landed at Charleville the Mayor asked where Miss Johnson was. 'Oh, she will be here in a minute,' replied Scott. More than an hour later a telephone message came from Quilpie, a small township 125 miles to the west where Amy had landed. At the time it was said that she had lost her way, but to Grabowsky she later confided that she had deliberately avoided the official lunch, and she told him why she had done so. 'Her explanation, as closely as memory permits me,' he recalls, 'was that because she was still feeling femininely unwell and was desperately tired she *had* to have a rest and the only way she could think of was to follow the Charleville-Quilpie railway line and find somewhere to land.'

[1] There is an amusing little sidelight relating to this coat. When Amy arrived in Sydney she was given a sealskin coat trimmed with squirrel by the Sydney Arts Club. Among her papers there is a letter written by the President of the Club to one of the reception committee's officials: 'It is genuine sealskin trimmed with natural squirrel. If you give this as an item to the Press would you emphasize the genuine part of it, as most seals are died [*sic*] rabbit, and I would hate for this to be described in the Press, as the Queensland gift was, as common rabbit.'

AMY JOHNSON

It was dusk when she finally arrived at Charleville, and over the bare red soil of the landing ground there was a blaze of light from the headlights of a score of cars. The townspeople prided themselves on their welcomes to aviators, and when *Jason* touched down the police were swept aside by the onrush towards the little plane. Amid frantic pushing and cheering Amy was trapped until rescuers fought their way to her. By the time she had been bundled into a car and driven to the hotel where she was to stay she was weeping hysterically. It is hardly surprising that during the next few weeks an irrational horror of crowds and strangers beset her, as it has beset others who have been overwhelmed by Australian welcomes.[1]

III

At Brisbane's Eagle Farm aerodrome, just after two o'clock on Thursday 29 May, the fourth day since Amy left Darwin, a crowd of twenty thousand waited eagerly for her arrival. She had already that day been welcomed at Toowoomba, and there, according to an eyewitness, 'Miss Johnson was literally dragged out of her machine and pulled through a surging and enthusiastic crowd to a waiting car.' The Brisbane crowd saw Scott's aircraft come in first – Amy had asked him to land ahead of her. Meantime *Jason* made a circuit over the crowds and at the end of it, so as to lose height, went into a steep sideslip. Then suddenly there were cries of 'Amy's crashed!' Touching down too fast and too late the aircraft had hit the far fence, plunged its way into a field of millet, reared up on its nose, somersaulted over, and finished on its back a crumpled wreck. Amy, fastened into her seat by a safety belt, was not herself hurt.

[1] Francis Chichester, on arriving in Australia earlier in 1930 (after his solo flight from England) suffered acute misery from what he termed 'agoraphobia' (i.e. 'a morbid dislike of public places').

'AUSTRALIA'S SWEETHEART'

Her own account of what happened appeared in the *Daily Mail* next day.[1] She attributed the crash entirely to engine trouble, though later in her tour she admitted that the strain of the receptions in Queensland, and the knowledge that thousands were waiting to greet her in Brisbane may also have contributed to the accident. 'I was flying high,' she explained, 'for we had come from a tableland over the mountains to the coastal plains. When I throttled back the engine, preparatory to climbing down[2] and circling the aerodrome, it spluttered frightfully. As I was going over the ground it stopped altogether. I did not have sufficient height to make a circle, and had to lose height rapidly. With a very steep sideslip I landed on the aerodrome all right, but unfortunately ran into a boundary fence . . . I knew it was inevitable when I saw the fence, and I sort of waited for it. It was all too fast for me to catch any impression . . . I was not thrown out, nor was I in any way injured. I was strapped into the cockpit and found myself still sitting there, but this time upside down. All I had to do was to undo the clip on the straps and slip out.'

A cheer went up as she was seen scrambling from the wreckage; then two huge policemen grabbed her under the arms and steered her towards the dais. There, amid thunderous applause, with her pullover torn and a gash in one boot, she waved and grinned with even more gusto than usual. 'People of Australia,' her voice came over the loudspeakers, 'I thank you from the bottom of my heart for the absolutely marvellous welcome you have given me. I have had splendid receptions everywhere, but this simply beats the band. I came here because I love flying, and if anybody else in England wants to fly I will say "Fly to Australia". I hope you will not forget my aeroplane, and the people in London who taught me to fly and to look

[1] Reports from Amy, prepared with the help of the *Daily Mail*'s agents on the spot, were being published almost every day at this time.
[2] This should, of course, read 'gliding down'.

after my engine properly. Please do not forget that it is for aviation that I have done this. You can see for yourself that I am not tired. I am as fit as a fiddle. That is because I fly.'

Next came the procession through the streets of the city, where the mobs jostled and peered and shouted, and many perched on the roofs of tramcars for a better view. Mounted police rode closely alongside the open car on which Amy was held upright by Cyril Westcott (who had just come from Sydney) while her right arm was raised in greeting by Captain Bird. On her face was a glowing smile, but when she reached Government House, where she was to stay, she collapsed in tears.

Only a few of her public engagements were cancelled after her accident, but it was announced that for the remainder of the tour, on doctor's orders, she would not herself pilot *Jason*, and the crash and its repercussions meant, of course, a hurried re-organising of some of the plans. In Melbourne Major de Havilland decided to fly immediately to Brisbane in his Hawk Moth,[1] taking with him the spares that were needed for the damaged *Jason*. On his arrival he met Amy and offered to fly her to Sydney, her next main stopping place, but Westcott had already accepted an offer from Charles Ulm, the enterprising Manager of Australian National Airways,[2] to put one of his airliners at her disposal for the trip. De Havilland however made a further helpful suggestion which was agreed to, that Amy should make the remainder of her tour, after Sydney, as passenger in his Hawk Moth.

[1] A six-seater cabin monoplane, VH-UNW.
[2] This pioneer airline had just been launched on its notable but brief career (it went into liquidation in 1932) and its leading spirits were Charles Kingsford Smith and Charles Ulm, who had become national heroes after their Pacific flight, the first from America to Australia.

'Australia's Sweetheart'
IV

While she was still in Brisbane news came from England
of her CBE, and along with it a spate of congratulations.
But there was also an anxious cable from her father:
'Alarming newspaper reports concerning your health.
Please cable me exact condition.' 'Do not believe report
my illness,' she cabled back. 'Am quite well but so many
functions are arranged for me that it is necessary to be
under doctor's orders in order to avoid overdoing things.
Don't worry, am doing fine. Prevention better than cure.'
Meantime to Jack Humphreys she sent a message which
showed even more clearly that she was in her usual lively
form: 'Am wearying of too much sugar. For God's sake
send salty cable at once.' Humphreys replied with salty
common sense: 'Your cable I understand. Be strong,[1]
and let me know your plans.' But he too added, 'Worried
your health.' Perhaps Amy's personal feelings at this time
are best shown in the answer she gave to a Brisbane
reporter who asked her what it felt like to find oneself
a world-famous figure overnight. 'I cannot realise it
yet,' she replied. 'I feel a person apart from all this – I
seem to be looking on at someone else whom the world is
acclaiming.'

On Wednesday 4 June she left Brisbane for Sydney,
travelling in the *Southern Sun*, one of ANA's eight-
passenger airliners (a three-engined Avro X). The trip
took over six hours, and on the way a 'picnic in the air'
took place – in those days a noteworthy happening –
with the four passengers seated round a specially
installed card-table decorated with poinsettias.

[1] Humphrey's advice 'Be strong' is of much interest in that it
links with a remark of Amy's while she was in Australia.
Speaking of her flight at a youth rally in Sydney she said 'A
friend gave me this advice before I started, "If you feel
yourself giving way, take a grip, don't be weak – stick it" . . . It
helped me.' The similarity between the two phrases strongly
suggests that Humphreys was the friend whose advice
sustained her.

Accompanying Amy, who was all in green and carrying a koala mascot, were Mrs Ulm as 'hostess', a reporter and Captain Bird (Westcott had gone on to Sydney the day before). Charles Ulm himself was the pilot; in Amy's log book she made a note of this and also wrote 'took the controls for part of the trip.' This must have been an exciting moment for her, the first time she had ever flown an aircraft larger than a Moth with a wheel instead of a stick. Her log-book entry does not however make any mention of Ulm's co-pilot, James Allan Mollison. There is not, in fact, any reliable evidence to show that her future husband, whom she thus met by chance for the first time, made much impression upon her on this occasion.

In *Playboy of the Air*, the gossipy and imaginative autobiography which Mollison wrote seven years later there is a short account of his first meeting with Amy; during the flight to Sydney he had the opportunity to chat with her. That evening, if she were not too exhausted, she was to attend a ball to be given in her honour by the Australian Flying Corps Association, and Mollison asked if he might partner her. By the time they reached Sydney, so he says, she had promised him two dances. That evening, against doctor's advice, she attended the ball. As she entered the Wentworth ballroom there was a rolling of drums and the dancers surged round her with a roar of 'She's a Jolly Good Fellow.' One admirer gave her a painfully hearty slap on the back and was rebuked by Westcott. According to *Playboy of the Air* Mollison conducted himself with much restraint, diffidence even. He was awestruck by the fact that the Governor, Sir Philip Game, who was escorting Amy, was a retired Air Vice-Marshal. 'Sir Philip, please, I have two dances with Miss Johnson, please. She promised them for me on our way from Brisbane today.' 'The Governor stared coldly . . . "Miss Johnson," he snapped, "is very tired now. She cannot dance".' After this frustrating experience Mollison did not see Amy again until two years later, by which time he was no longer an unknown airline pilot. By then he had followed in her footsteps and had become a successful long-distance flyer.

Midway through Amy's tour a popular Sydney news magazine, the now defunct *Smith's Weekly* (which has been described by one who knew it as 'a foul rag') launched a vitriolic attack upon her on the score of alleged avarice. It had probably been sparked off by an unfortunate decision on the part of Cyril Westcott to charge £100 on Amy's behalf for her personal appearances, but the attack was based on twisted evidence and was grossly unfair. It was also, in the context of aviation history, very ironic, for the financial gains from her flight (by comparison with those of some other long-distance flyers) were by no means outstanding. One must remember however that in 1930 there was much unemployment in Australia and money was very tight, therefore from the viewpoint of *Smith's Weekly* an 'exposure' of Amy's gains could be relied on to arouse scandalised interest. The campaign against her was especially unjust because in Australia the enthusiasm for pioneer flights was so great that it was ususal for the pilots to receive both Government grants and lavish gifts of money from fans as well as presentations and gifts in kind.[1]

The storm began to brew almost as soon as Amy reached Sydney, with criticisms in the *Labor Daily*. Next a reporter from *Smith's Weekly* interviewed Westcott, ostensibly with a view to preparing a case in her defence, and Westcott, with surprising trustfulness,

---

[1] During the previous ten years the Australian Government had given large sums to long-distance flyers. Ross and Keith Smith, for the first flight from England to Australia, had won an official prize of £10,000; Kingsford Smith and Ulm received £5,000 after their Pacific flight; Hinkler in 1928 was given £2,000. In the case of Kingsford Smith and Ulm the grant was more than doubled by donations from fans. The question of a money prize for Amy was in fact raised in Canberra just after she arrived in Australia, but the Labour Premier, Mr James Scullin, stated that a grant from the Commonwealth to the flyer was not justified.

briefed him very fully. Then, just after Amy left for Melbourne via Canberra (on 14 June), the newspaper published a heavily sarcastic attack, calling her 'The Air Digger of the Skyway' and 'The Gimme Gimme Girl.' It included a waspish lampoon in the form of an imaginary letter to her parents: 'I do loathe crowds staring at me for nothing. I don't mind them when they have been counted at the box office . . . My right palm is all itching, I must rub it on wood so that it's sure to come good, and then on brick, so it's sure to come quick . . . I'm sorry there is no Fishmongers' Guild out here, otherwise I'd have been on another £100 as their guest through Dad's association with that ancient trade . . . Your Johnnie, The Cash and Carry Girl.'

At this point *Truth*, another of Sydney's popular journals, assumed the role of Amy's champion, and for several weeks the whole of their front page was given over to denigrations of their rival's 'dastardly distortions and half truths.' One of these was the figure given for 'the big rake-off,' the total of the cash gifts said to have been received by Amy since she arrived in Australia, namely £12,675. This total had been reached by including not only various items that she would receive only when she returned to England (such as the estimated value of a Puss Moth which de Havillands were to present to her) but also the sum of £10,000 which the *Daily Mail* had announced they were awarding to her for her flight. But this £10,000 was not a gift. When, with appropriate fanfare, a few days after she reached Darwin, the *Daily Mail* had broken the news of their latest aeronautical 'award', they had called it – with reason – 'the largest amount ever paid to any woman for a feat of daring.'[1] But the fact that it was a payment (like

---

[1] The policy of the *Daily Mail* had long been 'to encourage the conquest of the air by all possible means,' and ever since 1906 they had given very generously to pioneers. Three of their prizes had been for £10,000 (one of these went to Alcock and Brown for the first flight across the Atlantic in 1919).

the £2,000 they were already paying to Amy for her exclusive story) was perhaps naturally not stressed, though it was mentioned briefly. The sum in question was in fact the price which Associated Newspapers, spurred by the competition of the *Express*, had contracted with Amy's father to pay for her services during the seven months immediately after her return to England as well as for her aircraft *Jason* (the full implications of this contract did not dawn on Amy till she was nearly home). Why was the award to Amy a payment not an outright gift? Feminists might argue that masculine prejudice was the real reason. But other likely factors were the depressed economic climate of 1930, and the fact that by this time the truly pioneering stage of long-distance flying had almost ended. Amy was just too late.

When the Sydney attacks began Westcott did his best to shield Amy from seeing them, while he himself replied in a restrained and dignified manner. 'Miss Johnson is not pretending she is a wealthy girl,' he explained, 'and she hoped of course to get something from her flight. All Miss Johnson's interest lies in aviation, and everything she gets is going back into aviation in some way. And it all means that she is furthering her ambition to do her little bit towards bettering speedy communication and quicker transport between England and the Dominions.' But when *Truth* came on the scene they sent a reporter to interview Amy at her Melbourne hotel, and he took with him a copy of *Smith's Weekly*. For *Truth* it was a rewarding interview, and the front page of their next issue was headed as follows: TEARS DISSOLVE AMY'S SMILE . . . RESENTS THE GIBE THAT SHE IS A GOLD DIGGER . . . IN GRIEF AND ANGER SHE THREW OFFENDING PAPER BEHIND THE PIANO

VI

The success of Amy's time in Australia was not spoilt by the Sydney attacks. Although she was upset and angered by them she smiled as unceasingly as ever and kept on saying the right thing in her impromptu, hatless little speeches (if she arrived at a function wearing a hat she would whip it off before she started speaking). 'Her tact in one so young and inexperienced is literally uncanny,' wrote a correspondent of one of the Adelaide papers. 'No one has heard her utter a word of complaint; the only shadow of a hint given of her secret sentiments has been a wistful remark that she would like to meet more young people.'

Nevertheless as the tour progress, during the second half of June, with Amy a passenger in Major de Havilland's Hawk Moth (they were accompanied by Ian Grabowsky, Bill Brash – a representative of Wakefields – and Miss Patterson, a secretary) the repetitiousness of the official welcomes became increasingly wearing. She was able to get a certain amount of rest, often sleeping while en route, but once or twice she was a trifle short-tempered in public. Yet as she and her companions stopped at place after place in Victoria, South Australia, and then in Western Australia, she conducted herself extremely well – this impressed both de Havilland and Grabowsky. And after she stayed for four nights at Government House at Adelaide, her hostess, Lady Hore-Ruthven, cabled to her parents 'Amy been staying with us. Standing tour wonderfully. Her head refuses to swell.'

The final stop of the tour was Perth, and when Amy arrived (on the afternoon of Saturday 5 July) outside the Savoy Hotel where she was to stay there was wild enthusiasm and confusion. In the turmoil a man pushed forward and tried to kiss her. She gave him a severe slap in the face and he retreated with a bleeding nose. Two days later, when Major de Havilland saw her off at Fremantle (she sailed for home on 7 July on board the P & O mail steamer *Naldera*[1]) he made a parting gift to her of a pair of boxing gloves, in order –

---

[1] A free passage had been given to her on the initiative of the line's Chairman, Lord Inchcape.

so he teased – that she should be able to defend herself against amorous fans.

Grabowsky has memories of Amy's stay in Perth which show that behind the scenes she also had an unpleasant experience. Bill Brash was a dedicated employee of Wakefields, and at Perth, to please a local aero club which used Wakefield oils, he insisted that Amy must fly a German aircraft, a Klemm, belonging to the club in question. She refused because although her tour was Wakefield-financed she was at this time intensely loyal to the British aircraft industry. 'I was walking to my room at the hotel,' Grabowsky remembers, 'and as I approached Amy's I heard a man's voice raised in anger and swearing. Without knocking I opened the door and there saw Amy lying on the bed crying and sobbing and saying "I won't, I won't." Standing over her was Bill Brash who was loudly and angrily saying somewhat as follows: "You're our servant – we bought you body and soul and you'll bloody well do what you're told and what we arrange."

'I'm afraid what I saw and heard,' Grabowsky continues, 'and the subsequent argument with Brash made me a veritable Sir Galahad, because I yelled at Brash "Shut up and don't you ever let me hear you swear at or abuse Amy again." Naturally Brash resented my interference and having told me to get out he then proceeded to explain that as far as he was concerned no one had any rights over Amy except himself, until she left Australia.' It was perhaps as well that Amy's stay in Perth was a short one.

23

FIASCO

July – October 1930

'They are putting up special barricades at Croydon Aerodrome. I'm afraid she is in for a terrific reception. I do hope she won't mind. It is all terribly exciting, isn't it?' While Winifred Irving was writing to Amy's parents, Amy herself, having left the *Naldera* at Port Said during the last week of July, was about to set off again by Imperial Airways on the final stages of her journey home. The leisurely tempo of air travel in 1930 meant two overnight stops between Egypt and England, and on the day when she was due to reach London, Monday 4 August, the biplane *City of Glasgow* left Vienna at 7 a.m. in hopes of reaching Croydon by six o'clock that evening. But it ran into violent storms and was already an hour late at Cologne. There Amy admitted to a reporter that she was dreading her return to England. Although she did not tell him so her anxiety centred chiefly round her obligations to the *Daily Mail*. She had not yet seen the contract which her father had signed for her while she was in Australia, but at Port Said a letter had reached her from the newspaper explaining that the official welcome at Croydon would be followed by a procession to Grosvenor House (where she and her family would be staying) and two days later there would be a public luncheon at the Savoy Hotel. After that the tour of Britain with her aircraft *Jason* would be launched with three days of welcomings in Hull.

FIASCO

Full details of the tour were unknown to Amy until, at Cologne, she received a letter from William Courtenay, the free-lance publicist whom the *Daily Mail* had engaged as organiser and manager of the tour (he was extremely air-minded and had recently helped Sir Alan Cobham to organise an 'air tour' of Britain). With the letter was a formidable programme covering a period of three months. After London and Hull, so Courtenay announced, Amy was to visit the following towns: Grimsby, Yarmouth, Clacton, Margate, Folkestone, Eastbourne, Bournemouth, Brighton, Portsmouth, Burton-on-Trent, Leicester, Hereford, Cardiff, Gloucester, Bristol, Llandudno, Blackpool, Morecambe, Liverpool, Plymouth, Glasgow, Edinburgh, Carlisle, Newcastle, Bishop Auckland, Manchester, Leeds, Lincoln, Sheffield, Stoke-on-Trent, Derby, Birmingham, Bedford, Norwich, Oxford, Cambridge, Colchester, Northampton and Reading.

'You will I feel sure like to go over this while on your way to Croydon,' Courtenay wrote with pride – for weeks he had been dashing about Britain making the multitudinous arrangements. 'I do not think you will find it too strenuous as it leaves three or four free days each week . . . The general plan has been to link up the tour with some outdoor annual festival such as a Civic Week or a Hospital Fete.'

II

Amy's commitments to the *Daily Mail* were not her only worry. She knew that the publicity concerning herself had got out of hand at home. Her father, whose judgment in handling her business affairs she accepted without question was out of his depth in the world of public relations. She had been shaken when she went ashore at Bombay to learn that a book entitled *Amy Johnson – Lone Girl Flyer*, by a journalist called Charles Dixon, had been rushed out without her knowledge or approval, and she had cabled at once to the *Daily Mail* asking that Crocker should act for her. But Vernon

Wood had cabled back 'The book contains nothing but praise . . . there is nothing to prevent anyone writing about you so long as he writes nothing defamatory or ridiculous.'

Not all the British publicity had been laudatory, however, though most of it was good-humoured. Lacking the presence of the heroine herself the press had fastened on her relatives and pestered them to discuss trivialities. After this a cartoon appeared in *The Graphic* showing a shopping street thick with placards and posters: 'Mrs Johnson gets her groceries here,' 'Fittem shoes – Amy Johnson's cousin wears them,' 'Eat more fruit like Mr Johnson,' 'Mrs Johnson's best friend buys her hats here.' In the newspapers too there had been signs of revolt, and the *Daily Express* published a letter from 'an Eton boy' begging 'Stop all this Amy Johnson stuff.' But such protests were few. As the *City of Glasgow* crawled on its way, against a strong headwind, the catch words of the song-book 'Amy' expressed the sentiments of the vast majority of the bank holiday crowds (estimated by the *Daily Mail* at about a million) that had congregated not only at Croydon but all along the streets of Norbury, Streatham, Brixton, Kennington and Westminster.

When the airliner eventually landed at Croydon it was three hours late and by the time the speeches were to be made dusk had fallen, and the dais was floodlit by means of a beacon used for night landings. This gave the occasion a pseudo-theatrical atmosphere, and seemed to accentuate Amy's youth and also her remarkably spruce appearance after her long, bumpy flight. Her elderly welcomers included Lord Thomson (Secretary of State for Air) and Sir Sefton Brancker,[1] also Miss Margaret Bondfield, Minister for Labour, who looked almost comically dowdy, in a shabby tweed overcoat and tea-cosy hat, as she congratulated Amy on behalf of the

---

[1] Both of these men, only two months later, lost their lives in the R101.

women of Britain and handed her a brown-paper parcel containing fan letters. Amy, in her own speech, seized the chance of saying that she felt the public must be as sick of the sight of her photograph and of her name in the newspapers as she was. She had never expeced such a result from her flight.

The twelve-mile procession to Park Lane was at a snail's pace, and by the time the cars reached Grosvenor House Amy was, according to her father, 'very much distraught' and also thoroughly chilled. But she still had to face a roomful of reporters and did not finally get to bed until about 2 a.m.

Next morning at nine o'clock, when the Johnson family were breakfasting in the Empire suite, with its silver walls and Changing-of-the-Guard decorations, they were joined by Bill Courtenay who had a suite next door. The dark, smooth-mannered, energetic young man regarded himself (so he wrote later in his autobiography) as adviser and 'Man Friday' to Amy.[1] But he was also at this time her taskmaster, a situation almost bound to cause friction. In subsequent years she employed him from time to time as her publicity agent, and relations between them were harmonious when he was no longer at the helm; in their first dealings sparks began to fly at once. 'Amy, in a simple canary-coloured frock, was toying with a grapefruit,' Courtenay reminisced in his book. 'I wanted from her a message for the evening papers about her experiences of the great drive from Croydon. I suggested she might say she found it a very emotional experience, for I had certainly found it so myself. "I am never emotional," she retorted quickly.'

Courtenay's assignment was not an easy one, and he had to deal with a succession of crises. One arose on the morning of the Savoy luncheon when Amy, who by

[1] The duties he assumed included vetting her fan mail, and he says he destroyed at least sixteen proposals of marriage, as well as various invitations from 'perverted females'.

now had a cold, was taken more seriously ill. A doctor diagnosed gastric trouble and a specialist was called in. Rest was what she desperately needed but could not have. Once more her will power triumphed, and most of the cheering crowds to whom she waved and smiled (a little wanly) all the way from Park Lane to the Strand could not see that she was propped up on cushions in the back of the limousine. Nor did the celebrities at the lunch – there were nearly three hundred of them – realise that while she was making her speech a doctor was close at hand, ready for emergency action if she collapsed. No wonder Esmond Harmsworth, presiding on behalf of his father Lord Rothermere, looked anxious as she spoke and as he handed to her the *Daily Mail*'s cheque for £10,000, along with a gold cup to commemorate her 'British Courage and Endurance'.

III

Later the same day she had to drag herself out of bed again to give a broadcast talk. It was not an impromptu effusion like her Australian speeches but had been prepared beforehand, and its slightly defensive tone is of interest as typifying her public statements at this time. 'I am afraid my flight has received far more than its due in publicity,' she said. 'I admit that I am a woman, and the first to do it . . . but in the future I do not want it to be unusual that women should do things; I want it to be recognized that women can do them. I want to assume that people who have taken the trouble to read about me have an interest in the more technical aspects of my flight. For example what preparations did I make? I didn't jump into an aeroplane at Croydon and say "Cheerio! I'm off" with no preparations at all. I do not see any sense in that. I worked jolly hard first . . . People often ask me if I think that many women have engineering minds. I do not at present, but I do believe that everyone can adapt themselves to anything. I believe when women first started motoring that everyone thought they were going to kill themselves, but that is certainly not the case now; and I look forward to the day when exactly the same thing is going to happen in aviation . . . Flying is one of those things that fascinates you; it grips you . . . There is nothing more wonderful and thrilling that I can imagine than going up into the spaciousness of the skies in a tiny light plane where you feel alone, at peace with everyone, and exactly free to do what you want and go where you will, and you need not come down to earth until your petrol runs out . . . Flying must be a heart and soul job, not a pastime, and I appeal to everyone who thinks of taking up flying to do it whole-heartedly. It is no good being lukewarm. If the job is worth doing it is worth doing properly. If you start, keep on.'

In these last two pieces of advice Amy voiced a desire that nagged persistently at her; the desire to be accepted as a 'regular' pilot and engineer. It was a desire which now could never be fulfilled, for she was trapped by her fame. But one of Amy's most influential admirers, Sefton Brancker, was clearly of the opinion that she could best serve 'the cause' as a public figure. 'She is really a splendid girl and I believe she will be a great asset to British aviation in the future,' he wrote to her father in reply to a letter of thanks for his help.

Just after Amy's return to England she saw a lot of Brancker, for he escorted her and made speeches about her at function after function, and also accompanied her to Buckingham Palace to receive her CBE.[1] Brancker also flew to Hull for her homecoming while she herself made the trip at the controls of *Jason* – her first cross-country since she crashed at Brisbane (while in London she had fitted in a few hours' flying practice, at Heston with Captain Baker). In her home town the exuberance of the crowds was almost up to Australian standards, and at one of the Hull functions, a youth

[1] Jimmy Martin drove them there in Amy's new MG saloon, the gift of Sir William Morris.

rally in the City Hall, the enthusiasm of the swarms of boys and girls inspired Amy to a sudden decision. On the spur of the moment, she told them, she had decided to use a purseful of sovereigns that had been presented to her by Sydney children to buy a gold challenge cup, to be won by a Hull child each year for some deed of courage. The idea took hold, and ever since 1932, when the trophy, inscribed 'The Amy Johnson Cup – For Courage' was given to the City of Hull, it has been awarded year by year.[1]

IV

Although the *Daily Mail* tour was timed to start immediately after the Hull visit, it was obvious that Amy must first have a holiday of some sort. A plan was made that she should escape to Wales with her sister Molly for a 'rest cure', but before this she had to be in London again for yet another public occasion, the presentation of the Gipsy Moth subscribed for by the readers of the *Daily Sketch* and *Sunday Graphic* (this was Amy's second new aircraft; the other was the Puss Moth from de Havillands). On a sunny Saturday afternoon Amy, escorted by Brancker, accepted the gift before a crowd of 100,000 in Hyde Park. Among the crowd was a small party of Amy's personal friends with whom she afterwards chatted – she had not seen them for some time. A tall old lady in black, accompanied by one of her daughters, was over from Switzerland (to visit her son Franz and his young wife). They had both

[1] This was not the only gift Amy made to the youth of her home town. From a fund that had been locally subscribed to make presentations to her there was a balance, and the Lord Mayor asked Amy what she would like done with it. She replied that she wished it to be used to finance an aviation scholarship, and as a result in 1931 the Amy Johnson Scholarship in Aeronautics was instituted at Hull University College (awards were made until 1944, but soon after this the university's Aeronautics Department was closed).

come to Hyde Park, and Franz was with them, to do homage to Amy's success. From snapshots we know that the reunion was a very cordial one; and it was thus, just two years after Amy's final parting from Franz, that she met him once more – it was the last time they ever set eyes on each other.

Next day Amy and Molly set off for Wales, driving in the new MG. Amy, with her hair scraped back and wearing glasses, posed as a school-teacher on holiday; they also chose small hotels and called themselves Ann and Moll Jones – yet they were recognised everywhere. Even the car's registration number, MG 720, acted as a magnet for autograph-hunters. Towards the end of the holiday they stayed two days at Harlech, and there they thought, mistakenly, that their fellow guests had not identified them. For once however their secret was not betrayed. Molly recalls that when Amy was stroking a dog belonging to an elderly lady in the hotel she heard its owner say, 'He knows you all right but he's too much of a gentleman to give you away.'

V

Back after only a week, Amy set off in *Jason* on 26 August for Eastbourne, the first seaside town on the *Daily Mail*'s revised programme.[1] At each resort there were to be welcomes and processions, banquets and dances, concerts and fireworks. As there was no aerodrome at Eastbourne, Countrenay had arranged that a farmer's field should be used for Amy's landing, with enclosures for the public, and he and the *Daily Mail*'s pilot, Captain C.B. Wilson, were on the spot when *Jason* came into view. One of the schoolboys present was Peter Masefield (now Chairman of the British Airports Authority) and he can still remember the scene. 'Courtenay was there like a ring-master

---

[1] Several of her appearances had had to be cancelled because of her holiday.

cracking his whip,' he recalls, 'in preparation for the ballerina's appearance. The field was not a very large one, and Amy tried four times to get down without success. Only on a fifth attempt did she manage to land.' He also remembers how tense and exhausted she looked that evening when she appeared on a balcony in the town – this was during a ball when she was greeted by an assembly of eight thousand. The *Daily Mail* must be overworking her, so people said, and her father, writing to her next day, remarked 'I notice you made a poor landing at Eastbourne . . . Do be careful.' He also commented with some anxiety on a *Daily Mail* announcement that Amy would break into her tour to speak for the United Empire Party's candidate at the Bromley by-election. Amy wired back that she had no intention of taking part in the 'Bromley affair'.

Courtenay claims that during the tour he took it upon himself to play the part of Amy's 'guardian and counsellor', but this seems a bit of wishful thinking. Although in the day-to-day arrangements she no doubt relied on him, for 'counsel' she now turned not only to her father but to Sefton Brancker and also to her former boss, Vernon Wood. But Courtenay was an efficient manager, and it appears he must have alerted the *Daily Mail*'s proprietors to the danger signals in Amy's demeanour at Eastbourne. For at Bournemouth, the next place on her programme, she received a telegram from Lord Rothermere saying he hoped she would not undertake too comprehensive a tour because she had already done enough for the *Daily Mail*. 'On the strength of that I could retire at once,' she wrote to her father. 'But I am morally bound to carry out the arrangements already made . . . I'm quite well but tired. Don't worry. Lord Rothermere has sent me a gorgeous diamond bracelet and he wants to see me when he comes back.'

Brighton, for a weekend, was next on the programme, and it was here that relations between Amy and the *Daily Mail* suddenly reached breaking point. Brancker came to Brighton on the Saturday for a dinner party in her honour, and he may well have urged her to 'resign' when he saw the effects the tour was having on her, though according to Courtenay 'ill-informed voices' had been trying since the tour began to persuade her to give it up, and he suggests that some of her flying-club friends had told her she was cheapening the cause of aviation.[1] In any case, on the Sunday at Brighton she told him she had made up her mind to abandon the tour as she found it too strenuous. Courtenay tried but failed to persuade her to change her mind; he then pointed out that according to her contract the aircraft *Jason* belonged to the newspaper. 'The climax came,' so Amy told her father, 'when they threatened to take it from me for their pilot to fly round on tour instead of me. I told them I would burn it sooner than let anyone else fly in it.'

Instead of burning her aircraft she took off in it and flew to Stag Lane. Jack Humphreys remembers that he was shocked to hear she had 'run away', but she was in such distress when she begged him to hide Jason that he agreed to do so. That afternoon Amy had a talk with the overlords of Associated Newspapers and as a result the remainder of the tour was called off, except for two final visits, to Portsmouth and to Ratcliffe in Leicestershire (where a new aerodrome was being opened) but in neither case was she to do any flying. 'The outcome of everything is that the *Mail* are letting me off my contract absolutely and are making the

---

[1] By a strange coincidence it was just at this time that another British woman-pilot was exploiting her success (and was being exploited) on the music-hall stage. Winifred Brown, a Manchester flyer, who had recently won the King's Cup Race – the first woman to do so – was appearing at the London Coliseum, wearing flying kit and with her winning aircraft beside her on the stage. Amy herself had consistently refused offers to appear in variety, but the publicity given to Winifred Brown's 'turn', and the disgust and ridicule it evoked in the aviation world, may well have contributed to Amy's revolt against the *Daily Mail*.

£10,000 a gift,' Amy told her father. '*Jason* belongs to me again and in the meantime . . . is locked up at Stag Lane.' From the viewpoint of Amy and her family there had to be a scapegoat for the failure of the tour and Courtenay was an obvious one. 'I am delighted you are to have a really long holiday,' Amy's father wrote to her, 'and that you are free of the *Daily Mail* tour (such a tour was never in my mind and was never intended – I believe it is only Courtenay who fascinated them with his ideas).'

VI

The 'really long holiday', although it lasted for only ten days took place, under Brancker's auspices, in peaceful and luxurious surroundings; Amy was invited to stay at Norton Priory near Selsey, the beautiful country house of Mr and Mrs Norman Holden. 'It's by the sea and the garden is perfectly glorious,' she wrote to her mother, and added that there were more than thirty peacocks. To her father she explained: 'I felt I could not stand another night in London. I was just afraid for one moment that I was going to have a complete nervous breakdown, but fortunately I have been able to come away in time to prevent that. Mr [Vernon] Wood is dealing with everything most efficiently and thoroughly, and it is such a relief to feel that now things will be seen to properly and not made a hash of by the *Daily Mail*.'

This last remark referred especially to a slip of Courenay's which rankled with Amy. Among the stacks of letters he had dealt with was one offering her a house near Stag Lane as a gift, and not realising that Amy would jump at this he had failed to mention it to her at once. By the time she heard of it and wrote to accept, her well-wisher had withdrawn the offer (and even the expertise of Vernon Wood failed to persuade him to relent).

Letters between Will Johnson and Wood provide some interesting comments on the *Daily Mail* debacle. Wood believed that if, after the first week of receptions,

Amy had been freed from all public duties for at least a month, so as to be able to put her own affairs straight, she would not have had to abandon the tour. 'We knew her personal affairs were worrying her,' her father wrote back. 'On several occasions I have tried to get hold of her in order that these could have some attention, but notwithstanding she has been in England since August 4th I have not had more than ten minutes real talk with her, and therfore I have been quite helpless in the matter . . . Immediately on her return I told her *all* arrangements were still subject to her approval and that if she preferred she could tear the agreement up. The fly in the ointment has undoubtedly been Mr Courtenay . . . I have a feeling she accepted [his] programme because she did not want to let Father down . . . The *Daily Mail* . . . have acted like perfect gentlemen and have been more than fair.'

After Amy's stay at Norton Priory she returned to London again, this time staying at Fleming's Hotel in Half Moon Street. Vernon Wood wrote to her father that the change in her was really wonderful: 'Amy is as bright and cheerful as a bird with two tails.' He was now helping her to find a flat, and also encouraging her to start writing a book about her adventures, but she was in no mood for this. 'I cannot settle down quietly for some time to come – I'm much too restless,' she told her father. 'It is a physical impossibility for me to stay on quietly in England . . . My object now is to clear up sufficiently to allow me to go abroad for a month or two . . . One point I should like to clear up is my liability so far as you are concerned.' After this there was a rendering of accounts, and she repaid to her father not only the £300 he had contributed to the cost of Jason, but every penny he had advanced for her other flying expenses.

VII

The improvement in Amy's health was short-lived. A fortnight later Humphreys was so gravely worried by her condition that through his eldest sister, who had been a VAD, he introduced her to a Harley Street physician, Dr Edmund Moore. Here it seems worthy of remark that there is no evidence, either in Amy's letters or in the memories of her friends, that her thoughts turned towards suicide at this time, even though Dr Moore later told her that when she came to him she was 'on the verge of insanity'.

On the advice of Dr Moore Amy entered a London nursing home for a fortnight of complete rest. While she was there she was shocked to hear of Brancker's death. 'Isn't the R101 disaster terrible,' she wrote to her mother. 'I had a lot of friends on board, and as a matter of fact, though you didn't know . . . I was nearly there myself. I told Sir Sefton Brancker I wanted to go on it and he used all his influence but no one quite knows why in the end all the women were forbidden to go . . . I've lost a good friend in him.'

She told her mother that after leaving the nursing home she would be staying with some new friends, Sir Archibald and Lady Weigall, who she thought would be of great help to her. Sir Archibald was a former Governor of South Australia, and Lady Weigall, as one of the Maple family, was well able to advise and help her with the furnishing of her flat. She was to stay with the Weigalls in their Mayfair house as 'Miss Audrey James' and only her parents and Crockers were to know her whereabouts. From the nursing home she wrote to her father, 'When I leave here I shall still be under doctor's orders. I am far from strong and have to go easy . . . It's taking me all my time to persuade the Doctor not to cancel my Engineers' Dinner. I've explained to him it's one of the most important events of my career.'[1]

It is obvious that Amy's parents, who were coming to London for the dinner and also for the Motor Show, did

---

[1] The Society of Engineers had asked her to read a paper about the maintenance she gave to her engine on the flight to Australia, and this 'serious' recognition delighted her. Jack Humphrey's helped her to prepare the paper.

not realise the state of her nerves, for they wrote suggesting that she might like to join them in visiting the show. Then, when they reached London, her father committed the solecism of telephoning to the Weigalls' house and asking for Miss Amy Johnson. This led to an outburst of uncontrollable temper from Amy, and her anger was still simmering when she wrote to them next day. 'What annoyed me so much,' she fumed, 'was that you couldn't even understand, or believe, that you had made things enormously difficult for me by phoning for me under my own name. Another thing you cannot realise is that I detest the publicity and public life that have been forced upon me . . . I have therefore been driven to tell you (rather too forcibly, I admit) what you cannot see for yourselves . . . that I am seeking hard to lose my identity of "Amy Johnson" because that personage has become a nightmare and an abomination to me. My great ideas for a career in aviation have been annulled, for a long time to come, by the wrong kind of publicity and exploitation which followed my return to England . . . I've had a complete collapse ever since the Engineers' Dinner and I'm not normal at present . . . I strongly resent interference and efforts to rule my life or control my actions . . . I've lived my own life for the last seven years and I intend to continue doing so.'

An interesting sidelight upon her state at this time is contained in a letter written by Dr Moore to Vernon Wood on 22 October, the day after the Engineers' Dinner. 'It was disappointing to find Miss Johnson's weight and blood pressure both down,' he wrote. 'I do not think she had any idea of establishing a physiological credit . . . Though she does not realise it, she wants a strong hand on her. I personally have not the same control now that she is away from the Nursing Home, and I am afraid I have not the time to run about after her.'

Amy stayed with the Weigalls for about three weeks, and towards the end of the time had to drop her alias, for her hostess was keen to display her famous protégée. 'I've just come back from a "tea fight" at

Viscountess Elibank's,' Amy wrote to her parents. 'How I loathe such stupid functions. On Friday I have to go to Princess Beatrice's Charity Dinner . . . I can't get out of it because it's Lady Weigall's pet scheme. She's getting just like everyone else – anxious to show me off – how I hate it! . . . I'm longing to get my own flat and be back living a grubby life at the aerodrome, or on another flight.'

One of the flight ideas Amy was toying with at this time was an attack on the long distance record; nothing came of it but the relevant correspondence provides a tailpiece to her association with the *Daily Mail*. It also shows that Amy was as single-minded in her financial planning as she was in carrying out a long-distance flight. It seems she wrote to her erstwhile patron Lord Rothermere (with whom she was evidently still on good terms) to ask for his backing, and also to suggest that the *Daily Mail* should buy back her aircraft *Jason* for £300, for the purpose of presenting it to the nation. To the first proposition Lord Rothermere said a firm no, but to the latter he said yes, and that is how the historic aeroplane G-AAAH found its way to the Science Museum.

24

HER OWN MISTRESS

November 1930 – March 1932

When in mid-November Amy moved into her new home, a flat in Vernon Court, a block overlooking the junction of the Finchley Road and the Barnet by-pass, she was relieved beyond measure to have her own establishment. With the cheerful company of a bull-terrier called Rough and within easy reach of her friends and her aeroplanes at Stag Lane, she rapidly improved in health. On 12 December she told her mother that she had just taken her 'B' Licence medical and she thought she had passed 'with flying colours'. 'It is extremely stiff and if one can pass that one must be very fit indeed . . . so you may rest assured that I am now quite well.'

But she still could not escape from the fan mail and the invitations, and her restlessness was insuperable. Flips to Hull and back could not satisfy her hunger for adventure and she confided to her father that she was hoping to go abroad again at the end of the year. 'I am not quite sure where I am going, but probably to China, a country I am extremly anxious to visit. Please don't breathe a word about it to anyone as I have a dread of it getting into the press . . . I shall have no peace at all until I am out of the country – the letters still pour in and I spend half my life answering them, and even then I only answer the essential ones. I've firmly made up my mind that New Year's Day shall be a definite new leaf, and after that . . . I shall undertake no further functions or answer any further letters except those from personal friends or in connection with my career.'

Her plans for a new long-distance flight took shape quickly – too quickly, in Jack Humphreys' view – and two weeks later she wrote to her parents, confirming that she was to set off on New Year's Day. 'Berlin is my first stop. Warsaw is the second, then Moscow, then . . . I follow the Trans-Siberian railway all the way to Peking and the aerodrome at which I stop depends on what information I get in Moscow . . . Please don't worry. I'll be very careful and let you know my movements as often as I can.'

II

The idea of a solo flight across Siberia in mid-winter was an utterly crazy one, espcially as Amy decided to make it in an open aeroplane, her Gipsy Moth *Jason III*, nicknamed 'God Willing' (*Deo Volente*) because of its registration letters 'DV'.[1] But with aircraft and money of her own she could now tackle any mad venture she fancied, and another long-distance flight would, so it seemed, rescue her from the chores of public life and yet keep her in the news in the interests of her career. Furthermore the planning for such a flight gave her the satisfaction of an over-riding purpose – something she otherwise lacked now that her life was an 'illimitable holiday'.

Through the British Embassy in Moscow she sought advice from the Osoaviakhim, the Soviet air propaganda organisation, and its Council's reply, though friendly, was most discouraging. 'The chief difficulty of the flight would be the exceedingly low air temperature . . . The Gipsy engine . . . has never been tried in these conditions . . . The Council warns the pilot about the aeronautical peculiarities of winter

1 This was the aircraft given to her by the readers of the *Daily Sketch* and *Sunday Graphic*.

flight in Siberia near the Pole where she will inevitably come across very thick fogs and snow storms.' The Council promised however that if Amy did proceed she would be given full facilities, even though they held that she was 'insufficiently prepared for such a serious and responsible matter.' When she left Stag Lane according to plan on New Year's Day 1931, having announced that she would change her undercarriage for skis at Warsaw, she had not yet received a permit to fly over Soviet territory.

Clad in a green leather flying suit Amy had to grope her way across Europe through icy mist and snow, losing her way time and again. After overnight stops at Liege, Cologne and Berlin she set off for Warsaw but once more got hopelessly lost, and about fifty miles short of her objective had to make a forced landing in fog. The red and white Moth crashed down on to a potato field, breaking undercarriage and propeller though Amy herself was unhurt. With help from a local priest, the British Embassy in Warsaw and the Polish Air Force she and her aircraft were transported to the capital and there she cabled home 'Not proceeding; Plans indefinite;' but in fact while her machine was being mended she did proceed (by night train) to Moscow, in order to pave the way for another trans-Siberian attempt later on in the year.

The visit to Moscow was a great success; Amy received a flattering welcome from various aeronautical leaders, became friends with Comrade Egorov (Chairman of the Osoaviakhim's Council), was praised by Lenin's widow as the best possible example for Soviet womanhood, and was given an hour's flight in a training aircraft. Rumours thereupon reached London that she was still intending to continue her flight eastwards. 'There's so many different reports that one cannot believe the press at all,' Jack Humphreys wrote to Amy's mother. 'I see in today's papers that still she may go on; I for one sincerely hope not . . . At Omsk the temperature is 100° [Fahrenheit] below freezing point. And petrol and oil will not stand that and I'm sure the engine cannot run below 60°. You see there's things we engineers can do flying in really cold weather, but not so cold and I'm very doubtful.' But he need not have worried. Before the end of January Amy was back at Vernon Court.

III

Chastened and realistic, she told Humphreys that she meant to try the flight again in summer, using her cabin aeroplane *Jason II* (the Puss Moth given to her by de Havillands). She then went on to suggest that he himself should accompany her. He was already by now acting as her mechanic: since the accident to his arm he had been unable to resume full-time work, for the complications of his injury were protracted, but when she had invited him to take care of her aeroplanes he had gladly accepted. This new business arrangement was in tune with a new development in their personal relationship, for since Australia Humphreys had become an Amy-worshipper, and although the easygoing banter between 'Jack' and 'Johnnie' was the same as ever, and he was still her most trusted confidant, he was no longer her 'tutor' but her devoted henchman. He had also become, by this time, an intimate friend of all the Johnson family. 'I'm teaching Jack to fly,'[1] Amy wrote to her father, 'as I have decided to take him along on my next flight. I need a mechanic and I'd rather have Jack with me than anyone else whom I don't know so well.'

The weeks and months of the summer of 1931 slipped by while Amy, based at Vernon Court, prepared for her flight. She did not mind living alone so long as she had a dog for company, and the flat suited her although she never really settled there. It was partly

---

[1] This remark is misleading. She was giving Humphreys a refresher course on the Puss Moth, which was very necessary as he had never flown one.

pied-à-terre, partly office (her fan mail now averaged about fifty letters a day). Two typewriters, letter cabinets, an enormous map of the world, a model of *Jason* and a cartoon asserting 'Ahr Amy has more backbone than her father's kippers,' were the items in the flat that caught the eye of a reporter who came to interview her there.

Apart from answering fan letters Amy's life at this time consisted largely of pottering about at Stag Lane and making sorties to other flying clubs; she was also taking daily riding lessons, which delighted her and much improved her health ('*I do love my horse!*' she exclaimed to her mother). There was an occasional uproarious party at the flat when she entertained her Stag Lane friends; she had now with relief sunk back into the social milieu where she felt most at ease, the cheerful, unpretentious happy-go-lucky milieu of the London Aeroplane Club. Her brief excursion into London 'society' had not brought any lasting friendships and she was now deliberately cutting herself off from it and declining almost all invitations to public functions.

Among her new flying-club acquaintances were three fellow-enthusiasts who were soon to make a mark in aviation, Dorothy Spicer, Pauline Gower and Winifred Spooner, while her admirers included a hat manufacturer, a scrap metal merchant, and two tycoons of the tailoring trade. She was not at present thinking of marriage, so she told an inquisitive reporter, who discovered that she nevertheless had an open mind on the matter and was not a man-hater. Her romantic aspirations were summed up thus by her interviewer: 'She wants somebody who has done more, seen more, than she has. Naturally hard to find.' And she was quoted as saying, 'I won't marry somebody who'll be known as Amy Johnson's husband.' Here it is perhaps pertinent to mention that Jack Humphreys believes Amy should have remained unmarried all her life, partly because when she was in one of her bad moods, 'you could do nothing with her.' In 1931 however he hoped that if she did decide to marry she might choose a young man whom she had met at the Leicestershire Flying Club, Peter Reiss, an aviation insurance broker who was a keen owner-pilot.

IV

Amy's new flight was timed for the end of July and she decided to aim for Tokyo, not Peking, in view of the worsening political situation in the Far East – this was just before Japan finally annexed Manchuria. Ciss Johnson, always a worrier, was full of anxieties. Apart from the threat of war there was always, of course, in these pre-radio days, the risk of a stranding in the wilds.[1] Amy tried to reassure her. 'You've no need to worry at all about this trip,' she wrote. 'You wouldn't if you could see how many aerodromes there are in Russia – about every twenty miles by the look of the map.'[2]

For the Tokyo flight she decided not to fit extra tanks in her Puss Moth for she wanted to show what could be achieved in a normal machine, but this meant that she and Humphreys would have to come down three or four times every day for petrol. On the first day of the flight, 28 July, after leaving Lympne before dawn, they stopped at Berlin, Konigsberg and Velikiye Luki before completing their first lap to Moscow late that evening. The two had agreed to take the flying in turns, and it was on that first day that Humphreys, at the controls, became aware of Amy's uncanny sense of direction. After crossing the Russian frontier he was doing a compass course over dense forests and the moon was rising. Amy had dropped off to sleep; then suddenly waking up she pointed off-course exclaiming 'Moscow's

[1] As portrayed by David Garnett in his terrifying novel *The Grasshoppers Come* which was published at just this time.
[2] During her stay in Moscow Amy had acquired a set of maps covering her intended route, showing all the 'civil airports' and 'aerodromes' laid down – at least in theory – under the First Five-Year Plan.

over there!' Her intuition disagreed with the compass course and there was no sign of a glow in the sky, but she was right. He also came to realise more clearly as the trip progressed that as a pilot Amy had definite shortcomings. He remembers that his most usual comment on her approaches was 'Woman! You'll have to go round again!'

For six days after leaving Moscow they flew on over the USSR, across the Urals, across the steppes, across the forests; following the trans-Siberian railway as much as possible, but often losing it as it tunnelled into the dark carpet of fir. At the Soviet 'airports' facilities were very crude but the Russians in charge – frequently women – were very friendly, and oil and petrol were supplied free. There were overnight stops at Kazan, Kurgan, Tiajin (near Tomsk), Irkutsk and Chita, and each evening Humphreys serviced the engine while Amy went off early to rest; then in the morning she was fresh for first turn as pilot. After the cordiality of the USSR they encountered a very different atmosphere in Manchuria. There the Japanese military authorities only permitted them to continue on condition that they kept scrupulously to a specified route, avoided all fortified zones, and refrained from taking aerial photographs.

When Amy and her 'mechanic' arrived at Tokyo on 6 August their flight from England had taken just under ten days; longer than they had hoped but better than the comparable lightplane record of eleven days between Berlin and Tokyo that had been set up by a Japanese pilot. In the world press their flight received little attention for it was somehow lacking in drama, and besides there were many other long-distance flights and flyers in the news. On the very day the trip was completed the American aviators Pangborn and Herndon also reached Tokyo on a round-the-world attempt, while meantime the Lindberghs were en route to Japan via Alaska, and three other Americans were already in Japan prior to tackling Pacific crossings. At the same time Francis Chichester, having crashed at Katsuura after completing his historic seaplane solo from Australia, was recuperating in a Japanese hospital (before Amy and Humphreys left for home they journeyed across Japan to visit him).

In the London papers on 7 August 1931 little mention was made of Amy's arrival in Tokyo, even though she had been welcomed with an embrace by General Nagaoka, the venerable President of the Imperial Aviation Society, whose whiskers were claimed to be the longest and whitest in the world. The headlines that day were devoted instead to the arrival in England of an unknown pilot from Australia – Jim Mollison. He had accomplished the amazing feat of making the trip solo in a Puss Moth in nine days, thus improving on the existing record by as much as forty-eight hours. It was a triumph of good planning, flying skill and endurance, and among the cables of congratulation he received was one signed 'Amy Johnson'.

V

The flying partnership between 'Johnnie' and 'Jack' worked so well that after their return to England in September Amy started to plan another trip with Humphreys – a very ambitious one – for the following summer. She wanted to make a flight round the world in a much more powerful aircraft than her Puss Moth, in order to challenge the eight-day record that had been established by the Americans Wiley Post and Harold Gatty. Full of confidence she wrote to Comrade Egorov for additional maps, persuaded Lord Wakefield to help with the backing, and began looking round for a suitable aeroplane: the Viastra, a new Vickers twelve-passenger airliner, seemed an ideal choice, and the company responded quite favourably to her first overtures. In the meantime, during the autumn of 1931, she decided to fill in time with a lecture tour, organised for her by a Liverpool concern, the Lecture League. Humphreys was to accompany her as indispensable man-of-all-work. Her talk with lantern slides, 'How *Jason* and I flew to the Land of the Golden

Fleece' proved very popular and she averaged a couple
of engagements a week.

For Christmas she was with her family, in Bridlington
not Hull, for her parents had just moved;[1] then she was
off again with Humphreys to lecture at various north-
country towns. But a sudden sharp attack of illness put a
stop to the tour: at Bolton she collapsed, stricken with
acute abdominal pains. She insisted that she must be
treated in London by the woman doctor who was now
attending her, and Humphreys had a nightmare drive
south through fog with Amy lying in the back of the car.
Two days later, in a London nursing home, she
underwent an operation which according to press reports
was for apendicitis. Letters from Amy to her mother at
the time, however, indicate that it was of a gynaecological
nature – probably some kind of hysterectomy. Amy and
her doctor had already discussed the need for such an
operation and the Bolton attack evidently precipitated it.
Several of Amy's close friends agree that the operation
must have been a drastic one for thereafter she was
incapacitated as far as child-bearing was concerned. At
the same time it obviously made her life easier as regards
her long-distance flying.

After three weeks in the nursing home Amy was sent to
a convalescent home near Colchester, which she found
very drab and depressing. She had been daydreaming of
a holiday in the sun and protested so loudly that after a
few days her doctor gave her permission to go to Madeira
instead, accompanied by a nurse. But when the
Winchester Castle reached Madeira she decided, on a
sudden impulse, that instead of stopping there she would
continue on the boat to South Africa. 'I intended to stay,
said goodbye and went ashore with the luggage,' she
wrote home later, 'but I didn't like the hotel and I didn't
like the people there. Gossipy, catty, society people they
looked. I'd gone all that way for sunshine, and it had
been raining there for six weeks. So I changed my mind.'

---

[1] This was a first step towards Will Johnson's retirement.

AMY JOHNSON

She loved the simple routine of the ship's life and the freedom from letters and telephones; she also amused herself by learning about navigation from one of the ship's officers. Before she reached the Cape she was enjoying herself so much that she had made up her mind she would not leave the *Winchester Castle* at Cape Town to return home on another ship, but would remain on it for the rest of its trip to Durban and rejoin it there for the voyage home. Thus she would not be back until early May and she cabled to Humphreys (who was acting for her with Vickers) that she would probably postpone her world flight with him until 1933; 'but,' she added, 'keep up negotiations until my return.'

Also while still at sea she heard the news that in South Africa the arrival of a long-distance solo flyer from England was awaited with much excitement. It was Jim Mollison, who was making the first light-plane flight to the Cape across the Sahara, and if all went well he would be reaching Cape Town on the same day as herself. Although Amy had cabled her congratulations to him from Tokyo the previous summer she had not met him since Australia. After she returned from Japan he was in Britain but their paths had not crossed.

25

JIM

March – July 1932

Jim Mollison reached Cape Town from England on
28 March 1932 almost incoherent with exhaustion
– during the trip of four days and seventeen hours he
had snatched only two hours' sleep – to find Amy
waiting at the aerodrome to meet him. In a tailored
travelling coat and close-fitting hat she looked neat and
a little shy. They exchanged banalities and after the
official welcomes she accompanied him to his hotel to
help him with his cables. Next day, when he had
revived somewhat and had his hair cut, and before the
Winchester Castle sailed for Durban, the two lunched
together and Amy, still in the hyper-impressionable
stages of convalescence, emerged from these
encounters dazzled and deeply in love.

What was Jim Mollison like in 1932? He was twenty-
seven, two years younger than Amy and only a trifle
taller, with bold blue eyes, full lips, and a charm of
manner that often proved irresistible to women. His voice
did not betray that he came from Glasgow for he had
acquired a drawl which has been likened to an Oxford
accent. Nor would one have guessed, from the dandyish
style he affected, that in the RAF (before his airliner days
in Australia) he had been a redoubtable boxer. (This is
well brought out in an anecdote told by one of Mollison's
Australian friends, the late Sir Gordon Taylor, in his book
The Sky Beyond. 'There is an authentic story of a night at
a dance in Melbourne. Some semi-drunk was foolish

297

enough to mistake the meaning of Mollison's waved hair
and to insult him in front of the lady with whom he was
dancing. Mollison quietly took the man outside, asked
him his address, got it; then beat him up into
insensibility, called and paid a taxi, and had the remains
delivered to the address.')

The meetings between the two flyers gave rise to
rumours of plans for a joint Atlantic flight, which Amy
denied as soon as she heard them, but there were no
hints of a 'romance' for as far as love interest was
concerned Mollison was already pigeon-holed: on the
day before he left England the popular press had
proclaimed his 'engagement' to Lady Diana Wellesley, the
tall, handsome eighteen-year-old half-sister of Earl
Cowley. The news was given special prominence in the
Evening Standard which Bill Courtenay had recently
joined.[1] The announcement was exceedingly premature.
Lady Diana had met Mollison at a Mayfair party – as a
new celebrity, living on his prize money at Grosvenor
House, he was being lionised at the time – and they had
since been enjoying a flirtation. But he was alarmed to
find that he was credited with serious intentions, and
was glad (so he later wrote) to be on the point of leaving
the country. In Cape Town he refused to make any
statement about himself and Lady Diana, and insisted
that nothing which had been reported about their affairs
had been authorised.

II

As far as Amy was concerned the emotional flurry of
her short stay in Cape Town caused a relapse in her
health, which was still very precarious. During the sea
trip alone[2] to Durban she was, so she afterwards said,

[1] Courtenay had been seeing a lot of Mollison for he was
ghost-writing an autobiography for him: it was published
later in the year under the title *Death Cometh Soon or Late*.
[2] Her nurse had left her at Cape Town to return direct to
England.

on the verge of hysterics, and on arriving there she was so 'done up' that she fainted and could not face anyone. This did not make her popular and she was distressed when she glimpsed a placard with the taunt 'BAD HEALTH OR BAD MANNERS?' A kindly millionaire, Mr W. Campbell, then came to the rescue and whisked her off to his country estate for ten days' complete rest. She stayed there sunbathing, with doctors and nurses in attendance, until just before the *Winchester Castle* sailed for England, and to a certain extent she recovered herself.

Waiting for Amy at Southampton was her mother, accompanied by Jack Humphreys, who knew at once from Amy's demeanour, that 'something was up'. A few days later he flew with her to Antwerp in her Puss Moth for an Aircraft Display and on their return they landed at Heston – to find Jim Mollison there.[1] Humphreys remembers that as soon as he saw Amy and Jim together he knew that 'something must happen' and indeed it did. Events now moved very swiftly. Mollison invited Amy to lunch with him next day (Monday 9 May) at Quaglino's, then one of the most fashionable restaurants in London, and at this tête-à-tête her bearing as well as her soignée looks attracted him increasingly (since her operation she was taking much more trouble about her appearance and had lost her former tomboy looks). Writing later of this lunch he made admiring mention of Amy's appearance – and also of her smile. Over the brandy he asked her to marry him and she accepted.

There is no doubt that the proposal was unpremeditated. When Mollison was asked next day whether there had been an understanding between

[1] Mollison's personal affairs were not in a satisfactory state at this point. He had got back to England (by sea) a fortnight ahead of Amy, to face an awkward interview with Lady Diana's mother, Clare, Countess Cowley, who during his absence had been denying that her daughter was engaged. But the situation had been patched up with a statement to the press that she and the young couple had agreed on a year's interval before any final decision was made.

himself and Amy in South Africa he replied without hesitation, 'No, there was no engagement then.' And in his autobiography *Playboy of the Air* he later emphasised that before the lunch at Quaglino's 'We had not considered, even momentarily, marrying one another. We had not discussed it in any way.' That afternoon the couple arranged that their engagement should be announced in *The Times* on the following day, and in the evening Amy broke the news first to her mother by telephone and then to the *Daily Mail*. That same evening she said to Jack Humphreys: 'I've got some news for you – you'll never guess!' 'You're going to marry Jim Mollison,' he answered. Meanwhile her fiancé was back at Quaglino's, in turn breaking the news to Lady Diana, who subsequently made the following statement: 'Jim Mollison is and always will be a very dear friend of mine . . . He and Miss Johnson have many interests in common, particularly as regards flying. I am sure Miss Johnson will be a most admirable partner for him.' One may add that Lady Diana herself was married during the following year and is now Lady Glentoran.

It seems that Bill Courtenay first learnt of the engagement from the paragraph in *The Times*. He had a thick skin and there is no evidence that he wasted time on feeling hurt because he had not been given an exclusive story for his paper. But he leapt at the opportunities that the 'romance' now offered him. This should not however be taken to imply that his congratulations to Amy and Jim were insincere: in his complex character, along with all the astuteness and showmanship there was a broad streak of romanticism and sentimentality. He lost no time in staging a lunch with the two 'to discuss the future of their flying careers,' and in his autobiography he claims that they took him into their confidence about all their plans and 'it was arranged that I should look after their joint interests and be associated with them in all their adventures.' This suggests that he became their press agent and manager on a regular basis straightaway but in fact he did not; he worked gradually towards such a position but attained to it only sporadically, by means of handling individual flights and 'stories'.

III

Among Amy's family, friends and acquaintances the reactions to her engagement varied from happy astonishment to dismay. Her parents were, with reason, taken aback by its suddenness, and her mother was at first very much upset to think that Amy was going to marry a man whom she had known for a total of less than twenty-four hours. She wrote to Jack Humphreys that she 'felt terrible about it,' and he tried to console her. 'They are both being really wonderful,' he wrote back, 'and are so very happy. In fact from Johnnie I get nothing but Jim, and from Jim nothing but Amy. Surely this is *all any* of us has wanted for years, and now we can only hope and pray for their continued happiness which I feel assured is already settled completely. I only ask you all to be very, very happy, for they are; and their understanding of each other is ideal.' Amy herself wrote to her father, 'Please believe that I'm *very, very* happy. Jim is a dear, and in spite of newspaper publicity, which seems to point to the engagement being only a business partnership, it is far more than that. To begin with I didn't realise it quite so clearly as I do now. I don't think I shall ever regret this big decision in my life.'

Together the engaged couple flew to Glasgow and in suburban Bearsden Amy was introduced to Jim's mother and to his step-father, Mr Charles Bullmore. Jim was an only child, and his mother worshipped him, though we know – from a letter she wrote subsequently to Amy – that there had long been difficulties between them, partly no doubt because of the unstable atmosphere caused by his parents' broken marriage.[1] This visit to Glasgow was the occasion of a

---

[1] Jim's father, Hector Mollison, and his mother (*née* Thomasina Addie) were divorced in 1915, when Jim was ten.

great gathering of Jim's relations. He prided himself on his Mollison blood, and what family links he kept up were chiefly with his father's relatives. Before the Scottish trip he had already introduced Amy to his Aunt Katherine (one of his five Mollison aunts) whose husband, Dr W. Alexander Hislop, practised in London – a warm friendship was soon to develop between Amy and both the Hislops. Amy's feelings for Jim's aged Mollison grandfather (a retired engineer surveyor) also later became very affectionate. But immediately after her first visit to Bearsden she wrote to her mother: 'Scotland was nearly more than I could stand. Jim's relatives nearly killed me! Well-meaning but of course I don't know them, and they're *so* dull, but quite nice.'

Jim's feelings about the Johnson family, after his first meeting with them at Bridlington, are not on record though a letter written afterwards by Amy to her mother, explaining that Jim had not been feeling well at the time, suggests that this occasion too was a sticky one.

IV

During the twelve weeks of Amy's engagement a revolution took place in her way of life. A year later, looking back to this time, she wrote to her parents (apropos of her health) 'I never really properly got over my operation . . . I got engaged and started a hectic life too soon after it.' Hectic indeed was the life of parties and publicity and prodigal spending that she was swept into as Jim Mollison's fiancée. The luxury of his standards at Grosvenor House – where he lived a gay life as long as his most recent prize money lasted – gave her a good excuse to leave Vernon Court (which she later sublet) and she installed herself first at the new Dorchester Hotel and then at Grosvenor House itself. 'I simply couldn't live at my flat any longer, I was getting to hate the place,' she wrote to her father from the Dorchester in June. 'It was damp and dark and far too much responsibility besides being very lonely. It is of course very extravagant to be living at a hotel like this . . . I pay forty-five shillings per day for a six-guinea suite . . . but this situation is only temporary. Most of my meals I appear to be having at the expense of other people, but I have spent quite a lot of money on clothes and have got some lovely new things, including a gorgeous fur coat[1] . . . I've got a beautiful engagement ring – a large single cinnamon diamond, with diamond shoulders. I'm giving Jim a gold cigarette case because he hasn't one and is always borrowing cigarettes, just like a true Scotsman!'

'Privately and between ourselves,' she told her parents, 'we are not going to have a big wedding and there will be no dressing up with bridesmaids and cake etc. I couldn't stand it. You mustn't be disappointed although I'm afraid many people will be. We've no idea yet when we'll get married, and we're still racking our brains to find out how we can escape publicity. We've been told on very good authority that all the registry offices are being watched.'

In the intervals between spending and merrymaking Amy and Jim busied themselves with projects for future flights. One of these schemes (which proved abortive) was that he should partner her on her round-the-world attempt instead of Humphreys. 'When Jim stepped in, I stepped out,' is how Humphreys himself cheerfully puts it, ignoring the offhand treatment he received at the time from the Jim-infatuated Amy; on 9 June she wrote casually to her father, 'I've given Jack a month's notice and I believe he's got a job abroad.'

Before the end of June Amy and Jim snatched a holiday in the South of France, then newly fashionable as a summer playground. In a letter home from Juan les Pins Amy described her gay doings and listed the film stars she had been meeting, but did not hide her uneasiness at her fiancé's careless attitude to life, not

---

[1] At this time she was still living on the proceeds of her Australia flight.

only about money – in Jim's view debts were a nusiance to be evaded.[1] 'I wish I didn't worry so much and take things so deeply and seriously – I think it's far better to take life lightly, but I'm not made that way.' Jim's hard drinking, already a long-established habit, was one of the things which she found she could not 'take lightly', but her chief worry, she confessed, was his next flight – it was to be a two-way attempt across the North Atlantic in a Puss Moth and was due to take place in a few weeks. There was talk of her accompanying him but this idea was dropped. From Grosvenor House on 21 July she wrote to her mother: 'I wish I could go to sleep and wake up a month hence when everything's all over. I can't settle to anything until Jim's done his flight. I know I'm going through now what you went through for me, but that doesn't make it any easier.' Then four days later she wrote home again: 'Don't believe what the newspapers are saying' – this referred to rumours that her marriage was to take place very soon.

V

At nine o'clock on the evening of 28 July Amy's parents received the following telegram: 'Jim and I are getting married tomorrow morning at ten o'clock but we are trying to keep it as quiet as possible. We should have much liked your presence but in the circumstances of Jim's approaching flight have decided to keep it an absolutely private affair between ourselves. Much Love, Amy.' Some panic telephoning took place between Bridlington and London, but after it was established that there was no early train which could get the family to London in time for the wedding Amy 'reconciled herself' (so she told a reporter next day) to the fact that they would have to be absent.

[1] When in 1928, at twenty-three, he came to the end of his RAF short service commission, he disappeared abroad leaving many unpaid debts behind him. In his autobiography *Playboy of the Air* he alluded openly to this.

JIM

Whose idea was it to exclude the Johnsons from the wedding? In the light of Jim's feelings about his mother there seems little doubt that it was he who insisted that no relatives should be invited. And even though Amy must surely have regretted this, one must remember that she was very strongly dominated by her fiancé at this time. In her dressing, for example, towards the end of her engagement she took to wearing only black and white to please him. Even for the wedding she wore black; a black coat-frock, with a swirl of silver fox round her shoulders and a little black cap trimmed with an eye-veil. Against this sombre background there was one striking note of contrast: white gauntlet gloves, and Amy's choice of these provides a strange echo of her first love affair. Seven years earlier she had told Franz that in one of her most vivid dreams she was aware that she could not be married to him because she 'could not find the white gloves.'

Amy and Jim were married (on the morning of Friday 29 July) at St George's, Hanover Square; the Ven F.N. Thicknesse, Archdeacon of Middlesex, officiated and only a handful of guests were present. Amy was given away by Kathleen, Countess of Drogheda – a flamboyant divorcee whose enthusiasm for flying was such that she had chosen 'Kathospeed, London' as her personal telegraphic address. The best man was Lieutenant Colonel Francis Shelmerdine, an air-minded civil servant who had succeeded Brancker as Director of Civil Aviation. Mollison later declared he would have preferred a registry-office marriage, 'but the public loves a big wedding.'

Outside in Hanover Street the crowds were agog and a huge Rolls-Royce was waiting to take Amy and Jim back to Grosvenor House when an elderly couple and two schoolgirls hurried into the church. Amy's parents and sisters had driven through the night from Bridlington in an agony of haste but hindred by heavy rain and skiddy roads. 'It was really a race against time to get there before 10 a.m.,' her mother wrote to her afterwards in much distress of mind. 'We could *not* manage it, try as we would; did not even stop to have any breakfast! We were so terribly grieved, so bitterly hurt, I was ill at the shock . . . What hurt us so much was that you had told us "not to take any *notice* of what the *papers* say." If you had told us . . . and asked us to keep it secret, we should not have minded so much, but to put us off so . . . was most terribly cruel and heartless.'

The family party went into the church and sat down in a side pew as though waiting for the ceremony to begin. They were told it was finished and the register was being signed, but the foursome remained paralysed in their pew while a smiling Amy, on her husband's arm, passed down the aisle without a glance in their direction. At the wedding breakfast at Grosvenor House, when she was told what had happened, she insisted that a search should be made by telephone, and hotel after hotel was questioned. But by this time her parents and sisters were on their way back to Yorkshire. They had slipped away from the church in anguished humiliation, but not before reporters had spotted them and made a 'story' out of their discomfiture.

26

BACK ON THE FRONT PAGE
1932–1933

The Mollisons' married life was fated to the glare of publicity from the start. Almost everything they did, almost everything that happened to them, was potential fodder for the news-hounds and the columnists. When Amy and Jim arrived in Scotland for their honeymoon, flying separately in two newly-acquired aircraft, reporters pounced on the 'air lovers' who were so soon to be parted by Jim's Atlantic flight. Jim enjoyed playing to the gallery and rightly regarded it as an important part of his job as a long-distance flyer, but there was also a certain simpleness in his nature, and his tongue was not in his cheek when he replied to the questionings of the press. 'Many people have wondered at me getting married to Amy before the flight,' he was quoted as saying, 'but our decision to become husband and wife was a sign that I was absolutely sure that I will succeed in my mission . . . If I accomplish the double journey in two and a half days I will be the happiest man in the world and Amy will be the happiest woman.'

The flight was so imminent that the honeymoon could not last for more than a weekend, but it was a weekend spent in a very sophisticated setting, for the Mollisons had been invited to stay at Kelburn Castle on the Firth of Clyde, where their hostess was Lady Bowden (wife of Sir Harold Bowden, the Birmingham bicycle manufacturer, who had rented the castle from the Earl of Glasgow). Then they rushed back to London, before dashing on to Ireland, for Portmarnock Strand near Dublin was the 'runway' Jim had chosen for his take-off. His new Puss Moth, the *Hearts Content*,[1] had to be very heavily overloaded and needed a run of over a mile.

Jim himself, as well as his aeroplane, required an abnormal amount of 'fuel' for a flight of this kind. One of his friends, Sidney Cotton (soon to become famous as a pioneer of photographic reconnaissance) has remarked wryly, 'Jim's long-distance flights differed from those of others in that others came down when they ran out of petrol, but Jim's ended when he ran out of brandy.' Jim himself made no secret of his dependence on drink: in the context of another of his flights he flaunted it. 'With me was brandy, lots of it,' he wrote in *Playboy of the Air*. 'If you ride in baby cars or catch trains and trams, you may sneer at me for drinking on the job . . . *You* drink next time you're cold, tired, frightened. Then understand why I did.' But he was unduly on the defensive when he wrote this. As his career continued his performances under the influence of brandy did not evoke sneers so much as incredulous surprise that he survived so many of them.

Amy waited for her husband in Ireland until the weather was favourable for the take-off (on 18 August) and then flew back to London to wait for news in the suite at Grosvenor House which was now her home. In these days, when contact with aircraft in flight is taken for granted, it is hard to realise that in 1932 there could be no news of a transatlantic pilot until his plane was sighted.

---

[1] Named after a Newfoundland village where he hoped to make landfall.

During the wait Amy had the companionship of Miss Doreen Pickering, Jim's tactful and experienced secretary, who had now taken on the additional burden of her correspondence. Also at hand was Bill Courtenay, whose small firm, Aviation Publicity Services, had a branch office at Grosvenor House. He was not Jim's manager for this particular flight, but with an eye to the future he made a point of hovering in the foreground, (and by the time of Amy's next grass-widowhood, six months later, it was part of his role as publicity agent to both the Mollisons to 'look after' her while Jim was away).

Amy, as Mrs Mollison, was already acquiring a certain poise as a public figure, and also a certain elegance. Although her bank balance was dwindling her celebrity-value brought many enjoyable perquisites. With the advice of Captain Molyneux himself she was learning how to wear simple day clothes, and at grand functions she could carry off her furs and her Cartier diamonds without looking nouveau riche. With her hair set in smooth waves, her eyebrows fashionably streamlined, and her make-up discreet and soignée, she might almost have been taken for a lifelong inhabitant of Mayfair. Only her speech betrayed her, for unlike Eliza Doolittle she never entirely lost her natural accent.

Under Jim's influence her whole attitude towards publicity had changed. Long ago, before her flight to Australia, headlines had seemed a glittering prize; after Australia they seemed a pestilence. Now she had come to regard them, as her husband and Courtenay did, as a measure of celebrity-value and thus of money-making capacity. She had also been learning, ever since her engagement, that the translation of celebrity-value into money or its equivalent calls for judgment and timing and subtle tactics. She had come to realise that at this level the publicity game is no longer merely a matter of tough deals with newspapers and testimonial seekers, but rather an art to be practised with a sensitive touch, in which the managers of luxury hotels and others whose trade stands to profit from gossip-column glamour – the jewellers and the couturiers, the vendors of fast cars and the maîtres d'hôtel of smart restaurants, make shrewd unspoken judgments and entice the famous to patronise their establishments.

Just after the marriage Amy's celebrity-value was especially high. Not only had her 'romance' enhanced it, but she was still a world-famous symbol of courage and adventure as well as a British national heroine. At Madame Tussaud's at about this time, when a query was set to girl visitors as to who they would most like to resemble when they grew up Nurse Cavell was voted first but Amy was second, and only after her, in third place, Joan of Arc. There was no doubt at this point that Amy was, in the jargon of the press agents, 'on the front page,' and her husband was on it along with her.

III

On Saturday 20 August, thirty-one hours and twenty minutes after *Hearts Content* took off from the Irish beach Jim, utterly exhausted, came down in a field in Newfoundland. He had made the first solo flight across the Atlantic from east to west, the first crossing of the North Atlantic in a light aircraft, the fastest crossing from east to west, and the longest duration flight ever made in a light aeroplane. The press shouted its feverish applause. But the superlatives excited only scorn from that influential commentator the editor of *The Aeroplane*, and a flow of typically jaundiced remarks soon appeared in his magazine. 'When a man has made himself a reputation as a record breaker,' wrote Charles Grey, 'he cannot well be employed as a joy-ride pilot or as a club instructor at a few pounds a week. So Mr Mollison finds that he has to do something which will put him in the public eye in order that he may keep in the public eye. So far as proving anything goes, Mr Mollison's flight proves nothing. Everybody knew that the average Gipsy engine will keep going for thirty hours, even without having the filters cleaned. And short of sheer bad luck in having ice formed on his wings or blocking the working of the controls, there was no reason why Mr Mollison should not cross the Atlantic. The only actual difficulty . . . is for the pilot to overcome his fear of falling in. And when one has the extreme incentive of earning one's living by keeping oneself in the public eye, or if one has such faith in one's future as not to be afraid at all, then an Atlantic flight loses its unpleasantness.' One can well imagine Jim's comments when these remarks by an arm-chair critic later met his eye.

In New York – the New York of the speakeasies – 'Cap'n Mollison' was given a lavish welcome, though he drew amused wisecracks from one of the columnists by reason of the smallness of his aeroplane; it was only half the size of the Ryan monoplane in which Lindbergh had crossed the Atlantic five years earlier. 'We grabbed a look at Captain Mollison's plane yesterday,' wrote Arthur 'Bugs' Baer. 'It's an English Moth and so small the Cap can steer himself with his ears . . . He doesn't climb into his plane and wave good-bye. He pulls it on like a hoopskirt, wiggles once or twice – and zoom – there he goes.'

Jim returned to England by sea, having been dissuaded from attempting the return flight by bad weather and by telephone appeals from Amy. She on her side, while he was away, occupied herself with a short course of blind-flying at the Air Service Training school at Hamble. There was still talk of an idea that she too might tackle a solo Atlantic crossing from east to west, and such a project would of course mean flying by night as well as by day. No woman had yet made this flight, though a few months earlier Amelia Earhart had flown the Atlantic solo in the opposite direction – the first women ever to do so.

IV

During a few weeks of the autumn of 1932 the Mollisons were able to 'settle down' to married life in London, and they busied themselves with cars and aircraft, and with the sort of things, social and official, which kept them as steadily as possible in the limelight. A month after Jim's return from America a behind-the-scenes row sent Amy rushing off to Yorkshire (by this time she was reconciled with her parents) but she was soon back at Grosvenor House and writing to them 'The troubles that brought me home are all over and we shall probably be much happier now and understand each other better.' There is no clue in her letter as to the nature of the 'troubles' but it seems likely, from a subsequent letter, that she and Jim quarrelled over some triviality.

Amy went on to tell her parents about a new long-distance venture on which she was to embark in a few weeks' time: she was to fly to South Africa and back by the West Coast route in a new Puss moth, *Desert Cloud*, 'I am going to try to beat Jim's Cape record – just as a sporting effort,' was how she put it, thus making the flight sound an easy undertaking. It was certainly a less arduous one than the Atlantic, but if she was to improve on Jim's Cape record it would involve quite a lot of night flying. She hoped however to avoid having to rely entirely on instruments by timing her hops in relation to the state of the moon.

Then, just before her start (on 14 November), she wrote again 'I shall leave Stag Lane tomorrow for Lympne, and if a fine night will leave soon after midnight. I'm looking forward very much to my flight . . . I want to make Colomb Bechar the first hop, then Niamey, Douala, Luanda, Walvis Bay, Cape Town . . . Courtenay is my "publicity manager" for this flight . . . I'm not fixed up with any paper. We are giving out the stuff wholesale until we see how the thing goes. You mustn't worry. If I'm missing Jim will come to look for me in the *Hearts Content*. The papers would give anything for that story, but we can't stage it and I hope it won't be necessary because it would mean my failure.'

Amy did not fail. She reached Cape Town safely on 18 November in four days and seven hours (ten hours less than Jim), but the flight had been a harrowing experience. 'My worst stretch was Douala-Benguela, all by night,' she wrote to Jim.[1] 'I'll never forget it. Thunderstorms, pouring rain, no moonlight through the clouds, and anyhow I left Douala at seven *with full load* and the moon didn't rise till about ten. I must admit it's frightened me of that coastline by night. It took me thirteen hours to do 800 miles, following the ins and outs of the coast with no forward visibility at all. I'm like you now – give me visibility and I'm all right, but take it completely away --- My scrappy bit of blind flying training was useless. I was out of control for a ghastly moment in a cloud because it's nearly impossible to concentrate on illuminated jumping figures in the dark when you're tired and the clouds very bumpy and high ground below. I have to do some of it by night coming back, but am arranging . . . to have two half nights instead of one whole night. It's much harder working out a schedule for the return than for going, because of doing Europe by day . . . I do loathe waiting . . . But isn't it thrilling to think that if all goes right I'll be with you two weeks tomorrow! . . . I'm getting very restless and nothing except the dark moon would keep me here a day longer than necessary . . .

'I wonder if it has occurred to you to write to me – I wish it would because I'd give anything for even a few words from you. I miss you so much that I can't really enjoy the blue sky and sunshine because I'm thinking all the time how much nicer it would be if you were here (and then I think maybe we'd quarrel about something and spoil it! But then maybe we wouldn't) . . . I'm sorry if you think it's silly and sentimental to write you and try to tell you how much I miss you, but you see all the time I have a most curious homesick feeling, and I know it's not for Grosvenor House, or foggy London, but just for you, all for you. It sounds ridiculous, but it's true.'

---

[1] This letter is the only one from Amy to Jim among her papers.

In spite of the wistful tone of these last remarks Jim was still at this stage an affectionate husband to Amy (never at any time was he a good letter-writer) and during her absence on the Cape flight his cables to her were worded with warm spontaneity. 'Marvellous show, Amy . . . Please wire. Love Jim,' he cabled to her to Benguela on the way out.

V

While Amy, at the Cape, awaited the next full moon, Bill Courtenay was writing to her father in keen excitement, with news that the *Sunday Dispatch* wished to run Amy's 'life story'. 'They want the first instalment the Sunday after her arrival or say it is no use,' he panted. 'If she lands at noon on a Saturday – as I would like – the *Dispatch* would have the story of the arrival and the homeward flight as first instalment. That would give us a week's breathing space to get the second ready . . . It is vital to have something ready for her to inspect and alter as soon as she arrives. Can you help by letting me have some early history and early photos. I suggest the best way is for me to come to Bridlington one evening and spend a night when we could have a yarn about her early life and I could type it down as you recounted it.'

Courtenay brought off his coup, and the *Sunday Dispatch* serialised Amy's ghost-written life story just after she completed her return flight from the Cape. Her double flight in record time was a notable *tour de force* and brought her a new wave of popularity. She even earned praise from the aeronautical press, and was also awarded the Segrave Trophy for 1932, as the British subject who had accomplished during the year 'the most outstanding demonstration of the possibilities of transport by land, air or water.'

That Christmas she and Jim enjoyed a gay holiday at St Moritz, and for Amy this was probably the happiest moment in the whole of her marriage. She was fit and well and radiant with success, but chiefly she was content because her so easily bored playboy husband was not yet bored with her. 'I am as happy as I can remember ever being,' she exclaimed in a Christmas note to her family. Then in a letter to her mother she described life at the Palace Hotel. 'There is a most interesting cosmopolitan crowd here, amongst them being Harold Lloyd, Clara Bow, Rosie Dolly, Ann Dvorak, Mr Goulding (the man who produced "Grand Hotel") and many others. We are lucky to meet them all and we have some good parties and real fun. I like Harold Lloyd the best of them all – he's totally different from what you'd imagine.

'We spent a day in Paris on the way out and Chanel has given me a most marvellous evening dress and she has offered to dress me at cost price.' Then she added an astonishing admission: 'However I have all the clothes I want at the moment.' 'I don't want to go back,' she continued, 'but Jim is already getting tired of it. He doesn't like sports particularly, whereas I like them tremendously. He is going off in about three weeks' time on another flight. What a life we lead!!'

This next flight of Jim's was to be from England to Brazil, again in the *Hearts Content*, which he had equipped with two compasses in case one went wrong. Sidney Cotton recollects that when Jim proudly told him this he asked him how he would know which one had gone wrong unless he fitted three. Jim, impressed by Cotton's logic, fitted a third. And since this South Atlantic flight of his was successful[1] it is of interest to quote briefly here from a letter which Amy later wrote to a member of the US Navy Department's Hydrographic Office, describing the nevigational methods to which Jim introduced her for their long-distance flying together. 'On our flights we do not carry out navigation as it is generally understood on board ship,' she explained. 'We fly on dead reckoning only,

---

[1] It won for him, along with his North Atlantic solo, an award of the Johnston Memorial Air Navigation Trophy.

making visual calculations of drift. This is quite easy to do over water and we find that we steer a far more accurate course over water than over land. Our compasses are P.4 Horizontal large bowl, Aperiodic, and we have three of them.'

In February 1933 Jim flew the South Atlantic in record time and also established three other 'records'. He was the first person to fly from England to South America, also to fly across the South Atlantic from east to west, also to fly solo across both North and South Atlantics. These achievements did not arouse the admiration of *Flight* or *The Aeroplane* but a year later they won for Jim the Royal Aero Club's Britannia Trophy, for 'the most meritorious performance in the air during 1933,' and at the time they were crowned with the glossy tribute of a portrait frontispiece in the *Tatler*.

VI

It had again been an anxious time for Amy, and when Jim decided to return to England by sea she went to Madeira to meet him. While she was awaiting him there she received a letter from his mother (the only one from Mrs Bullmore to Amy that has survived) which is of outstanding interest for what it shows not only of Jim and his mother but also of Amy herself. 'I am sorry to learn that you have been nervy,' she wrote, 'but I am not surprised, as Jim's hazardous flight on the top of your own was enough to cause it. In fact, both of you have been living at high tension since you were married, and it is bound to react. I can sympathize, for I have gone through so much in my life, and have had to fight nerves many times. I think you did a wise thing in going to Madeira – there is nothing more soothing than a sea voyage, and the fact that you are going to meet Jim will hasten the cure. I like the frank way you admit your love for him and I thank God for it. We both love him – but a Mother's and a wife's love are totally different and can't clash . . . I should like you always to think of me not as a mere mother-in-law but as an understanding friend . . . I feel that where I have failed in understanding him since he came to manhood, you will succeed. His ideals and mine have often clashed, and he has sometimes hurt me terribly, but though he has a good streak of his father in him, he has a lot of me too, and we are bound to be fundamentally alike in many ways. I naturally am very proud of you both, and am greatly interested in all you do. I think you are ideally suited – both being air-minded with the same interests. It would never have worked if Jim had married a girl who had only social and domestic interests. You make a wonderful combination. I used to think what a mistake my first marriage was and that it had wrecked my life, but now I look at it differently. I believe there is a Divine plan in everything and probably it was fore-ordained that Hector Mollison and I should be joined together and produce a pioneer like Jim. I dreamed dreams for him as a boy, and I still do. I think he has it in him to go far yet, and I hope he will go down in history not only as a pioneer in Aviation, but as a great man. Your name also will go down in history, and I am very ambitious for you both.'

By the time Jim reached Madeira, and he and Amy sailed together for home, plans were well advanced, under Courtenay's care, for a 'next' long-distance flight which if all went well seemed quite likely to go down in history. Timed for early summer it was ambitious in the extreme. 'I liked conceiving my plans on a grand if not on a grandiose scale,' Courtenay later remarked in his autobiography. But in fact by 1933 unless plans for a long-distance flight were on a grandiose scale it had little chance of attacting attention. 'Ordinary' trans-oceanic flights, and even round-the-world solo attempts were by now two-a-penny, and it was not easy to think up something original to compete with subsidised enterprises such as that summer's Italian 'Air Armada' – a sortie by twenty-four military flying boats from Rome to Chicago.

The project that Courtenay and Jim and Amy had agreed upon centred round an attempt on the world's

long-distance record. In a twin-engined de Havilland
Dragon, a new transport plane in which the passenger
seats were being replaced by three extra tanks, the
'Flying Sweethearts' were to aim first for New York.
There they would stop for only a day, and then set off
for Baghdad – this 'leg' of the flight would be the record
attempt. Next, with hardly a pause, they would fly back
again to London. It was a daunting programme – some
thought a foolhardy one.

A fortnight before they were to start Amy got a
friendly letter from C.N. Colson of *Flight* pleading with
her to change her plans. 'I do want to beg you to give up
this plan of flying to New York before making your real
record attempt,' he wrote. 'It is asking too much, both of
yourself and of the funnly little devil called "Fate" . . .
You have such a good chance of putting the record
above anything any other country is likely to touch that
it seems foolish, to me, for you to take any undue risks
before doing so. Do reconsider the matter. Put the
Dragon in a box and then fly from Croydon to New York
when you have broken the record, if you *must* go on
doing these things.' *Flight* was not in good odour with
Amy at this time, for it had recently published some
criticisms made by the Royal Aero Club of inaccuracies
in her *Sunday Dispatch* life story. Her reply to Colson
was cool and stiff. 'Much as I appreciate your thought
for our safety,' she wrote, 'yet I am afraid it is
impossible to alter our plans. Our reason for flying the
machine to New York instead of shipping it is that it
appears to us to be a reflection both on the
serviceability of our aircraft and on the possibilities of
aviation in general to put a perfectly good aircraft on to
a ship to be carried across the water.'

The perfectly good aircraft had now been named
Seafarer and had been painted black – 'Jim's favourite
colour'. Courtenay had arranged a 'tie-up' with the *Daily
Mail* and to enhance the human interest Jim's mother
and Amy's family were to be present at the send-off.
'This flight means a tremendous lot to Jim and me,' Amy
had written to her father. 'Please let Betty come. What

does school matter in comparison to this? . . . Without unduly stressing matters, there is always the risk that this may be the last you see of us. We ourselves put our chances of success at 10–7, and anyhow if the fates are only kind everything else is already in our favour, so you must not worry. We flew the machine yesterday and it is really perfect. We are really looking forward to it, but can appreciate that it must be an anxious time for you . . . The take-off I think should be interesting.' This last remark was, so it was soon to prove, an understatement of extreme irony.

At Croydon early on the morning of 8 June 1933 Amy in a white flying suit and Jim in black overalls bade farewell to their relatives and then, with a plentiful supply of St Christopher charms for luck, they boarded their jet-black aeroplane. In the still air of early morning the overloaded *Seafarer* needed such a long run that Jim taxied beyond the edge of the aerodrome on to the rough adjoining grass. This proved disastrous. As the aircraft started its bumpy run, down a slight incline, it hit a gully, bounced, slewed round as the undercarriage gave way, and finished up flat on its belly. THE MOLLISONS CRASH . . CROYDON CROWD SEE MISHAP BEFORE START . . . HEAVILY LADEN PLANE DAMAGED . . . TO TRY AGAIN. Photographs of Amy and Jim taken just after the accident show how genuinely it had shocked and distressed them. But their failure, viewed from a dispassionate publicity angle, was a most gratifying success: their enterprise had now become a 'drama' instead of just one more long-distance flight. Next day Amy's father wrote to her: 'As regards Thursday morning . . . I hope you are not taking it too seriously; it was an incident that could happen to anyone. I don't want to develop the superstitious thought too much, but you did have a lot of St Christophers on board. Well, instead of thinking these haven't proved lucky . . . try and think that something worse might have happened – thus in that event they *have* brought you luck.' Something worse might indeed have happened. When the *Seafarer* collapsed it had 450 gallons of aviation spirit in its tanks.

A month later the aircraft had been repaired and was ready for a second attempt. This time, so as to try to ensure a good start, Amy and Jim decided to take off from the expanses of smooth hard sand at Pendine on the Carmarthenshire coast, and on 3 July, a couple of days after Amy's thirtieth birthday, they flew there hoping to leave in a few days. The little Beach Hotel was soon overrun with inquisitive holiday-makers. 'We are living as quiet a life as possible with such crowds around,' Amy wrote to her parents during the first week of July, while waiting for suitable weather over the Atlantic. 'We are sleeping away from the hotel because it's impossible here. Crowds are camping on the beach all night and we get no peace. Don't tell Trevor [her sister Molly had just married a Welshman, Trevor Jones] but although the Welsh are very warmhearted, they've no manners.' Soon the warm-hearted Welsh became so overpowering that Amy and Jim withdrew to London until the weather was right, and not until 22 July did they return to Pendine in the *Seafarer*, with Courtenay huddled in the back behind the extra tanks. On the way he amused himself by composing an account of the forthcoming flight entitled 'Our Story, by Jim and Amy Mollison'.

At noon the *Seafarer* took off – safely. In view of the Croydon accident Jim had chosen to load a minimum of fuel so as to lessen the strain on the undercarriage. 'Now for the greatest adventure of my life,' Amy exclaimed to the reporters just before she left. She was looking strained, so they said. 'This may be my last spectacular flight,' Jim had put in, 'I hope it isn't too great a venture.' Jim was at the controls at first, and throughout the flight Amy scribbled occasional notes which form an interesting log of their progress. 'Took off Pendine 12.00 BST with 428 gallons petrol' was her first entry. '[Take-off] Run about 1 mile (60 secs) approx. Low Cloud and fog to Mizen Head. Passed over Mizen Head 2.20 BST. Clouds and fog. Flew over them at 2,000 ft coming down to 1,000 about 400 miles out. Practically no wind. Bad weather from about 600 miles out to about 800 or 900. Twilight lasted till midnight . . . Good night over clouds – rarely saw the sea – Appeared calm.

'Began to get light about 6.00 BST. Sun rose about 8.30 . . . Over clouds and fog until about 100 miles from land – then clear. Sighted icebergs and drift ice.'

Then, when they had been in the air for just twenty-four hours she wrote: 'Saw land (N. corner of Newfoundland).' After this, the final entry in her 'log' was as follows: 'Economising petrol to try to make N.Y.' She wrote this towards evening on the second day of their flight, and she later told Courtenay that she herself had wanted to land and refuel at Boston while there was still daylight. But Jim, so it seems, was intent on 'making New York non-stop'. They were over Connecticut near the Bridgeport aerodrome – within fifty miles of New York, when their fuel ran out. Jim circled the aerodrome again and again and the landing lights were turned on to try to help his approach. But by this time he was almost blind with exhaustion, and he landed down wind, overshot badly into the marshes beyond the boundary, and the *Seafarer* crashed over on to its back. When the rescuers arrived they found Amy crouched moaning over Jim who was unconscious, his head and face gashed and bleeding. By the time the two were in hospital a horde of souvenir hunters had swooped down on the *Seafarer* and left it a naked shell. Even Courtenay could hardly have wished for his clients a more attention-catching arrival. As at Croydon the 'failure' of the Mollisons was their success in terms of publicity – as measured in column-inches.

27

BREAK-UP

1933-1935

'I like America very much and wouldn't mind staying over here for some time. Jim doesn't like it, though.' So wrote Amy to her parents in the autumn of 1933, several months after the Bridgeport crash. When she and Jim started from Pendine they had expected to stop in New York for precisely a day, but in fact she stayed on in the United States for as long as seven months, and during this time became an ardent America-lover. Also, but more fleetingly – only so long as 'the blonde adventuress of the skylanes' was in the news – the Americans became Amy-lovers. Her happy smile and her sparkle, her candour and her unpretentiousness, as well as her gift for saying the right thing in public, won hearts in America just as they had in Australia and in England.

Amy was given much more attention by the American press and public than was her husband, for he had already been feted the year before after his North Atlantic solo. Jim had liked America well enough when he held the stage alone; now, having to play second string to his wife, he was critical and surly, 'loathed America', and was often away from her. Indeed his very natural jealousy of her latest popular success certainly contributed to the disintegration of their marriage which from now on began to set in.

Whispers of 'troubles', and even of the likelihood of separation or divorce soon began to appear in 'some of the unimportant press,' as Amy's father phrased it. But he had also seen an indignant denial by Jim. 'We were of course very pleased to read that,' he commented, 'and do hope you and Jim are getting on very nicely indeed; of course one can understand after the disappointments you both experienced that your nerves were very much frayed.'

There had, it is true, been a whole series of disappointments in connection with the projected long-distance flight, but Amy's nerves, and Jim's too, had also been frayed by the continuing strain of living in the public eye, without any chance to recover in peace from the shock and injuries of the *Seafarer* accident. Even during the first hours after the crash a crowd of press photographers had invaded Bridgeport Hospital, and though officially banned from the sickroom they had burst in with their flash-bulbs and secured 'sensational' pictures of the two flyers lying swathed like mummies; Jim had had thirty stitches in nose and cheek; Amy's left arm and both hands were bandaged and one of her legs was injured. Then after less than twenty-four hours the pair were dressed, propped up in wheelchairs, lifted into a transport aircraft, and flown to New York where they were installed in the ornate twin beds of the Plaza Hotel's imperial suite.

A week later, on a sizzling August day, 'Amy and Jimmy', still partly bandaged, were given a ticker-tape welcome – described by the *Herald Tribune* as 'a sort of shirt-sleeved Mardi Gras.' For Amy this was an exciting new experience (though less so for Jim, who had been through it all before) and she made a conquest of the Mayor of New York, John P. O'Brien, who did the honours with gusto although it was the fourth such welcome he had presided over in the space of ten days.[1]

---

[1] The other long-distance flyers concerned were Wiley Post (who had just completed a round-the-world flight), James Mattern, back after a similar attempt which had failed, and the officers of the Italian Air Force who had flown from Rome to Chicago.

AMY JOHNSON

II

Amy's New York success gave her stay in America a stimulating send-off but it was less significant for her future than the weekend she and Jim spent with Amelia Earhart and her publisher-husband George Palmer Putnam (who was also her manager) at their Connecticut home – a weekend which included a luncheon with the Roosevelts at Hyde Park.

The Mollisons had first met Amelia in England the year before, just after she made her solo Atlantic flight, and Amy had taken to her at once though Jim had reservations. He later described her as 'that strange, charming woman,' and one can understand how strange the teetotal Amelia must have seemed to the playboy Jim, even though her beauty and charm obviously captivated him – as they did everyone. 'Lady Lindy', with her superficial resemblance to Lindbergh, with her short fair curls, starry eyes and fresh youthfulness, was at the same time an intelligent, thoughtful, naturally elegant woman, tall and slim, with lovely tapering hands (not unlike Amy's). Unassuming and friendly in manner, she had plenty of practical commonsense but also poetic depths; her private philosophy of flying was that all pilots love to fly because of the beauty of flight – whether they know it or not. As Amy saw more of her in the summer of 1933 admiration merged into heroine-worship, and Amelia's influence is so evident in Amy's subsequent life that the resemblances and differences between the two women, the one so American and the other so very English, are of considerable interest.

Amelia was five years the elder of the two, and had first sprung to fame in 1928, a couple of years before Amy. She too came from a modest home; her father was a small-town lawyer in Kansas. When she took up flying in her early twenties and became an enthusiast she regarded it – as Amy too did at first – as an enthralling off-duty sport. She was nearly thirty, and absorbed in a job as a social worker, when she was persuaded to join an Atlantic flight attempt (as a passenger) for the publicity she would bring by being the first woman to cross the Atlantic by air. Amelia possessed a balance that Amy lacked and she was not overwhelmed by the onrush of fame. She accepted the irksome responsibilities of public life and meantime set out to prove herself a 'serious' pilot by undertaking her solo crossing of the Atlantic in 1932. Besides this she flew autogiros as well as aeroplanes in the United States, and helped to operate one of the first regular passenger services between New York and Washington. At the same time she dedicated herself to the cause she cared most about, the interests of women in the contemporary world. She founded the first society of women pilots, the 'Ninety-nines'[1] and also campaigned for their professional recognition, rather as Lady Heath had done in Europe (but in a calmer and more dignified manner). Although as regards long-distance flying Amy may have excelled her in sheer courage and in refusal to accept defeat, Amelia won for herself the kind of position in the world of 'serious' achievers that Amy pined to attain to in England. Her active, creative life made Amy's social round in London with Jim, amid idlers and hangers-on who liked to be seen about with flying celebrities, seem more than ever a stifling hot-house. 'Now I've broken away from the London society life which I hate so much I could never return to it for long,' Amy wrote to her father while she was in America. 'It's a pity I can't like living at Grosvenor House and doing nothing, because it's the only sort of life Jim likes to lead, but I can't help hating it, and I did give it over a year's trial.'

---

[1] So named because there were ninety-nine founder members.

Amy Johnson

III

In spite of the damage to the *Seafarer* Jim and Amy were able to persevere with their plan to attack the world's long-distance record, for Lord Wakefield offered to provide a replacement. Thereupon Jim sailed from New York in mid-August to supervise the completion of the new machine. 'Whether we do the same flight again or change our route depends on when the plane is ready,' Amy told her father in a letter from the Plaza where she was still living. Then she asked a question which showed that she, not only Jim, set store by the attitude of press and public: 'What is the reaction in England to my staying here whilst Jim comes home?' she asked, but then hastened to justify herself. 'I am staying here,' she explained, 'because I don't want to go back to London where there is nothing to do, when there is so much of utility and interest to do here that I don't know where to start . . . This hotel will remain my headquarters and . . . to show you I'm well looked after I have a secretary, a maid, a nurse who acts as chaperone, companion and everything combined, and a man called [Vernon] Stuart whom Jim knows well is helping me with advice [on public relations]. I am constantly in touch with Amelia and her husband and am well in with the White House and the Government at Washington (or I think so – anyhow one evening they sent a couple of men to see me specially on trying to get women interested in using the airlines) . . . On Friday I am motoring to Boston with Amelia . . . She is the first woman Vice-President of an airline, which is being opened at Boston, so we are going together for the inauguration.'

Under Amelia's auspices Amy was given an opportunity that thrilled her, the chance of acting as co-pilot on a scheduled airline flight to the West Coast. 'I am going to fly on one of the largest American Airlines (TWA) as a co-pilot, in order to get experience,' she wrote. 'It is a great compliment to allow me to do it, although of course it will give them a good advertisement, but it's never been allowed before and you know how hard it is in this world to try to do something new.'

Jim arrived back from England by mid-September and he and Amy then hurried to Toronto, for at Amy's suggestion they had decided to start their record attempt from the Wasaga Beach, the shore of one of the Canadian Lakes, which provided a three-mile run of hard sand (Amy had pointed out that New York was by now sated with long-distance flights and flyers, whereas the Canadians were still enthusiastic). When however in the first week of October, after weeks waiting for suitable weather, the Mollisons tried three times to make a start, they were unable to coax the overloaded aircraft safely off the ground.

After this they abandoned the whole project, and returned to New York en route for a Bermuda holiday. Amy, whose health had been deteriorating, and who had had a riding accident in Canada, then went into a New York hospital for a check-up. It soon proved that her stay would have to be prolonged, and Jim went on to Bermuda alone. After almost a month in hospital Amy wrote to her parents, 'They found various odd things, but the chief was an internal ulcer, so of course I had to stay and have it seen to . . . The doctor says I need six or eight months' rest, and I'm not surprised . . . My plans are to go to Bermuda for about a month to convalesce, and then I'll probably go travelling for about three months . . . I really must get fit . . . I don't know what Jim will say – I haven't seen him for three weeks.'

IV

When Amy finally rejoined her husband, early in November, she was still very nervy as well as physically weak. Photograhs taken at a Bermuda swimming pool show both of them looking sad and unsmiling. Jim, in his autobiography, likened his six-week holiday in Bermuda to a second honeymoon, but he did not mention that less than a fortnight of it was with Amy. Here it may be added that according to legend Jim spent much of his first honeymoon in an alcoholic stupor; also that Amy later told more than one of her friends that when Jim was drinking heavily she found she too had to drink heavily – to drown her disgust.

Before the end of the month the two parted company again. Jim returned to the bars and nightclubs of London while Amy went on to Florida to continue her convalescence. More than ever she was enamoured of America, although she soon admitted in her letters that she was homesick for England and also for Jim, though not for his playboy existence. 'I am almost sure to be over here again soon,' she wrote to her father from Palm Beach. 'This place is ideal, but the people are impossible, with a very few exceptions. Most of them are old millionaires, extremely snobbish and very uninteresting . . . I'm very brown and feeling better than I have been for a long time . . . The honest truth is that my nerves have been all to pieces, and I'm only just beginning to get right again . . . I needed months to myself and I still need longer but I'm so homesick and want to see Jim so much that I can't bear to be away any longer . . . Nothing would have induced me to do any flying for the last few months, but at last I'm beginning to feel I want to get back to it again, and that's a good sign . . . It isn't very pleasant to feel one's self control slipping away, and to have violent nerve storms over every slightest thing that goes wrong.'

One occasion just before this when Amy's self control slipped right away was much publicised at the time, and in this same letter she described what had happened. She had been driving back to Palm Beach from Miami in the early hours of the morning after several parties. In an irritable mood, she let out her Mercedes and was run in by two speed cops in plain clothes. Fearing they were gangsters she tried to make a getaway, failed, was grabbed by the cops and hit one of them across the face. She was then taken to a courthouse and subjected so some unpleasant cross-questioning. 'I tried to smooth them over,' she told her father. 'If I'd had a hundred dollars I could have "fixed" it. You can fix anything here if you have enough money.' Then a few days later she had to appear in court, and she got off with a fifty-dollar fine and twenty dollars' costs – but with a nervous relapse.

She stayed on in America until mid-February 1934, then sailed for England and joined Jim who was by now full of plans for the forthcoming England–Australia air race: she had agreed to partner him in a new machine that was being designed specially for the race by de Havillands. The £15,000 in prize money offered by the Australian magnate Sir MacPherson Robertson (to commemorate the centenary of Melbourne and the State of Victoria) was attracting a strong entry, particularly from America, and de Havillands had decided to meet the challenge. Their Comet racer, a fast twin-engined monoplane that has been likened to a streamlined petrol tank, had many avant-garde features including a retractable undercarriage and variable-pitch propellers. Three Comets were to be built, the Mollisons were to pilot one of them. Amy, who at the time of her TWA flight to California had been given a sight-seeing tour of the Douglas factory, was not enthusiastic. 'Jim has ordered this special machine for the Australia race,' she wrote before she left the States, 'and I shall go with him, but we haven't a chance. The Americans are sending machines over which will make any British one look silly. The only chance we have is if they all lost their way and we don't.'

V

Although so scathing about British chances in the race Amy reached England in a mood of optimism and initiatives. With the example of Amelia before her she was overflowing with ideas for her own future in aviation. Already several months earlier she had written to Colonel Shelmerdine – as Director of Civil Aviation he was, so she evidently felt, well placed to advise and help her.[1] 'I am quite sure you will agree with me that "stunt flights" are at an end,' she had written, 'although I think there is still plenty of scope for what might seem to be spectacular flights but which are really of some scientific and technical value . . . Do you think there is any possibility at all of my being given anything satisfactory to do in aeronautics in England?' Ideas she had in mind included 'some kind of position with Imperial Airways, or simply experimental flights to collect data, on the same lines as Lindbergh is doing for Pan American,' 'some kind of job for the Air Ministry which would help to expand civil aviation,' or 'any sort of good-will flights.'

There is no evidence that Shelmerdine responded helpfully to this, but Amy, on her return, tackled other influential acquaintances with suggestions that reflected Amelia's influence, and one of her schemes bore fruit. Amelia was aviation editor of the monthly *Cosmopolitan* and in April 1934 Amy was appointed aviation editor to the *Daily Mail* – she was to write a weekly article headed 'Plane News'. Temporarily living with Jim at Grosvenor House again, her new mood of energy also found an outlet in learning to play squash rackets, with the encouragement and help Peter Reiss, who was a player of championship class.

Then in May Jim and she took a country cottage, at Lurgashall in Sussex, and she wrote glowingly to her father after the first few days: 'I'm so happy to be away from London and Grosvenor House at last. This is the next best to having my own home.' But it was only for the summer, and the ever-restless tempo of the Mollisons' life, as well as the ever-grandiose standard of their living, may be judged from other remarks in Amy's letter. 'I have sold the *Seafarer* and am very sorry,' she reported, 'as it's terribly awkward without an aeroplane just when the fine

---

[1] This letter is incidentally of special interest as the first indication since Amy's marriage that she intended to plan her career apart from her husband's.

weather has arrived. I don't know what to get instead as there is nothing here I really want. I may go back to America to get one.' She had ordered a new car, but one car was nothing like enough. 'I hate driving this old borrowed Delage,' she complained. 'I'm longing to get my Hispano . . . I have also sent to America for the Mercedes I had there, as we need a "hack" car for the country. Jim won't let his new Buick be used by anyone.'

After a month at Lurgashall she announced that she was sailing for America. 'It's a sudden decision,' she told her father, 'I'm going over (privately) to see the Beech aircraft people, as I may buy one of their aeroplanes and take the agency for this country . . . It will give me an interest.' She would keep on writing her weekly articles for the *Daily Mail* while she was away, though she was already tiring of her editorship (it lasted no longer than her six-months' contract). 'It's not much fun writing for newspapers,' she concluded. 'They're so impersonal and inhuman.'

The visit to America was short, but quite long enough for her to come to an agreement about the agency. Stifling her feelings of disloyalty to the British aircraft industry, Amy became the agent in Britain for the American company and ordered one of the new Beechcrafts, a resplendent four-seater cabin biplane. Then she dashed off for several weeks to Arizona where the exhilarating climate suited her to perfection. 'I feel nearly ten years younger,' she wrote from the Grand Canyon airport.

Hurrying back again to England before mid-August, she was again based at Lurgashall, but did not spend much time there, for she volunteered to fly de Havilland Dragons on the Paris run of a service operated by the airline pioneer Edward Hillman from Abridge in Essex. This engagement lasted only a few weeks, but it was a landmark in her career, the first time she had worked as a fully-fledged professional pilot. It also gave her, by chance, an intimate knowledge of the cross-channel air trip to Le Bourget, a first step towards her much closer links with Paris that were to come.

By the end of September the thoughts of both Amy and Jim were focused anxiously on their prospects for the Australia race, for which they were not at all well prepared. Only two weeks before the starting date, 20 October, Amy wrote to her father: 'We are terribly worried about the time factor. We have not yet got delivery of our machine nor have we been flown in it, never mind flying it ourselves. We both of us must have some practice and when we shall get it beats me . . . We have a tremendous lot to do – our maps aren't ready, nor our permits, nor have we got our flying-suits, lifebelts, flares, etc., etc. . . . I wouldn't be surprised if this race is a flop – I have always thought it would be, but am quite willing to be proved wrong. I would much rather be wrong!' A few days later however de Havillands had completed and tested the Mollisons' Comet and Amy wrote, 'We've got our machine now and it's beautiful and very fast, but very difficult to fly. I hope it will go all right in the Race.'

The start was to be at dawn on 20 October from Mildenhall in Suffolk, and at 6.30 a.m. the Mollisons in their *Black Magic* were to be the first away. As they boarded their racer Jeffrey Quill, one of the three RAF Flying Officers who had volunteered for starting-line duties,[1] caught a memorable glimpse of them. 'I saw Jim and Amy climb into their Comet,' he recalls. 'He looked as white as a sheet and as if he had been sloshed for forty-eight hours – which I suspect he was. She looked very nervous and apprehensive and I felt desperately sorry for her having to climb in behind that rather raffish character for such a venture as this.'

Nevertheless for the first laps of the race, as far as Baghdad and Karachi, 'the good old Mollison genius for finding the way seemed to work,' as Quill puts it.

---

[1] The other two were Flg Off K.B.B. Cross and Flg Off A.E. Clouston.

'Theirs was the only Comet to reach Baghdad non-stop and on schedule. It was a remarkable and impressive achievement.' The Mollisons' time to Karachi was 22 hours and they thereby halved the existing record. But then the mishaps began. After two false starts from Karachi they lost their way, reportedly owing to a misjudgment of the wind combined with compass trouble. When they landed to check their whereabouts they refuelled with ordinary motor-car spirit, and just after that, before reaching Allahabad, one engine seized up. While the rest of the field sped on, and Charles Scott and Tom Campbell Black in another Comet won the race for Britain, the Mollisons were miserably stuck at Allahabad for nearly three weeks while their damaged engine was repaired. They made the homeward flight together as far as Europe, then Amy flew on from Athens by Imperial Airways and arrived at Croydon alone. Bill Courtenay, who met her there, afterwards wrote to her father that he had serious misgivings about the prospects ahead of both Amy and Jim.

'Amy told me a lot of things which of course I would not use in the press or in a book,' he wrote, 'and I am rather worried about the future for her . . . I think it is essential that she should not let her name drop out of the public eye. *Between ourselves* I want her to resume operating flights on her own as I feel her judgments are best and that both as regards the Atlantic and the race she might have pulled things off if she were captain of the craft. This is not to say anything against Jim of course but I can tell you better what is in my mind when I see you. Sooner or later I think he will have to get down to a job of work and it would be wise to do it now while there is a certain amount of sympathy about due to their misfortunes in the Race. Besides every year counts against a man once he is nearing thirty.[1] I've put one or two good ideas up to him but whether he will act on them or not I don't know . . . They have to remember that Fleet

[1] Jim was now 29; Amy 31.

Street considers them off the front page now, although Amy should always be good copy because of her Australia and Cape flights and because she is a girl. Getting back on the front page which is vital to them unless they had a large income and could retire, is not going to be too easy and I hope they will be amenable to advice.'

One piece of advice which Courtenay offered to the Mollisons just after this must have seemed ironic to Jim, and to Amy laughable or perhaps even offensive. 'I wish you and Jim would beat it from Grosvenor House,' he wrote to Amy after a chat with her husband, 'and take a nice home somewhere where you can be together more. I told him you should both have a babe and get Wakefield as godfather before the old man dies! Don't leave it too late! It will make a lot of difference to your joint happiness.'

More in Courtenay's line than acting as uninvited marriage counsellor was the publicising of a programme of aviation debates, one of them between Jim and Amy, that had been arranged for the early months of 1935 by the Women's Engineering Society – or rather by its energetic Secretary, the well-known feminist Miss (later Dame) Caroline Haslett. Amy's membership of the Society dated from before her Australia flight, and when she became famous it naturally looked to her to take a lead in its doings. Just after her marriage she was elected Vice-President, and now she had become President.[1] The debates had been

---

[1] Her tour as President lasted for three years, from 1934 until 1937. Here it should be mentioned that Miss Haslett, after Amy's death in 1941, initiated an appeal to establish a scholarship in her memory, in order to help women pilots towards attaining professional status. The first Amy Johnson Memorial Fund Scholarship was awarded in 1954, under the auspices of the Women's Engineering Society. More recently, in January 1967, responsibility for the Fund was handed over to the British Women Pilots' Association. (This scholarship for women pilots is not connected with the Amy Johnson Scholarship established in 1945 by the Society of British Aircraft Constructors to finance five-year apprenticeships for girls.)

specially planned to coincide with the start of her tour of office. In the first of the series the Mollisons were to discuss record-breaking flights, Amy holding that they no longer served a useful purpose and Jim presenting the opposite case. But although Amy spoke with conviction and made her point well, Jim, when his turn came, spoilt things by insisting that he really agreed with his wife, and was only arguing against her for the sake of the debate.

VII

After this the Mollisons did not meet for many months. Without telling Amy his plans Jim departed in mid-January 1935 for America, and Amy wrote to her father 'I am leaving Grosvenor House for good and am storing all my stuff.' She went briefly to Malvern for a riding holiday with her sister Betty, then early in February sailed for Madeira for a 'real rest'. But lazing in the sun with pleasant holiday companions could not cure her malaise. Bronzed but still sick at heart she wrote again to her father 'I have not been well for a long time and cannot discover what it wrong . . . I know almost everyone here, and there are some very nice people; my loneliness is only due to my own frame of mind and feeling so rotten.' Her father urged her to confide her troubles to him, and the frank reply she wrote to him from Madeira provides a most illuminating survey of her feelings and ideas at this time.

'Jim of course has been my undoing,' she confessed, 'but I would do just the same if I had the chance over again. Women are fools enough to love the men who hurt them most . . . I am still very much in love with Jim, but am as unhappy with him as away from him . . . I have no idea what is going to happen to my married life – there are difficulties I cannot tell anyone. I am merely doing what I hate most doing – waiting to see.' These poignant remarks suggest that Amy had at last become aware of Jim's habits as regards other women – habits which were common knowledge to most of his friends and acquaintances, for he usually made no secret of them whatever. 'Mollison was woman-mad and a great many women were Mollison-mad,' was once said of him by a man who knew him quite well, and his attitude towards his feminine conquests can be judged by the observation he once made to a woman friend who teased him by remarking that he probably did not even remember their names. 'My dear,' he drawled, 'I never ask their names.'

It was fortunate for Amy that she could pour out her troubles to someone as understanding as her father. 'There is Income Tax to pay,' she went on, 'but I cannot deal with this except through Jim, and I've got an idea he's cleared the country for good. I've heard nothing from him since he left. It's strange, isn't it, giving up a home, money and security to get married, and I haven't even a husband now either . . . Please don't worry about me. I learn my lessons and usually profit by them. I shall never starve, and experience is good for me . . . I have a lot of Yorkshire shrewdness and a fairly good business head.[1] What I lack most at present is stability. I am off my balance, indecisive, ill, unhappy, but with underneath still a great zest for life, and I am sure it still holds adventures for me.'

As regards finance, she was not in debt but her assets were dwindling. 'I have now to decide what is best to be done. To capitalise everything and invest it safely would not bring me in enough income to live on, nor does it appeal to me to go back to living on £3 a week . . . I am trying to get some sort of job, but am still able to pick and choose . . . I can always turn to lecturing, or accept one of the many things I now turn down as uninteresting or beneath my dignity. I am not yet concerned with old age, and refuse to spoil the next few years, when I can enjoy life, by trying to save for when I am over fifty.

[1] This was a persistent illusion of Amy's.

'I am therefore going to spend my money seeing the world and keeping a weather eye open for opportunities of making money . . . It is better to splash a bit now and run out of money whilst I am still young and have a name and reputation, than to eke it out missing life and opportunities . . . You must agree from the human standpoint if not from an economic one.'

She then went on to jot down a list of the jobs she had 'up her sleeve', a list which is fascinating for the insight it gives into her current tastes and ambitions, and also for what it shows of her social contacts.

1 Offer from Sir Alan Cobham to join his Air Circus this summer.
2 Try to sell some Beechcraft planes, for which I hold the agency. I make about £200 profit per plane.
3 Join Phillips and Powis of Reading who have joined the Miles Aircraft Company (they made the Miles Hawk, one of the outstanding light planes of today). This quite appeals to me, but there would be very little money to begin with, but opportunities.
4 Join my Screw Products Co.[1] Would take me away from aviation except as a hobby. Would also take me away from London. Not much money to begin with, but opportunities.
5 Lecturing – I have a standing offer to join two leading lecture agencies.
6 Go on the music-hall stage. I have an offer of £300 a week!
7 Write air fiction in collabration with Harry Harper.[2] I shall do this one day in any event.
8 Go to America to carry out a ranch scheme I have thought of. This appeals to me, but would take me away from England, and it's highly speculative.
9 Join Dorothy Spicer and Pauline Gower in their activities.[3] Nice girls, but little money to be made.

[1] A precision engineering company in which Amy had shares.
[2] The *Daily Mail* air correspondent.
[3] Air-taxi work and joy-riding.

Even all this did not exhaust Amy's imaginative gropings; in a postscript she added three more possibilities she had in mind. The first was to pay Courtenay commission to get her jobs, either as a technical adviser or as a writer on aviation. 'I have not approached him, but think he could do it. The reason I have not tried this yet is that it always savours so much of the film-star to have a manager or agent, and I am trying so hard to build up a serious reputation and get away from the "stunt" category.' The second idea was 'to try to persuade some factory' to take her on as 'a sort of apprentice in test flying.' 'I am terribly keen on this and it is the only way to get the necessary experience. No money in it, but it's the work I'd like most,' Her final idea was to suggest to a friend of hers, Miss Rose Taylor, 'head dress designer of Fortnum and Mason' to join with her in a shop to specialise in 'cruising, seaside and holiday attire.' 'There is a lack of this in England – Palm Beach is the acknowledged leader of Beach Wear, and it would be rather fun travelling and ordering things.'

VIII

Not one of Amy's ideas materialised. After her return to England in April 1935 everything seemed to go wrong; it was a time of frustrations, money worries, driving and flying accidents. As soon as her new Beechcraft arrived from America she damaged it in a crash landing. 'It was my own fault,' she admitted afterwards to her father. 'I had never worked this new undercarriage before . . . and apparently didn't handle it right. Anyhow, it has shown me how safe it is to land without wheels in the unlikely event of my ever having to. I was quite afraid of it before. No accident is wasted if one learns anything from it.'

For some weeks she stayed in St John's Wood with some Madeira friends, Colonel and Mrs Ingham Clarke, then in May she moved to the Savoy Hotel. By this time Jim was back at Grosvenor House. Amy, still in love, still miserable, was unable to hide that she was at his beck and call. She clutched at a scheme which would have involved their working together – an abortive project which she insisted (to her father) was *not* a crazy one. It would be, she said, 'the first commercial Atlantic freight service', and she and Jim, as sole directors, would themselves operate a shuttle service between England and America, each making a return trip per week, which she reckoned would earn them a weekly 'clear profit' of £6,000.

But behind the façade of the Mollisons' shared interest in flying, mistrust was poisoning their relationship, and their marriage was tending more and more towards an open breach. In the summer and autumn of 1935 various happenings took place which may perhaps best be described by quoting from the statement Amy later prepared for her solicitors at the time of her divorce action. After explaining that since her Madeira holiday she had stayed first with a woman friend, then alone at the Savoy, while her husband, since his return from America, had been living at Grosvenor House, she then went on: 'I begged him to return with me, as right up to this time I had no evidence of infidelity on his part, although I was filled with somewhat vague suspicions. He maintained that he preferred a bachelor life and refused to live with me. However, sometime in July or thereabouts, during my last week's stay at the Savoy, he changed his mind and came to live with me there. During this week I received my first active suspicion of infidelity. I returned earlier than expected from a theatre and came home to the Savoy to find my husband lying on the bed in our bedroom with a woman whom I did not know. I ordered her to go, and after her departure accused my husband of being unfaithful and told him he must leave at once. He absolutely refused to go, and gave as his excuse that both he and the woman were very drunk (which was obvious) and that they were merely sleeping it off. I could not turn him out by force, and had nowhere to go myself, it being by this time the early hours of the morning. He swore to me that he had never been unfaithful and I had no choice but to believe him as I had no proof. However, my suspicions were well aroused, and I therefore left the Savoy Hotel and went to stay with another woman friend in the country. My husband visited me here from time to time, but we saw very little of each other, and although outwardly good friends, we never really made things up.

'This state of affairs continued until about November (1935) when I came to London where I took a furnished house[1] for a period of four months. My husband also visited me here during the first week of my tenancy, but it seemed useless to effect a reconciliation as I could not quite believe his protestations of fidelity. He then decided to go to America, and before he left I suggested that I should divorce him as I could not see the point of continuing to live in this most unsatisfactory manner. He asked me to leave things for the time being, saying he would take about a six months' holiday and we could both think things over.'

[1] Belgrave Cottage near Eaton Square.

28

VIE PARISIENNE

1935–1937

One of Amy's address books is devoted entirely to Paris. For during nearly two years, at the time when her marriage was finally breaking up, Paris was her base – or rather her perch – almost as much as London. It was a gilded perch, and the address book of '*la glorieuse aviatrice anglaise*', as *Paris-soir* once called her, included many 'society' names, as well as some of the great couturiers and milliners: Paquin, Mainbocher, Rose Valois. This chapter of her life is little known but it is an important and interesting one, not least for what it shows of her moral standards, while it also brings out some of the contrasts in her character – the naiveté and the shrewdness; the ambition and the caution; the warmth of heart and the sharp temper.

During most of her 'Paris period' she was able to live a life of *grande luxe* owing to the support of a powerful tycoon, the late M François Dupré, who was one of her most persistent admirers. Then in his late forties (he was fifteen years her senior) he had already established an international reputation as a hotelier; already too his racing stables were famous, and since he was also keenly airminded his amorous pursuit of Amy was tinged with heroine-worship. The two probably first met during the summer of 1935 when Amy (at about the time of her thirty-second birthday) made several trips to the continent in her Beechcraft – not only to Paris but to Budapest, Vienna and Biarritz; and by

November, soon after Jim went off to America, she was giving as her Paris address the Hotel George V, which was owned by Dupré. Shortly after this a suite there was put permanently at her disposal.

Amy's first sight of Paris had been long ago with Franz, on their journey back to Hull from Switzerland, but since then, although she had made various fleeting visits (with Winifred, with Jim, and also as a Hillman pilot) she had never until late in 1935 stayed in the city for more than a few days at a time. The reason which brought her to decide on a longer stay was a prosaic one: she was worrying about her teeth and wished to consult a fashionable American dentist who practised in Paris. Thereupon she proposed herself to Winifred's sister Isabel,[1] and stayed with her while she kept her dentist's appointments and also enjoyed gay evenings out which brought her film-star bouquets next day.

On this occasion she did not use her Beechcraft for getting her to and from Paris; she was short of money and had decided to hire it out to charter (both of her ventures in this field were ill-fated; the first, when her 'customer' was Mr Stanley Grove Spiro, foundered in a legal wrangle, and the second ended in a crash). Other attempts to scrape up additional income included designing beauty cases for Elizabeth Arden, trying to write 'air fiction', and briefing a ghostwriter who was tackling a new presentation of her life story.[2]

But another much more ambitious scheme that took hold of Amy's fancy after Jim's departure was the floating of an air-tour company which, so she envisaged, would mean plenty of flying for herself as well as plenty of profits. It would be called 'Air Cruises', and her plan was to purchase a second-hand de Havilland Dragon and then, with herself as pilot, take

---

[1] Who by this time was Mrs Harry Venton: she had married an Englishman whose job was in Paris.
[2] This eventually appeared early in 1937 as a series of articles in *Thomson's Weekly* under the title 'Behind it All'.

parties on pleasure trips to European capitals and elsewhere. She pictured a 'dignified' service, in collaboration with luxury hotels, which would attract a fastidious clientele. By the beginning of 1936 she had found potential backers in the directors of a Mayfair car-sales company, but she had qualms about working with them for she regarded their ideas as niggardly.

At this point Dupré entered the lists as an alternative backer, and in February 1936 Amy first mentioned him to her father. 'I have become great friends with a director and prime mover of the George V Hotel in Paris (equivalent to the Dorchester),' she wrote, and she then went on to report that he was 'young, wealthy, likes me and is very interested in the [Air Cruises] idea. He has position which these other people completely lack, and he has the sporting spirit which I like . . . He says he will buy the machine outright, and won't grumble if the thing's a failure. It sounds grand, but . . . I don't know whether one can entirely trust a Frenchman . . . I feel somehow that English people and capital are more reliable, but I prefer the freedom of the other offer.'

'My friend in Paris is called François Dupré,' she wrote in her next letter. 'He owns the largest studd farm in France, is a director of several large companies, and only originally took up the hotel business as a side line. He has now taken on lease the Plaza, another big hotel in Paris . . . He has his own aeroplane and pilot, speaks English perfectly, and has interests in Canada and the USA. He is used to dealing with the wealthy class I want to attract and sees the need for proper treatment of them.

'He will put up £5,000 to start the company. He wants me to order a *new* Dragon with de luxe furnishings and wireless. He is so keen on the idea of cruises round France for his hotel guests that he will do them anyhow, even if I drop out. However, he is very generous and fair and wants to please me.'

There is no doubt that Dupré wanted to please her; he was by now very much smitten. The letters and cables from him that she kept are discreetly worded but their tone betrays his feelings. In March 1936, when he was away on a business trip to America and Canada he cabled from New York, 'Wish you were here . . . Don't think partners should part so much.' By this time Amy had accepted his backing for Air Cruises, the company had been formed, the Dragon purchased, and the news of her project had been released to the press with May as the date of the initial cruise.

But the prospects ahead of the venture were precarious, for its success would depend largely upon a normal seasonal influx of rich visitors from across the Atlantic. A letter from Dupré from Montreal reflects his anxiety as regards the mounting international tensions in Europe.[1] 'If things are not better by the end of the month,' he wrote, 'and if it appears that there are serious possibilities of a war between Germany and France, we might think it advisable to postpone our plans. People on this side seem very much impressed by the war talk in Europe!'

II

Meanwhile in London Amy herself – still without Jim, who had by now drifted on to Australia – had moved to another 'cottage', the Gate House in Ennismore Gardens, and was installed there, when not in Paris, with a maid-housekeeper (Jessamine James) a secretary (Nancy Mudie) and a little dachshund (Tina). She was already acquiring a Parisian elegance which could not fail to arouse admiration in London: the time was ripe for new ventures. And at just this moment an unexpected opportunity arose for her; a chance, in Bill Courtenay's phrase, to get back on to the front page.

One of her London friends, Captain H.L. Farquhar, who owned a fast new Beechcraft (its power was almost twice that of her own) offered to lend her his plane for an attempt to regain the London–Cape Town record – a

[1] Hitler re-militarised the Rhineland on 7 March 1936.

new record had just been set up by the Phillips and Powis test pilot, Flight Lieutenant Tommy Rose, flying one of his firm's machines 'on a normal business trip'. To Amy the timing seemed providential. Such a flight, if successful – and she never seems to have doubted that it would be – might earn her some good money, would help to give Air Cruises a send-off, and could also 'tie-in' with the new life story.

The idea in its original form came to nothing. On the first occasion when Amy flew her friend's machine she damaged it slightly an on the second made a disastrous forced landing near Birmingham. 'I flew the new aeroplane up and broke the undercarriage,' she wrote to her father from Castle Bromwich. 'I don't like the machine very much and I don't know yet how this will affect my flight.'

Yearning for an alternative aeroplane she was glad when a new suggestion was made to her by a friend who knew the Sahara well, Colonel R.V. Jellicoe. He advised her to drop the Beechcraft idea, and make the flight in a British aircraft, a Percival Gull. Several successful long-distance flights had recently been made in cabin monoplanes of this type, notably Jean Batten's crossing of the South Atlantic. Only a few days after the Beechcraft mishaps Amy came to an agreement with Percivals and they offered to lend her a Gull fitted with special long-range tanks.

Acting upon her father's advice she decided to employ Courtenay as her manager and publicist for the flight: there was much to be said for an agent who knew her preferences. Courtenay knew, for example, that unlike her husband she strongly believed in withholding information from the press until she was on her way. But this virtually ruled out a 'tie-up' with a newspaper; in any case press interest in such ventures was now exceedingly hard to come by, and Courtenay was very pessimistic about the likely rewards. The situation as to Amy's personal publicity was also a tricky one. 'We must be careful how we put the story over once she gets to the Cape,' he wrote to Will

Johnson. 'It must not be a question of staging a "come back" but merely a personal point to re-win the record.' Another delicate piece of public relations concerned Jim. Amy had heard nothing from him for months but if he were not forewarned of her flight he might well put his foot in it when the news reached him, and a renewal of rumours that the Mollisons marriage was breaking up would tarnish Amy's halo. So she wrote to him with news of her plans and he replied by telephone from Australia, having scented publicity in which he himself would share, especially if he were on the spot. He was returning to England by 'air mail', he said, to greet her on her return from the Cape.

Meanwhile the reactions of François Dupré to her project were warmly enthusiastic, and he made no complaint when she had to delegate the organising of Air Cruises. 'As far as we are concerned,' he wrote from Montreal, 'the main thing is for you to accomplish your flight. I have the greatest admiration for your pluck and the most complete faith that you will accomplish what you are setting out to do. All my thoughts are with you always.'

III

The flight was to start from Gravesend airport, the Percival headquarters, and at dawn on 3 April 1936 (the date had been chosen to coincide with a full moon) Amy was given a send-off by her father, her sister Molly, Courtenay and a handful of old friends including Peter Reiss and also – this was the first time she had met him since her marriage – Jack Humphreys (by now he had recovered sufficiently from his 'dismissal' to accept her invitation to see her off).

Like the pale blue aeroplane she was to fly Amy herself was streamlined and glistening; in keeping with the theme of a 'normal business trip' she had chosen elegantly simple travelling clothes, a Schiaparelli suit of navy-blue serge with a divided skirt, and a warm overcoat to match. Her first stop, during the afternoon, was to be on the northern edge of the Sahara, and she planned to fly across the desert during the night. The initial lap was uneventful; she reached Colomb Bechar at 3.45, landed on the large but stony aerodrome and was most efficiently received by the French military authorities. But then the unexpected occurred. In her own words (written a week afterwards) 'Everything was ready for me and in less than an hour the machine was filled with petrol and oil, my Thermos replenished with coffee, water flasks filled; maps, torches and wireless data put ready for the long flight by night over the Sahara. I changed my navy serge suit for a cooler suit of cream silk, drank a cup of refreshingly hot tea and settled myself in the cockpit, a little tired but quite ready for the next stage. I had filled up completely with petrol and had enough for 2,300 miles. It was not necessary to take so much, as I had only about 1,500 miles to cover, but one never knows what may happen and perhaps the extra petrol might be needed. Alas for this ironically wasted caution. The aerodrome is a mass of stones, large and small, and with my heavy load the take-off was too difficult. I gathered speed, then suddenly the machine swung violently to the left. Quickly I throttled down but it was useless, it continued to turn and I was soon in a very rough ground near the boundary . . . She spun round, there was a loud tearing noise and the poor Gull collapsed. I was terrified of turning over and bursting into flames, but I was luckily spared this. I do not know what had happened and still do not know. Either the tail wheel had burst or I had caught a large stone with the metal fairings on the wheels. People watching me thought it was the wind which was very gusty . . . Such a stupid accident. Everything finished so quickly.'

Next day the news went out that the flight was abandoned. But for Amy the misfortune served only as a spur, and the same reserves of will power and courage that had taken her to Australia came into play: the Gull must be repaired and she would fly it back to Gravesend and try again at the next full moon. It appears that Amy – though shaken and distressed – never had any doubts whatever about this decision, which was in fact very typical of her. (An experienced pilot of the same era as herself has said that to his mind the thing that stands out most of all about her character as a flyer is her 'amazing guts'. Her ability 'to pick herself up, dust herself off, and start right over again' is to him the most remarkable thing about her.)

In England Peter Reiss did his best to obtain spares quickly for her, but Amy in her keyed-up state found the delays exasperating. 'Already it is the fifth day here,' she wrote to her father on the 9 April, 'and I am still only receiving telegrams asking for details of damage. If only they would hurry up.' On this same day a cable came from Reiss announcing that he was about to leave for Colomb Bechar in a Leopard Moth, bringing with him the spares and a Percival mechanic. But Amy's patience was exhausted and she felt she could trust no one but herself: next day she flew back to Brussels by Sabena airline – there Reiss met her in the Moth and took her on across the Channel.

When she left England again for Algeria, just over a week later, she was piloting the Air Cruises' Dragon, and with her were Peter Reiss, her sister Molly (for the jaunt), the Percival mechanic, and the spares. On 29 April she was back once more at Gravesend in the resuscitated Gull; 4 May was the deadline for the start of her new attempt. At this crucial point, two days before she was to leave, Jim arrived in London from Australia. He came to the Gate House, told Amy he wanted to start life over again with her, and she took him back to live with her in her house. In a hurried note to her parents just before she left on her flight she told them 'Jim's looking after things here,' and at Gravesend on the morning of 4 May the press photographers were able to record a farewell embrace between husband and wife.

Amy's second attempt to recapture the Cape record was a resounding success. Not only did she improve on Tommy Rose's record by eleven hours but she established records for the return flight and also for the round trip. Her back-to-the-wall persistence caught the public's fancy and despite the apathy of the press to her first attempt, the *Daily Express* bought the rights to her exclusive story and *Paris-soir* relayed it in French. And not only the popular press acclaimed her; *The Times* gave her two editorials and made a flattering verdict: 'Her last flight is no mere flash in the pan but an achievement in keeping with a distinguished aeronautical career.'

There are some interesting parallels between Amy's 1936 Cape flight and her Australia flight six years earlier. In both cases she flew in aircraft which was not the one originally planned; in the course of both she overcame devastating setbacks by means of her tenacity and will power; at the end of both she won ecstatic applause for her personal achievement. Once again, too, the word 'wonderful' echoed through the fan letters from high and low. 'My dear *Wonderful* Amy Mollison,' wrote Violet, Duchess of Rutland. 'I want to tell you just that big word! My little grandson of six, John Julius Cooper, said on your arrival back "What she now ought to have is sleep." I thought that so understanding.'

Another of the fan letters was from a distinguished authoress whose command of language prevented her from resorting to 'that big word'. Rebecca West, convalescing from an illness at a sanatorium in Austria wrote 'You must be weary of hearing from strangers – but my excuse is that you may have heard of me as a writer, and perhaps that might be taken as an introduction, if you are kind. I wanted to tell you that my convalescence from a tiresome fever I picked up in the Balkans has been immensely brightened by your new success. It is always a joy to me to think of your power and courage; and I have an elder sister feeling towards you because I suspect you are the same breed as me, a woman who loves her work but hates the racket of public life and gets the jitters through it, and often seems to herself like a puppy-dog that's got tangled up in its lead. My blessings on you, now and always.'

In May 1936, soon after Amy's return from the Cape, she and Jim had 'a long talk'. 'For the first time,' so she later wrote, 'he admitted to numerous infidelities extending over a period dating from about one month of being married. I was naturally terribly upset at this definite corroboration of my suspicions, but on his promise to live a different life in future I agreed to give him a fresh start . . . I tried things out during the summer months.' Several of her women-friends told her, at about this time, that she ought not to let Jim 'treat her like a doormat', but she ignored their advice for she was still under his spell.

Through June and July the Gate House was the Mollisons' home and they attended various public functions together. They both spoke (very amusingly) at an 'Atlantic' aviation dinner at the Forum Club; they also attended an occasion at Bridlington when Amy, swathed in a Parisian mink coat, performed the opening ceremony of a local mansion, Sewerby Hall, which with its estate had been acquired by the Borough as a public park.[1]

In the meantime they were both full of plans for new flights, but for one reason or another none of them came off. They revived the idea of a joint round-the-world venture, and tried, without success, to acquire one of the Comet racers for it. Then there was talk of a 'formation flight' in two smaller aircraft: 'spectacular but suicidal' was how Amy described the scheme to her father. A few weeks later the whole thing had been dropped and they were trying to find a machine for the 1936 Johannesburg Air Race. Meanwhile in July Amy took part in the King's Cup Race (flying a British Aircraft Eagle) but without success.

---

[1] In 1959 Amy's father presented her trophies and awards to the Borough of Bridlington, and they have since been on permanent exhibition at Sewerby Hall.

One result of Amy's new attempt to make her marriage work was that she had no time at all for Air Cruises and she temporarily withdrew from the company. Dupré does not seem to have raised any objections; he bided his time, and her place as the company's pilot was taken by Mrs Beryl Markham, a blonde from Kenya whose flying exploits were in the news at the time. But life with Jim was not easy and as the summer progressed Amy began to lose confidence in his resolve to turn over a new leaf. As a last resort she suggested that they should go off together on a holiday in the South of France for a month or so 'to put things finally to the test.'

From Juan les Pins she wrote to her father 'We couldn't get a machine for the Johannesburg race so there's nothing to hurry back for. We've no plans (too busy watching the European situation).' She was also busy watching Jim, and during this holiday she came at last to the conclusion that he was 'incapable' of remaining faithful to her and that they must part.

Back in London in September 1936 she instructed Crockers to start divorce preliminaries and asked Jim to leave the Gate House (before he went he admitted to many more infidelities). He moved to the Hyde Park Hotel, having agreed to 'give her her evidence' before leaving for America in a month's time, but after only a week he left the country without a word to her. When Amy learnt of his departure (from a newspaper report) she was in Paris again – with Dupré. 'It was a shock to find Jim had gone to America,' she wrote to her father a day or two later from Lausanne. 'I am only here for the day – I came in the Air Cruises Dragon with my partner Dupré. I am taking up my company again and it is nice flying in the Dragon after so long.'[1]

It was also nice to be in Paris in early autumn, buying jewels and new clothes, and having French

---

[1] In fact Air Cruises never again became a going concern and the company was wound up in January 1937.

lessons and skin treatments and sessions with the dentist and 'nerve treatments by a very clever Indian doctor'.[1] 'I'm quite happy and content and looking forward to my future,' she told her father. 'I've heaps of ideas and plans.' One of her plans was to make a trip to America in November, 'then Africa for Christmas . . . Dupré is going, his French pilot, a Frenchman called Pierre Lyautey, who is the nephew of the famous General Lyautey, and who knows the Sahara and Morocco very well and is arranging for us to be received everywhere. We first of all go to Kenya where we are going to join Lord and Lady Furness on a large big-game hunting expedition. I have always longed to do that. We shall be out in the bush for Xmas – New Year in Nairobi . . . I've persuaded Dupré to buy a new plane instead of the Dragon. He's having a fast French Caudron machine and I'm intensely looking forward to flying it.'

In this same letter she confided to her father her personal feelings about the Frenchman upon whom her 'plans and ideas' depended, and the passage concerned provides a fascinating glimpse of how things stood between Amy and François at this time. 'This man Dupré is a strange man,' Amy told him. 'He's generous and kind to me in the extreme, so much so that I was worried and had a long talk with him. He told me he was "madly in love with me and wanted to marry me when I was free!!!" You've no idea what a joke it is! I can't stand him at any price and I told him I would never marry again and I could never love him. He wants anyhow to carry on with all our arrangements so I said I would. What is a girl to do? if I threw him over I'd have no aeroplane and couldn't make this [Africa] flight, and I'd lose a great many other advantages beside. He seems quite content with the situation . . . He admits I've never encouraged him and he says I'm to regard myself as under no obligation whatsoever. Of

---

[1] Amy's Cape flight had temporarily restored her finances, as well as her celebrity-value.

course I do a lot for him indirectly, as it [Air Cruises] must be good publicity for him – although he wants to remain in the background.'

Amy's 'ideas and plans' for the end of 1936 were not destined to come off; she did not go to America in November nor to Africa for Christmas. On 20 October, returning to Croydon from Paris in her Beechcraft, she crashed when making a forced landing in fog at Chelsfield in Kent, and her injuries included a broken nose and dislocated shoulder. That evening reporters besieged the Gate House and Amy, very badly shaken, disclosed the news that she and Jim had agreed to separate. She did not however mention his unfaithfulness or the possibility of divorce; she blamed the breach on the publicity which had always prevented them from settling down. Her statement set off an explosion of news stories on both sides of the Atlantic, and for Jim in New York, preparing to make yet another transatlantic flight (in an American Bellanca), the publicity was a godsend. He added to it by announcing that he had named his aircraft *Miss Dorothy* after a London revue actress, thus turning a spotlight on to the current 'romance' between himself and Dorothy Ward. Amy meanwhile, after a few days in a nursing home, went to stay with friends in Buckinghamshire (and there Dupré came to visit her).

As the autumn of 1936 drew on – it was the time of the Abdication crisis – Amy resumed her gay life in London and Paris. But she had not fully recovered from the Chelsfield crash and during December her health broke down and she retreated to a Swiss clinic for a month's rest, accompanied by her sister Molly. By February 1937, however, when Dupré and another Frenchman joined the two in Austria for some ski-ing she was her exuberant self again. 'If only you could be here too,' she wrote to her mother. 'Blue skies, brilliant sunshine, shining white snow and always feeling so well and full of energy. You would never hear me say now that I'm wearied and worn out!'

Dupré and his 'backing' still dominated Amy's life during the first half of 1937 and they were often together. After Austria she was in Paris, then he came to London (where he met her father and got on very well with him), then they were both in New York – at the end of March she sailed for America (with a new wardrobe by Mainbocher)[1] and did not return until June. She had several motives for making this trip, foremost among them fresh trouble with her teeth. She was now dissatisfied with her Paris dentist and had decided to consult a Fifth Avenue practitioner. And not only her teeth were given expert treatment while she was in New York: she stayed with an American friend Gloria Bristol, who was a beauty specialist, and as a result before she returned to Europe she was looking as enamelled and orchidaceous as a film star (one columnist described her as 'the outstanding feat of glamorizing ever performed outside the Hollywood factories').

Apart from the campaign to improve her appearance Amy's main preoccupation was a forthcoming air race from New York to Paris, sponsored by the French Government. It was to take place in August 1937 to commemorate the tenth anniversary of Lindbergh's flight, and she was to compete in Dupré's new Caudron Goeland, a silver and scarlet six-seater (an alternative possibility, suggested by Courtenay, that she should fly a twin-boom Burnelli aircraft had promised well at first but then petered out). In the race she would be accompanied by a navigator, but despite this she had set her heart on learning to navigate by sextant 'all by herself', and one of the purposes of her trip to America was to follow up an offer of special coaching in navigation that had been made to her by an affable American, Lieutenant Commander P.V.H. Weems of the

---

[1] The couturier of whom it has been said that he could not only make a woman look like a lady, but as if her mother and grandmother had been ladies too.

US Naval Academy, whom she had met in London the previous autumn.

Early in May she wrote to her father from Annapolis, 'I am here for a fortnight especially to study celestial navigation with Commander Weems, who is admittedly one of the world's experts. He is very charming and I am thoroughly enjoying the hard work I am putting in.'[1] She took her navigation very seriously: Harriet Cohen, still a fan but now also a friend of Amy's, remembers that when she saw her in New York she found her as much obsessed with navigation as she herself was with the piano. But Amy's hard work with Weems was of no immediate use to her; while she was still in America the Atlantic race was cancelled. The US Department of Commerce, keen to ensure the success of the first transatlantic air services, feared that if crashes occurred during the race they would put off potential passengers. Amy was disgusted at the decision but she had other 'plans and ideas' to fall back on: with Dupré behind her she hoped at last to make a flight round the world.

Hardly was she back in Paris however than she and François fell out. Amy's temper got the better of her when she discovered that Dupré was planning to use his new aircraft for a continental trip at a time when she seems to have assumed it was at her own disposal. 'François has thrown me out,' she wrote to her mother. 'Not really! But I have left the George V. Things were

---

[1] Amy's studies at Annapolis were so much publicised that they evoked an amusing protest from a local misogynist who wrote to Commander Weems: 'I deeply regret, and am sure that all of the real men that have been trained at the Academy resent, your bringing a female (Amy Mollison) to this fine Institute and giving her instructions in navigation. This Academy is sacred to men and I beg of you to use your great knowledge and experience in this science on behalf of men only . . . Let us strive to keep this a Man's Country, and this can be done if all men will cooperate and rule with a strong hand and retain the rights nature gave them.'

getting a little difficult . . . No more flights for me, I'm afraid, so you can finish worrying.' Her mother's health was very frail at this time and she was glad to be able to spare her: a few weeks later (in July 1937), when the news came that Amelia Earhart was lost over the Pacific, she wrote again to her mother. 'No more flights so no need to worry! Poor Amelia!'

VI

When Amy returned to Europe the fact that she and Jim were divorcing was public knowledge, for Jim had already let it out to the press. Amy herself had also taken steps towards resuming the use of her maiden name. Jim was living in London at this time, writing his reminiscences (with the encouragement of the *Daily Express* air correspondent, Victor Ricketts) and Amy, in spite of the break with Dupré, felt she would prefer to make Paris her main base. 'I have just taken a lovely little apartment in Paris,' she told her mother. 'I'm letting my house in London . . . I don't really like hotel life and know I shall be happier in a home of my own. It is a pity to give up my pretty London cottage but it is much too expensive to keep it on, and anyhow I am never there.' To her father she explained 'I am only continuing with my plan to live in Paris as it is so much cheaper to live there and I can live on a lower standard much more easily than I could in London. For example it would be very difficult and lead to much talk [in London] if I moved . . . to some very cheap flat in the suburbs, and in any event that would be much more expensive than Paris, especially now with the fall of the franc . . . In the meantime I shall make an attempt to start my book[1] or to do some writing of some sort. I think that's the only future for me worth while, but it is awful hard work to write and I am afraid I am not specially gifted for it . . .

---

[1] She may already have been planning her book *Sky Roads of the World* which she wrote during the following year.

What a business life is, and how futile it seems sometimes.' She also asked her father for advice about Dupré. 'I shall drop him altogether, don't you think? I feel better without him anyway and am not at all sure that I want to do anything in co-operation with him even if it is business.'

Soon after this Amy and her father had a talk about her relations with Dupré and subsequently (on 16 July 1937) he wrote to her at some length on the subject, gently encouraging her towards a reconciliation. 'Somehow or other I feel that you will hear much more of F.D.' he told her. 'He likes you very much indeed and it would probably please him to continue to be closely associated with someone he likes as much as yourself and at the same time someone who was perfectly honest and straight; such an experience would give him pleasure and he can afford that pleasure . . . I advise you to be much nicer to him, that is more polite and not try to make him feel so uncomfortable . . . I think he DOES look upon you differently from other girls . . . You won't find it easy to get anyone to come up with big money, therefore when you are in touch with a man like F.D. who is really willing to spend generously then you ought to try and make the atmosphere as smooth as possible rather than make it more and more irritable, which no man would stand.'

Amy took these remonstrances to heart. 'After lots of hard thinking,' she replied, 'I am wondering whether I have made a hopeless mess of things . . . The funny thing is that, away from F.D., I can more easily see his good points which when I am with him get lost in my quite inexplicable dislike of him . . . It's awfully difficult constantly forcing oneself to be nice to someone who irritates one. Sooner or later something is bound to blow up.'

In her next letter[1] she continued her 'F.D. Narrative',

[1] Written on 30 July 1937 from Versailles – she was using the Trianon Palace Hotel as a temporary *pied-à-terre*.

as she called it. 'When I got back [to Paris] I telephoned F.D. and went to see him at the Hotel George V . . . He said that he was quite willing to help me to fulfil some plans if I had any, but he did not think it wise to give me any money as it would only be a temporary solution to my difficulties . . . Already he is getting on my nerves again. I just can't help it, I'm afraid. He then invited me to go to his Stud Farm and I accepted, after a lot of hesitation as it is quite against my better judgment. I don't think there is any doubt at all that he still likes to have me around and he is extremely clever at getting his own way. It makes me afraid to watch his tactics. I don't like people who are so clever . . . He seems to have been trying to convince me of all the wonderful things I am missing by showing me pictures of his girl friends with him in Venice, Budapest, Rome, etc. etc. and telling me of all his plans for his plane . . . and of how neglected I look now with no-one to look after my clothes, cars, etc., and so on . . . It's all very difficult, and I have a feeling that no matter how hard I try with F.D. it will always end in disaster as he has this most peculiar effect on me of irritating me almost to the point of madness.'

The next instalment of Amy's 'narrative' followed a fortnight later (it was written from a small hotel outside Cannes). 'I went to the Stud Farm for the weekend and with difficulty avoided the purpose for which I had quite obviously been asked. I tried to be very agreeable yet not to give anything away. It worked so long as I was holding out any promises for the future. It was all arranged that I came on my holidays and on the 19th [of August] was to be in Paris at the George V, meet F.D. and go with him to Switzerland for a three-weeks cure. He was very nice and held out hopes of helping me, although I now have no illusions whatever as to what he wanted in return, and again all the help was just so much bait. For example he suggested my starting a career in Canada, and later I found out that he is intending to spend half his time in that country. Anyway I was still hopeful of handling things well.

Unfortunately (or fortunately, I don't yet know which) things were not left in my hands.'

This last remark refers to a contretemps which was a most embarrassing one for Amy. Dupré, who had been planning to fly to Cannes for a brief visit early in August, discovered by chance that Amy's 'holidays' were to be spent in the South of France with another Frenchman, a friend of his own, a man of much charm but of considerably less affluence than himself. This, it seems, decided Dupré that he had had enough of Amy's ways. 'When I arrived down here,' she went on, 'I called in at the Carlton Hotel to see F.D. He was very sweet but quite firm. He declared that I had chosen between himself and . . . [his friend] and that our ways now lay apart. It was useless to argue. Looking back I still can't make up my mind what I should have done. There is no doubt at all that I have missed a life of luxury as F.D.'s mistress (which wouldn't matter much if I liked him, but I can't bear the idea of sleeping with someone for the sake of what I can get). So that's that. I am living in a cheap hotel counting every penny when I might have been having everything I wanted . . . Maybe it's a pity . . . maybe it's the best thing that could have happened. One can't see these things clearly at the time. I acted more by instinct than by reason I think.'

'I am convinced you have done right,' her father reassured her. 'Our conscience is the thing we've to be clear with . . . Get ready now for some hard work and real work and I'm sure you'll pull through. I would forget the F.D. episode entirely as there would only be one end.' After this Amy seldom made any further mention of Dupré in her letters home. Writing to her father on 1 December 1937 – four months after her final break with 'F.D.' – she remarked 'he has sailed today for the US taking a beautiful Hungarian girl,' but so far as we know she did not make any comment when later the marriage took place between M François Dupré and Mlle A.S. Nagy.

29

HAND TO MOUTH

1937–1940

'A brave, naive *déracinée*: that is how Amy was described by Lord Vansittart, who interviewed her at the Foreign Office at the beginning of the last war when, searching for work to which she could dedicate herself, she begged him – in vain – to take her on for 'some dangerous mission in Secret Service.' But a more sensitive summing up of her as she was in her mid-thirties, just before the war, was recently given by a man who knew her as a personal friend, the novelist John Moore. 'She was a *good* girl. Genuine and generous-spirited, straight, dead honest and reliable. She wasn't having a very happy time. I always thought she was still in love with that so and so Jim Mollison. On the rare occasion when she drank too much it was because she was unhappy, and sometimes when she was tight she was a bit reckless and apt to let fly; I remember her telling me she had a frightful scene with a policeman in Bristol or Cardiff or somewhere when she had called him everything under the sun and was lucky not to be roped in for being drunk in charge.'

Among Amy's friends there is some difference of opinion as to how much she resorted to drink – one of them hotly denies that she was in any way addicted to it – but the incident she mentioned to Moore (which occurred in September 1939 outside Cardiff) was not her first scene with the police when driving late at night; there had been the clash with the Florida cops five years earlier. Then – as Amy Mollison – she had been deeply unhappy because her marriage was cracking; now, Amy Johnson once more,[1] she was beset by miseries of many kinds. She yearned for a settled home yet was always restless, always moving. She missed being married, but most of the men she fell for were not 'the marrying kind'. She schemed and battled for a worthwhile, challenging job in aviation and meantime spent herself on ephemeral odds and ends. An intensely busy life gave her little time to brood and sometimes, especially when she embarked on a new venture or went to live somewhere new, she believed that she was happy, but this euphoria never lasted long and her true state of mind could be guessed from the expression of deep sadness on her face when in repose.

The love of her family and of her few close friends was almost the only constant in her life at this time. She wrote as much as ever to her parents – especially to her father – and her letters form a sombre but most interesting narrative of these years, when she drifted from place to place, from one enthusiasm to another, from man to man and from one financial crisis to the next. The letters to her father are packed with details of money troubles, for after the extravagances of her life with Jim, and the experience of being 'subsidised' by Dupré, Amy found it impossible to control her spending, and her attempts to make ends meet were futile. She sold her aircraft, her mink coat, some of her jewels, most of her few investments, but the proceeds were swallowed up at once. Eventually she was glad to accept an allowance of five pounds a week from her father.

But all this was behind the scenes. On public occasions, to the press and to any she chatted with, Amy appeared smiling, self-possessed, calm and enigmatic – there was nothing of the hectic divorcée about her. The patina of Paris and the 'glamor' of New York still clung to

---

[1] She resumed her maiden name by deed poll on 22 March 1937, at the same time that she began divorce proceedings.

her, and one newspaperman who met her briefly at a party wrote of her as follows: 'I suppose one might describe her as "feminine" but the word is not sufficient. Her personality wrapped her like an aura. One just knew at once that she was someone very unusual . . . She was quiet and almost shy to talk to; and she had very calm, blue eyes. She seemed to be altogether self-contained.' Another chance acquaintance, Michael Daunt the test pilot, who met her with John Moore, also remembers her restrained manner and her charm. But it was the look of tragic unhappiness that he glimpsed on her long little face that chiefly remained in his memory.

II

In the late summer of 1937 Amy's plans for an apartment in Paris collapsed and she withdrew to England. Her relations with Dupré had not been embittered by the break, but naturally her Swiss cure with him had been cancelled, and instead she went alone for a few weeks to a health clinic near Tring. At this poing she decided that she no longer wanted to live in London, and by a stroke of luck was able to stay on in the Chilterns for she was offered (on loan for a month) a charming old cottage at Haddenham near Aylesbury. It belonged to the Hislops, Jim's aunt and uncle; the fact that she was divorcing Jim had not alienated them, indeed to the end of her life she and they remained warmly affectionate friends. Her feelings towards Jim himself were however temporarily worsened at this time by the publication of his memoirs, *Playboy of the Air*.[1] The allusions to herself in it, though not unkind, were made in a patronising way which infuriated her – so much so that her first impulse was to issue a writ for libel, though she was dissuaded from this by a legal friend who consoled her by calling Jim 'a drunken bounder who has boasted publicly of his vicious life.'

[1] The book was dedicated to Dorothy Ward.

HAND TO MOUTH

Amy liked the Chilterns so much that in November 1937 she took a furnished cottage in Princes Risborough (a picturesque little timber-framed house adjoining the churchyard and variously known as Monks Staithe, the Old Vicarage, and the Old Rectory) and from this new base she threw herself into a breathless round of activity. 'I adore my little house,' she wrote home exuberantly. 'I am extremely fit and enjoying life . . . I ride horseback and bicycle a lot. Mr Dupré has given me a saddle for a Xmas present. Jessamine loves it here too and so does Tina. The Ford car is running very well.' Each morning she bicycled to some nearby stables and went off riding; frequently too she hunted with the Old Berkeley, and meanwhile was also taking up two new sports, gliding and motor-racing.[1] But in her big Ford car she was always dashing up to London and her engagement book for the first half of 1938 bristles with dates at the Savoy, the Ivy, Claridge's; it also shows many appointments for elocution lessons.

Amy's speech had by now taken on a Mayfair idiom, but she had been forced to a painful awareness that her accent still betrayed her origins by an impersonation which Florence Desmond was giving in cabaret and on the music halls. Among Amy's papers is a pencilled account of the occasion when she herself chanced to witness it (she seems to have been planning an article to show how well she eventually got over her mortification). One evening she was taken by an American friend to a London restaurant where Florence Desmond was the cabaret star; after the caricatures of Mae West and Garbo there were cries of 'Amy Johnson, We want Amy Johnson.' 'My heart started thumping,' she recalled, 'and I had a funny feeling inside. The brilliant actress came back and rendered her masterpiece. "Does my voice

[1] The motor rallies, hill climbs and track races in which she took part brought her a good deal of publicity but very few prizes.

sound like that to you?" I asked my companion anxiously, and to his swift "Not in the least – let's get out of here," I thought "He's only saying that as it's easiest. No man tells the truth when he's with a woman".'

Between her trips to London and her many sporting activities (which did not at this time include much flying) Amy found time for quite a lot of writing; chiefly articles for the *Daily Mail* and similar papers but also the beginnings of her book on the world's airlines, a foreword for Pauline Gower's *Women with Wings*, and the essay about her childhood and youth which was published in *Myself When Young* (she described it at the time to a reporter as 'not a stereotyped autobiography but a psychological study'). Furthermore she was now embarking upon a campaign of job-hunting which she herself described as 'desperate'. The word is not an exaggeration. If Amy had been any less persevering by nature the rebuffs and disappointments she suffered might well have led her to despair. She had already been a victim of publicity; now she was a victim of the British tendency to distrust the publicised. With characteristic ingenuousness she wrote openly in one of her articles of this impasse in her life. 'Often it happens that your very name is against you in applying for a serious job. It is hard to persuade some hard-boiled business man that you have any brains behind a windowfront name. It is harder still to escape being captioned "stunt pilot" and considered as good for nothing except to take rather unnecessary stupid risks that no ordinary mortal would dream of taking. It rather seems to go with sitting on flagpoles and going over Niagara Falls in a barrel.'

One of her schemes was for an appointment at the Air Ministry, but when after a long wait she was offered a post as a Junior Operations Officer at five pounds a week she was disgusted (and also embarrassed because Sir Francis Shelmerdine, Director General of Civil Aviation, had taken great pains to help her). 'Oh dear, whatever made me think I would like to go into the Air Ministry,' she wrote to her father. 'How on earth can I live on £5 . . . I am living here at the rate of about

£20 a week . . . I am so happy nowadays living this peaceful country life, riding, hunting and gliding, and going to town every now and then . . . [for] my voice production lessons . . . If I don't take the Air Ministry job, my plans for the future would be just to carry on as I am doing now . . . I meet lots of nice people and would keep a lookout for a nice rich husband.[1] My two main assets, being Amy Johnson and a woman, are disadvantages at the Air Ministry, and unfortunately nowadays I've so lost my enthusiasm for flying that I can't take on such a job for the pure love of it. I've been in the game for a long time and am pretty fed up with it now. I saw Jim yesterday and he has offered to lend me his new aeroplane, his maps and everything if I would like to do a flight, but I refused. Life seems too good to waste it that way.'

III

Such was the life that Amy was living when her tenancy of Monks Staithe ran out. She tried to find an alternative in the same district, but discovered nothing suitable and in August 1938 moved to a country club (Rossley Manor) near Cheltenham. The Cotswolds suited her even better than the Chilterns. 'I love my new home,' she told her parents. 'All the people here are nice, and it's quiet and homelike. It will be far cheaper than Monks Staithe . . . I like Cheltenham too, and also the people. They are so friendly – so different from Princes Risborough and High Wycombe.' After a couple of months she rented a cottage called Old Rowley at Stoke Orchard, a pretty village between Cheltenham and Tewkesbury, and there, for

[1] This was written a few days before Amy's decree nisi was granted on 8 February 1938 (it was made absolute on 24 August). Mollison was remarried on 12 November 1938 to Mrs Phyllis Hussey, an heiress; this marriage was dissolved in 1948. In 1949 he made a third marriage, to Mrs Mary Kamphuis, widow of a Dutch Air Force colonel, and she survived Mollison's death in 1959.

the remainder of the nine months she lived in Gloucestershire she continued her busy round. But she was less often in London now, and participated occasionally in local doings: in Cheltenham she gave a talk at the Ladies' College, and the functions she agreed to attend included a laundry-workers' ball at which she presided over the election of a beauty queen.

She was still busy writing. Her book on the airlines of the world (for Chambers, the Edinburgh publishers) was soon to be serialised in *Chambers' Journal*, and as usual she was churning out articles for the popular press, most of them on aviation, but some on subjects of general interest to women. She took serious pains with her writing (her library included quite a few text-books on journalism) and it seems that her work usually satisfied her editors, for many of her typescripts are almost identical to the published articles. But she never found it easy to work as a regular contributor to a newspaper; for a few months in the autumn of 1938 she was engaged by the *Sunday Graphic* as special correspondent on the Civil Air Guard,[1] but the assignment ended prematurely.

What Amy had been hoping for was an appointment in the Civil Air Guard itself, and she felt 'very hurt', so she told her father, when she was not invited to participate. 'I have written to Sir Kingsley Wood [the Air Minister] for an interview,' she told him. 'I thought of asking him point-blank why there is no room for me in his schemes to make the country air-minded . . . Maybe he thinks I am not respectable enough, and should merely out-stunt his stunt.' Her interview with Sir Kingsley was an 'unqualified failure', even though he was 'very nice and sympathetic'. 'He said he wished he could have given me something . . . [in] the Air Guard scheme, but that as all the jobs were voluntary he had not considered me for them as he knew I would want something paid! He told

---

[1] A scheme to attract would-be pilots into a 'second line' reserve by heavily subsidised tuition at the flying clubs.

me that I could still have the job of Junior Operations Officer if I wanted it, but I told him I now had a job with the *Graphic* at three times the salary with a hundredth part of the work and ten times the power. I don't know whether he liked that.'

Although her lucrative job with the *Graphic* did not last for long she had plenty of other writing to do; by now she was turning her attention to motoring and for a short time was editor of a newly-launched monthly *The Lady Driver*. But all her writings and doings were brought to a standstill when early in 1939 she was involved in a road crash. On 8 February, driving back to Gloucestershire from London, she collided with another car, and although she had a lucky escape she suffered a knee injury and was very much shaken. This setback did not however damp her initiative, and while still on crutches she set off to New York to recuperate. 'The sea voyage ought to be useful as convalescence, and I shall be without motoring for a month,' she explained to her father when she warned him of her plan; she also warned him that she would probably have to ask him for 'a small loan', even though she intended selling a pair of ear-rings that Mr Dupré had once given her. It was a quiet trip, very much on the cheap; when Amy returned early in April she was still in a mood of discouragement, and she told the press that as her services as a pilot were not wanted she had volunteered for National Service as a lorry driver. She had not fully recovered from her accident and was far from well; soon after this she suffered from a poisoned finger and had to have the nail off. The publication of her book *Sky Roads of the World* did nothing to raise her spirits. 'Am sending you and Daddy a copy of my book,' she wrote to her mother. 'Personally I think it looks horribly dull and I'm most disappointed.' The jacket of Amy's book was drab and uninviting, and the book itself was hardly better. Although certain passages are interesting it is a hotch-potch of information and reminiscences, and much of it reads like a travel brochure. Perhaps Amy should have stuck to the popular journalism that was within her range.

AMY JOHNSON

IV

Some of the best of the articles Amy wrote are on gliding, and her passion for the sport continued for over two years – until war came. 'Real flying for You' was the title of her first piece on the subject. 'The slowness, the peace, the tranquillity . . . The silence, broken only by the soft swish of the wind in my hair, is rapture after the deafening roar to which I have been accustomed for so many years.' Why had Amy never before tried her hand at it? We know that two experts who were Stag Lane friends of hers (Joan Price, later Mrs Meakin, and Captain R.S. Rattray) had repeatedly urged her to do so. The answer is that ever since she learnt to fly she had been far too much preoccupied with powered flight; furthermore her only two contacts with the gliding world had been unfortunate ones. Seven years earlier, just before she flew to Australia, she had once been on the point of making a flight in a glider as a publicity stunt – a news agency wanted to photograph her as the first woman in England to try the new sport – but chance prevented it, and her next contact with the movement was almost as abortive. On her return from Australia she was persuaded by Sefton Brancker to become a Vice-President of the British Gliding Association, which had been formed in a belated attempt to follow the lead of Germany in popularising the sport. But she was not personally interested at the time, and in a letter written to the Association's Chairman, E.C. Gordon England, in 1932, she prophesied that gliding would 'never really be popular or profitable in this country' (whereupon Gordon England replied, 'If you could ever fly over to the Wasserkuppe say during their annual competition period I think your whole attitude would undergo complete modification, as you would then see what can be accomplished with a little support').

By the late summer of 1937 Amy's prophecy had been proved wrong. Gliding in Britain was by this time no longer confined to elementary 'air tobogganing'; the techniques of soaring had been introduced from Germany, and this was resulting in a surge of new ardour at the gliding clubs. Such was the state of affairs when Amy, while at Tring for her 'cure', drove over to Dunstable to investigate the London Gliding Club. 'I joined the club in much the same way as I joined the London Aeroplane Club,' she subsequently related. 'I wandered on to the premises, and asked how much it would cost to join. The only difference this time was that I was made an immediate member and started instruction within ten minutes of joining . . . It is not that I am well-known. Everyone is treated alike. There is a friendliness, enthusiasm and sporting spirit such as I haven't come across for a long time.'[1]

She found the same friendliness, enthusiasm and sporting spirit at the Midland Gliding Club (at the Longmynd, above Church Stretton) and at the Yorkshire Gliding Club at Sutton Bank near Thirsk, and both of these hill-top camps became favourite haunts of hers, especially at weekends. She often made her way to them by road, driving her Ford rather less speedily than usual because she was towing a trailer carrying a sailplane (or rather its disassembled components). At one of the international crises of 1938 a Sunday newspaper invited her (along with other celebrities) to say how she was going to spend the 'crisis weekend'. 'I am spending a quiet weekend gliding in a remote part of England, where I can enjoy for two days the illusion of peace,' she replied. 'If only Hitler could likewise relax for two days and forget himself.' As a glider pilot, much of whose time was spent waiting for weather, she found herself becoming far less impatient than usual. 'It's good for our characters, and I'm

---

[1] Although Amy was much liked in the gliding fraternity and never exploited her fame she was pursued by fans even to the wilds of Shropshire. At an Easter Camp at the Longmynd in 1938 £26 was taken in fees for admission to see her and for signed photographs.

developing quite a tranquil temperament nowadays,' she wrote to her father from Sutton Bank in August 1938. 'Today is a heart-breaking day. A gorgeous west wind, but too strong. My Kite is already rigged, but hidden around the corner away from the wind which is blowing a young gale. I've been ready since early morning to set off to get my Silver C,[1] complete with barograph and everything ready but the wind still howls and it isn't worth risking. It's all right in the air, but it's coming in to land that is dangerous . . . Without an engine you can't take chances.'

With an engine Amy continued as usual to take chances, as John Moore discovered when he accompanied her in a borrowed light aeroplane on a flight to the Longmynd for some gliding. 'Despite her enormous experience Amy was not a very polished flyer,' he writes. 'She didn't give the impression of handling an aircraft *superbly* well and her landings were always a bit casual. She would just bang the aircraft down with a sort of air of "OK that's that. We've arrived." On this occasion on the Longmynd she chose a patch of rough heather in which to bang down her aeroplane. We went bounding along for thirty yards or so, then one wheel got caught in a rabbit hole and that indeed was that. However we had a lovely day's gliding. Although I had done a little gliding before, I had never flown a sailplane, never had the exciting experience of watching a buzzard almost at my wing-tip doing exactly the same thing as I was, only so much better. Amy looped her single seater sailplane, which seemed to me very adventurous and alarming. Some friends fetched us home that evening, and we left the aircraft at the top of the Longmynd to be salvaged later.'

Another new friend of Amy's (who got to know her at the Longmynd) also discovered that her abilities as an airwoman did not match her fame. This was Dick Atcherley who as a Schneider Trophy pilot in 1929 had

---

[1] An international gliding certificate.

been one of Amy's heroes. 'We both belonged to the Midland Gliding Club, and she most kindly lent me her glider,' he recalls. 'I gave her a bit of link trainer at Tern Hill to hot up her instrument flying, which of course was necessary for gliding. I was shocked to find how incapable she was of flying blind and marvelled at (and admired) her long flights, which must have put her in the most ghastly (blind) circumstances.'

V

In June 1939 – just before her thirty-sixth birthday – Amy at last succeeded in securing a flying job. 'Folks, you've got the chance of being flown by a world-famous air pilot for five bob a time!' proclaimed the *Daily Mirror*, for she had been taken on by the operators of the Solent air ferry.[1] 'You will probably think I'm foolish not to stick to writing,' she wrote to her father from Portsmouth, 'but I need a more active life and don't really like writing although it's useful as a sideline . . . My job here is pretty strenuous.' This was an understatement, for the ferry company had army cooperation contracts, which meant almost non-stop flying by day and by night, whenever weather permitted. But she was so delighted to be earning as a pilot and so determined to prove herself as a professional that she stuck to the job for nearly nine months, until wartime reorganisation brought it to an end.[2]

Meanwhile in her off-time she was making new friends and discovering the enchantments of sailing. 'Last night I went sailing and thoroughly enjoyed it,' she wrote to her mother after a few weeks at Portsmouth. 'Can't think why I haven't tried it before.

---

[1] The Portsmouth, Southsea and Isle of Wight Aviation Ltd.
[2] This army cooperation work meant flying aircraft on pre-arranged courses to provide surprise targets for the searchlights and range-finders of local anti-aircraft batteries. The pilots were paid £1 per day plus 10s per hour for day flying and £1 per hour for night flying.

It's much more exciting than flying.' Very soon she was toying with the ideas of a little racing boat of her own, of a sea holiday from the Clyde that summer, and of perhaps one day a voyage round the world under sail. 'I have two different people in mind to go with,' she told her father, 'so if one fails me I have the other. This is something to look forward to and gives me a definite aim, which is what I have been needing for some time.'

With the cottage at Stoke Orchard still on her hands she started living in lodgings in Portsmouth, but quickly tired of 'digs', and only a fortnight before war was declared announced to her father that she was about to take 'a lovely bungalow' at Old Bosham. 'I'd sooner live here anyway even if my work here was finished.' Then a week later she suddenly became aware that war was impending. 'I don't know whether I am taking a particularly gloomy view of things,' she wrote to her father on 24 August, 'but everyone at the airport seems to think war is as good as declared . . . It's terrible isn't it, and so criminally stupid.' She did not however envisage that hostilities would interfere with her sailing plans. 'I'm writing this on a boat in Portsmouth Harbour,' she went on. 'The boat belongs to a man called Bill Long, who has been away five years on it going all round the world. He is teaching me all about sailing, etc. and he is one of the people I have in mind if ever I get a chance to get away on a sailing trip.' But would she? 'All the submarines have just gone out, and there are no battleships left in the harbour. The weather seems to fit in with the general tension – it is heavy and dull. Mother tells me that you will probably go to Blackpool, but I shouldn't think that would be a very safe place . . . Don't worry about me, because I shall just stick with the Company . . . We have been ordered to Cardiff (this is a "secret" destination) . . . and we are all under orders to stay within contact with the aerodrome and be ready to vacate at a minute's notice.'[1]

---

[1] Amy's employers were one of the independent air transport companies which at the outbreak of war were taken over by

A week later she was still at Portsmouth, and on 31 August wrote again to her father: 'It's awful this waiting, isn't it? I'm trying to carry on as much as possible with a normal life, and all the time I get off I go out sailing and get away from everything . . . I don't know whether you will think I have been very unwise or not but I have taken the bungalow today. The owner . . . is agreeable to my taking it and sub-letting it to another prospective tenant . . . if war comes and I can't move in myself . . . I wish something would happen soon. Things seem pretty grim in Portsmouth, but one can't keep at high tension point indefinitely. All shipping is controlled and everything except sailing ships and the ferries have guns. The harbour is patrolled and sandbagged and there are guns everywhere. At night there are no lights, although there are as yet no regulations about car lights or house lights. We are still under a two-hour notice to go to Cardiff, and I've been living all week with my suitcases packed. We're doing quite a lot of flying, but no machines are allowed up at night without radio . . .

'I had a notice from the Civil Air Guard calling on me to stand by for duty as a ferry pilot.[2] I replied to say I was with the Portsmouth Company and was under orders to go to Cardiff but that if they had any more important or suitable work for me I would be prepared to go anywhere and do anything required . . . Don't let the tension get you down. We've certainly got to stand up against this "war of nerves".'

---

the Air Ministry, and put under the control of a new organisation, National Air Communications (NAC), which was to have a major base at Cardiff.

[2] Air Ministry moves were now afoot (following the initiative of Gerard d'Erlanger, a Director of British Airways) towards forming the Air Transport Auxiliary (ATA), a pool of experienced pilots who were ineligible for the RAF. Originally it was planned that these pilots should undertake miscellaneous transport work behind the lines, but when the ATA came into being it concentrated almost entirely on ferrying aircraft between factory airfields and RAF bases.

On the day after Britain entered the war Amy wrote to her parents, 'You can be thankful you've only got daughters and not sons! . . . Hope you're not worrying too much.' She was writing from Heston where she had been sent to await orders. 'Everything's so uncertain. So far as we know, our headquarters are at Cardiff (a detestable place!) and we just fly where we're instructed by the Air Ministry. This morning there was a terrific rush on to come here, and we've simply been sitting here all day . . . It's gloriously fine . . . but how I hate doing nothing . . . The airport here is absolutely dead. Everyone has evacuated and the Air Ministry hasn't yet taken over . . . All flying has to be done to strict orders, but so far we've no official position – no uniforms or anything of the kind . . . We're to fly officers, equipment etc. to wherever they want to go.'

Her next letter (dated 12 September 1939) was from Cardiff, for the Heston 'posting' had been countermanded. 'This waiting about is beginning to get me down,' she groaned. 'The trouble is we have to be at the airport the whole time in case we're wanted . . . It does seem an awful thing that everyone's lives are spoilt for no good reason at all – just at the mercy of a madman. It's incredible how such a situation ever could arise in this modern so-called civilised world. Apparently the only hope of finishing things off at all quickly is internal trouble in Germany, but the opposition has no leader and they're all so mortally afraid.'

The phoney-war period was a tedious time for Amy, as it was for most of her colleagues. They still had their army cooperation work but instead of the rush of communications flying they had expected there was not nearly enough to do. In Cardiff she and two fellow-pilots took a house together, and she enjoyed this until the two others were sent elsewhere. 'I'm on my own here,' she wrote to her parents at the end of November. 'One of the pilots has gone to Newcastle till the end of the year and the other is still "somewhere in France".'

She was very well she said, and was playing squash several times a week, but was feeling frustrated as regards her work, for she was once again up against 'woman prejudice', which in this case meant that she was no longer given a chance to make communications flights to France.

At the end of the year she discussed with her father a new development in the ferry work of the ATA which since it started had employed only men pilots. There was now to be a women's section with Pauline Gower in charge. 'Had I played my cards right and cultivated the right people,' she wrote. 'I could probably have had the job Pauline Gower has got. But honestly I wouldn't like to have it. I'd much rather work in a proper commercial aviation company with men pilots than be one of a team of women sort of being given the crumbs to keep them quiet. They're not really doing anything much and the pay is very poor. They're only to fly open machines like my original *Jason*. I'm not doing much myself now anyway, but the pay's good and there may be opportunities later . . . '

Still in the employ of the Portsmouth company, and still doing army cooperation work, Amy was moved in mid-January 1940 from Cardiff to Reading, and from Woodley aerodrome she wrote, 'I am happier now than I have been since the war started. I am my own boss here and am in charge, which is so much nicer. Also I get every weekend off, and I get more expense money and I like the people so much more and have a lot of friends.' But after just over a month at Reading there was bad news. 'I'm feeling rather worried today,' Amy wrote on 21 February, 'because I've just had definite confirmation that the Air Force are to take over all Army Cooperation flying . . . That puts me out of a job! . . . Most of the men will be taken over by the RAF but of course I haven't a chance at all . . . The prejudice against women pilots is still very strong. You may have read about the "ATA Girls"? There are nine of them, headed by Pauline Gower . . . I'd hate to join them but I do want to keep a flying job.'

A fortnight later the axe had fallen. 'We've all been

given a month's notice,' she wrote from a small hotel at Wargrave. She had already filled in an ATA entrance form, but was still hoping for a flying job more to her taste. She wrote letter after letter to influential friends and hurried to London for lunches and interview, but as one disappointment followed another she confided to her father 'If I don't get a job soon I am thinking quite seriously of getting away out of all this mess. I might even try for a job in Kenya.'

Then in April, a few days after the Germans invaded Denmark and Norway, she had to make up her mind ('In a month's time I can definitely have the ATA job at £6 a week . . . I should be afraid to turn . . . [it] down . . . as if I did I could never apply for it again'), and during the first week of May 1940 she finally decided to join the women's section of the ATA, which was based at Hatfield. Nevertheless she felt awkward about her decision, and in a letter to her father from the Castle Inn at Benson in Oxfordshire (to which she had moved from Wargrave) she described some of the embarrassments it involved for her. 'Pauline Gower told me that she had to have a pilot by the 1st of May,' she wrote, 'and that there was no doubt at all I should be chosen as no one could come anywhere near up to my qualifications. I therefore went ahead to make plans to take up this job on May 1st. Nothing at all happened until I had a circular letter asking for my log book and Licence . . . Then came a circular letter "Dear Madam, If you are still interested in this job kindly note we are holding flight tests and interviews on Monday next the 6th inst and let us know whether you intend to be present." . . . I telephoned Pauline . . . and duly turned up. As I parked the car I saw another applicant all dolled up in full Sidcot suit, furlined helmet and goggles, fluffing up her hair etc. – the typical CAG[1] Lyons-waitress type. I suddenly realised I could not go

---

[1] Civi Air Guard.

in and sit in line with these girls (who all more or less look up to me as God!), so I turned tail and ran. I telephoned a few minutes later to leave a message regretting that I had flu and couldn't come. The more I thought about it the more my pride was hurt, and the more I dreaded having to take on this job, which I never liked from the first. Yesterday I telephoned them to say I felt better, just so that I could get their reactions. I asked for the man at the top, and rather to my surprise he told me the job was being kept open for me and that the test was a pure formality and when could I come.'

Next day, the day after the first onrush of the Germans into the Low Countries, Amy wrote to her mother 'Isn't the news terrible! Things are happening now so rapidly one hardly knows what to do. All the same I don't think we shall have raids over here just yet . . . I'm going to join the ATA after all.'

30

HAPPY ENDING?

June 1940– January 1941

Towards the end of her life Amy had no doubt as to how she would die: long-distance record-breaking flyers always 'copped it' in the end. 'I know where I shall finish up – in the drink,' she told one of her friends. 'A few headlines in the newspapers and then they forget you.' Nevertheless she did not dwell morbidly on the subject of death, and during her last seven months, from June 1940 until January 1941 (the time of Dunkirk, the Battle of Britain and the early part of the Blitz) she became progressively happier and more contented. For she was able to feel, as at thirty-seven she settled to work as an ATA ferry pilot, that the aim she had set herself more than ten years earlier had at last been attained; she had been accepted in a 'serious' flying job. Furthermore her service life gave her few opportunities for extravagance and for the first time since childhood she was almost free from money worries.

After her death her sister Molly, with whom she spent her last evening, recalled that she had never seen her looking so happy and well; Pauline Gower declared that Amy had told her, not long before her last flight, that she was happier than she had ever been, and Jim's aunt Mrs Hislop, whose house in Holland Park Amy frequented when off-duty in London, told her mother (in a letter of condolence) that Amy had been 'so much happier these last months.' Mrs Hislop enclosed a snapshot which she said 'must be I think one of the last photos taken of Amy – in a little cottage in Bucks where she visited a friend of mine.' It shows a radiant Amy, off-duty in civilian clothes and 'knitting for the Air Force', with a smile on her face that is serene and calm.

This new happiness was undoubtedly real, even though beneath it there still lay a tragic discord in Amy's emotional life. In spite of the fact that she seems at last to have grown away from her passion for Jim Mollison it is clear that the role of a gay divorcee did not suit her; where matters of the heart were concerned she was not in the least hard. And she was often irresistibly drawn towards the very men who did not shrink from exploiting her. Spontaneously generous towards those she found attractive, she was wounded if the ardour of an admirer cooled before hers, and one of her friends in the ATA, a woman of perception and sympathy, remembers feeling distressed to see how hurt Amy was by the cavalier treatment she received from such men. Reviewing Amy's time in the ATA this friend says 'She seemed to me unhappy. I think she missed being married to Jim Mollison, or anyway being married to someone.' This same point was echoed, from a different angle, in a letter which Amy's parents received after her death from Bill Courtenay. Among his reflections upon Amy's life was the following remark: 'I would have liked to see her happily married to a man in a fitting station as I know you would.'

Nevertheless in the summer of 1940, amidst the pressures of her new work and the excitement of wartime, it appears that she did not often pause to consider the unsatisfactory personal situation into which she had drifted. And meantime her warm heart and usual cheerful spirits, along with her lack of conceit and infectious zest, endeared her to her women colleagues.[1] 'She fitted into Hatfield like a hand in a

---

[1] When she joined the ATA there were less than a dozen pilots in the women's section but the numbers soon increased.

glove,' Alison King has written in her book *Golden Wings*. 'She settled down, simply, to do a job of work.' Yet Miss King goes on to explain that this did not in the least mean that Amy sank into obscurity in the ATA. 'It was quite a revelation to go out on a trip with her, especially to the RAF airfields. The moment she stepped from her aircraft and was recognised she would be surrounded by embarrassed but determined airmen wanting her autograph, and then would come the squadron leaders and wing commanders . . . It was the same too on the civil stations and indeed in the hotels or wherever she went.' Yet despite all the fan-worship Amy managed to keep up to schedule with her deliveries of aircraft; she was indeed hyper-scrupulous on that account.

Such was the impression Amy made on those around her at Hatfield, but her letters home show that her enjoyment of her new work did not begin immediately she joined the ATA (on 20 May 1940). Just at first, as a very new Second Officer in a very new uniform (like the men the women wore navy-blue slacks and tunics and jaunty forage caps) she felt frustrated and miserable, even though Pauline Gower, now her commanding officer, tried to put her at ease. 'I dislike intensely being with the ATA,' Amy wrote to her parents after a few days at Hatfield. 'I'm too much of an individualist to work as a cog in a wheel, however necessary I see it is, and that it is the only thing for me to do.' Her next letter, a note written a few days later, was less dismal ('I'm quite well and settling down to my job. Pauline is grand') but after another few days she was again overwhelmed by pessimism. 'Did you see in France they're having women in the French Air Force? They'll never do that here . . . I'm hating this job more and more and am getting really depressed and miserable. It's not only the boredom of the actual flying we do, and the fatigue of flying in slow, open machines . . . but I find it so difficult to conform to the sort of life the rest of the girls live. It is so like a girls' school, with the same favouritisms, jealousies, cattinesses etc. We are only united on one thing – that we should be allowed to fly more advanced machines – and even then, no account is taken of experience.[1] For example, I am the last comer, so I am last in everything. I *hate* being treated like a "new girl" . . . It's because I hate unfairness and favouritism that I submitted with as good a grace as possible to undergoing the same red tape as the rest. The whole of my flying career has just been one long fight against jealousy, and I'm right up against it here. I keep very much to myself, and so far haven't let anyone have the slightest idea that my pride is badly hurt. What's the use anyway! Probably everything is my own fault, but I never could get on with a team of women. Do you remember when I was at Morison's Advertising Agency, how the other typists hated me and made me do the menial work because I was the newcomer? Well, I seem to be back in those days again. At the moment I'm sitting in the sun writing letters whilst the ATA boys are coming over to fly away the Hurricanes.'

II

At the end of her third week in uniform she was writing home in a newly optimistic vein. 'Am much less depressed today,' she told her mother. 'It really seems at last as though we are going to be allowed to do more interesting flying. Pauline dined two evenings ago with Air Vice-Marshal Courtney,[2] who was perfectly charming and asked her to tell him exactly what she wanted. She told him the whole story and things have started improving at *once*! Our numbers are to be doubled and we've got ten people coming for tests on Monday. We're to fly more advanced machines and are actually this afternoon fetching some Proctors from

[1] When Amy joined the ATA she had 2,285 hours of flying experience (she acquired a further 275 hours during her ATA service).
[2] Air Chief Marshal Sir Christopher Courtney was then Air Member for Supply and Organisation on the Air Council.

AMY JOHNSON

Luton. We are to do all our own testing and training here ourselves and very shortly five of the most experienced pilots are to go for some training on Masters, Hurricanes and things like that! I am very thrilled at the prospect.'

She was by this time quite often escaping from the girls'-school atmosphere by spending as much of her off-duty time as possible at the house of some old friends who lived in a village not far from Marlow: the drive from Hatfield took an hour but she felt so much the better for the change that she did it often. Now, however, as the war situation became blacker, she was growing anxious for her parents, even though they had left the East Coast and were at Blackpool with Molly and her husband. Amy urged them to go to Canada, taking with them Molly and her baby daughter Susan. 'Why not?' she wrote on 23 June, the day when Churchill proclaimed that Britain would fight on alone. 'Go and join Uncle Tom in Vancouver . . . I think there's going to be hell let loose here . . . Don't delay too long – once it starts there'll be no opportunity. You're better going now than as a refugee! And you can always come back if our fears are groundless. I can't understand the French packing up. I feel they lack leaders and any real sort of inspiring ideals. Thank God we've got Winston Churchill but I still feel we're not doing enough.' Then she gave them the latest news on her work: very soon, she said, she and the other girls were going to ferry Oxfords, 'twin-engined bomber training machines.' They would be promoted to this after taking a conversion course at the Central Flying School.[1] 'I've had a terribly busy week – two trips up to Scotland,' she went on. 'It is very tiring ferrying a slow aircraft all the way and then getting home again as best we can, including a night on the train, but actually, I don't mind it very much as we manage to get some fun out of it.'

[1] Amy, after her conversion course, was promoted to the rank of 1st Officer with effect from 1 July 1940 (her thirty-seventh birthday).

HAPPY ENDING?

A month later, a week or so before the Battle of Britain began in earnest – she wrote with intensified enthusiasm. 'I am finding life much more exciting than before the war and am thoroughly enjoying my job these days,' she said. Another reason for her good spirits was that she had now arranged with her friends near Marlow that their home should be her own home base (it remained so for the next five months, until her death). This meant of course a thirty-mile trip to work, but since the White Waltham aerodrome, now the central headquarters of the ATA, was not very far from them she planned to commute by air. 'I've fixed it so that I fly to White Waltham each night and back to Hatfield next morning,' she explained. 'It's a grand arrangement . . . I've all my things there, and it's much more pleasant than digs.'

From her new home she wrote to her mother in September, during the first week of the Blitz: 'Don't let Daddy come to London . . . it truly isn't safe. Bombs are dropping just anywhere and as one must take shelter, one can't get any work done anyway . . . I've had to give up going there for shopping . . . My uniform has been blown up! I took it in to my tailor in Savile Row for alterations, and the place has been completely destroyed by a direct hit. Eighteen guineas gone west, together with all the time and trouble spent on fittings and alterations.' 'I simply don't have a minute these days,' she went on. 'Up at 6.45; on the go all day; back for supper about 7.30 and what with a bath and a letter or so it's bedtime. I'm very fit and very busy, and so far have escaped any serious raids.'

Amy's letters at this time brought news to her parents not only of herself but of her sister Betty (now aged twenty-one and engaged to an RAF pilot, Ronald Falconar-Stewart) who since late July had been working at Hatfield in an ATA secretarial post. 'She really is getting on fine with her job and is very popular,' Amy reported. But she worried about Betty too, for her billets were not far from the aerodrome, which was quite often an enemy target. 'In some ways I wish she was further away,' Amy wrote from her friends in October. 'But this night bombing is such a chance anyway . . . and we've simply got to be fatalistic about it . . . We thought we were as safe as anywhere here, but the night before last we were driven to our shelters! A huge bomb dropped at the top of the hill.'

III

'Jim has joined the ATA and is at White Waltham!' So Amy announced to her mother during the early weeks of the Blitz. 'It's a nuisance, and he always makes a beeline for me and keeps on asking me out, and on these days of bad weather when we're hanging about all day it's impossible to escape him. However it will sort itself out, and it surely must be obvious to him I'm no longer interested. Honestly, he bores me stiff!!!' Can we be sure that Amy really meant this? Certainly her wording in this letter is unequivocal. But whatever her true feelings towards her ex-husband may have been at this time the fact that she and Jim were occasionally seen together again gave rise to much imaginative gossip. The popular press which earlier, when she was still Jim's wife, had pounced upon every hint of a 'rift', now – ignoring Jim's second marriage – began to drop broad hints of a new 'romance'. Lord Castlerosse for example wrote in his column in the *Sunday Express*: 'It looks to me as if Providence has taken to writing beautiful fairy stories . . . While both on duty they met. Amy came home and had tea with Jim, and she came across a box of old gramophone records and they played the tunes they liked when they were first married.'

Amy made hardly any other mention of Jim in her letters home; in any case she was too busy to write much. Her work now consisted chiefly of flying one of the Anson 'taxis' for her Pool, which meant transporting up to eight of her women colleagues to the various aerodromes where they were required for their ferry flights. 'We're having guns in the Ansons and I have my own special gunner (a man)!' Amy told her father. 'What a curous anomaly, when there's all this terrific prejudice against women even ferrying Hurricanes without guns to aerodromes for storage. I'm trying to work up an agitation about the women getting equal pay for equal work . . . We all only get £8 a month flying pay whilst Jim, for example, walks straight in and gets £700 a year to my £450, or something near . . . The men now have a marriage allowance too, and most of them are amateurs as against most of our women being professionals . . . We can't expect equal pay for types we don't fly, but we ought to have the same when we're doing precisely the same job, the same hours and the same aircraft, don't you agree?'[1] Then Amy added a remark which brings home the drastic change the war had caused in her standard of living. 'It's a question of principle,' she said, 'as we don't really need more money.'

In December 1940 she was back again on ferry jobs, mostly to Scotland, and from the Orangefield Hotel at Prestwick she wrote home on 9 December 'I brought an Oxford up here yesterday and stayed the night at this pub. It's very nice to get away for a change. However, it's a lousy day today and we look like being stuck for the time being. There could be worse places.' In this same letter she told her parents the good news that she was to have a few days leave at Christmas and hoped to join them at Bridlington (they had now returned to their own house from Blackpool). This would be the first time she had seen them since July. But then came a rush of work. 'We have a lot of machines for Scotland,' she wrote ten days later, 'and I think I have to take one north on Sunday [22 December]. Heaven only knows when I'll get back . . . I feel very fit and am still enjoying my work. I do hope you have a nice Christmas, and don't feel too awful about it if I can't be with you. Christmas doesn't mean much this year.'

---

[1] They did later get equal pay for flying the same types.

This last remark proved very true in Amy's case: on Boxing Day she wrote to her mother that prolonged bad weather had again been holding her up at Prestwick. 'Just a note to let you know where I am. I've had the lousiest Christmas stuck up here.' Back at Hatfield on 29 December she wrote home again. 'This isn't a proper letter . . . I just wanted to put a note in with Betty's letter to let you know I received the five pounds safely . . . It's grand of you to send me such a generous Christmas present and I am most grateful . . . (I think I shall buy Savings Certificates with it. I've already got fifty I've saved up!) . . . I came back from Scotland on the night train finally, after being stuck up there for six days!! I wasn't half fed up with it. All the very best for the New Year, and lots and lots of thanks . . . Dearest Love, Amy.' That letter was the last her parents ever received from her.

IV

AMY JOHNSON BALES OUT, MISSING . . . The papers on the morning of Tuesday 7 January 1941 were full of it. The first newspapers were fragmentary, but there was no doubt that a plane piloted by Amy had crashed into the Thames Estuary on the afternoon of Sunday 5 January – a bitterly cold day with fog, snow showers and an east wind – for she had come down close to a convoy and her identity had been established from various salvaged items. By an extraordinary chance Drew Middleton, the American newspaperman, happened to be on board one of the ships of the convoy's escort and was an eye-witness of the crash, from a distance of a couple of miles. He reported that he had seen Amy's plane flying at about 750 feet, but could hear no sound of the engines. 'Something white fluttered out and dropped into the sea. It might have been a parachute, but if it was it was a desperate jump, for the plane was less than 200 feet up. The plane jumped up as it hit a wave, hung suspended for a moment, and nosed over.'

In the wartime press, when last flights were daily occurrences, Amy's name might hardly have been expected to reappar in the headlines the following day, but it did so thanks to a press release issued by the Admiralty on the Tuesday evening which provided material for a further 'sensational' story. According to the Admiralty the crew of the trawler HMS *Haslemere* (the ship nearest to the crash) saw two survivors in the sea – one of them a women. When all their attempts to rescue the woman had failed, the trawler's commanding officer, Lieutenant Commander Walter Fletcher,[1] dived overboard to try to save the other survivor, a man. He reached this second person, and managed to support him in the water while the trawler's lifeboat approached. But it could not fight the strong wind and heavy breaking sea. A naval motor launch then arrived and picked Fletcher up (no trace however was found of the man he had tried to save). He was by then unconscious, and suffering from extreme exhaustion and exposure, and he died soon after having been landed and taken to hospital.

This release naturally gave rise to a spate of rumours and also in some quarters to incredulity. That afternoon the *Evening News*, after interviewing an ATA official, came boldly out with a heading ADMIRALTY REPORT CALLED 'MISTAKE'. 'In the rough sea and in poor visibility,' the official had said, 'we think a natural mistake has been made, and that the second object in the water was not a body.' The *Evening Standard* however suggested that Amy, having landed at an intermediate aerodrome because of the weather, had responded to an urgent appeal by a service man going on leave for a lift. Pauline Gower pooh-poohed this. 'The theory that she picked anyone up during an emergency landing because of weather is improbable. If she landed because of weather she could not take off again. Besides, she was most conscientious about the

---

[1] Fletcher was then 34. His naval career had included the unusual experience of polar exploration; when 27 he had been attached to the 1934 expedition to the Canadian Arctic led by J.M. Wordie.

ATA rule about not carrying passengers.[1] Only a life or death appeal would have moved her, I am sure. I personally am convinced she had nobody aboard with her.'

Meanwhile a formal rebuttal of the 'mystery passenger' theory was issued by the Ministry of Aircraft Production. This second official statement gave a reconstruction of Amy's flight based on the evidence of those who were last in touch with her, including ground staff at the Blackpool aerodrome, Squire's Gate, from which she had taken off on the Sunday morning. 'It has now been established that when Miss Amy Johnson left the [Squire's Gate] airfield at 1045 a.m. on Sunday no passenger accompanied her. The weather report given to Miss Johnson was bad. "All right," were her parting words. "I am going over the top." This indicated that she proposed to fly above the weather[2] . . . Her scheduled flight should have taken one hour.[3] Nothing more was seen of Miss Johnson's plane until 3.30 p.m. when it came down over the Thames Estuary . . . Three hundred airfields have been signalled for any news of Miss Johnson having landed to refuel. None has yet reported having seen her . . . It is believed that Miss Johnson lost her course in bad weather. After flying round for several hours her petrol became exhausted and she finally bailed out . . . It is possible that she saw the naval convoy and endeavoured to alight as near as possible to one of the vessels.'

This statement, which appeared in the Thursday morning papers, of course added fuel to the

---

[1] It was forbidden to give casual lifts. But service men in uniform were in fact often taken as passengers (when official permission had been obtained).

[2] Strictly according to ATA regulations this was forbidden, because for security reasons aircraft being ferried were not equipped with R/T wireless. In winter, however, the rule was often ignored by 'press-on' pilots.

[3] She was bound for Kidlington near Oxford. An aircraft storage unit of the RAF was then based at this airfield as well as a ferry pilots' pool.

controversy, and on Friday the *Daily Express* asked WHERE DID AMY PICK UP MR X?, while the *Daily Mail* insisted SHE WAS ALONE, and in the *Daily Sketch* Bill Courtenay, claiming the prerogative of long friendship, sought to dispose of the 'base, cruel and slanderous rumours' which, so he said, had been circulating the day before. His reference was to gossip which by this time had got about (a friend of Amy's father wrote to him that it was 'common talk in the RAF') that Amy had not only landed in a field to pick up 'a pal', but that her purpose had been to fly him out of the country on some sinister mission.

After this, for the general public, the 'mystery' of Amy's death faded into the background. But for her family the hurt of the unpleasant rumours lingered on, and at the time when evidence relating to her last flight had to be produced in the Probate Court so that her death could be presumed, her father asked Sir William Crocker to do his utmost to clear her name. More than two years passed before the necessary statements were collected – it was a difficult matter, especially in wartime, to contact all the naval peronnel concerned – but at last in December 1943 the case came before the Court.

V

From the viewpoint of the historical record, the affidavits and statements which were collected for the Probate case (and of which the following narrative is a summary) provide invaluable evidence. Together they establish in some detail many of the facts of Amy's last flight, though they do not by any means solve all the 'riddles' involved.

Pauline Gower, one of the main witnesses, stated that she last saw Amy on Friday 3 January, when she instructed her to fly an Oxford aircraft from Hatfield to Prestwick and to collect another similar machine from Prestwick and fly it to Kidlington aerodrome, Oxford. 'At this time her demeanour was perfectly normal and she seemed keen to make the flight. Later that day I received a signal that owing to bad weather she had landed at Tern Hill near Birmingham.' Amy stayed the night at the Hawkstone Park Hotel, Weston-under-Redcastle, and on the following day Pauline Gower received a further signal that she had arrived at Prestwick, delivered her aircraft and then taken off again on the southward journey in the other Oxford. The engineer in charge at Prestwick, Thomas Scarborough, testified that he himself strapped Amy into the Oxford (V 3540) and was quite certain she was alone in the plane when she took off at 4 p.m.

Then the story was taken up by Amy's sister Molly (Mrs Trevor Jones) whose home was at Newton Drive, Blackpool. 'On Saturday 4th January my husband and I, after spending the afternoon out, returned to our home . . . and found my sister there . . . We spent the evening together . . . It was a cold night with some mist and in the course of conversation my sister said she had a rather sticky passage from Prestwick but that she had fortunately been able to reach Blackpool and was very glad to make the landing . . . During her visit she mentioned that she thought the compass of her aeroplane was a little out of adjustment. My husband offered to telephone the aerodrome to have it put right but my sister said she wanted to get away fairly early because she was anxious to complete her journey, . . . [and] that she would "smell her way" to Kidlington . . . [She] left us at about 10 a.m. on Sunday in the very best of spirits.'

At the Squire's Gate aerodrome several of the ground staff saw or spoke with Amy when her plane was being filled up. Harry Banks, a refueller, remembered that just before she entered her aircraft she had a conversation with some RAF pilots who were near and asked them about the weather. Then she got into the aeroplane and started up the engine, and as the weather 'came up a bit nasty' she said she would wait to see if it would blow over. Banks got into the aircraft with her and they sat talking and smoking together for some time. At this point a rigger, Frank Sutherland, came up and told Amy that the Duty Pilot advised her not to take off; she replied that 'once she was off the ground she would get over the top.' Banks stated that visibility was then very bad, also that he sat in the plane with Amy until she moved off, and that there was no possibility that she could have taken anyone on board after he got out. The signal book at Squire's Gate recorded her departure at 1149 hrs.[1]

'The first I knew of anything being wrong,' Pauline Gower continued, 'was when I received a message from White Waltham aerodrome to the effect that a plane had crashed into the Thames Estuary and that Miss Johnson's papers had been found.[2] White Waltham sent an enquiry to all aerodromes to ascertain whether Miss Johnson had landed at any of them and the answer was in the negative.' Then she went on to give her views on the likelihood of what had happened. Amy's Oxford, she stated, if fully loaded with petrol, would have a maximum flying time of three and a half to four hours. 'That type of aeroplane could not safely be landed anywhere except at an aerodrome and Miss Johnson was too good a pilot and had much too strong a sense of loyalty and discipline to attempt a perilous landing on some open space . . . I am satisfied that Miss Johnson having taken off alone from Blackpool was alone in the aeroplane at the time of the crash and that she did not land anywhere to take up a passenger after leaving Blackpool.

'In my opinion she struck ice-ing conditions and probably made attempts to get down to the ground but was unable to break through the fog cloud. When her petrol had either been exhausted or she knew it was on the point of running out, she may have lost control of the machine because of the accumulation of ice or decided to bale out as the only chance of saving her life.'

[1] Not 1045 as had been stated in the MAP release; that was the approximate time she had hoped to leave.
[2] Two bags of Amy's had been picked up near the aircraft wreckage by a boat from HMS *Berkeley*.

The statements obtained for the Probate Court from the naval officers and ratings who had been eye-witnesses of the crash gave an equally convincing picture, though a very different one. Lieutenant Patrick O'Dea, Fletcher's second-in-command, stated that he was on the bridge of the *Haslemere* at about 3.30 p.m. on the day in question. The weather was rough and there was a heavy swell. 'Our ship was in convoy. Suddenly I saw a parachutist come through the clouds . . . Shortly afterwards a plane came into view through the clouds near the parachutist . . . I did not hear any machine gun or other fire . . . The Commanding Officer . . . who was on the bridge with me altered course and rang full speed ahead on both engines . . . The parachutist landed on the water when the ship was about half a mile away . . . At about this time we became aware that the ship was aground and the engines were put to slow astern . . . After about ten minutes the ship was afloat again and the engines were stopped . . . By the time the ship was afloat a person had drifted in towards the stern of the ship.'

One of the seamen on the *Haslemere*, Nicholas Roberts, was looking over the bulwark and heard the person in the water shout 'Hurry, please hurry'. 'It sounded like a small boy's voice at first,' he said, 'and then I realised it was a woman's.' He had already thrown out a heaving line, but although it fell very close to the woman she made no attempt to get hold of it. (This is hardly surprising. Amy, who was always susceptible to cold, must have been completely numbed by the icy water.)

Another of the *Haslemere*'s seamen, Raymond Dean, also tried desperately to make a rescue. 'I mounted the bulwark aft and got over on to the rubbing board,' he said, 'and I sprawled out flat on the rubbing board holding on to the ship with my arm through the fairlead . . . I reached out with my hand towards the parachutist who came to within about five feet of it and shouted "Hurry, please hurry". It was definitely a woman's voice and she looked young. She was wearing a flying helmet. She appeared to have a life-saving jacket on which was keeping her afloat. She did not appear to be swimming, there was no action of her body at all. Some heaving lines had been thrown to her by members of the crew on deck . . . I saw two lines thrown. One landed in front and one beside. She could have reached them but she made no attempt to grasp them.'

'The person I thought to be a woman was now quite close in under the stern of the ship,' said Roberts. 'The ship was heaving in the swell and the stern came up and dropped on top of the woman. She did not come into view again.'[1]

Then the *Haslemere* witnesses went on to the evidence which had given rise to the 'mystery passenger' theory. Already before 'the woman' lost her life, so they unanimously agreed, a second 'person' had been seen in the water, farther off than the woman, and also drifting towards the ship. Both Roberts and Dean, and also O'Dea, insisted that 'beyond a shadow of doubt' they saw two persons in the water at the same time. They also confirmed that Commander Fletcher (realising with horror, so it seems, that nothing further could be done to save the woman) leapt overboard to try to save the second person. 'I stripped off and was going over the side,' said Dean, but Commander Fletcher told me to get back inboard and he went over the side himself.' 'He swam out towards the person,' said O'Dea. 'One of our lifeboats had been launched and was making its way round our bow . . . but the sea was rough and there was a strong tide running.'

Additional evidence, from water level, was given by another *Haslemere* seaman, Vivian Gray, who was one of the lifeboat's crew. 'The sea was rough and it was very difficult to manage the lifeboat,' he said. 'I saw Commander Fletcher . . . and we pulled towards him . . .

---

[1] It seems from this statement that Amy's death was more probably caused by the impact of the ship's stern than by drowning.

When we were first drawing up close . . . I saw another person in the water . . . [whom] I took to be a German airman on account of the flying helmet that was worn.' Dean, on the *Haslemere*, had also noticed 'the person' seemed to be wearing a flying helmet, and added that there appeared to be a scarf or something muffled up round the neck (an interesting detail since a muffler was part of the normal gear of an operational pilot). O'Dea said that Commander Fletcher, who must have been a very strong swimmer, reached 'the person' before the lifeboat did, and several of the witnesses agreed that he supported him in the water for a short time. Then the two separated, and 'the person' disappeared altogether. Since Fletcher, when he himself was rescued, was unconscious, and remained so until his death in hospital, there was afterwards no means of obtaining any further first-hand evidence about the accident.

VII

Amy Johnson died in the Thames Estuary on 5 January 1941. No doubts were left on that score after the Probate Court granted permission to presume her death. But nagging doubts remained, and they still remain, on the question as to whether there was a passenger in her plane – and this despite all the persistence and ingenuity that Sir William Crocker brought to bear in his efforts to 'clear Amy's name' at the time of the case in 1943.

Sir William, undeterred by the assertions of the naval witnesses, claimed that the alleged head of the alleged second person in the water had in fact been the larger of Amy's two bags, which as one of the salvaged items he had inspected and considered very closely. The shape of the bag, which fastened with a zipper, was roughly that of a rounded pyramid; it was airtight and consequently, so he pointed out, would not sink; its rectangular base measured eighteen inches by seventeen, it was about twelve inches deep. His hypothesis was that Commander Fletcher, when he reached the bag and found it was not a human being, rested on it briefly and then abandoned it. 'This gallant gentleman,' he argued, 'who sacrificed his life in the attempted rescue would not abandon a person he was endeavouring to save, in order to save himself.' One may add however, with all respect to Sir William, that this would hardly apply if Fletcher had found that 'the person', when he reached him was on the point of death or already lifeless. It is also difficult to reconcile the buoyancy of Amy's bag with the testimony of the eye-witnesses that the 'person' to whom Fletcher swam disappeared entirely from view (they furthermore agreed that no objects from the wrecked aircraft were seen in the close vicinity of the *Haslemere*).

Another quite different possibility, which seems much more convincing, was put forward during the Probate case by Mr C.A. Marshall-Reynolds, representing Amy's executors. In January 1941, Mr Marshall-Reynolds pointed out, dog fights were frequently taking place in daylight over the Thames Estuary, and the 'person' whom Fletcher tried to rescue may well have been a survivor or a victim of one of these fights – a pilot of the RAF or of the Luftwaffe who had either baled out or been shot down.[1] It is rather surprising that this suggestion, which if correct would reconcile all the conflicting evidence, was not given much attention at the time. Nor has it often been mentioned since, while Sir William's 'bag' theory, and variations of it, have become part of the Amy Johnson legend.

One last question must be asked concerning the 'mystery passenger'. How did the original 'Mr X' theory, which of course stemmed from journalistic renderings of the Admiralty press release, develop further into the

---

[1] According to Air Ministry records there was an air-raid warning in Canterbury in the late morning of 5 January 1941, so it is by no means impossible that the 'person' in the Thames Estuary that afternoon was a member of the crew of one of the raiders (no RAF casualties were reported at this time).

rumour that Amy's last flight was some sort of shady smuggling operation? A relevant possibility that has not heretofore been suggested concerns the 'common talk in the RAF' to which Will Johnson's friend referred. Doubtless some of the personnel who contributed to this talk had been in France during the phoney war, and they may well have had vivid recollections of seeing Amy there (at the time when she did, in fact, make occasional communications flights to the Continent from Cardiff). After her death the *Daily Mail* air correspondent Noel Monks gave the following lively account of one of her appearances at Reims, which was then the French headquarters of the RAF. 'She walked into the bar of the Hotel Lion d'Or, crowded with RAF pilots, and ordered a lemonade. She had just flown an unarmed transport plane from England through the danger zone to Reims. A young Hurricane pilot recognised her. "There's Amy Johnson – Let's toast her!" he cried. And Britain's first woman air ace was toasted in vintage champagne.' Amy Johnson . . . flying through the danger zone . . . turning up in France . . . Is it not likely that some such association of ideas – some such jumble of champagne-tinged memories – may have combined with the tenuous clues provided by the first reports of Amy's crash to give birth to a completely fictitious rumour?

VIII

In February 1961 there was another 'Amy Johnson riddle' in the form of a macabre echo of her death. The bones of a woman that were washed up at Herne Bay were suspected of being hers. Five months later however the Coroner for East Kent informed her father that it had been established beyond doubt (with the aid of Mr Nickolls of Scotland Yard and Dr Keith Simpson) that the bones could not be those of his daughter. 'A few headlines in the papers and then they forget you.' The bitter epitaph that Amy had forecast for herself was not an apt one. 'A few headlines in the papers and then they *remember* you,' would have been a far truer one. Publicity, which had shaped the course of her career during her lifetime continued, and still continues, to focus upon her after her death. In a sense the 'mystery' of her last flight and the 'Mr X' rumours were a most appropriate ending to her life. It was strangely fitting that in her death on active service – the kind of death 'in harness' that she would have wished (as many of her friends have pointed out) – she was at the same time a heroine to the public and also its victim. Her end was in character with the Amy Johnson legend, the legend of a woman who, despite every obstacle, not only earned a permanent place in the history of aviation, but also became a world-famous symbol of adventure, tenacity, and courage.

INDEX

INDEX

399

INDEX

INDEX